TRAVELER

istanbul &
western turkey

NATIONAL GEOGRAPHIC

TRAVELER

istanbul &
western turkey

by Tristan Rutherford
& Kathryn Tomasetti

National Geographic
Washington, D.C.

CONTENTS

TRAVELING WITH EYES OPEN 6

CHARTING YOUR TRIP 8

History & Culture 12
Istanbul Today 14   Istanbul's History 22   Land & Environment 36
Food & Drink 40   The Arts 44

ISTANBUL 52
The Old City 54
Topkapı Palace & the Archaeology Museum 58   Hagia Sophia 66
Blue Mosque & Around 70

European Istanbul 98
Galata & Around 102   The Northern Golden Horn 112
Taksim Square & Nişantaşı 116   Tophane, Çukurcuma,
& Cihangir 120   Beşiktaş & Ortaköy 124   North of the Bosporus Bridge 130

Asian Istanbul 136
Kadıköy & Around 140   Üsküdar & the Asian Bosporus Shore 146

Istanbul Excursions 152
Black Sea Beaches 156   Princes Islands 160   Bursa & Uludağ 166
Ankara 170

WESTERN TURKEY 176
Troy & Gallipoli 178
Gallipoli 182   Troy, Çanakkale, & Bozcaada 186

Ephesus & Roman Turkey 192
Çeşme Peninsula 196   Ephesus & Around 198   Pamukkale & Hierapolis 204

The Turquoise Coast 206
Göcek to Kaş 210   Kekova to Antalya 216

Cappadocia 220
Göreme & Around 226

TRAVELWISE 232
Hotels & Restaurants 242   Shopping 260
Entertainment 262   Activities 264

INDEX 266   **CREDITS** 270

A tea seller outside the Hagia Sophia in Istanbul

TRAVELING WITH EYES OPEN

Alert travelers go with a purpose and leave with a benefit. If you travel responsibly, you can help support wildlife conservation, historic preservation, and cultural enrichment in the places you visit. You can enrich your own travel experience as well.

To be a geo-savvy traveler:

- Recognize that your presence has an impact on the places you visit.

- Spend your time and money in ways that sustain local character. (Besides, it's more interesting that way.)

- Value the destination's natural and cultural heritage.

- Respect the local customs and traditions.

- Express appreciation to local people about things you find interesting and unique to the place: Its nature and scenery, music and food, historic villages, and buildings.

- Vote with your wallet: Support the people who support the place, patronizing businesses that make an effort to celebrate and protect what's special there. Seek out shops, local restaurants, inns, and tour operators who love their home—who love taking care of it and showing it off. Avoid businesses that detract from the character of the place.

- Enrich yourself, taking home memories and stories to tell, knowing that you have contributed to the preservation and enhancement of the destination.

That is the type of travel now called geotourism, defined as "tourism that sustains or enhances the geographical character of a place—its environment, culture, aesthetics, heritage, and the well-being of its residents." To learn more, visit National Geographic's Center for Sustainable Destinations at *www .nationalgeographic.com/travel/sustainable.*

istanbul & western turkey

ABOUT THE AUTHORS

Tristan Rutherford has been a freelance travel writer since 2002. He writes envy-inducing travel features for *The Independent* and the *Sunday Times Travel Magazine* among others. He also lectures in travel journalism at Central Saint Martins and Kingston University in London. Of the 60 countries he has visited, Rutherford still rates Turkey as the best, having been smitten by his first grilled squid and *rakı* dinner by the Bosporus in 1995. Outside of Istanbul, he rates the sprawling Roman ruins south of Ephesus and the tranquil fishing villages of the Aegean as his favorite Turkish sites.

U.S.-born, Italian-raised **Kathryn Tomasetti** writes travel stories and guidebooks for the likes of *The Guardian* and *Rough Guides.* Her library of travel photos—snapped from as far afield as China, Syria, and Chile—has been published by *Time Out, Dorling Kindersley,* and *The Independent.* Tomasetti has hunted down archaeological ruins and nuggets of culinary knowledge throughout Turkey, often traveling by the country's magical sleeper trains. But Istanbul remains her personal highlight, and she urges visitors to take in the Egyptian Bazaar and the street markets of Kadiköy, as well as the famed Grand Bazaar.

Tomasetti and Rutherford have worked on about 25 guidebooks together across the Mediterranean, and are based between Nice and Istanbul. Both are members of the British Guild of Travel Writers.

Charting Your Trip

Istanbul, Turkey's cultural capital and largest city, is the gateway to this fabulous country. It combines the museums and restaurants of a vibrant 21st-century destination with a historical legacy as the capital of Roman, Byzantine, and Ottoman Empires.

A plane hop away, ancient ruins and fine sand beaches stretch for hundreds of miles along Turkey's sun-blessed Mediterranean coast. Inland await the dynamic diplomatic capital of Ankara and the "fairy chimneys" of Cappadocia.

How to Get Around

Luckily for the visitor, Turkey's major sites are clustered close together, either in Istanbul or along the Mediterranean coast. Getting around is quick, efficient, and easy. The only difficult part is choosing how to go!

The original means of crossing between Europe and Asia, ferries are a major form of transport—either across the Bosporus that bisects Istanbul, or to the alluring islands that dot the coast. These short hops are great fun, with bars and at least a handful of open-air seats for that wind-in-your-hair experience. The municipal ferry company, Istanbul Deniz Otobüsleri, has schedules and maps at *www.ido.com.tr*.

Driving is not recommended. Inexpensive taxis are ubiquitous in Istanbul and along the coast. In the countryside, drivers are easy to hire and tours straightforward to arrange. Your hotel concierge will be the first in line to help.

For longer distances—including the journey from Istanbul to the south coast that many travelers reading this book will make—most destinations are served by bus or air. Long-distance buses are extremely comfortable (though they lack a restroom) and make frequent stops for meals and a stretch. However, trips over six hours can quickly become tedious.

Air services from Istanbul to southern Turkey's four airports—İzmir, Bodrum, Dalaman, and Antalya—are frequent. Prices are only a bit more than the equivalent bus trip if booked in advance, as three or four airlines usually compete on each route. There are several reliable bus companies and airlines; see Travelwise p. 236 for lists.

Trains are a magnificent way to travel. They slice through Turkey's open countryside in ultramodern style, with seat-back TVs on high-speed services, and luxurious beds on the sleeper routes. Three rail lines are relevant to readers of this guide: The Istanbul to Ankara high-speed and sleeper lines; the Ankara to İzmir sleeper service;

Glasses of Turkish tea

and the Istanbul to Cappadocia (Kayseri) sleeper service. Visit the Turkish State Railways website at *www.tcdd.gov.tr* for information.

If You Have a Week

Turkey has so much to offer that it's impossible to see everything on a short trip. Fortunately, if your senses become overloaded on the country's awe-inspiring mosques, ruins, and markets, a beach or a lazy island is almost always nearby.

Nearly all visitors to Turkey start their trips with a stay in bustling Istanbul. Three days or so allows you time to see many of the city's must-see sites, most of which are in the **Old City,** an area known locally as Sultanahmet. Although it's easy to walk between all of its fabulous sites, bear in mind that the Old City does get its fair share of tourists, so to avoid the crowds head out early or late. Start at the **Topkapı Palace,** once the fairy-tale playground of the Ottoman Sultans. The wealth inside, from bejeweled daggers to religious relics, is fascinating. Be sure to leave time to visit the stunning **Archaeology Museum** on the palace grounds. Just outside the Topkapı gates is **Hagia Sophia,** one of the largest buildings of the ancient world. Now a museum, this 1,500-year-old temple displays mosaics that are guaranteed to leave you speechless. Across the garden from Hagia Sofia is the enormous yet graceful **Blue Mosque.**

The Old City is also a prime venue for shopping—a national pastime in Turkey. Pick up Turkish delight and handmade ceramics in the **Grand Bazaar,** a few minutes walk west of Hagia Sofia, or the **Spice Market** (also known as the Egyptian Bazaar) near the Galata Bridge at the Old City's northern edge.

Istanbul has several other sites that you simply can't leave without seeing. North of the

NOT TO BE MISSED:

Lapping up Turkish cuisine, meze, kebabs, and seafood included **40-43**

The Topkapı Palace, from the harem to the treasure room **58-65**

The mosaics and magnitude of the Hagia Sophia—ex-church, ex-mosque, now museum **66-69**

Taking a boat tour along the Bosporus **106-107**

The ruins at Ephesus or Pamukkale at dawn or dusk **198-201, 204-205**

Hopping along the Turquoise Coast by boat, foot, *dolmuş,* or car **211-215, 218**

A hot-air balloon ride over Cappadocia in **227**

Mosque Etiquette

From the cathedrals of Europe to the temples of Thailand, places of worship make up the most beautiful and culturally significant sights of many countries. The thousands of mosques in Turkey are no different. Some, like the Old City's Fethiye Mosque (see p. 89), are former Christian churches. Others, like the Atik Valide Mosque in Üsküdar (see pp. 146–147), are soaring reminders of Ottoman-era splendor.

Mosques are places of worship first and foremost, but visitors are welcome provided they avoid prayer times and Friday mornings. Both men and women should dress modestly, and footwear should be left in the rack by the door. A respectful silence should be observed inside. Snapping photos of worshippers is a no-no, but pictures of the building are fine. It's courteous to leave a donation to help fund the mosque's maintenance.

Turkish Lira

The currency of Turkey is the Turkish lira (Türk lirası, abbreviated as TL). One lira is made up of 100 kuruş, although half lira (50 kuruş), quarter lira (25 kuruş), and 10 kuruş coins are the smallest that travelers will use. Bills come in denominations of 5, 10, 20, 50, 100, and 200 lira, each with a portrait on the back side of Turkey's founding father, Mustafa Kemal Atatürk.

Any problems? The 5 and 50 lira notes look alike, and can sometimes confuse. Be wary when receiving change from a taxi driver, as these bills are occasionally switched. When settling a restaurant bill, it's normal to run through the figures with the waiter—locals do this, too, to avoid any discrepancy.

During the 1990s inflation was so rampant that there were more than a million lira to the dollar. The currency is now stable, and the offending six zeros were officially lopped off in 2005, even though *milyons* still crop up in common parlance. In particular, small figures are sometimes referred to by the million, so a two-lira soda may cost *iki milyon*, or two million!

Golden Horn, in European Istanbul, a stroll down the Parisian-style boulevard of **İstiklal Caddesi** is an absolute must: Great restaurants, inviting side streets, and world-class boutiques await. A wander around the **Istanbul Modern** art gallery is also recommended, and a **Bosporus cruise** is a good way to get an overview of the whole city in just a few hours. Other attractions in European Istanbul include the massive **Galata Tower** and a climb up the 18th-century **Kamondo Stairs**. In Asian Istanbul, east across the Bosporus, the towering mosques of **Üsküdar** or the street theater of **Kadıköy** will round out any Istanbul trip. And don't depart before you've had a traditional Turkish hammam, an Ottoman feast, and a glass of local firewater *rakı!*

Ankara, Turkey's diplomatic capital, is overlooked by 99.9 percent of visitors to Turkey, but its superb museums just an hour's flight or overnight train from Istanbul are certainly worth visiting for a day. Few travelers omit the fairy chimneys of **Cappadocia,** a few hours southeast of Ankara via car, bus, or rail, from their itinerary. These hollowed-out homes in the rock have been inhabited for two millennia and were one of the birthplaces of Christianity; today many have been transformed into luxury cave hotels. **Ephesus,** on the Aegean coast, and **Pamukkale/Hierapolis** inland— both a flight or an overnight bus from Istanbul or Cappadocia—are the most visited ancient ruins in Western Turkey. A trip to either of them will be amply rewarded, as will a side visit to a nearby beach or quieter archaeological site such as **Laodicea** (6 miles/10 km south of Hieropolis).

Istanbul Travel "Card"

An electronic key fob known as an AKBİL is the smart way to pay for public transport in Istanbul. Credit can be stored on this little device, which is available from most newsstands, streetside kiosks, or transport stations for a TL 6 refundable deposit. When you jump on any of the city's trams, trains, ferries, buses, and funicular lines, simply punch your AKBİL at the electronic barrier and hop on board. And AKBİL-holders don't just jump the line for *jetons* (transport tokens)—they also get a small discount on each journey!

If You Have More Time

With ten days or two weeks, visitors can really begin to scratch the country's surface. Spend half your trip in Istanbul, scheduling time to discover less trodden sites like the **Süleymaniye Mosque,** the **Church of Pammakaristos,** the hip suburb of **Nişantaşı,** or the street markets of **Beyoğlu.**

A night away from the city can add a touch of magic to the trip. Book a hotel on the **Princes Islands** or near the **Black Sea beaches** in summer, or at the **Yalova** spa or **Uludağ** ski resort during winter. Each of these destinations is around an hour or two away from Istanbul by bus or ferry.

Turkey's heaven-sent coastline will delight those visitors with time to spare. History buffs should choose the **Gallipoli Peninsula** and ancient **Troy,** each five hours by bus from Istanbul and the site of epic battles.

Heading farther afield to the southern coast requires a flight or overnight bus ride. Action adventurers should base themselves in **Kaş** or **Göcek,** where sea kayaking, coastal walks, and diving are all on offer. If you're really looking to relax, the long beach and vine-covered ruins of **Çiralı,** outside Olympos, several hours by bus east of Kas or south of Antayla, are sublime. And for an absolute escape, kick back on a **"Blue Cruise" boat tour** of Turkey's turquoise bays and green islands. The cruise can be joined in Kaş, Göcek, or any of the Turquoise Coast's other major resorts.

Visitor Information

A wealth of helpful visitor information is available at *www.goturkey.com,* Turkey's official tourism portal. The site is overflowing with maps, practical travel information, and details on the country's history and culture—plus you can book flights, hotels, and package tours. Another great resource is *www.kultur.gov.tr,* the official website of the Ministry of Culture and Tourism.

The abandoned village of Kayaköy, south of Fethiye, has been preserved as a museum.

History & Culture

Istanbul Today   14-21

Istanbul's History   22-35

Feature: Eight Great Ottoman Sultans   25

Experience: Browsing Historical Bookshops   27

Feature: Atatürk   28-29

Land & Environment   36-39

Food & Drink   40-43

Experience: Learning to Cook Turkish Food   40

Feature: Ten Most Famous Dishes   42

The Arts   44-51

Experience: Whirling Dervishes   48

A worshipper studies his Koran by the ornate carved minbar of the Blue Mosque in Sultanahmet, Istanbul.

Istanbul Today

As the bridge between Europe and Asia, Istanbul is often described as a symbol of Turkey as a whole, a meeting place of conflicting ideas and forces. Many argue that this is the place where East meets West; where traditional values clash with modernization; where secularism vies for power against political Islam.

But the crossroads metaphor is not just simplistic. It simply doesn't ring true. Turkey is not a nation confused about its future, nor is Istanbul some kind of ideological battleground. Rather, they are a city and a country on a fairly straight path to the prosperity and international respect that befits one of Europe and Asia's newest regional powers and one of its oldest and finest cultural centers.

Young Istanbullus relax at a trendy café on the Galata Bridge.

Barring economic or political disaster, Turkey should soon surpass the Netherlands as the world's 16th richest country, somewhere on a par with Australia. Even the 2007-2010 global financial crisis has merely dented, rather than destroyed, Turkey's strong annual economic growth rate.

Confidence in the Air

Head to any town listed in this book and you'll see a country with a spring in its step. Istanbul, a city of almost 13 million, buzzes with excitement and individuality, a stark contrast to the increasingly homogenized capitals of Europe, or strip-mall sameness that is spreading through the United States and the Middle East. Creative industries thrive on every corner of the Beyoğlu and Nişantaşı zones: design, architecture, music, publishing, and more.

Where once fashions would have been imported from Europe, style is now very much a homegrown affair. The world-class Istanbul Modern museum (see pp. 121-122) is a disused warehouse turned waterside arts complex that wouldn't look out of place in New York, Berlin, or Seoul, and showcases primarily local art, not foreign works. Players from the city's big soccer clubs once looked abroad for success. Now these clubs take on all comers in the European Champions League, attracting global stars to Istanbul.

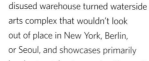

Barring economic or political disaster, Turkey should soon surpass the Netherlands as the world's 16th richest country.

The western triangle between Ankara, İzmir, and Antalya covered in this book boasts a similar vibe, yet with more diversity. The coast's package resort industry has faced a three-pronged attack: Consumer tastes have switched from all-inclusive fortnights to culture-rich mini-breaks; budget airlines now allow bespoke, independent trips to the country's south; and Turkey's tourism authorities have been relentlessly promoting their awe-inspiring ancient ruins and hidden beaches over hotel swimming pools and discount sunburns. A few of this guide's ritzier hot spots, such as the Çeşme peninsula's Alaçatı, are a cocktail of fusion cuisine, warm seas, and hip hotels modeled after France's St. Tropez and Florida's Miami Beach.

Conversely, some idyllic fishing villages—where life revolves around games of *tavla* (backgammon), cups of tea, and wondrous fish dinners—haven't changed in decades. Let's hope they stay that way.

The Roots of Today

This shift in Turkey's fortunes has been achieved in spite of, rather than because of, political and economic events over the last 30 years. After an economically disastrous military coup in the early 1980s (generals rarely make good economic stewards) Prime

Istanbul Blogs

Checking out Istanbul's great range of blogs is an informative way to get a handle on the latest local happenings. Some of the city's best include:

- **www.Istanbuleats.com**
  Istanbul Eats: By Ansel Mullins and Yigal Schleifer, photographed by Jonathan Lewis—ideal for the city's off-the-beaten-track restaurants (see p. 87).
- **www.Istanbulfood.com**
  Istanbul Food: Local chef Tuba Şatana offers her favorite spots to sample local cuisine—and those to avoid.
- **Istanbulstreets.wordpress.com**

Istanbul Through My Eyes: A beautiful photo per day from city resident Ozgur.
- **www.pukkaliving.com**
  Pukka Living: Listings ranging from the weekend's concerts to fashion workshops.
- **www.taranoble.com**
  Tara Noble & Her Works: Amusing ruminations from an American living in Turkey.
- **www.sublimeportal.com**
  Sublime Portal: The forum of choice for resident Americans—perfect for picking up tips or asking a specific question before you arrive.

Minister, and later President, Turgut Özal (1927–1993) led the country to a brief recovery. The strategic status of NATO's largest Muslim member—and the military alliance's second largest army—was cemented by the first gulf war (1990–1991) and the collapse of the Soviet Union (Özal was on the first plane out to the newly independent Turkish-speaking "Stans" in Central Asia).

Following Özal's sudden death from a heart attack, Tansu Çiller was sworn in as Turkey's first female prime minister in 1993. Characterized as the country's answer to the former British prime minister Margaret Thatcher, Çiller proved to be just as divisive but much less competent, often resorting to petty nationalism as her economic policies broke down. It was during this period that the PKK, the outlawed Kurdistan Workers Party, reached its apogee, fighting military and civilian governments in turn, whose first response was a heavy-handedness akin to Britain's bloody initial encounters with the IRA in Northern Ireland. The Kurdish language was essentially banned—a law recently overturned by today's pragmatically competent government of Recep Tayyip Erdoğan.

> As mayor of Istanbul from 1994, [Recep Tayyip] Erdoğan cleaned up the city in a similar manner to former New York City mayor Rudy Giuliani.

As mayor of Istanbul from 1994, Erdoğan cleaned up the city in a similar manner to former New York City mayor Rudy Giuliani. Chugging and unsafe old buses were replaced with eco-friendly versions, chaotic traffic was re-routed, and municipality debts were repaid. In 2001, he formed the pro-EU Justice and Development Party (AKP), taking on the mantle of prime minister in 2003. An austere personality with a strong sense of social justice, Erdoğan hacked at corruption, boosted education and health care spending, and steered Turkey clear of both the Afghanistan and Iraq conflicts. It's no surprise that United States president Barack Obama chose Istanbul for his first state visit to a Muslim country in 2009. Erdoğan has twice been listed as one of *Time* magazine's "100 most influential people in the world."

The finishing line in Turkey's long road to full participatory democracy—and perhaps the milestone of Erdoğan's career—came in September 2010 when Turkish citizens voted 58 percent in favor of changing the country's constitution. The generals' junta of 1980 drafted Turkey's previous constitution. In many ways it served to protect the perpetrators of the coup and silence critics of it. In future, those who plot to take over the nation by military means should now be tried in civilian courts, and those dismissed from the military will hold the right of civilian appeal.

In another passage, the rights of unions, associations, and even striking workers will be enshrined in law—enforcing yet another check and balance on the country's future rulers. And a juiced-up supreme court should now allow for army commanders and government ministers alike to be openly placed on trial. In the words of Germany's Foreign Minister Guido Westerwelle: "The reform of the constitution is another important step by Turkey on the road towards Europe." Erdoğan's Greek counterpart, Prime Minister George Papandreou, claimed that, "The Turkish people reaffirmed (their) commitment to the European perspective."

Selling Turkish flags in front of the Yeni Camii (New Mosque), in Eminönü, Istanbul

Regional Politics & Economics

Turkey's largest trading partner, the European Union, has long treated its eastern neighbor like a casual girlfriend, rather than a married partner. After 25 years of accession talks (the political equivalent to "making out"), the wedding date was never set. The positive fact for Turkey is that its 70.6-million-strong population is better educated than ever. More importantly, 67 percent of Turks are of working age, which may become a key asset as the European Union's population gets older. The Turkey-EU Customs Union signed in 1995 lets Turkey trade with Europe, without the Union's well-documented bureaucratic and Euro currency issues.

The sentiment that "Turkey is not a part of Europe and will never be part of Europe" from current EU chief Herman Van Rompuy rings similarly from many European capitals. With this attitude in mind, Turkey has been looking elsewhere for trade and mutual alliance. A photographic spread in *Newsweek* magazine in 2010 showed Prime Minister Recep Tayyip Erdoğan shaking hands with every leader from each of Turkey's neighboring countries, from Iraqi Kurdistan to Greece. This policy has overturned Turkey's once negligible role in the area, the latter stemming from Ottoman colonial rule in Arabia, Turkey's military partnership with Israel, and local water and energy issues. Long-standing rivals have now become close friends.

It's now Israel that incurs the wrath of its former regional best friend—Turkey chastises Israel for its policies in the occupied Palestinian Territories on humanitarian grounds. The shooting of nine Turks on an aid convoy to Gaza by Israeli commandos on May 31, 2010, brought relations to a new low.

In terms of energy issues, Turkey's position as a long-term net importer of oil and gas may change with the discovery of huge amounts of fossil fuels off its Black Sea coast. In regard to energy politics, the geopolitical web has been woven in its favor too. In a politically stable country, Turkey's Mediterranean coast is now the hub and terminal of the Baku–Ceyhan oil pipeline. In 2009, a deal was signed to run Russian natural gas from its Black Sea reserves through Turkey and on to Europe.

But Turkey's greatest foreign policy triumph today is the settling of its traditional animosity with Greece, with whom it fought a savage war in 1923 (see pp. 32–33). Relations improved after the "earthquake diplomacy" in 1999, when both countries literally pulled each other out of the rubble. Over the following decade Greece's current prime minister, George Papandreou, worked tirelessly to bring the two sides together. In 2010, Turkey and Greece hosted a joint cabinet meeting in Athens. This unprecedented act of friendship should usher in deep cuts to both countries' defense budgets in the coming years.

A final policy objective is the peaceful reintegration of Cyprus. This Mediterranean island nation has been divided since 1974, when a coup orchestrated by the Greek military junta initiated a military invasion by Turkey to protect the island's ethnic Turks. Nearly four decades since the conflict, a Berlin-style wall still divides the Turkish north and Greek south. In an era when tens of thousands of Greek holidaymakers roam the streets of Istanbul, and advertisements from the Greek tourist authority urge Turks to travel to their country, the division is now seen as even more of a tragic anachronism than ever before.

Cultural Dos & Don'ts

Turks are comfortable with foreigners and are extraordinarily welcoming, particularly outside of the tourist-centered Old City. Following these tips will win you an extra smile.

- Some sections of society—and some parts of the city—are very traditional. Don't wear skimpy clothes: All visitors must observe dress codes when visiting mosques.
- Armed with these six Turkish words and phrases, you can't go wrong: *merhaba* (hello), *iyi günler* (good day/good-bye), *evet* (yes), *lütfen* (please), *teşekkür ederim* (thank you), *özür dilerim* (sorry).

- Women, do expect to take the lead when shaking hands with an older gentleman. Men, do warm up to kissing male acquaintances on both cheeks.
- Do score points with Turks by chatting about their three favorite subjects: children, their hometown, and food.
- Don't be surprised at good-natured questions about your marital status, job, or income. Make up stock answers if you'd rather protect your privacy.
- Do be assertive in lines and restaurants or you may not keep your place or get served. There is no need, however, to be rude or push in front of others.

Old sores may heal slowly in the Mediterranean, but in an age where Turkey's President Abdullah Gül makes state visits to former adversaries Armenia, Syria, and Iraq, anything is possible. In 2008 the symbolic Ledra Street crossing between the island's divided capital of Nicosia was reopened with great fanfare, although not without aggravation on the ground. Greek Cypriot President Dimitris Christofias was elected the same year with a manifesto of reconciliation. The 2010 election of nationalist politician Derviş Eroğlu in the north may put the brakes on the process, but talks continue under the auspices of the UN.

On balance, modern Turkey stands out as a beacon of success. It is a country that has managed to transform itself from a feudal monarchy to a modern, democratic republic in the space of a single lifetime.

Transport

The bumpy buses of Turkey's past have been transformed into a world-class transport system. Five or six inexpensive airlines (see p. 236) now run against superb coach services, all bookable online. New high-speed trains (see sidebar p. 39) ably complement these routes, and will reduce the journey time from Istanbul to Ankara to just over three hours in 2013. To support Turkey's burgeoning population, additional high-speed routes are be also being constructed between the huge central Anatolian cities of Ankara and Konya, with projects on the board to link Ankara and İzmir with an additional three-hour line.

However, commuting in Istanbul isn't pretty. Summer is hellish in the heat, especially during rush hour. Istanbul mayor Kadir Topbaş, who was re-elected in 2009, has increased the number of trams, buses, funicular lines, gondolas, and ferry boats, but it won't be until 2013 that the pressure on them all will be reduced, when the Marmaray undersea tunnel (a Metro line running under the Bosporus; see sidebar p. 36) is finished. On completion, it is hoped that around a quarter of local city journeys will be taken by rail, the third highest in the world. Other engineering plans include a third bridge over the Bosporus and a new Metro line over the Golden Horn, which will speed passengers from the fringes of the Black Sea to Istanbul's Atatürk Airport, and all points in between.

The Bright Future

On balance, modern Turkey stands out as a beacon of success. It is a country that has managed to transform itself from a feudal monarchy to a modern, democratic republic in the space of a single lifetime. Turkish soap operas are broadcast across the Middle East showing a modern, liberated, and tolerant country. Year-on-year, Turkey's citizens are more educated and wealthier—but remain just as welcoming. The country now lives in peace with its eight neighbors. And its beaches, museums, and archaeological sites are now better protected from the ravages of industrial development than ever before.

Perceptions may have changed, but has the city? In 2010, it seems, it really did. Events from U2 concerts to open-air opera performances and film screenings took place on a daily basis. All were well organized and publicized, too. The city's key sights, including the Hagia Sophia (see pp. 66–69), the Süleymaniye Mosque (see pp. 87–88), and parts of the Topkapı Palace (see pp. 58–64) were given a new lease on life. And aside from the countless new galleries and boutiques, the new Museum of Innocence in Beyoğlu also opened its doors.

One of the few certainties about the future of Istanbul is that the city will continue

Kayaks are a great way to see Turkey's historic Turquoise Coast.

to grow at what many Turks believe is an alarming rate. Istanbul has always been regarded as a "world city" or "global city," one of the great urban centers that hum with economic activity, breed cultural trends and movements, and have an importance in politics beyond their own nation. Location is at the root of Istanbul's significance. It is a transportation hub between Europe and Asia, between the Mediterranean and Black Seas, between West and East. These factors still hold and the metropolis dominates Turkey and the region.

Today, Istanbul is a city of more than 12.5 million people, nearly one-fifth of Turkey's population. Already home to half a million people by the start of the 19th century, the city has expanded ever since. The only exception was during the immediate post–World War I period when it was occupied by British, French, and Italian forces. By 1965, greater Istanbul was home to 2 million people, rising to 4.8 million in 1980 and 7.6 million in 1990. Since then, the population growth has been steeper, bringing a whole new set of problems for city planners. The face of the city changed: multistory buildings became commonplace, industrial suburbs developed, modern highways were constructed, and districts of poor housing mushroomed to accommodate the new workers.

Unbridled Growth

From the 1950s through the 1970s, much of the new housing development was illegal. Around the urban fringes, migrant workers built squatter settlements, known as *gecekondu* (meaning "set down at night"). Yet, no sooner had the city authorities extended facilities to these districts then new settlements appeared, as the flow of the poor from the countryside became a flood. By the 1970s, more than 60 percent of new homes built in Istanbul were illegal. Even in the early 21st century, there are still neighborhoods without electricity and proper sanitation.

Urban growth brought environmental problems. Household and industrial waste issues raised concern; air pollution increased; and the supply of water for domestic use and for industry became a worry. Gecekondu are being demolished and replaced by districts of mass public housing, but the influx of newcomers continues. Many of the new residents are Turkish Kurds from eastern Turkey, who differ in language and culture from other Turks. The main centers of economic and industrial activity remain along the European shore. The Asiatic shore, which is home to one-third of Istanbul's people, is increasing in importance, and towns and cities up to an hour's journey away are becoming part of the metropolitan area.

However, while Turkey won't revel in Olympic or World Cup status—a coming-of-age spotlight for developed states such as China in 2008, or Brazil in both 2014 and 2016—the future of this modern, democratic, peaceful state looks bright. Atatürk (see pp. 28–29) would have been proud. ■

A Multireligious Society

Although Turkey is a predominantly Sunni Muslim country, it is also a liberal, secular republic. Religious practices tend to be moderate, and non-Muslims are enthusiastically welcomed everywhere, including mosques. Many of the world's major organized religions are also represented in Istanbul. The Ecumenical Patriarchate of the Orthodox Christian faith resides in the city, and Istanbul is home to significant numbers of Greek orthodox and Armenian Christian residents. A close-knit community of Jews worships at synagogues in Galata and Balat, and two prominent Catholic churches sit on İstiklal Caddesi.

Although Istanbul is a cosmopolitan, modern-thinking city, it's still likely a more conservative place than your hometown. Be aware that revealing clothing will draw stares, such as plunging necklines on women or shorts on either gender (although this attire is acceptable at resorts and on the beach).

Istanbul's History

Southeastern Turkey, between the Tigris and Euphrates Rivers, was one of the cradles of civilization. The fertile plains of Anatolia nurtured Neolithic cultures nearly 10,000 years ago and the remnants of more complex Hattian, Akkadian, Assyrian, and Hittite cultures date from 2500 B.C. The city now known as Istanbul was founded under the name of Byzantium, in the seventh century B.C.

In the second to first centuries B.C., independent states like Phrygia (based at Górdion where Alexander slashed through the eponymous knot, see p. 174) and Lydia (where the proverbially rich King Croesus minted the world's first fortune) were the successors to the seminomadic wanderers who made southeast Turkey their stomping ground. Both these regions were eventually subsumed into the Persian Empire by Cyrus the Great—the first clash in a long battle between Western and Persian cultures. Coastal states like Caria (with its bases at Didyma and Miletus, see pp. 202–203) and Lycia (at Myra, Olympos, and Phaselis, see pp. 216–219) were influenced by Hellenic forces from Troy. However, these communities, too, were transformed into Persian satrapies, paying tribute to Persepolis in modern-day Iran.

Greece & Rome

The tiny town of Byzantium (later known as Nova Roma, Constantinople, and Istanbul) came under Roman protection in the first century A.D.

In 334 B.C., centuries of creaky Persian rule were swept away when Alexander the Great conquered the Persian Empire. A few great men have battled their way across Anatolia, but surely the 22-year-old Alexander the Great (356–323 B.C.)—the son of the conquering King Phillip II of Macedon (382–336 B.C.), tutored in his youth by Aristotle (384–322 B.C.)—has few equals. Hellenistic culture, with its grand architecture, art, and civil politics, followed in the wake of Alexander's conquering army. When he died a decade later, having fought all the way to northern India, his vast empire was divided between his four generals.

Without Alexander's world-conquering zeal, however, these Hellenistic kingdoms dwindled and weakened. By the time the Roman Empire reached present-day Turkey, it had little trouble defeating its divided kingdoms. Lycia reverted to Rhodes before becoming a Roman province itself. Caria came under Roman stewardship, too. The Roman ruins in this vast coastal area, some lost in forests, others commanding lonely headlands, some, like Simena (see sidebar p. 218), lying half-submerged in the Mediterranean, are some of the finest in antiquity. Many rank among the most heart-stoppingly beautiful in the world.

The fairy chimneys of Cappadocia, together with the tiny town of

Byzantium (later known as Nova Roma, Constantinople, and Istanbul), came under Roman protection in the first century A.D. As long as young men, materials, and tributes flowed westward, these eastern provinces positively flourished. This situation was particularly true under the Pax Romana, the two centuries of Roman Peace in the Mediterranean, which was ushered in by the great emperor Augustus (63 B.C.–A.D. 14), who chose Ephesus (see pp. 198–200) as his capital of Roman Asia. Emperor Hadrian (A.D. 76–138), the best traveled of all the Roman rulers, passed through Anatolia circa A.D. 122, and visited the thriving city of Ephesus, then the world's second largest city, a few years later. But an even greater gift, the transferral of the Roman Empire's seat of power to Istanbul, was yet to come.

Capital of an Empire

Emperor Constantine the Great (A.D. 272–337) was cut from a different cloth than his predecessor, Emperor Diocletian (A.D. 244–311). Diocletian wanted to restore the power and culture of Rome's golden age—he persecuted Christians and attempted to reverse the

Excavated Roman theater in ancient Myra, near Demre

fragmentation of the empire, but ended up retiring to grow vegetables in his native Dalmatia. The Christian convert Constantine, on the other hand, proclaimed religious tolerance with the Edict of Milan in A.D. 313 and embarked on one of the grandest and most unlikely schemes in the empire's history: The relocation of the imperial capital to the small Greek colony of Byzantium.

It proved an inspired move. In one swoop Constantine annulled the growing barbarian threat to the empire's capital, simply by moving the capital away from the barbarians. Powerful old elites were left 1,000 miles away in Rome and his kingdom now controlled the strategic bottleneck of the Bosporus, where navies and armies could drive both east and west. Moreover, the move allowed Constantine to stamp his authority over his realm. But what name should be given to this glorious new city? The powers that be decided on Nova Roma, or "New Rome," but it didn't stick. Its citizens called it Constantinopolis, meaning "Constantine's City," which had a much more enduring ring to it.

The new capital was glorified with a six-year building spree. The city walls were extended to make way for churches, civic buildings, and houses, the houses encouraged by the gift of free land to imperial citizens. In a mirror of ancient Rome, a vast hippodrome (see pp. 71-73) was constructed, the footprint of which forms the heart of Istanbul's present-day Old City. Constantinople was finally consecrated in A.D. 330, protected by relics such as the True Cross and the Rod of Moses (the former was stolen during the Fourth Crusade, see p. 30, the latter now resides in the Topkapı Palace; see pp. 58-64). Constantine's enlightened rule benefited Anatolia, too. Roads ran east into the plains, Ephesus was rebuilt, and, in far off Cappadocia, Christians felt safe enough to emerge from their underground caves.

> Constantine . . . embarked on one of the grandest and most unlikely schemes in the empire's history: The relocation of the imperial capital to the small Greek colony of Byzantium.

In the long history of Istanbul and Anatolia, however, one trend rings true: As the great man falls, the empire falls with him. On Constantine's death, the realm was divided, and squabbled over, by his three sons. Theodosius the Great (A.D. 347-395), who ably patched up the empire, can be considered the last true Roman emperor. Goth and barbarian invasions along the Danube were either put down or halted at the Theodosian Walls, a defensive structure that still rings the city today. When Theodosius died in Milan it was deemed sensible to split the unwieldy empire in two, each governed by one of his sons, the western, broadly Latin-speaking half based in Rome, the eastern, broadly Greek-speaking half in Constantinople. Although they came close, these two empires would never be united again.

The Byzantine Empire

It wasn't until the splendid reign of Justinian the Great (A.D. 483-565) that the eastern empire, known as the Byzantine Empire, flourished once again. However, his rule got off to a flimsy start. The emperor was forced to flee the Nika Riots that convulsed the city in A.D. 523 via a secret passage that led through to his palace. But from the city's ashes (and on top of the bones of the 30,000 rioters he put to the sword) a vast new empire was built, with a new taxation system and a new legal code—the Codex Justinianus—that now forms the basis of Western European law. The period's crowning glory was the Hagia Sophia church (see pp. 66-69), inarguably the finest building of the age.

Eight Great Ottoman Sultans

Today's Turkey—from its city skylines to its liberal outlook—has been shaped by this ruling dynasty. Of these leading eight sultans, some were good, some were bad, and some were just plain dangerous to know.

Osman I (r. 1299–1325): Founder of one of the world's greatest political dynasties and father of Orhan, the conqueror of Anatolia and Bursa (see p. 166). Apparently foresaw his illustrious empire in a dream.

Bayezıt I (r. 1389–1403): Bursa-born sultan who added to the victories of his father, Murad, in the Balkans, earning himself the sobriquet of Yıldırım, or "Thunderbolt." Bayezıt's encirclement of the beleaguered Byzantines culminated in a siege of Constantinople. It was only checked by the rampaging Tamerlane (Timur), who defeated the Turks at Ankara in 1402.

Mehmet II (r. 1451–1481): As if speaking seven languages wasn't enough, Mehmet Fatih ("the Conqueror") breached Constantinople's city walls in 1453 at the tender age of 21. His awesome tomb at the Fatih Mosque (see p. 89) is a place of pilgrimage.

Selim I (r. 1512–1520): Selim "the Grim" was a born fighter. Muscular and tall, he dismissed any succession issues by putting his brothers and cousins to the sword before assuming power. He extended the empire to Syria, Palestine, Egypt, and Saudi Arabia, and brought the Islamic Caliphate to Istanbul.

Süleyman I (r. 1520–1566): Europe breathed a collective sigh of relief when the all-conquering 45-year reign of Süleyman the Magnificent came to an end. During his lifetime he presided over the world's most powerful nation, leading conquering armies across eastern Europe and the Middle East. The riches he brought back to the country initiated an architectural and cultural golden age.

Abdülmecit I (r. 1839–1861): Great reformist whose alliance with Britain and France in the Crimean War blocked Russian designs on the empire for a brief period. In his 20-plus years in power, Abdülmecit received the world's first

Osman I, founder of the Ottoman Empire

Morse code message, overhauled the army, and had seven wives and countless sons, four of whom became sultans.

Abdulhamit II (r. 1876–1909): The dour Abdulhamit traveled widely in Europe with his camera and captured much of the empire on film. He formed an alliance with Germany to stymie growing British, French, and Russian power, but was dealt an inevitably losing hand. Eventually exiled to the Beylerbeyi Palace (see pp. 148–149), where he excelled at carpentry.

Mehmet VI (r. 1909–1918): Born in the Dolmabahçe Palace (see pp. 126–128), circumcised in the Topkapı, and left Istanbul on a British battleship in 1922 as Atatürk pushed for modern Turkey's independence. Died in San Remo on the Italian Riviera.

EXPERIENCE: Browsing Historical Bookshops

Fancy delving into an 18th-century description of Istanbul's hammams and harems? Need a selection of yellowing early 20th-century street maps for your wall back home? Well, look no further. Even the most amateur historian could spend their entire trip in Beyoğlu's historical bookshops.

Denizler Kitabevi (*İstiklal Caddesi 199, tel 0212/249 88 93, www.denizlerkitabevi .com*): Beautifully presented maritime maps and specialist naval history.

Homer (*Yeni Çarşı Caddesi 12, tel 0212/249 59 02, www.homerbooks .com*): Bold, beautiful photography books

and historical texts just about İstiklal Caddesi, plus culinary, cultural, and language titles.

Librairie de Péra (*Galip Dede Caddesi 8, tel 0212/243 39 91, www.librairiedepera .com*): A glorious mixed bag of out-of-print Istanbul guides and libraries of Turkish arts, culture, and music.

Robinson Crusoe (*İstiklal Caddesi 195, tel 0212/293 69 68, www.rob389.com*): Ancient Anatolian travelogs and modern Turkish history, plus plenty of translated novels and contemporary titles from Turkish authors, such as Yaşar Kemal (see p. 50).

Key to Justinian's success was his brilliant general Belisarius. After all, it's certainly handy to have one of the greatest military tacticians the world has ever seen fighting in your corner. Byzantine rule spread to Persia, Egypt, North Africa, nearly all over Italy—including Rome—and southern Spain, while riches flowed in the opposite direction. The world lay in Justinian's grasp, but for one vital weakness: his conspiring wife, Theodora. The daughter of a bear-keeper at the Hippodrome and a full-time courtesan and dancer, Theodora was thought of by her opponents as little better than a prostitute. Only the thoroughly modern man Justinian, who changed the law to let different social classes wed, would even consider marrying so far below his status. Fiercely jealous of Belisarius' fame—she considered him a threat to her and her husband's power—she had the military genius slandered and temporarily imprisoned.

> **Meanwhile, another storm was sweeping across Byzantine positions in Syria, Egypt, and Anatolia: Islam.**

The empire's demise due to plague, combined with assaults by the Bulgars, Vandals, and Persians, was only checked by Emperor Heraclius (A.D. 575–641). So sorry was the situation when he took power that he considered transferring the capital, like Constantine, to Carthage in modern-day Tunisia. Meanwhile, another storm was sweeping across Byzantine positions in Syria, Egypt, and Anatolia: Islam. Arab armies mounted two nearly successful sieges of Constantinople. But the city was saved each time, first when the Islamic standard-bearer Ebū Eyyūb el-Ensari (see p. 93) was slain, then by the timely arrival of a Bulgarian Christian horde.

Little thought was given to the imperial borders, as the empire tore itself apart during the iconoclastic debates (see p. 66) under Leo III (ca 685–741). Mosaics and icons were removed from the Hagia Sophia, nobles were exiled on the Princes Islands (see pp. 160–163), and worshippers went back underground in Cappadocia. Instead of

(continued on p. 30)

"The Deësis" mosaic at the Hagia Sophia, formerly a Byzantine church

Atatürk

Mustafa Kemal Atatürk is idolized in Turkey—and revered abroad—as the soldier-statesmen who carved a victorious modern state from the wreck of an empire. As the nation's father figure (he took the name "Atatürk," or Father of Turks, after ordering all his citizens to adopt surnames in 1934), his modern, liberal, secular ideology guides current Turkish politics and policy.

Perhaps his most enduring legacy is neatly summed up by one of his most famous quotes: "Peace at home, peace in the world." Since Kemal became Turkey's first president in 1923, the country has steered a neutral course in a divided neighborhood, carefully avoiding the horrors of World War II, local Arab-Israeli conflicts and the recent Afghan and Iraq wars.

Kemal was born in Thessaloniki in 1881, in present-day Greece. The genetic makeup of his parents is testament to the diversity of the rapidly shrinking Ottoman realm: his mother, Zübeyde Hanim, was a blond, blue-eyed Balkan, while his father, Ali Rıza Efendi, was said to be Albanian. In a typical break from family traditions, he enrolled in a military high school, before excelling at the Harbiye Military Academy, now the Istanbul Military Museum (see pp. 118–119). His first taste of conflict, both political and military, came as he joined the Young Turks Revolution in 1908 (see p. 32), only to be sidelined in military roles in Damascus, Libya, Bulgaria, and on the crumbling fringes of the empire.

But as the empire faced a siege by the British, French, and Russian entente in 1915, it was all hands on deck. Kemal was awarded a division at the bloody Battle of Gallipoli (see pp. 182–184). On day one of the conflict he counterattacked at the head of an exhausted platoon in order to stop the Anzac's initial advance, telling his troops: "I don't order you to fight, I order you to die." Subsequent actions cemented both his reputation and a promotion to colonel.

As the Allies eventually occupied Istanbul and planned to dismember the rest of the empire, Kemal fled to Samsun to rally the nationalist rebels. Lightning attacks pushed the Greeks—and their French and Italian backers—all the way to İzmir and into the Aegean. The Ottoman old guard fared little better: the corrupt sultanate was abolished, the caliphate dissolved, and Kemal proclaimed president in the new capital at Ankara.

Atatürk as Reformer

The enlightened dictatorship that ensued ushered in a modern, secular and eventually democratic

The Philosophy of Kemalism

The political credo of Atatürk, Kemalism, is based on several pillars: republicanism, statism, populism, secularism, nationalism, and revolution. These principles are still at the center of political philosophy in Turkey, with different factions, including the armed forces, believing that they are the true guardians of Kemalism. Kemal Atatürk believed that only republicanism expressed the true wishes of citizens and that a secular society—one in which religious bodies have no influ-ence on the state and vice versa—was the ideal. His nationalism was not a nar-row ethnic sentiment but a "Turkishness" based on language, common history, and an allegiance to the new republic. His policy of statism centered on state regu-lation of the economy, while his concept of populism implied pride in a shared Turkish citizenship. Atatürk thought that only his revolution could sweep away the corrupt, undemocratic regime of the old Ottoman Empire.

and artisans and traders were invited to build ports, naval fleets, and palaces, not least the Topkapı (see pp. 58–64). The new Ottoman capital was renamed Istanbul (although the moniker "Constantinople" survived another five centuries).

The Ottomans

The new empire expanded under sultans Bayezit I and Selim I (see p. 25). By the reign of Süleyman the Magnificent, it had eclipsed the Byzantium's greatest splendors. In 1529 even the gates of Vienna were pounded by the Turks. Fabulous public works, many of them by the royal architect Sinan (see pp. 90–91) following military victories, include the Süleymaniye (see pp. 87–88), the mosques in Üsküdar (see pp. 146–150), and the renovated Hagia Sophia (Sinan added the minarets)—the highlights of any visit to Istanbul today.

But just as Justinian's conspiring wife set Byzantium on the road to ruin, so Süleyman's bride Roxelana (see sidebar p. 60) ushered in 400 years of Ottoman decline. Both a grand vizier and Süleyman's favorite son—a revered and capable sultan in waiting—were murdered on Roxelana's orders, paving the way for her idiot child Selim II to take the throne. It was now viziers who ruled the empire, as it was chipped slowly away by the trading powers of Europe (who obtained imperial trading concession in Istanbul) and by decades of palace intrigue.

Haydarpaşa Garı (Haydarpaşa Station)

Taking a ferry across the Bosporus to Haydarpaşa must rank as one of the best commutes in the world. Boats from European Istanbul pull up to this gothic castle of a railroad station—which would look more at home in Bavaria than on the shores of Asia—and passengers march off to catch a train home. Although most of the travelers will be heading to the suburbs of Asian Istanbul, a few will be catching an overnight train across Anatolia. Others might be booked on the regular services that still chug all the way to Aleppo in Syria, and Tehran in Iran.

To understand how a mock-German castle ended up on the Bosporus, a short history lesson is required. As the ailing Ottoman Empire limped into the 20th century, British and French intrigue in Turkey's Middle Eastern possessions grew. Sultan Abdülhamid II allied his empire with Germany's Kaiser Wilhelm II who—as a self-styled "Protector of Islam"—never missed the opportunity to ingratiate himself with a potential anti-British partner. Wilhelm thus gifted Haydarpaşa to the Turkish people, and architects Otto Ritter and Helmut Cuno completed the twin-turreted edifice in 1908. As World War I (1914–1918) reared its head, the Turks and their German allies constructed railroad links from Istanbul to Syria, Saudi Arabia, and almost into Iraq, all seen as potential theaters of war.

A century later, the station still looks stunning. But after admiring the magnificence of the building, walking around the station today imparts a forlorn feeling. Haydarpaşa was built to be the literal crossroads of East and West, but in an age of jet planes and long-distance buses, the station's restaurant, bar, waiting rooms, and newsstands lie curiously underpopulated. The station remains, however, Turkey's largest and grandest.

Including a train ride in your Turkish experience is great fun. The nearest point of interest to visitors is Bostancı, a faded seaside resort and ferry hub for the Princes Islands (see pp. 160–162), a 15-minute ride south.

Greek-Turkish Population Exchanges

Following the empire's defeat in World War I, the 1920 Treaty of Sèvres sought to dismember the Ottoman Empire. Greece, with the support of its wartime allies (Britain, France, and Italy), landed armies in İzmir with a mandate to protect the Christian populations. This Greek force was defeated by the Turkish nationalist forces led by Kemal Atatürk.

In the resulting peace agreement, the 1923 Treaty of Lausanne, Turkey, Greece, and the League of Nations agreed on a population exchange based on religious identity. It was hoped that this forced evacuation of a half million Muslims from Greece and 1.3 million Orthodox Greeks from the newly founded Republic of Turkey would "tidy up" the ethnic map of Europe and water down the fuel for future conflicts. In an area known for its multiculturalism, this tragedy split up neighbors, families, and friends alike.

Periods of Decline

The 16th- and 17th-century Sultanate of Women, where valide sultans (the sultans' mothers) ruled by proxy as their sons indulged in carnal stupor inside the harem (see pp. 60–61), balanced the empire somewhat. The Tulip Period in the early 18th century witnessed Sultan Ahmet III, as he introduced literature, printing, and a flower craze into the empire, combined with inspired diplomatic politicking outside of it. The mid-19th-century Tanzimat Period, personified by reformists like Mahmud II and Abdülmecit I (see p. 25), further reformed the empire's military, administration, and legal codes, and eventually moved into the European-style Dolmabahçe Palace (see pp. 126–128). But endemic corruption coupled with foreign crippling loans to the empire tainted it as "The Sick Man of Europe." Migration during the Balkan, Caucasian, and Crimean Wars "Islamicized" the empire greatly, yet churches and foreign quarters of the city sprang up to serve modern waves of European immigrant communities in Istanbul. It was clear that the center couldn't hold.

New ideas from Europe, including nationalism and democracy, found favor with the Young Turks movement, whose membership included the future leader of modern Turkey, Mustafa Kemal Atatürk (see pp. 28–29). Poor, dithering Abdul Hamid II was replaced in a civilian coup in 1909, as the clouds of war funneled along the Gallipoli Peninsula (see pp. 182–185) and across the empire's revolting Arab and Armenian borders. Millions from every ethnic group died in the ensuing period, both from war and its famine-stricken aftermath. What was once the world's most powerful empire was occupied now by foreign powers. It fell to Atatürk to lay the seeds for the modern Turkey we know today.

Greek Culture in Modern Turkey

If you're hoping to hunt down the ancient Greek roots of European culture, it's best to do so along the Turkish coast in Troy (see pp. 186–187), Pergamon, Ephesus, Priene, Miletus, and Didyma (see pp. 198–205). In Istanbul itself, any vestiges of pre-Roman settlement have been built over by successive Byzantine, Ottoman, and modern Turkish states. Although many gravestones, pillars, and columns are inscribed in Greek, the majority of these date from Byzantine rule in the fourth and fifth centuries, when the Orthodox faith became the official state religion and Greek replaced Latin as the empire's lingua franca.

Centuries later, ethnic Greeks made up a sizable proportion of the polyglot Ottoman Empire's merchant class. Particularly large populations resided in the ports of Istanbul, (especially along the Golden Horn, Kadıköy, and the Princes Islands), İzmir, Trabzon, and along the Aegean coast. Many distinctive Greek stone houses and schools remain, such as the red-brick Greek school in Fatih.

Istanbul once had a large Greek population, but the effects of the Greco-Turkish War (1919–1922) and subsequent population exchanges between Greece and Turkey (see sidebar opposite) greatly reduced the number living in the city. The upheaval expelled families that had lived in Istanbul for generations, as Turkish families were similarly expelled from Greece. Whereas before the war, some 120,000 Greeks lived in Istanbul, there were fewer than 65,000 by the mid-1950s.

Greeks have left an indelible mark on the face of Istanbul. Today, the Fener neighborhood boasts echoes of a glorious history of Greek culture. Here visitors can see Saint George's Church—the headquarters of the Orthodox patriarchate—as well as three Greek schools, several small Greek churches, and typical Greek family homes with characteristic decoration on their façades. The Ecumenical Patriarchate of the Orthodox Christian

Worshippers light candles in St. George's Greek Orthodox church in Istanbul.

Faith—the highest see and holiest center of the Orthodox Christian Church—still resides in this area. Over 50 Greek churches are open to worshippers and respectful visitors across Istanbul.

The Oldest Relics Return

While the small remaining Greek districts may be relics of Constantinople, there are often discoveries in Istanbul of an older past, the pre-Roman city of Byzantium. During the construction of the Marmaray undersea tunnel (see sidebar p. 36) project in 2004, a vast ancient port was discovered near Yenikapı, a transport hub on the edge of the Old City. It's still too early to assess the significance of the finds, but the excavations have so far revealed over 30 sunken ships, a Byzantine city wall, and graves containing 8,000-year-old skeletons from a Stone Age settlement, the city's earliest known relics.

Experts have referred to the finds as some of the most fascinating nautical pieces ever unearthed. The huge 60-foot (18 m) cargo boats, loading vessels, amphora carriers, and sailing craft have turned our knowledge of shipbuilding, and thus history and maritime trade, on its head. The harbor itself is considered an engineering feat.

Also uncovered were the bones of lions, elephants, and ostriches, evidence that points to exotic animal importation on a grand scale, perhaps for private entertainment, perhaps for public battles staged inside the Hippodrome. A new exhibition space that will house these unique maritime treasures is currently in the offing. When up and running, it will complete the near ten-millennia story of this great city. Unsorted remnants of the Yenikapı finds can currently be found in Istanbul's Archaeology Museum (see pp. 64–65).

Turkish à la Française

As Atatürk introduced Latin letters to the Turkish alphabet in 1928—and the country embraced such modern inventions as hair stylists, taxis, and elevators—any words that were missing from the dictionary were simply purloined from French. Visitors will see scores of examples all over Turkey, including:

English	French	Turkish
alcohol	alcool	alkol
ticket counter	guichet	gişe
match	match	maç
shock!	choc!	sok!
buffet	buffet	büfe
elevator	ascenseur	asansör
ticket	billet	bilet
ham	jambon	jambon
pantyhose	collants	kulots
gymnastic	gymnastique	jimnastik
funny	comique	komik
hair stylist	coiffeur	kuaför

Since the 1980s, many new words have been introduced, this time from the English language. Can you work out the following? *Kontakt lens, deesk, faks, flaş.* (Contact lens, disk, fax, flash.)

Legacy of the European Capital of Culture

The mantle of Capital of Culture, given to a different European capital every year, is one of Europe's most prestigious titles. For Istanbul, the award of European Capital of Culture 2010 (*www.en.Istanbul2010.org*) allowed it to show off more than its historical assets as the capital of three vast empires, or the current Istan-cool status as the world's fourth largest, and possibly hippest, city.

The legacy of the European Capital of Culture—or Istanbul2010 as it's known locally—is bestowed in the title. First of all, it shows that Istanbul is a firmly modern European capital.

Turkey's President Abdullah Gül (center) during Turkey's 2009 EU membership negotiations

Recent visitors would argue that it's edgier than London, has more experimental restaurants than Paris, and is a hundred times friendlier than Berlin, not to mention larger than all three of Europe's leading cities. While Istanbullus (the local term for the city's residents) have never considered themselves any less European than their cousins over the EU border, it's nevertheless heartening for them to know that their art, fashion, architecture, and music industries are on par with, if not better than, their counterparts farther west.

The second key legacy is an association with culture. When most tourists think of Turkey they think of sunshine, food, beaches, and world-class shopping. How many first-time visitors to the country know that Istanbul was the capital of the Roman Empire for 900 years, or that the Ottoman Empire was once the most powerful force on the planet? Moreover, few visitors previously considered Turkey's cultural heritage—the ruins, temples, mosaics, mosques, and amphitheaters—to be a principal reason to make the trip.

As a European Capital of Culture, Istanbul has ushered in a whole new class of visitor. According to Yılmaz Kurt, General Secretary of Istanbul2010, the number of independent visitors is through the roof, each contributing greatly to the local economy as they look for the hip hotels and offbeat designer stores that have sprung up to cater to this new market. As this new style of city traveler—enabled by discounted airfares from almost every European city—trumpets modern Istanbul to their friends, the legacy looks set to last. ■

Land & Environment

Turkey is almost a continental landmass in its own right. Not only does it bridge Europe and Asia, it's also blessed with ecosystems from both continents, from alpine valleys and rocky deserts, to palm-fringed islands and endless fertile plains.

At 302,535 square miles (783,562 sq km) the country is larger than Texas, and significantly bigger than any European state. Turkey's European territory, north of Istanbul, is a land of flat plains and gently rolling hills dotted with pine forests. Conversely, Asian Turkey, which makes up some 97 percent of the country, is more rugged and mountainous and has of some of the most diverse geographical regions on the planet. These lands, beyond the Bosporus and Dardanelles straits, are commonly known as Asia Minor, or Anatolia (Anadolu in Turkish).

A Varied Nation

Over the millennia, raging rivers and seismic activity have folded, pockmarked, and sculpted Turkey into four distinct geographic areas, each with their own unique ecosystems and landscapes: the Mediterranean, the Black Sea, central Anatolia, and eastern Turkey. The Mediterranean coast, along which lie most of the country's ancient ruins, has always been a fertile and forgiving region. Mild, wet winters and gloriously sunny summers have made possible mass cultivation of citrus, vines, and—inland on the

Tunneling Under the Bosporus

In 2004, after many years of planning, work began on the Marmaray project (*www.marmaray.com.tr*)—a railway tunnel under the Bosporus linking Asian and European Istanbul. Embarking on such a task in a city like Istanbul, which is home to 12.8 million people and sits on a tectonic fault, was never going to be easy. A large part of the tunnel had to be built from earthquake-proof concrete and steel pipes, which were then lowered to the seabed in 425 feet (130 m) long sections. The tunnel was completed in 2008, but various setbacks—such as the discovery that one of the project's key sites was also the location of a long-lost Byzantine port (see p. 34)—mean that the Marmaray won't open until 2013.

Those few who have walked through the tunnel report that it's a spooky place—one of the busiest shipping sea-lanes in the world sits right overhead, but down below it's dark and silent. Bizarrely, though, mobile phones still get excellent reception.

When it opens it will, in theory, allow comfortable rail passage from Aberdeen, Scotland, to Tehran, Iran, without stepping off a train platform (journey time will be six days). The Marmaray Tunnel is part of a wider 47-mile (76 km) project that will link Istanbul's suburbs and airports, drastically reducing the number of vehicles on the road. At peak times up to 75,000 commuters will be shuttled from Europe to Asia every hour.

Mountainous landscape of Cappadocia, scattered with fertile fields and valleys

flood plains—grain. More natural vegetation, such as fig, olive, pine, and cypress trees thrive in the wilder spots, particularly where the Taurus Mountains stretch right down to the coast.

Turkey's northern Black Sea coast is hemmed in by the Pontic and Kaçkar mountains, and has long been geographically and culturally isolated from the rest of Anatolia. Fertile mountain rivers flow through thick alpine forests, then flood down to the generally damp coast. Tea and tobacco are produced here in equal abundance. Before mining (and recent discoveries of oil), fishing was the primary industry, especially for anchovies, or *hamsi,* also a pejorative term for the many Black Sea coasters who have brought their well-known business skills and liberal outlook to Istanbul.

Both the Taurus and Pontic ranges encircle central Anatolia, a vast plateau rising between 2,000 and 4,000 feet (600–1,200 m). Rainfall is scant, winters bitter, and the summers dusty and scorching. Beyond the capital at Ankara and the fairy chimneys of

A hot-air balloon journey over Cappadocia's "fairy chimneys"

Traveling to the Interior with Style & Speed

Connecting Europe's major urban centers by high-speed train is very much in vogue. In the last decade, super-fast routes have opened between Paris and Marseille, Milan and Rome, and Madrid and Barcelona. Linking Istanbul's 12.8 million residents with Ankara's 5 million will not only slash traffic on one of the world's busiest air routes, but will trounce jet travel in terms of comfort and speed, connecting city center to city center in just three hours by 2013.

The eastern half of the track (Ankara–Esenkent, Ankara–Sincan) is already in operation, allowing passengers to travel between cities in just over five hours at speeds of up to 155 miles (250 km) an hour. So what's it like? It certainly beats the bus, and the current four-times daily service is quicker than the airplane once check-in, security, and transfers are taken into account. Seats are "business class" with mini-TV screens and pan-oramic picture windows through which you can watch Turkey zoom by.

Follow the track's progress at *www.railway-technology.com/projects/ankara-Istanbul.*

Cappadocia (themselves caused by ashy volcanic fallout, see p. 222) is eastern Turkey, a soaring, twisted knot of mountains culminating in majestic Mount Ararat (16,854 feet/5,137 m). Nomads still crisscross the high plains, as do golden eagles, porcupines, wildcats, lynx, brown bears, deer, and—if locals are to be believed—wolves the size of ponies. Grazing livestock, not the cultivation of food crops, has always been the mainstay here. These snowy climes have preserved many ancient cultures, although the area—bordering Armenia, Iran, Iraq, and Syria—is still recovering from the lawlessness common in many of the world's remote border regions.

Protecting Turkey

Much of Turkey is geographically unique and of key historical importance, and over 40 national parks protect the country's most treasured sites. World War I battlefields on the Gallipoli Peninsula (see pp. 182–184) and the skiing station of Mount Uludağ (see pp. 168–169) are sheltered from overzealous development by their placement in the national park system. Several of Turkey's attractions, including Troy, Pamukkale, and parts of Istanbul, benefit from UNESCO protection as World Heritage sites.

> **Several of Turkey's attractions, including Troy, Pamukkale, and parts of Istanbul, benefit from UNESCO protection as World Heritage sites.**

Pollution is an ever present problem in fast-growing countries, particularly ones with large refining, oil transportation, and petrochemical industries. Turkey now has a nascent oil production industry its southeastern regions and along the Black Sea coast, too, the latter an already heavily polluted sea. In the towns and cities, you will find that litter is still thrown with casual abandon, although attitudes are changing.

But most of Turkey remains a haven, far removed from the highways, strip malls, and crowded beaches that clog up parts of Europe and the United States. The 30-million-plus visitors who are welcomed to Turkey each year are encouraged to help. Recycling your rubbish, limiting consumption of the ubiquitous plastic water bottles, and sharing your thoughts on environmental issues with your hosts is a great way to start. ∎

Food & Drink

With a vast, mixed terrain that lays claim to mountain terraces, sheltered orchards, and thousands of miles of coastline, Turkey is home to a hugely varied cuisine—even the ubiquitous kebab comes in hundreds of varieties.

Many of the ingredients we've come to rely on in everyday cooking are indigenous to Anatolia, including chickpeas, wheat, broad beans, walnuts, and apples. Yogurt? The ever popular breakfast food, snack, and smoothie component originated here. Like other Mediterranean cuisines, local dishes using fresh seasonal ingredients developed for consumption in times of plenty, while dried, salted, and preserved ingredients were put to use during the lean winter months.

Ottoman Cuisine

During the Ottoman Empire's peak, an army of over a thousand chefs pounded, diced, and fried away in the sumptuous Topkapı Palace kitchens, feeding tens of thousands daily. Tack on the exotic ingredients and cooking techniques that were plucked from the edges of three continents, and it's little wonder that Ottoman menus were whittled into an elaborate display of culinary leaps, loops, and arabesques. Imperial banquets included ornate creations such as pigeon stuffed with pine nuts, mint, and dried apricots and pilaf with chickpeas—except the chickpeas were replaced by gold nuggets.

To sample Ottoman dishes in Istanbul, visit Tuğra at the Çırağan Palace (see p. 125), where head chef Uğur Alparslan re-creates recipes found in the Topkapı Palace libraries.

Turkish Cuisine Today

Each of Turkey's regions is renowned for its own special dishes. But you needn't travel far to try the countryside's finest, as being in Istanbul—a veritable Turkish melting pot—means you can sample them all. Refer to our picks in Travelwise (see pp. 243–259), or look for authentic, family-run spots that sport *yemekevi* (home-style) signage. From the Black Sea come *hamsi pilavı* (anchovy pilaf) and corn bread. Aegean specialties concentrate on fresh fish and seafood, while from Gaziantep—the traditional home of Turkey's finest cuisine—*baklava* and syrupy desserts are the order of the day.

One of many *döner* kebab shops, Istanbul

EXPERIENCE: Learning to Cook Turkish Food

Fallen for Turkish cuisine? Yearning to re-create minty *ezogelin* soup, melting *imambayıldı*, or syrupy sponge cakes? Longtime Istanbul resident Dutch-born Eveline Zoutendijk is Cordon Bleu–trained. Together with Turkish chef Feyzi Yıldırım, Eveline teaches intimate half-day courses at her cooking school and restaurant, **Cooking Alaturka** *(Akbiyik Caddesi 72a, Sultanahmet, tel 0212/458 19 19, www.cookingalaturka.com, $$$$)*. Each hands-on, three-hour cooking lesson is followed by a five-course meal (non-chefs are welcome to attend). Other Turkish cooking courses are offered at the **Istanbul Culinary Institute** *(Meşrutiyet Caddesi 59, Tepebaşı, Çamlık Sokak, tel 0212/251 22 14, www.Istanbulculinary.com, $$$$)*.

Ten Most Famous Dishes

Although each region in Turkey offers an infinite variety of local dishes, the following are the country's most consistently popular picks.

Çorba (soup): Most meals begin with *çorba*. *Mercimek çorbası* is made from lentils and vegetables; *ezogelin çorbası* blends bulgur, red lentils, and mint. The pale, tripe-based *işkembe çorbası* is believed to prevent hangovers: Note the late-night vendors along İstiklal Caddesi! Traditionally, çorba is also eaten for breakfast.

Dolma (the stuffed): From zeytinyağlılar to *yaprak dolması* (stuffed vine leaves) and *Imambayıldı* (eggplant stuffed with tomatoes, onions, and herbs), these cold dishes make a light first course or refreshing summer meal. When a dolma is *etli*—stuffed with meat, such as *soğan dolması* (lamb- or beef-stuffed onions)—it is served hot as a main course.

Pide, a sort
of Turkish pizza
stuffed with cheese and meat

Kebabs: Now a worldwide staple, kebabs can be prepared in hundreds of ways: Sizzled on a skewer (*şiş kebab*); slow-roasted on a spit (*döner*); topped with foaming butter, tomato sauce, and cream (*İskender*); sprinkled with chili pepper (*Adana*); interspersed with eggplant (*patlıcan*); or studded with pistachios (*fıstıklı*).

Köfte (meatballs): Unpretentious yet delicacies unto themselves, *köfte* are usually a blend of lamb, beef, egg, and seasonings. Other common variations include *çiğ köfte* (raw beef or lamb, mixed with bulgur) and *mercimek köfte* (a vegetarian version made with red lentils).

Lahmacun & pide: Both with crispy dough bases, *lahmacun* is thin, round, and topped with minced lamb, parsley, and chili flakes, while thicker *pide* (also referred to as "Turkish pizza") is long and oblong with fillings like *kaşar* (cheese) or *sucuk* (spicy sausage) pinched between its pointy ends.

Lavaş: Huge, paper-thin *lavaş* bread features in two of Turkey's most popular snacks: *dürüm* (a tasty version of an American lunchtime wrap where lavaş is crisped up, seasoned, and rolled around a—usually meat-based—filling) and *gözleme* (where lavaş are filled with cheese, potatoes, or spinach, folded, and cooked on a searing hot plate).

Mantı (stuffed pasta): Similar to miniature Italian ravioli, *mantı* consists of tiny beef- or lamb-stuffed pasta doused in a garlicky yogurt sauce. Vegetarians can look for *patatesli mantı,* stuffed with potato instead.

Menemen: A breakfast dish comprising eggs scrambled with tomatoes, onions, and sweet green peppers. It's often topped with *peynir* (cheese) or *sucuk* (spicy sausage), and you'll find it at streetside cafés at all hours.

Meze: Somewhere between appetizers and tapas, *meze* make up the first course of most restaurant meals. Dozens of tiny tastes are laid out or rolled over to your table on a trolley. Take your pick of *soğuk mezeler* (cold meze), which may include *patlıcan salatası* (eggplant puree), *börülce salatası* (black-eyed pea salad), or *lakerda* (marinated bonito). *Ara sıcaklar* (hot meze), such as *kalamar tava* (fried squid), can be ordered off the menu.

Zeytinyağlılar: Seasonal vegetables are cooked in *zeytinyağı* (olive oil), along with lemon, sugar, and salt, cooled and served at room temperature. Depending on the current harvest, you'll find *enginar* (artichokes), *taze fasulye* (green beans), *kabak* (zucchini), *bakla* (broad beans), and *patlıcan* (eggplant). Vegetables stuffed with rice and spices are a type of *zeytinyağlılar.*

Regional specialties offer an extra dimension to a tasty cuisine. In the north, fish is normally fried, coated in corn flour, and is served with a sauce or yogurt. Restaurants along the Black Sea coast delight diners with their fried anchovies *(hamsi)* and corn bread. The southeast is known for particularly spicy kebabs. Around Istanbul and Bursa try the local Iskander kebab. Cooks in Gaziantep, in the east, favor local pistachios and other nuts in a variety of dishes.

A Refined Cuisine

Turkey's cuisine is increasingly appreciated by international food lovers. Based on fresh ingredients, Turkish dishes are healthy and appetizing. The nation is almost self-sufficient in food. In the south, citrus fruits, melons, hot peppers, and a wide range of vegetables are grown, while parts of the north grow tea as well a variety of cereals. Olives, figs, pistachios, eggplants, oranges, and lemons are widely cultivated while upland pastures support many sheep. Lamb and chicken are the most commonly served meats, and beef is also popular. In Muslim Turkey, pork is not on the menu. Western and southern areas, in particular, are home to vineyards and many homes have a vine scrambling up to the balcony.

Lamb and chicken are the most commonly served meats, and beef is also popular. In Muslim Turkey, pork is not on the menu.

The sea provides a rich bounty with enviable catches in the Aegean, Black, and Mediterranean Seas and in the Sea of Marmara. *Kılıç* (swordfish), *kalkan* (turbot), and *lüfer* (bluefish) as well as shrimp *(karides)* are popular. Seafood restaurants along harborsides often rely upon the day's catch for their star dishes. Watch which cafés the locals go into and you can be assured of a good meal.

Breakfast usually features bread, honey, yogurt, cheese, and tomatoes. Lunchtime may be *ev yemek,* literally "home food," a mix of vegetables and stew, or perhaps pilaf, a rice or bulgur (cracked wheat) dish that can include peas, beans, or eggplants. Dinner is the day's main meal, culminating in a dessert of tempting fruits or a sweet pastry. Salads are prominent on the menu, often including spicy herbs with tomatoes and cucumbers. The motif of Turkish cuisine is simplicity and excellent ingredients. Preparation is uncomplicated; presentation is important. Food is seldom covered by sauces, and spices are skillfully used to great effect and in moderation.

Drinks

In the daytime, hot tea is popular, served strong and black in tulip-shaped glasses. In the evening or after a meal, coffee is the preferred drink in Turkey but forget the range of Western coffees—although these are now available alongside Western-style dishes, fast food, and take-outs in the cities. Turks drink strong, slightly bitter coffee in small cups, which normally appear on the table alongside dessert. The national drink is *rakı,* a powerful aniseed liqueur to which water is added. Turkey also produces a selection of good wines, most of which are dry. Experience the best by tasting the local wine in each region. Non-alcoholic options include freshly squeezed fruit juices. While orange juice is a firm favorite, pomegranate and apple juices are also popular—and why not try a refreshing carrot juice? In winter, some traditional drinks appear, such as *boza,* made from fermented millet, and the very sweet *sahlep,* made from orchid roots and served hot with cinnamon. ■

The Arts

From ancient Roman frescoes to abstract video installations, the arts in Turkey run the gamut from traditional heritage to cutting-edge contemporary.

Architecture

Local architecture includes crumbling Roman amphitheaters, Byzantine cathedrals, thousand-year-old caravanserais, and magnificent domed Ottoman mosques, all interspersed with the pared-down appeal of the Istanbul Modern (see pp. 121–122) and the attractive town houses of the city's residents. In whatever era or style your passion resides, you'll find plenty to feed your architectural interests in and around Istanbul.

Visitors to Turkey are frequently surprised to discover the seemingly endless enclaves of ancient ruins that dot the countryside. There's no risk of forgetting the first-millennium B.C. here—reminders of the Hellenic and Hellenistic (approximately 1000–250 B.C.) empires, overlapping with all-encompassing Roman rule (through A.D. 334) are everywhere. For a peek at fine theaters, agoras, and stadiums, head to Ephesus (see pp. 198–200), Hierapolis (see p. 205), and Aphrodisias (see p. 203).

Constantinople (Istanbul) was established as the Roman capital in A.D. 334, and with the fall of Rome less than a century later, the city was soon headquarters to the new Byzantine Empire (sixth century A.D.–1453). Architectural experimentation was cultivated, particularly in the scores of structures built under Emperor Justinian (A.D. 483–565). Distinctive features of the grand buildings of the era include domed roofs, copious use of gold leaf, and intricate mosaic work. The Hagia Sophia (see pp. 66–69) is a shimmering example, and generally considered the zenith of Byzantine architecture. Istanbul's city walls were also constructed during this period.

During this same period the Seljuks—a tribal empire that crashed from Persia into Anatolia around the middle of the 12th century—were also developing their own building style. Their legacy includes caravansaries, or *kervansaray* (a kind of combination warehouse and inn, where traveling traders could board with their wares and animals for the night), *madresseh* (religious schools), mosques, and hammams. Most were built around an open (or occasionally covered) courtyard; another distinguishing feature is the ornate stone carvings around a structure's entranceway, such as Bursa's Yeşil Cami (see p. 167).

In 1453 Mehmet the Conqueror seized control of Constantinople, ushering in the enduring reign of the Ottoman Empire. Seljuk and Byzantine architectural traditions

---

Mimar Sinan's Architectural Wonders

Imperial architect Mimar Sinan's (see p. 46) genius is on display throughout Istanbul. Some of his most impressive buildings are: the Hammam of Roxelana (see sidebar p. 68), located close to the Hagia Sophia; Rüstem Paşa Mosque (see pp. 86–87) in Eminönü; Old City's Süleymaniye Mosque (see pp. 87–88); Kılıç Ali Paşa Mosque, Tophane (see p. 120); and Atik Valide Mosque in Üsküdar (see pp. 146–147).

The domed and vaulted ceiling of the Süleymaniye Mosque, designed by Sinan

fused and intensified, with new elements, such as vast suspended domes, thrown in. Imperial architect Mimar Sinan (1490–1588; see pp. 90–91) is considered to have been the greatest of all Ottoman designers. A visit to Istanbul would not be complete without a visit to one of his masterpieces (see sidebar p. 44), which range from imperial mosques, constructed on a monumental scale, to humbler structures like public baths, schools, and, tucked away in a side street near the Süleymaniye mosque, Sinan's own elegant but modest mausoleum. Topkapı Palace (see pp. 58–64), Ottoman center of command, was also built at this time; later Ottoman architecture (18th century) includes the wooden waterside *yalı* (private mansions) that line the Bosporus.

As Ottoman influence petered out, locals began to turn westward for inspiration, and European influences eased their way into 19th-century Istanbul. Art nouveau's twirls and whirls can been seen along İstiklal Caddesi (see pp. 110–111) in the Beyoğlu district, while the royal family's transfer to Dolmabahçe Palace (see pp. 126–128) in the Beşiktaş district in 1856 was a carefully considered "modern" move, away from the extravagant 16th-century splendor of the Topkapı Palace.

Art and art lovers at the 11th Istanbul Biennial in 2009

Today, much contemporary architecture skirts Istanbul's edges. Local fashion label Vakko's new headquarters (2010) is a cube of glass and steel. Bending walls play with indoor space and outdoor areas at Kanyon Shopping Mall (2006, see sidebar p. 134). Across the Bosporus, Üsküdar's Şakirin Mosque (2009) was designed in part by leading female architect Zeynep Fadıllıoğlu (b. 1955). And in a city as densely populated as Istanbul, it's no surprise that 21st-century architecture is also often a new take on the old. Seek out industrial-chic Santrallstanbul (see p. 114), formerly a power station, now a contemporary exhibition space.

Art & Photography

During the Byzantine Empire, art was often closely inter-twined with the era's architecture. Intricate mosaics adorned church interiors, such as the recently restored examples at Hagia Sophia (see pp. 66–69), while gold-steeped icons, such as the artworks on display at the Greek Orthodox School of Theology on Heybeliada (see p. 162), were often hung in period churches. The beautiful

> As Ottoman influence petered out, locals began to turn westward for inspiration, and European influences eased their way into 19th-century Istanbul.

icons made in Constantinople were highly sought after throughout the Orthodox Christian world, and these Byzantine icons remain the prized possessions of many churches in Russia and Ukraine even today.

Islamic scripture warns strongly against depicting people or animals in art, asserting that only God has the ability or right to create life. Historically, this restriction meant that the most popular forms of artistic expression during Ottoman times were calligraphy, carpet weaving, and ceramics. Calligraphy, in particular, was elevated to a breathtaking level of beauty and complexity by Ottoman artists, whose work decorates the interiors of Istanbul's finest mosques and palaces. Istanbul's Museum of Turkish & Islamic Arts (see pp. 78–79) provides a crash course on close to three millennia of Middle Eastern art.

Towards the end of the 19th century, figurative art rocketed in popularity. In 1914, the local government sent a group of the country's finest artists to Paris to absorb modern painting methods, including Impressionism. Their return to Turkey resulted in an exciting injection of new techniques. In 1937, President Atatürk decreed that Dolmabahçe Palace's former crown princes' apartments be converted into the Museum of Painting and Sculpture (Resim ve Heykel Müzesi, see p. 124). Today the museum houses more than 7,000 Turkish and international artworks.

Photography has been a favorite Turkish artistic medium throughout much of the past century, kick-started by the Abdullah Brothers, the Ottoman Empire's official photographic chroniclers. Visit Antalya's Suna-İnan Kıraç Kaleiçi Museum (see p. 219) for their 19th-century shots of city life. Istanbul-based Ara Güler displays shots of contemporary Turkey at his café, Ara (see Travelwise p. 249), while the Istanbul Modern (see pp. 121–122) boasts an exhibition space dedicated to photography.

Today Istanbul's local art scene is buzzing, as Europe looks east for inspiration. Along with over 250 contemporary art galleries (see a few of the best sidebar, p. 103), the city hosts the annual festival **Contemporary Istanbul** *(Nov., www.contemporaryIstanbul.com)*, as well as the **Istanbul Biennial** *(Sept.–Nov., odd years, www.iksv.org)* every other year. For banks, prominent local companies, and business magnates, including the Koç and Sabancı families, patronage of the arts is a priority. In 2010, and with much international fanfare, the Vehbi Koç Foundation inaugurated the new contemporary space **ARTER** *(İstiklal Caddesi 211, tel 0212/243 37 67, www.arter.org.tr, closed Mon.).* Also worth seeking out is **Proje4L** *(Elgiz Museum of Contemporary Art, Meydan Sokak, Beybi Giz Plaza B Blok, Maslak, tel 0212/290 25 25, www.proje4l.org, closed Sun.–Mon., Tues. by appointment only)*, a private museum founded by Sevda and Can Elgiz in 2001.

To learn more about the contemporary art found in Turkey today, or pick up a copy of Hossein Amirsadeghi and Maryam Homayoun Eisler's *Unleashed: Contemporary Art from Turkey* (2010), which includes profiles of 90 top artists, as well as interviews with notable Turkish gallery owners and curators.

Music & Dance

You're in a boisterous Istanbul *meyhane* (traditional restaurant) and in walks a group of musicians. The noise level rises a notch as they tune their instruments, then launch into a romping traditional tune, probably drowning out your dinner companions. As you scan the room, even the trendiest of Turks laugh, raise their arms, snap their fingers, and sing along.

Welcome to Turkey: a culture that embraces song and dance with refreshing abandon. Perhaps most immediately associated with the country are both whirling dervishes (see pp. 49–50) and belly dancing. The latter's erotic origins are unknown, but it earned a favored place here under the Ottoman empire. Unfortunately, most of Istanbul's belly-dancing performances today hover between touristy and downright seedy.

But there's plenty more to the local music scene. Popular types of Turkish music include Arab-influenced arabesk and modern *fasıl* (of which you'll hear variants in the meyhane), as well as local pop. Folk instruments are still studied and widely played. They include the *mey* (flute), *davul* (drum), *saz* (Turkish lute), and *kemençe* (Byzantine lyre), all of which can be seen along "music street," Galip Dede Caddesi.

Today, Istanbul's Süreyya Opera House (see p. 141) and the Atatürk Cultural Center (see p. 117) are great places to take in concerts,

---

EXPERIENCE:
Whirling Dervishes

The Galata Mevlevileri perform most evenings at the **Hodjapasha Culture Center** *(Ankara Caddesi, Hocapaşa Hamam Sokak 5–9D, tel 0212/511 46 26, closed Tues. & Thurs., www .Istanbuldervish.com)*, a 500-year-old hammam near Sultanahmet's Sirkeci train station. On Thursday nights, you can also see a *sema* ceremony at **Silivrikapı Mevlana Cultural Center** *(Mevlânakapı Mah., Yeni Tavanlı Çeşme Sokak 8, Fatih, tel 0542/422 15 44, www.emav.org).* In addition, the **Galata Mevlevihanesi** (see p. 108) presents sema performances in their *tekke*, or religious hall.

Young *mevlevi* perform their famous whirling dance in traditional attire.

modern dance, and opera, while all sorts of Turkish dance performances take place at the Hodjapasha Culture Center *(Ankara Caddesi Hocapaşa Hamam Sok No: 5-9D, Sirkeci, tel 0212/511 46 26, www.turkishdancenight.com)* on Tuesday and Thursday nights. For a more intimate experience, look for posters advertising smaller performances, or ask around for local recommendations.

Whirling Dervishes

Hypnotic *mevlevi*, known in the west as "whirling dervishes," are synonymous with Turkey. They feature on tourist board posters, and it seems that every major city herds tourists into weekly, or even nightly, spectacles. It may be an art, but the twirling isn't just for show. It's also a form of worship.

Mevlana Celaleddin Rumi (or simply "Rumi") founded the Sufi religious order of mevlevi in his hometown of Konya during the 13th century. Its core practices included *sema*—when mevlevi perform a spinning ritual dance until they enter a kind of trance that they feel brings them closer to the mind of God. Sufism and its mystical practices remained popular throughout the Ottoman Empire until mevlevi were banned during the 1920s, at the start of the enthusiastically secular Turkish Republic. Sema ceremonies remained underground until 1975, when the ban was revoked.

Today, clad in fitted shirts and long white skirts, topped with a kind of elongated fez-type hat and spinning with abandon, mevlevi are a unique sight. If you're keen to learn more about the mevlevi, don't miss the opportunity to experience a sema performance (see sidebar p. 48).

Poetry & Literature

Against a backdrop of Byzantine chronicles and ornately formulated Ottoman lyrical verse, modern Turkish poetry and literature is based on folk traditions of oral storytelling, epics originally sung by traveling bards *(aşık).*

More recently, 20th-century Turkey's renowned poets include Nazım Hikmet (1902–1962), communist, political agitator, and mentor to Orhan Kemal (see p. 123), and Mehmet Akif Ersoy (1873–1936), author of the lyrics to the Turkish national anthem. Heybeliada-born satirist Aziz Nesin (1915–1995) poked acidic fun at Turkish society and politics throughout the 1950s and 1960s. Today, the country's most famous literary exports are Kurdish author Yaşar Kemal (b. 1923), author of *İnce Memed,* or *Memed, My Hawk* (1955); poet and writer Enis Batur (b. 1952); Elif Shafrak, who penned the controversial *The Bastard of Istanbul* (2007); and Nobel Prize-winner Orhan Pamuk (see sidebar p. 118).

In the tradition of travelogs and memoirs, Turkey has captured the heart of plenty of foreign authors, too. For a few of the finest, see "Further Reading" (Travelwise p. 234).

Scribes of Istanbul

The following eight great historical titles are all still in print. Each lucidly uncovers a different era of Istanbul, from its Byzantine beginnings to the city in the 1970s. Some of the early European travelers—such as Edmondo de Amicis and Pierre Loti—witnessed the empire's upheavals and palace revolutions firsthand. Others, including John Julius Norwich and Lars Brownworth, discuss historic battles and events from a modern perspective. You can pick up titles by Orhan Pamuk and John Freely in any of Istanbul's leading

Hollywood . . . in Turkey?

Long before "talkies" took the world by storm, the craze for moving pictures swept through Istanbul. Public screenings began during the 1890s, when films were only a few minutes long. Local movie production peaked during the "Yeşilçam years" (1950s–1970s), when Turkish movie studios were based around Yeşilçam Sokak in Istanbul, an area that became known as Turkey's Hollywood, producing hundreds of movies a year.

Turkish film has experienced a renaissance over the last decade. Recent Turkish films have earned critical acclaim and box-office popularity all over the world. Director Nuri Bilge Ceylan's *Üç Maymun (Three Monkeys,* 2008) was nominated for an Oscar, while in 2010, the third film of director Semih Kaplanoğlu's *Bal (Honey)* trilogy won the Berlin Film Festival's prestigious Golden Bear award. At home, Turkish-produced movies attract viewers in droves. Themes ranging from slapstick comedy like *Recep İvedik* (2008), to political sagas like *Büyük Adam Küçük Aşk (Big Man Little Love,* also titled *Hejar* in Kurdish, 2001).

Istanbul has two annual film festivals: The newer !f Istanbul *(www.ifIstanbul .com)* runs for ten days each February; the International Istanbul Film Festival *(Uluslararası Istanbul Film Festivali,* known as the IKSV, *www.iksv.org)* consists of two movie-laden weeks in April, culminating in its Golden Tulip awards ceremony. Both festivals screen films with subtitles.

bookshops. Books by the other authors are best bought before you depart on your trip.

Seyahatname by Evliya Çelebi: Republished in 2010 as *An Ottoman Traveler* by University of Chicago professor Robert Dankoff, Çelebi's (slightly exaggerated) accounts of his trips from Istanbul to Russia, Hungary, and Mecca make him the key chronicler of 17th-century Ottoman life.

Costantinopoli by Edmondo de Amicis: A late 19th-century romp through Istanbul's highlights, including vivid descriptions of the Basilica Cisterns (see pp. 73, 76–77) and the Galata Bridge (see pp. 102–103).

Pierre Loti: Travels with the Legendary Traveler by Lesley Blanch: Writing mostly from the panoramic cafés of Eyüp, Orientalist Loti breezes through turn-of-the-20th-century Istanbul society with aplomb.

> **Handmade decorative art items are made using skills and sometimes even tools passed down from one generation to the next.**

Istanbul: Memories of a City by Orhan Pamuk: Nobel laureate Pamuk touches on the lost city of his youth, a procession of endless weddings, childhood fantasies, and tales from the Bosporus. Like most of his books, it was translated into English by Maureen Freely, daughter of John Freely and former Istanbul resident.

Strolling through Istanbul by John Freely and Hilary Sumner-Boyd: The city's definitive walking guide. Freely, an American scholar based in Istanbul on and off for five decades, is the acclaimed author of over a dozen books about Turkey.

Lost to the West by Lars Brownworth: Effortless sweep through Byzantium's highs and lows. Brownworth's free podcasts about Byzantine history (*www.12byzantinerulers.com*) are also highly recommended.

Byzantium by John Julius Norwich: Lucid, powerful, and eminently readable trilogy from the master historian. Provides a comprehensive overview of the empire's rise and fall.

Tales from the Expat Harem by Anastasia M. Ashman and Jennifer Eaton Gökmen: Stereotype-challenging firsthand accounts from foreign women who married Turkish men.

Literature for Turkey as a whole? Many travelers find Herodotus' *The Histories* an excellent companion. In a similar manner, Homer's epic *The Iliad* uncovers the politics and siege of ancient Troy. Two more recent books provide an excellent introduction to modern Turkey. In Tom Brosnahan's *Bright Sun, Strong Tea*, the writer breaks bread with tribal chieftains and Ottoman nobles as he authors the country's very first guidebook in the 1970s. Jeremy Seal's *A Fez of the Heart* goes on the trail of Turkey's traditional head gear in 1993 and is touching, illuminating, and hilarious all at once. (For our full reading list of cultural, fiction, and guidebooks, see p. 234.)

Crafts

Generations of Turks have produced high-quality craft items and these traditions are kept alive to this day. Handmade decorative art items are made using skills and sometimes even tools passed down from one generation to the next. The best known Turkish crafts are rug- and carpetmaking. *Kilims* are rugs hand woven on a loom. Unlike carpets, kilims are flat with no pile. Both are usually made by women and, while they follow decorative themes, each is unique. Leatherworkers make clothes and bags, as well as cushions and small goods from leather scraps. Colorful enamel tiles, with ornate decoration and a thick glaze, are produced in Iznik and Kutahya. Wood craft has a rich history, from vernacular furniture to inlaid, gilded, and engraved art objects. ■

Istanbul

The Old City 54–97 ■ **European Istanbul** 98–135
Asian Istanbul 136–151 ■ **Istanbul Excursions** 152–175

The historical, colorful core of Istanbul, headquarters of the Byzantine and Ottoman Empires, and home to myriad ancient sites

The Old City

Introduction & Map   56-57

Topkapı Palace & the Archaeology Museum   58-65

Experience: Taking a Course at the Caferağa Medresesi   64

Hagia Sophia   66-69

Blue Mosque & Around   70-97

Feature: Hammams—Ancient Turkish Baths   74-75

Experience: Visiting Sultanahmet's Baths   75

Experience: A Shopping Trip in the Grand Bazaar   82

Experience: Istanbul Eats Culinary Tours   87

Feature: The Life & Times of Mimar Sinan   90-91

Experience: A Boat Trip Up the Golden Horn   93

Walk: Around Eyüp & Pierre Loti   94-95

Hotels & Restaurants   243-246

Pages 52–53: Maiden Tower at sunset, with the city of Istanbul stretching out behind it
Opposite: Interior of Hagia Sophia

The Old City

Istanbul's imperial heart for over 1,500 years, the Old City (Sultanahmet) sits between the Golden Horn to its north and the Sea of Marmara to its south; the Bosporus tumbles past Seraglio Point (Sarayburnu), its eastern tip. Fragments of fifth-century walls ring this narrow, almost triangular peninsula, interspersed with luxury hotels, fish markets, and crumbling wooden homes.

A fish market along the Bosporus strait in Istanbul, its fish kept fresh by the crisp winter air

The Old City has a half dozen must-see sights—but no one would blame you if you gave them all up in order to visit Hagia Sophia twice. Upon completion in its current form in A.D. 537 it became the largest cathedral—as well as one of the largest buildings—in the world, a distinction it held for nearly a thousand years. When the Hagia Sophia's patron, Emperor Justinian, first gazed at the candlelit golden dome and dazzling mosaics, it must have looked like heaven on earth.

The perfect symmetry of the Blue Mosque (Sultanahmet Camii), built under Sultan Ahmet I, so dominates the panorama that it lends the Old City its Turkish moniker, Sultanah-met. Ottoman princes from the nearby Topkapı Palace (Topkapı Sarayı) worshipped under its great dome for generations. Sultan Ahmet I's harmonious gift to the city has been marveled at by characters as disparate as former U.S. President Bill Clinton, Pope Benedict XVI, and Iranian President Mahmoud Ahmadinejad (not that that trio is likely to be spotted sharing a pot of çay together).

But it's not simply the well-established sights that appeal. During the construction of the Marmaray Tunnel (see sidebar p. 36), the peninsula's southern neighborhood of Yenikapı was discovered to be sitting atop Constantinople's Harbor of Theodosius. The port was a nautical hub from the 4th through the 14th centuries, and the site has been fertile hunting ground for a gamut of seafaring vessels. In addition, plenty of ancient artifacts, some dating from 4000 B.C., have also been unearthed, making the planned creation of a museum to permanently display these treasures a given.

Aside from the occasional tourist bus visiting the incredible mosaics at the Church of St. Savior in Chora (Kariye Camii), or the handful of foreigners taking in the incredible view atop Eyüp, visitors seldom venture just west of Sultanahmet proper, up the Golden Horn's southern bank. A pity, as this area hosts many of Istanbul's most offbeat sights, including portions of the ancient city walls and the Church of St. Stephen of the Bulgars—a cast-iron church that was flat-packed in Austria and floated down the Bosporus. Some of these sights would be tricky to find even if they weren't so woefully signposted. The solution? Point to the listing and any local will wave you on your way. ■

NOT TO BE MISSED:

Topkapı Palace: Istanbul's most popular sight and epicenter of the Ottoman Empire for centuries 58–64

Trying your hand at calligraphy at the Caferağa Medresesi 64

Hagia Sophia, with its renovated interior shimmering with gilded mosaics 66–69

The six-minareted Blue Mosque, its gallery decorated with more than 20,000 İznik tiles 70–71

Shopping for gifts, Turkish Delight, and treasures at the Grand Bazaar and the Spice Market 79–85

Getting steamed, scrubbed, and invigorated at one of the Old City's historical hammams 74–75

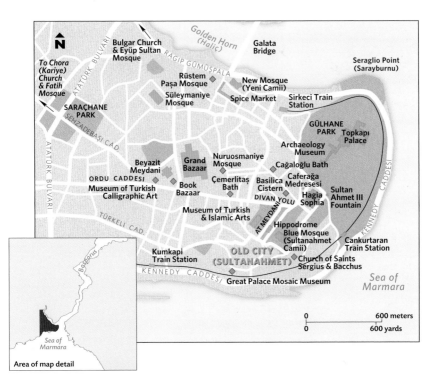

Topkapı Palace & the Archaeology Museum

A UNESCO World Heritage site and the epicenter of the Ottoman Empire for four centuries, Istanbul's most visited attraction—Topkapı Palace—exudes opulence. Befitting such a historically important capital, it housed the Imperial Treasury, the Imperial Mint, and a harem of the realm's most beautiful women, and was home to generations of sultans. Next door, the Archaeology Museum hosts a treasure trove of fascinating historic artifacts.

The regal site of Topkapı Palace, as viewed from the Golden Horn's natural harbor

Topkapı Palace

Sultan Mehmet the Conqueror (1432–1481) began work on the palace (sarayı) in 1459, a few years after his capture of Constantinople. Topkapı was expanded and modified over the years, primarily thanks to the conquering glories of Süleyman the Magnificent (1495–1566) and the skill of the indefatigable royal architect Sinan (see pp. 90–91). Entrance into the complex is via the imposing **Imperial Gate** (Bab-ı Hümâyûn). Traditionally, no commoners were allowed past this point. Inside the **first courtyard** is Gülhane Park (see sidebar p. 63), the **Hagia Eirene church,** the ruins of the Imperial Mint, and Istanbul's Archaeology Museum (see pp. 64–65). By the **Fountain of the Executioner** (Cellat Çeşmesi)—the spring where the palace executioner washed his hands after dispatching prisoners—is the Topkapı ticket office.

The **second courtyard** was once home to thousands of staff,

INSIDER TIP:

To cut to the chase, hire your own Topkapı Palace guide. Guides offer their services outside the main ticket booth in front of the Gate of Salutations, cost about 50 Turkish lira ($35) per hour per person, and can jump the long ticket lines.

—CLIVE CARPENTER
National Geographic contributor

including the sultan's advisors, and his private army of Janissary guards. It also contains the palace kitchens and imperial stables. The **third and fourth courtyards** were the private domain of the sultan and his family, and bear such unimaginable displays of wealth that it can make a visit overwhelming. It's best to go slowly, savor the sights, and let your mind wander back through the Ottoman Empire's glory days.

The Second Courtyard: The twin-turreted **Gate of Salutation** (Bab-üs Selâm) leads through to the tree-dappled second courtyard. Originally only persons on official palace business could pass through this vast portal. All visitors were also required to dismount, as only the sultan could proceed on horseback.

To the right of the entrance gate are two **scale orientation models** of the palace; these are useful in getting a grip on the overwhelming size and layout of the grounds.

The second courtyard is much as it was when Mehmet the Conqueror first laid out the complex, although tropical birds and animals, plus a few worried-looking viziers (court advisors), would have been strutting through the gardens too.

To the right of the courtyard are the **Palace Kitchens** (Saray Mutfakları, see sidebar this page). These reopened in 2010 after extensive renovations and are identifiable from the rows of chimneys on top. In Topkapı's golden era, the kitchens were responsible for feeding up to 4,000 people a day, and twice as many if there was a banquet.

Today the kitchens are filled with a stunning display of Far Eastern porcelain, which was prized by the Ottomans, as the dye used in its production was supposed to neutralize poison. For this reason, Chinese ceramics were imported along the Silk Road. Indeed, as

Topkapı Palace

✉ Bab-ı Hümâyûn Caddesi, Gülhane

☎ (0212) 512 04 80

🕐 Closed Tues.

💲 $$$$ (Harem additional $$$)

🚇 Gülhane

www.topkapisarayi .gov.tr

Feeding the Thousands

The Topkapı Palace Kitchens were staffed by up to a thousand cooks, on call to feed the sultan and his inner circle around the clock. Split into various subdivisions, the Palace Kitchens included a creamery, a beverage kitchen, an out-service kitchen, and the harem kitchen—serving up dishes for the sultan's family and concubines.

China's Cultural Revolution in 1967 laid waste to much of that country's original stock, the "china" collection at the Topkapı Palace is now the largest outside of Asia. Find thousands of Song, Yuan, Ming, and Qing dynasty pieces, alongside European porcelain from

Limoges and Sèvres, in France. One room in the kitchens displays elegant silver services—some gifts from foreign dignitaries—and another room shows the kitchen as it would have looked in its heyday, with the huge iron pots, pans, and ladles that were used in cooking for the servants and sultans alike.

Directly on the other side of the courtyard, inside the **old treasury,** is a vast display of vintage weaponry. The loot piled up here, which includes swords, bows, and armor plundered from all over the Middle East, Europe, and Asia, tells a vivid story of Ottoman expansionism. In the north corner of the courtyard is the **Imperial Stables** (Istabl-ı Âmire). These once housed the sultan's and princes' horses, but were renovated in 2010 as an outstanding temporary exhibition space and display a selection of various sultans' horse carriages.

The Harem: Although a visit to the harem incurs an extra charge

($$$, 9:30 a.m.–3:30 p.m.), the chance to glimpse what was haram, or forbidden, for over four centuries is worth every cent. The harem served as the sultan's private chambers, as well as that of his close family, a fact made clear by the sheer level of opulence on display.

The scores of small rooms, fine latticework, and stained-glass windows give the impression of a gilded cage, which is exactly what it was for several sultans-to-be, who were imprisoned in paradise lest they threaten the current sultan's throne. Ibrahim I (1615–1648), better known as Ibrahim the Mad, was wheeled out to rule as sultan on the death of his brother Murat IV (1612–1640) after two decades in the harem. Ibrahim had an obsession with obese women that bordered on zealotry, eventually finding companionship in the 330-pound Sheker Pare, or Sugar Cube, as her nickname translates. More perversely, he had every harem girl

Roxelana & the Harem Women

In addition to the four wives permitted by Islamic law, the Ottoman sultans allowed themselves an exuberant variety of concubines. The most beautiful girls from across the empire—most of them Christians from Crimea, Greece, and the Caucasus—were brought from slave markets to stock up the sultan's harem. The two most powerful women in the harem were the sultan's mother, the Valide Sultan, and the sultan's official first wife, the First Kadın.

Many harem women rose to great power, not least Roxelana (1510–1558), a Russian slave girl captured in what is now

Ukraine. As Süleyman the Magnificent's First Kadın, she made every effort to retain power during tumultuous times. She even persuaded Süleyman to dispose of his grand vizier and lifelong friend, İbrahim Paşa (see p. 78), by spreading rumors about his royal ambitions. After İbrahim was strangled in his sleep, another blot on her ambitions appeared in the guise of Mustafa, Süleyman's much admired son from a different marriage. To pave the way for her own son Selim to take the throne, Roxelana conspired a hate campaign against Mustafa, which led to his nocturnal strangulation.

INSIDER TIP:

The harem at Topkapı Palace is very popular and gets booked up quickly. As soon as you enter the palace grounds, buy a separate ticket for the harem at the kiosk in front of its entrance and view some of the palace's other sights while awaiting your designated time slot.

—SALLY MCFALL
National Geographic contributor

Traditionally dressed guards at Topkapı Palace's harem

drowned in the Bosporus during a palace intrigue late in his reign. After steering the empire toward rapid collapse, he was eventually assassinated by his Janissary guard.

The narrow **Golden Road** (Altınyol) connects the harem's key rooms, including the **Imperial Hall** (Hünkâr Sofası), a rococo playground for the sultan and his family, and the deliciously beautiful **Apartments of the Queen Mother** (Valide Sultan Dairesi), a central figure in Ottoman palace society. Of key historical importance is the **Courtyard of the (Black) Eunuchs** (Harem Ağaları Taşlığı). These castrated figures administered the harem. Although they couldn't physically take part in harem scandal, they were the instigators of many a conspiracy within what was literally a cutthroat world of several hundred women, all jockeying for supreme status and power.

The Third Courtyard: Entrance to the third courtyard, or "inner palace" as it was often known, was strictly controlled. Even the grand vizier, the sultan's chief adviser, could only pass through the ornate **Gate of Felicity** (Bab-üs Saadet) into this secret sanctum with special permission. A stone in front of the gate marks where the banner of the Prophet Muhammad once flew. In wartime, this flag would be entrusted to the Grand Vizier, who would carry it into battle.

The sultans would have spent their days in the lush gardens and ornate buildings of the third courtyard. Behind the gate is the **Throne Room** (Arz Odası), otherwise

Tilework outside the Circumcision Room at Topkapı Palace

INSIDER TIP:

For tired tourists, Gülhane Park is the ideal spot to rest on the long sightseeing walk around Topkapı Palace and the Archaeology Museum.

—CLIVE CARPENTER
National Geographic contributor

Behind the throne room is the **Library of Ahmet III** (Enderûn Kütüphanesi). Its soaring dome is frescoed with an intricate weave of orange and blue flowers. Light is filtered through glass stained with Koranic inscriptions below İznik tiles thick with delicate tulips. Key manuscripts on religion, law, and history—written in Persian, Arabic, Turkish, and other languages of the empire—were once kept here.

To the left of the library is the **Chamber of the Sacred Relics** (Kutsal Emanetler Dairesi), one of the most arresting sights in the palace. The pavilion contains some of the most important relics in the Islamic world, most of which were brought back by Sultan Selim I (Selim the Grim, 1465–1520) from his campaign to subdue Arabia in 1517. These artifacts include a tooth and a footprint of the Prophet, the ancient keys to the Ka'aba—the most sacred site in Islam, found in Mecca—and one of Muhammad's finely inscribed swords. The star exhibit, protected behind glass, is the mantel once worn by Muhammad. These rooms are a place of pilgrimage for thousands of Muslims each year; out of courtesy, it's

known as the Chamber of Petitions. Here military leaders and imperial advisers would have petitioned the sultan, who would receive news of his far-flung empire while reclining on a golden plinth in this lavishly decorated room. Foreign ambassadors, many of whom would have kissed the hem of the sultan's clothing, were occasionally granted an audience here.

kind to allow them enough space to pray freely.

The **Imperial Treasury** (Hazine-ı Âmire) takes up the entire east wall of the inner courtyard. This shimmering collection of diamonds, emeralds, and gold has few rivals anywhere in the world. It's literally priceless and the size of the gems makes a mockery of even the most extravagant modern-day engagement ring. Read each inscription carefully, as the story behind each emerald-encrusted sword or diamond headdress is fascinating. Most valuable of all the exhibits is the Spoonmaker's Diamond, a brilliant 86-carat gem lit up by a surrounding double row of 49 additional diamonds.

Imperial Costume Collection: This permanent exhibition next to the treasury is captivating, as it shows the dandified side to the sultans' lives. Like most of the Topkapı's collections of treasure, ceramics, or armor, only a fraction of the entire anthology of clothing is on display, which here includes a vast Italian velvet costume made for Süleyman the Magnificent.

Murat III's short gown covered in Islamic verses is displayed next to Mahmud II's white sailor's outfit, an elegant take on a European admiral's uniform.

The Fourth Courtyard: This leafy area was a sanctuary for the sultan and his family. Full of elaborate kiosks and parks, it is blessed with expansive views and serves as a welcome respite after the ostentatious overload of the third courtyard.

The **Circumcision Room** (Sünnet Odası) is decorated with highly unusual Chinese-inspired tiles. They portray pheasants reminiscent of a Ming dynasty vase, the birds' eyes once studded with real diamonds. Scores of young princes no doubt cried through their rite of passage under the sunny blue-and-white-tiled interior. One of the last was Mehmet VI (1861–1926) in 1870. The Ottoman Empire's final ruler from 1918, he left Istanbul on a British warship when the sultanate was abolished in 1922, spending his final years in the resort of San Remo on the Italian Riviera.

Next to the Circumcision Room is the golden **İftar Pavilion,** where

Museum of the History of Science & Technology in Islam

✉ Gülhane Park
🕐 Closed Tues.
💲 $
🚇 Gülhane

Gülhane Park

Gülhane, "Rose House Park" in Turkish, is Istanbul's oldest public park. It lies just east of Topkapı Palace and shares the same entrance gate as the palace and the Archaeology Museum. A shady place for a stroll, its spacious landscape of trees and flower beds has long been a favorite with picnicking families and courting couples. The sultans used the park as a private domain and built boathouses, kiosks, and viewing platforms to watch the ships ferrying in trade from every part of their empire. A few teahouses occupy the place where sultans once pontificated.

On the western edge of the park is the **Museum of the History of Science & Technology in Islam,** housing replicas of inventions in astronomy, physics, geography, and more, from the 8th to 16th centuries.

Archaeology Museum

✉ Osman Hamdi Bey Yokuşu, Topkapı Sarayi, Gülhane

☎ (0212) 520 77 40

🕐 Closed Mon.

💲 $$$

Ⓜ Gülhane

www.istanbular keoloji.gov.tr/ archaeological_ museum

the sultans would have broken their fast during the Muslim feast of Ramadan. The views are jaw-dropping. The nearby **Baghdad Kiosk** commemorates Murat IV's Baghdad Campaign and capture of the Mesopotamian city in 1638. It's a classically Ottoman reclining room with fine carpets and cushions, where sultans would have chatted and smoked with friends and relatives. The silver stove in the middle of the room was a gift from King Louis XIV of France, himself no stranger to gross ostentation.

The remaining buildings in the fourth courtyard, most of which are closed to the public, include the **Chief Physician's Chamber** (Hekimbaşı Odası), which served as the court drugstore, and a fine European pavilion known as the **Grand Kiosk** (Mecidiye Köşkü),

which hosts a fine Ottoman-inspired restaurant called **Konyalı** (tel 0212/513 96 96, www .konyalilokantasi.com, closed Tues.; see Travelwise p. 244).

Archaeology Museum

In any other place, this museum would be the city's must-see sight. In Istanbul, however, the Archaeology Museum (Arkeoloji Müzesi), built in 1881, competes with the neighboring Topkapı Palace, plus the nearby Hagia Sophia and Blue Mosque, so viewing its million-strong exhibits is normally a calm, contemplative voyage of discovery.

The museum's displays are world class. It has two entrances (one located in the first public courtyard of Topkapı Palace and the other from Gülhane Park) that lead you into marble halls, passageways, and grand chambers stuffed with exquisite ancient artifacts, Roman splendor, and the finest treasures of the Ottoman world outside of the Topkapı Palace. Two ancillary museums on site add other dimensions to the visit. The **Tiled Kiosk** (Çinili Köşk), housing the **Museum of Islamic Art,** built as a pleasure palace by Mehmet the Conqueror in 1472, is filled with an unrivaled collection of Ottoman ceramics, stained glass, carpets, and porcelain. The **Museum of the Ancient Orient** began as a fine arts college in 1883. It is noted for its collection from pre-Islamic Arabia and its clay tablets inscribed with cuneiform script. Look for the Treaty of Kadesh, the world's oldest peace accord.

Allow two hours for even a brief tour of the Archaeology Museum's

---

EXPERIENCE: Taking a Course at the Caferağa Medresesi

Tucked between the Topkapı Palace and the Hagia Sophia, the **Caferağa Medresesi** (Caferiye Sokak, Soğukkuyu Çıkmazı No: 1, Sultanahmet, tel 0212/513 36 01, www .caferagamedresesi.com) was originally a religious school built by Sinan. The ornate classrooms and the 15 former dormitories that ring a delightful courtyard garden were turned into an Ottoman crafts workshop in 1989. They now host day- and week-long courses in mosaics, calligraphy, music, photography, ceramics, gilding, marbling, and more. Instruction is in both English and Turkish. The center's schedule is very flexible, so stop by in person to arrange your instruction.

The Alexander Sarcophagus, originally (and mistakenly) attributed to Alexander the Great

principal collection in the main building. As the Ottoman Empire spread over North Africa, the Levant, and present-day Syria, Iraq, and Saudi Arabia, the wonders piled up in Istanbul. Additional treasures from southern Turkey and present-day Lebanon were rounded up in the empire's dying days by curator Osman Hamdi Bey, whose bust sits prominently in the museum's entrance. (Bey's *Tortoise Trainer* canvas is the highlight of a visit to European Istanbul's Pera Museum; see p. 109).

Sarcophagi: The museum's most popular room contains a collection of sarcophagi. These Lycian, Egyptian, and Phoenician tombs are all impossibly grand. Some are solid polished stone; others are decorated with scenes of hunt-

ing, war, and daily life from two millennia ago. The most elegant is the **Alexander Sarcophagus.** Its splendor and decoration once confused curators, who wrongly ascribed it to Alexander the Great; it's now thought to be the resting place of a provincial governor. Carvings along the side depict Alexander routing the Persians and hunting lions.

Over three additional stories, the museum takes in Hittite history, Roman jewelry, and a selection of those finds not purloined by Troy excavator, Heinrich Schliemann (see sidebar p. 188). Its most recent exhibition displays 30 boats discovered and excavated from an archaeological dig that uncovered the remains of a Byzantine harbor. Make time for a cup of tea in the sarcophagus-strewn grounds. ■

Hagia Sophia

Hagia Sophia has dominated the Old City's history, geography, and politics since its completion as the world's largest cathedral under Emperor Justinian in A.D. 537. Its majesty and beauty is undeniable and the fact that its dome is no longer spread with gold leaf, and that a few of the mosaics have gone missing, is testament to its tumultuous history.

Stunning view of the Hagia Sophia amid landscaped gardens with the Bosporus as a backdrop

Hagia Sophia

✉ Osman Hamdi Bey Yokuşu

☎ (0212) 520 77 42

⊕ Closed Mon.

$ $$$

🚇 Gülhane

It's to be expected that Hagia Sophia (Aya Sofya)—a building that has crowned the Istanbul skyline for some 1,500 years—should have suffered a little wear and tear. The tears were more sudden than the wears, however, and the first came as religious debate ripped apart the Byzantine Empire. The iconoclastic Emperor Leo III (ca 685–741) banned the worship of graven images during the late 720s and the spellbindingly beautiful mosaics were removed from the Hagia Sophia. They made a swift return, thanks to the icon-revering Empress Irene (752–803). She ruled as regent for her son Constantine VI (771–797)—who couldn't see the mosaics in later life, as his eyes had been gouged out on Irene's orders! But the next dose of iconoclasm, combined with several earthquakes and woeful economic mismanagement across the Byzantine Empire, paled in comparison with the sacking the

Hagia Sophia endured by the Christian crusaders in 1204.

These Latin invaders desecrated the church as if it were a pagan temple. Gold leaf and silver artifacts were plundered as loot, and relics were shipped off to churches across Europe. Wily Doge Enrico Dandolo (1107–1205), the Venetian leader who essentially bamboozled the crusaders into taking Constantinople for his own serene republic, is allegedly buried inside the church.

The last Byzantine emperor, Constantine XI Dragases (1404–1453), uttered the cathedral's final Christian liturgy on May 28, 1453, as Ottoman forces pounded the city walls. The invasion's cultured leader, Mehmet the Conqueror, rode directly to the Hagia Sophia after Constantinople's fall the next day. By the following Friday the cathedral had been converted into a mosque. The Ottomans kept it in perfect repair, adapting it without harming the original structure or its glorious decoration. The mosaics were covered, rather than destroyed, and additions like the minarets were carefully matched to the building's style. In short, the Hagia Sophia is a masterpiece. Its glory has now been enlivened

INSIDER TIP:

Gaze at the faces of seraphim—angels of the heavens—brought to light for the first time in centuries after a 17-year-long restoration in Hagia Sophia.

—RÜYA KÖKSAL KUDU
National Geographic Expeditions

by a recent full-scale renovation, which was completed in 2010. And although it's the current vogue to find and capture each mosaic with a cell-phone camera or monster SLR, it's also worth wandering aimlessly or gazing up at the soaring dome, the 40 windows of which cast a supernatural light over the cavernous interior.

Touring Hagia Sophia

Most visits begin in the long **gold-ceilinged narthex.** Look up for the **mosaic of Emperor Leo VI** bowing down before Christ Pantocrator. To gauge the Hagia Sophia's grand scale it's worth heading straight up to the horseshoe-shaped **upper gallery.** Here, an observation disk highlights the location of all the building's major mosaics, although

Using a Guide in the Hagia Sophia

As one of the world's most important buildings for the last 1,500 years, the Hagia Sophia is stuffed to the gills with history, anecdotes, and hidden corners. Hiring a guide, in addition to using a guidebook, can be truly beneficial. Museum guides (all of whom should be wearing an official identity card) ply their trade outside the building, and can seemingly converse in any language from Farsi to Mandarin.

Prices are around $$$$–$$$$$ for 45 minutes, although more in-depth tours are also offered.

Secret Sites Around Hagia Sophia

Four free, little-visited sites ring the gated Hagia Sophia complex. Within the complex itself, but only accessible via a different entrance 100 yards (91 m) west of the main gate, is the Sinan-designed, 16th-century **mausoleum of Selim II**, plus the tombs of his son Murat III (1546–1595), grandson Mehmet III (1566–1603), and great-grandson Mustafa I (1591–1639). None of them was a model leader: Selim was a drunkard, Mehmet a bully (he murdered at least 39 family members), and poor Mustafa a neurotic weakling. But the exquisite tilework, so fine that the raised glaze can be caressed, plus the additional eerie graves of each sultan's family members (Selim's alone is circled by 44), makes for a fascinating tour.

The nearby **Hammam of Roxelana,** Sultan Süleyman the Magnificent's ever conspiring wife (see sidebar p. 60), is another Sinan-designed mini-masterpiece. The staff of Hagia Sophia would have used the hammam in times past, as the world's most powerful woman obviously had her own private bath in the Topkapı Palace.

Farther around the complex is the **Çeşme of Sultan Ahmet III,** an ornate calligraphy-covered fountain that proudly proclaims itself "the most beautiful street fountain in Istanbul." Finally, turn left halfway down the cobbled street for a peek at the **Caferağa Medresesi** (*tel 0212/513 36 01, www.caferaga medresesi.com; see p. 64*).

each one is also clearly annotated should you prefer to stumble upon them instead. A green disk just in front of the observation disk marks the spot where Byzantine empresses would place their thrones and gaze over proceedings—they certainly picked the best view in the house!

Head right from here to the south gallery for a pantheon of glowing mosaics. First is the **Deësis mosaic,** depicting a humble Virgin Mary and fine-featured John the Baptist casting their eyes down at Christ and imploring him to show forgiveness. Past Doge Dandolo's small cenotaph are two equally glorious works.

The **Empress Zoe mosaic** portrays Christ Pantocrator, supposedly flanked by Emperor Constantine IX Monomachus (1000–1055) and his beautiful Empress Zoe (978–1050). In fact,

it's likely that Constantine's face was the third to grace the wall, with Zoe's first two husbands replacing each other in turn. The neighboring **Comnenus mosaic** depicts the Virgin and Child, flanked by Emperor John II Comnenus (1087–1143) and his wife Empress Irene (1088–1134). Their son, Alexius Comnenus (1106–1142), is represented on an adjacent panel. From both sides of the upper gallery there is a wonderful view of the **Virgin and Child mosaic,** which dominates the apse.

The **ground floor** delights in equal measure. Even if you can't fathom every carved pillar, burial chamber, or mini-mosaic, revel in the space nonetheless. Look out for the **weeping column,** normally conspicuous by its line of hopefuls; it's said that if you twist your thumb around the hole in the moist rock, your wish may come true.

As a Mosque: Remnants of Hagia Sophia's five centuries as a mosque are apparent throughout. Note the marble minbar (from which the imam would preach), an ornate ablutions fountain, huge pendant chandelier, plus eight suspended green disks inscribed with the names of Allah, the Prophet Muhammad, the first four caliphs, and Muhammad's first two grandsons. The two huge marble urns near the entrance were most likely carted here from the ancient city of Pergamon, 310 miles (500 km) southwest of Istanbul by Sultan Murat II (1404–1451). As in most mosques, the floor was richly carpeted until 1935, when Atatürk transformed the mosque into a public museum.

More than five million visitors share this sight each year, so it pays to arrive early, or just before closing. If you find the interior overwhelming, take a break in the tearoom. Even the nearby grounds are littered with architectural fragments from an earlier Theodosian incarnation of the church.

After the collapse of the Ottoman Empire, and before the final peace treaty with the new Turkey, the Hagia Sophia was the object of conflicting ambitions. Greece and Italy both staked a title to the church. But as the partition of western Turkey, which the Western Allies initially envisioned, never occurred, it remained Turkish. Claims by Orthodox and Catholic communities lingered but the building was deconsecrated in 1934, turning it into today's museum. ■

Admiring the details from the upper gallery of Hagia Sophia

Blue Mosque & Around

The six minarets of the Blue Mosque lend a magical air to the Istanbul skyline. Egyptian obelisks and Roman columns mark out the ancient Hippodrome adjacent, the city's center-piece in Byzantine times. All now lie on the appropriately named At Meydanı, the Square of Horses. Leading westward, the boulevard of Divan Yolu boasts scores of shops, a tram, and one of the main entrances to the Grand Bazaar.

Narrow streets open on to the majestic presence of the Blue Mosque.

Blue Mosque

The name Sultanahmet Camii (Blue Mosque) comes from Sultan Ahmet I (1590-1617), the pious—although consistently unlucky—sultan under whom this grand temple was constructed. In part, the Blue Mosque served as an attempt to appease Allah for Ahmet I's losses against infidel armies on both the eastern and western flanks of the Ottoman Empire. A gifted ex-pupil of the great Sinan, Sedefhar Mehmet Ağa (1540-1617) was chosen to oversee its seven-year construc-tion. Just as the mosque was completed, what little luck Ahmet I had ran out and he succumbed to typhus at the age of 27.

It's easy to imagine the Blue Mosque as two near-perfect squares, one containing the interior, the other the courtyard. It's surprising that the deliciously calm forecourt comes without

INSIDER TIP:

To see the Blue Mosque in another dimension, make sure to take in the daily light-and-sound show staged after dusk from May through October.

—SALLY MCFALL
National Geographic contributor

the rococo touches seen on other grand mosques, like the Yeni Valide in Üsküdar (see p. 147) or the Süleymaniye up the Golden Horn (see pp. 87–88). Although, in common with these two mosques, the complex once included a school, market, religious college, caravansary, and kitchens. Note the ablutions fountain and the rooftop domes that climb over each other in perfect symmetry, all the way up to the skies.

Inside, eyes are instantly drawn upward to the great dome and succession of semi-domes, each one covered by spellbinding geometric frescoes (although these are not the mosque's original decoration). Four great stout columns hold aloft

this hypnotic sight. The gallery, just a short way above the richly carpeted floor, is ringed with over 20,000 fine İznik tiles. Some are patterned, while others depict floral representations of tulips, roses, and carnations.

Of key importance are the mihrab, the carved niche that denotes the direction of Mecca, and the minbar, the pulpit used for Friday prayers. Both are of finely carved white marble. The upper gallery left of the mihrab contains the royal loge, where the sultans themselves would have prayed.

Be aware that the mosque is still a working one. A polite notice asks visitors to stay hushed and be respectful, and not to take photographs of those at prayer. Shoes must be removed and female visitors must don a headscarf from the mosque's amusingly varied collection upon entering the inner sanctum.

The Hippodrome

The Hagia Sophia was Constantinople's most sacred building, but the Hippodrome was always its most popular. When Emperor Constantine moved his

Blue Mosque

- ✉ At Meydanı 17, Sultanahmet
- ☎ (0212) 518 13 19
- 🕐 Closed Fri. a.m.
- 💲 Donation of $$ recommended
- 🚊 Sultanahmet

Mystery of the Blue Mosque's Six Minarets

Ordering a mosque with six minarets—the same number that bedeck the Grand Mosque in Mecca, Islam's holiest spot—was considered a tad presumptuous on Ahmet I's part. Two rumors surround the construction. The first is that the sultan actually demanded gold minarets (*altın*), not six minarets (*altı*), but the instructions became lost in translation—although surely it's hard to miss the construction of an extra minaret or two on your doorstep. Another legend claims that Ahmet I—as caliph of the Muslim world—was thus shamed into adding an additional seventh minaret on Mecca's Grand Mosque, although this seventh minaret may have been completed some years before.

capital from Rome to the shores of the Bosporus in A.D. 324, he embarked upon a building scheme of grandiose proportions. The new eye of the empire needed pomp and pageantry—and this was delivered in spades by the Hippodrome, a 492-yard-long (450 m) racetrack where a crowd of 100,000 could clamor for victory. Modeled on the Circus Maximus in Rome, charioteers careened around the *sphendone* curve—above which the emperor sat—an image perfected by Charlton Heston in the 1959 movie *Ben-Hur*. The track's layout roughly follows the U-shaped road in present-day At Meydanı.

The reasons why the Hippodrome maintained a hold on the Byzantine psyche are numerous. The Romans loved sport, and a season of games served to placate the populace. Races also served as a link between ruler and ruled. The emperor could arrive directly at his private loge to cheer the display via a tunnel from the adjoining Great Palace, the old

INSIDER TIP:

Admire the oldest dome of Little Hagia Sophia Mosque— the former church of Sergius and Bacchus, built in 526.

—RÜYA KÖKSAL KUDU,
National Geographic Expeditions

Byzantine royal residence building, which was subsumed by the Blue Mosque a millennium and a half later. Finally, the Hippodrome was used to mark great victories. The Byzantine general Belisarius was awarded such a "triumph" in A.D. 534, parading his war loot and captured Vandal soldiers around the capital.

Hippodrome Spoils: Various statues and spoils were lined in the Hippodrome's center, or *spina*. Several survive today. The **Obelisk of Theodosius** was pilfered from Luxor in Egypt in A.D. 390. The hieroglyphics, still in near mint condition, celebrate Thutmosis III's (d. 1425 B.C.) victory in the distant Euphrates some 3,500 years ago. Scenes of Theodosius and his retinue toiling away are engraved on the rock base beneath.

The somewhat pathetic **Serpents Column** was once a snake-headed statue brought by Constantine to the city from Delphi. One of the heads now lies in the Istanbul Archaeology Museum (see pp. 64–65), while a drunken Polish diplomat allegedly knocked off another several centuries ago.

The Million

At the start of Divan Yolu, a few steps from the entrance to the Basilica Cistern, on Caferiye Sk, is the diminutive Million Taşı (or Million Stone). This tiny column once was the point from which distances from the Roman Empire's new capital at Constantinople to destinations all over the empire were measured, making it literally the center of the world. The idea was not a new one: Emperor Augustus had erected a Milliarium Aureum, or "golden milestone," in Rome a few centuries earlier.

Relief of Emperor Theodosius on the base pedestal of the Obelisk at the Hippodrome

The **Walled Obelisk,** today little more than an extremely tall tower of bricks, was once covered in valuable bronze plaques. Like much else in the city, these items were pillaged during the ignominious Fourth Crusade in 1204, when the Great Palace was also definitively sacked. Familiar with those four gilded horses that lie in St. Mark's Square in Venice? They once graced the Hippodrome's southern corner.

Church of Saints Sergius and Bacchus

This tiny former church, a five-minute descent southward from the Blue Mosque, is aptly known as Küçük Ayasofya, or Little Hagia Sophia. Not only does the Church of Saints Sergius and Bacchus resemble its giant big brother, its history is a mirror of the Hagia Sophia's too. A grateful Emperor Justinian dedicated the smaller (and older) of the two churches in tribute to Sergius and Bacchus. These early Christian soldier-martyrs appeared in a dream to his uncle Justin, demanding clemency for Justinian whom he held incarcerated at the time. Both churches were showered with mosaics and gold leaf, and a rough frieze depicting St. Sergius, Justinian, and his conspiring wife Theodora remains. Both buildings were later converted into mosques, this one during the early 16th century.

Basilica Cistern

This vast subterranean space, one of the most visually

(continued on p. 76)

Church of Saints Sergius and Bacchus

 Küçük Ayasofya Caddesi

🕐 Closed Fri. a.m.

💲 Donation of $ recommended

🚇 Sultanahmet

Hammams—Ancient Turkish Baths

The exact origins of hammams remain unclear, but it's believed that they were adapted from Roman and Byzantine thermal baths. Within Islam, physical cleanliness is equated with spiritual cleanliness. However, the Turks—and particularly Turkish women—took the simple steam bath a few steps further, transforming their bathhouses from a place of ritual cleansing to a beloved social space, ideal for keeping up with local news, exchanging gossip, and meeting friends.

Men relax at a Turkish hammam.

Each of life's milestones was traditionally celebrated in the hammam, such as the bath of the bride, the bath of the bridegroom, post-circumcision, and post-childbirth. Each hammam-goer brought their own special tools, including a rough scrubbing mitt (kese), etched metal bowl for washing, cotton towels, and wooden clogs. At the zenith of Ottoman rule, the empire was peppered with thousands of hammams, whether royal, private, or public. The intriguing rituals that took place within these bathhouses featured in travelogues written by visiting Europeans, popularizing hammams throughout the West.

Modern Hammams

Today hammams throughout Turkey are still fairly similar. Most hammam-goers, particularly outside of Istanbul, continue to conscribe to the experience as a social one, and visit in large, same-sex groups, but don't be surprised if local cityfolk friends have never visited a hammam. Although communal baths are making a comeback, many people consider hammams antiquated. As all homes now boast private bathrooms, why would you want to bathe with a bunch of strangers? You only need to try it once to see how quickly that sentiment dissipates.

A hammam has three interconnected chambers. The first, the *sıcaklık,* is the hot room, typically with a large dome punctuated with small windows. A marble stone at the center, the *göbek taşi,* is where patrons lie to heat up with steam and receive a massage. Beyond the sıcaklık is a room of intermediate heat where bathers wash. The final chamber, the *soğukluk,* is cool—a place to relax and enjoy a cold drink.

INSIDER TIP:

Visit a hammam or traditional bathhouse. Çemberlitaş [see sidebar below], just outside the Grand Bazaar, is divine. Men and women disperse to mosque-like chambers for a spiritual cleansing costing the equivalent of about $45.

—MARLEY GIBBONS
National Geographic contributor

EXPERIENCE: Visiting Sultanahmet's Baths

Visiting a Turkish hammam is high on any visitor's list. Whether you're a hammam virgin or addicted to the steam, here's what to expect when you hit one of Sultanahmet's popular bathhouses.

Despite website photos to the contrary, in traditional Turkish hammams men's and women's baths are always separate (unless within a hotel). In fact, many even have individual entrances for each sex.

A "menu" lists fees for a basic entrance, often comprising a scrubbing mitt *(kese),* soap massage, and oil massage. Once you've chosen what you'd like, you pay on the spot. You may be given a token that you'll eventually give to the masseur inside the hammam.

You'll be provided with a towel (a lightweight, rectangular wrap) and clogs, then shown to a communal (single sex!) changing room with lockers or a small, lockable cubicle. Take off all of your clothes (including underwear) and wrap yourself in the towel, then make your way into the baths. Note that most women disrobe entirely within the hammam itself, while men must keep the towel around them at all times.

Once inside, pour cool water over your body using one of the bowls positioned at the fountains that edge the walls, and use the kese to scrub your skin. Lie down on the hot marble *göbek taşı* (navel stone) in the center of the room. If you've opted for it, one of the masseurs will scrub and massage you with soap here. Relax for as long as you like; eventual oil massages will take place outside of the steam rooms.

In Sultanahmet, two historical hammams vie for (mainly tourist) custom. Royal architect Sinan (1490–1588) designed **Çemberlitaş Hamamı** *(Vezirhan Caddesi 8, tel 0212/522 79 74, www .cemberlitashamami.com.tr, $$$$$)* in 1584, under the patronage of Selim II's wife, Nurbanu Sultan. **Cağaloğlu Hamamı** *(Kazım İsmail Gürkan Caddesi 34, tel 0212/522 24 24, www.cagalogluhamami .com.tr, $$$$$),* built in 1741, has hosted the likes of Kaiser Wilhelm II, Florence Nightingale, Tony Curtis, Rudolf Nureyev, and Kate Moss.

Other favorite hammams in the city include Beyoğlu's **Galatasaray Hamamı** *(www.galatasarayhamami.com)* and Üsküdar's **Çinili Hammam** (see p. 147).

Basilica Cistern

- Yerebatan Caddesi 13
- (0212) 522 12 59
- $$
- Gülhane

arresting sights in all Istanbul, knows almost no equivalent anywhere else in the world. Despite occupying a space of 105,000 square feet (9,500 sq m) almost directly underneath the Hagia Sophia, it has been lost to the world for centuries at a time.

Like the Hagia Sophia, the Basilica Cistern (Yerebatan Sarnici) was constructed on the orders of Emperor Justinian (483–565). Around 7,000 slaves toiled on the project for years at a time. When it was completed, the cistern could hold 100,000 tons of water and was filled by an intricate series of aqueducts that stretched to the Belgrade Forest (see pp. 132–133). Thanks to the 336 pillars that rose from the waters to support the roof, it became known as the "sinking palace."

INSIDER TIP:

It's hard to believe that a cistern would be considered a must-see sight, but the Basilica Cistern is like nothing you have ever seen before. It exudes atmosphere in spades— you'll be glad you made the downward journey!

—SALLY MCFALL
National Geographic contributor

The cistern fell out of favor after the Ottoman Conquest of 1453, as the Turks preferred running water, not stagnant pools, in their palaces. The often-used local idiom *kadın sesi, para sesi, su sesi*—"the sound

A monumental head of Medusa, upside down, at the Byzantine Basilica Cistern

of women, the sound of money, the sound of water"—gives an inkling of the Turkish love of bathing and fountains, although the Ottomans still used the cistern's water for the palace gardens.

Common knowledge of the cistern thus became scant. It became known to the West through the explorer Petrus Gyllius (1490–1555), who was documenting the city's Byzantine ruins in the mid-1540s. Gyllius came across local residents who drew fresh water from the ground and, more bizarrely still, caught fresh fish from their basements. He must have been staggered as he descended into the fascinating subterranean abyss, armed only with a torch, to discover a dauntingly vast void, silent only for the drip, drip, drip of water slowly flooding in.

That same moist, eerie silence greets visitors today. A wooden walkway now loops through the columns—some plain, some ornate, some visibly buckling under the strain—but the feeling is completely otherworldly. Families of carp swim around the complex. At the far end of the cistern, holding up two great pillars, lie two huge Medusa heads carved out of stone. Undoubtedly from an earlier era, they were possibly used as pedestals, as they were pagan images. These heads make for a great photo, with scores of hauntingly lit columns lined up behind them.

Even after almost a century and a half, the words of Edmondo De Amicis, the Italian travel writer who dipped into the cistern in 1874, still ring true:

"I descended to the end of dark,

humid steps and found myself under the domes of the Great Basilica Cistern of the Byzantium...

"The greenish water that is partly enlightened by washing-blue light— which further increases the horror of the darkness—vanishes under the dark domes while the walls shine with the water running down thereon thus dimly discovering the endless rows of columns everywhere like the trunks of trees in a pruned forest."

The Cisterns in Celluloid

Many visitors will already be familiar with the Basilica Cistern thanks to the 1963 James Bond movie *From Russia With Love*. In the movie, a young Sean Connery paddles through the spooky cisterns in order to spy on the Soviet Embassy— which, in reality, of course, lies over the Galata Bridge on İstikal Caddesi in the European Beyoğlu district. The movie not only ranks as many viewers' favorite Bond flick, it also takes in sights and sounds from 1960s Istanbul. Other backdrops in the movie include a boat trip past the Dolmabahçe Palace, and Sirkeci station, from where Bond and a Russian assassin catch the Orient Express.

Sogukçeşme Sokak

North of the Hagia Sophia, running from the Imperial Gate to an entrance to Gülhane Park, is Sogukçeşme Sokak, a charming street that looks like the set for a movie. You may be surprised how such an historic byway has survived in this busy, central location. It is, however, an illusion. In the 1980s, a rundown row of traditional wooden houses along this street was demolished and replaced by a modern concrete

Museum of Turkish & Islamic Arts

✉ İbrahim Paşa Palace, At Meydanı Sokak 46

☎ (0212) 518 18 05

🕐 Closed Mon.

💲 $$$

🚇 Sultanahmet

structure onto whose facade was fixed replicas of the old carved wooden decoration and pastel colors of the nine former dwellings. The reconstruction is now a boutique hotel, the Ayasofya Pansiyonlari (see Travelwise p. 243).

Museum of Turkish & Islamic Arts

The Museum of Turkish & Islamic Arts (Türk ve Islam Eserleri Müzesi)—the first museum in Turkey to exhibit local artworks with those sourced from the Middle East—opened in 1914. The rich collection of more than 40,000 ancient ceramics, calligraphy artworks, miniatures, and carpets was originally housed in the kitchens of the Süleymaniye Mosque (see pp. 87–88). In 1983, the collection was moved to the renovated **İbrahim Paşa Palace** (İbrahim Paşa Sarayı), opposite Sultanahmet's Hippodrome, where they are displayed today.

The 16th-century İbrahim Paşa Palace takes its name from İbrahim Paşa, the first of Sultan Süleyman the Magnificent's grand viziers.

A Greek slave sold to Ottoman royalty when just a young boy, İbrahim was a good friend to the youthful Süleyman. The boys grew up together, İbrahim playing an enthusiastic second fiddle to Süleyman's illustrious ascent. When Süleyman was crowned sultan in 1520, İbrahim was named his grand vizier, married the sultan's sister, and was gifted this sumptuous palace.

Although İbrahim Paşa kept his prestigious position for 13 years, the royal world was a place of fickle loyalties. Whether the grand vizier became inebriated with his own power, or Süleyman's wife Roxelana grew jealous, İbrahim Paşa was strangled by his father in 1536. All his belongings reverted to the sultan, including his home. Parts of the ostentatious palace were destroyed, being deemed simply too extravagant. Over the following four centuries, the building was used as barracks, a clothing factory, and a prison.

Today, just a small portion of İbrahim Paşa Palace is dedicated to the Museum of Turkish & Islamic Arts, with artworks exhibited

Turkish Contemporary Art

It's not all ancient history in Istanbul. As enchanting as these traditional pieces are, Turkey is also pushing to the forefront of international contemporary art. The local scene continues to grow, with wealthy patrons such as the Koç family promising to sponsor the Istanbul Biennial—a biennial contemporary exhibition—through 2017. Look out for documentary filmmaker Kutluğ Ataman, whose installations featured at London's Whitechapel Gallery in 2010, the striking female figures painted by Kezban Arca Batibeki, Hale Tengers' controversial sculptures, videos by Kurdish artist Fikret Atay, or Taner Ceylan's hyperrealist photo-like paintings. For the best of Istanbul's contemporary art, visit the Istanbul Modern (see pp. 121–122) or a handful of the city's 250 galleries.

around one of the complex's four courtyards. Upon entering the museum, visitors are funneled directly into a leafy courtyard. It is home to a pleasant café, edged by fragrant rosebushes, and a small terrace with great views overlooking the Hippodrome and Blue Mosque.

Upstairs, small rooms neatly chart Islamic art, beginning with carved ivory objects and mosaic fragments from Damascus' Umayyad dynasty, which date from around A.D. 700–800. Various ornate wooden doors and shutters include the stunning doors and double dragon door knocker, from Cizre's mosque. Elaborate flowers adorn 16th-century İznik tiles and 19th-century glassware. Anatolian calligraphy and vibrant miniatures splash color and golden highlights throughout the exhibitions.

With the **Great Ceremonial Hall** at its center, the extensive collection of carpets is the museum's true jewel—knotted carpets from Konya dating from the 13th century; 16th-century carpets from Uşak, center of the Carpet Design Revolution, featuring octagonal stars, or three circles and two wavy lines, originally a Buddhist symbol; Iranian carpets decorated with flowers, birds, and the tree of life; and Caucasian carpets with striking contrasting colors.

Down the steps, a final hall is dedicated to the museum's **ethnographic section.** There's a re-creation of a nomadic yurt (with diagrams if you're interested in making your own), plus dioramas of village life.

Certificate of pilgrimage to Mecca, dated 1193, displayed at the Museum of Turkish & Islamic Arts

Grand Bazaar

The Grand Bazaar—called Kapalıçarşı, or "covered bazaar" in Turkish—is one of the world's oldest shopping centers. Constructed from 1461 under the reign of Sultan Mehmet the Conqueror, then expanded by Sultan Süleyman the Magnificent, the bazaar is a heady mix of carpets and kilims, Kütahya and İznik ceramics, Middle Eastern antiques, and endless souvenirs.

Make no mistake—covered it may be, but the Grand Bazaar is no mere mall. A massive 484,380 square feet (45,000 sq m), the bazaar encompasses more than

A stroll through Istanbul's Grand Bazaar (Kapalıçarşı) is a must for any visitor.

3,500 shops spread over 64 streets. It's a city unto itself, with restaurants, banks, its own police force, post office, and mosque, not to mention the daily dramas of its 22,000 workers. At least a quarter of a million visitors pour through one of its 22 gates every day, with the number closer to half a million in summertime.

The massive market is subdivided into sectors, with shops selling similar items generally grouped together geographically. These "neighborhoods" include jewelry, carpets, clothing, antiques, leather,

INSIDER TIP:

Hammam supplies from Derviş or Abdulla found in the Grand Bazaar make authentic gifts. Laurel-scented soaps, hand-loomed *peştemal* towels, and copper bathing bowls are traditional luxuries.

—ANASTASIA ASHMAN
National Geographic Traveler
magazine writer

souvenirs, and fabrics. **Sandal Bedesteni** and the Byzantine **İç** (or Cevahir) **Bedesten**—the bazaar's original vaulted buildings, where precious items were bought and sold, then safely locked up come nightfall—sit at the heart of the market. The latter is built atop the city's Roman agora, and is said to be connected to the Spice Market (see pp. 84–85) via a myriad of underground tunnels. At the bazaar's eastern edge, **Nuruosmaniye Mosque** (Nuruosmaniye Camii, 1748–1755) is currently under renovation. You may be able to peek at its pretty, peaceful courtyard.

Grand Bazaar

⊠ Various entrances, including main gates Nuruosmaniye Kapısı (Nuruosmaniye Caddesi) and Çarşı Kapısı (just north of Beyazıt Meydanı)

☎ (0212) 519 12 48

⊕ Closed Sun.

🚇 Beyazıt

www.kapalicarsi .org.tr

Bartering Etiquette

When making a purchase, most Grand Bazaar vendors assume that you will barter, particularly if you plan to buy more than one item. To do so successfully, keep the following tips in mind.

- Begin by asking the item's price (*ne kadar?*). Even if you are convinced you'll be purchasing it, don't look too convinced, as overt enthusiasm is bound to raise the asking price. Never, ever be coerced into stating how much you think the item is worth first. The vendor's asking price will give you a lead. Your final price will probably end up somewhere between a third and two-thirds of the first price requested.

- Decide how much the object of your desire is worth to you. Take into account the amount of work that has gone into creating it, its age, and its rarity—and bear in mind that the bazaar's wares range from dirt-cheap Chinese imports to 300-year-old rugs.

- Counter with a price that's half of what you're prepared to pay. Note that most

vendors are veritable polyglots—otherwise bartering is enacted through punching numbers into a calculator, then flashing it back and forth, so don't worry if you're still working on your Turkish numbers!

- Raise your price in slow increments. Your final price should meet the vendor's somewhere in the middle.

- Don't be afraid to walk away. If the vendor is willing to lower his or her price further, you'll be called back. If not, and you're willing to pay the last price discussed, there's no shame in returning a few minutes later.

- Above all, remain composed and friendly at all times. Aggressive haggling will get you nowhere, particularly in Turkey. Instead, this exchange should be akin to a playful dance.

There are also a few shops in the Grand Bazaar where the prices are fixed. Respect the vendor's choice, although, of course, there's never any harm in asking for a discount!

EXPERIENCE: A Shopping Trip in the Grand Bazaar

An Istanbul resident since 1998, journalist turned expert personal shopper Kathy Hamilton offers unique trips through the Grand Bazaar. Whatever your passion—from general window-shopping to hunting down a collector's obsessions—Kathy's market know-how, fluent Turkish, and solid relationships allow shoppers to slip easily below the bazaar's simmering surface.

Between April and October, when tourists flood Istanbul, Kathy Hamilton (tel 0536/ 884 92 26, www.İstanbul personalshopper.com, $$$$$) spends a few days each week at the Grand Bazaar. Her shopping trips have proved popular with pop stars, Middle Eastern royalty, and American TV personalities, as well as plenty of resident expats. So much so, that Kathy now has two equally knowledgeable colleagues to assist her.

Weaving adeptly through the warren of antiques and sparkly jewelry stalls, Kathy steers visitors to a few of her favorite spots, including **Nick Merdenyan's Calligraphy shop** (İç Bedesten 24, tel 0212/513 54 73, www .lordoftheleaves.com). Nick uses cat-hair paintbrushes to portray Jewish, Christian, and Muslim imagery on Floridian dieffenbachia leaves.

Ceramics and textiles make popular gifts or souvenirs. Kathy recommends **EM-ER** (Takkeciler Sokak 100, tel 0212/514 22 65, www.em-er.com), for their high-quality, affordable, hand-painted ceramics. Nearby, **İgüs** (Yağlıkçılar Caddesi 80, tel 0212/512 35 28, www.igustekstil.com) stocks decadently soft wraps.

Textile collectors should head directly to Osman's treasure trove, at **Semerkand** (Yağlıkçılar Caddesi, Astarcı Han 25–32, tel 0212/ 526 22 69). Ottoman kaftans and batik scarves are interspersed with ancient money pouches and worn leather booties. Kathy's connections extend outside the bazaar walls too: Ducking down an alley near Çarşıkapı Gate, she dips into **Pillows Store** (Çarşıkapı Caddesi 13, tel 0212/528 99 73, www .pillowsstore.com), where bolts of fabrics can be transformed into pretty cushion covers, bedspreads, and tablecloths.

Personalized shopping trips can be booked Monday through Saturday, 10 a.m.– 3 p.m. The maximum recommended group size is four, although special requests are welcome.

Traditional Turkish rugs for sale in the Grand Bazaar

Take in the heady aromas of Istanbul's Spice Market—a cornucopia of herbs and spices.

INSIDER TIP:

When shopping in the bazaars, don't rush, check around to compare the best offers at other sites, and take your calculator to work out the exchange rate.

—CLIVE CARPENTER
National Geographic contributor

The Grand Bazaar is an ideal place to pick up great value souvenirs, including silver bangles, pashmina scarves, carved wooden printing blocks, hammam towels, and Ottoman kaftans, among many other treasures. Note that main streets are signposted—however,

these indications can be somewhat confusing. A better option is to pick up a map of the Grand Bazaar from one of the shopkeepers (although only a smattering of shops stock them) or ask around to find a specific area or item. Otherwise, rejoice in the discovery that awaits via an aimless wander.

If you're a keen shopper, don't limit yourself to the covered bazaar itself. The warren of streets surrounding the Grand Bazaar and threading downhill toward Eminönü is packed with overflowing shops. These Aladdin caves stock everything from bolts of printed fabric to red tulle wedding dresses. Look out for quality mohair and wool, buttons and crafting supplies along **Mahmutpaşa Yokuşu** and in

Sahaflar Çarşısı

  Beyazit Mh., off
Kalpakçilarbasi
Caddesi

Beyazıt Meydanı

Kürkçü Han, while cluttered shops along **Marpuçcular Caddesi** and **Fincancılar Sokak** stock shiny costume jewelry and hair accessories.

Head west out of the bazaar and you'll stumble into the **Sahaflar Çarşısı** (Book Bazaar), just north of Divan Yolu and the Beyazıt Meydanı tram stop. Although the bulk of the modern and antiquarian books on sale here are in Turkish, this petite bazaar is a great spot to pick up colorful

Turkish miniatures. On sale are both antique miniatures, and contemporary ones; the latter are often painted on the yellowing pages of old Ottoman manuscripts.

Spice Market

The Spice Market was constructed during the 1660s to provide a valuable income for the large New Mosque (see opposite) complex nearby. It is referred to in Turkish as the Mısır Çarşısı (Egyptian Bazaar), as it's believed that funding to build the L-shaped shopping arcade was garnered from taxes levied on Egyptian imports.

Both locals and tourists frequent the Spice Market, an enchanting domed structure that's somewhat lower key than the Grand Bazaar. Inside, there are around 90 shops, which originally sold strictly spices, herbs, and medicinal mixes. Today, you can expect to find piles of *kırmızı pul biber* (spicy red pepper flakes), deep yellow turmeric, strings of tiny okra or preserved vine leaves, and dried eggplant shells for *dolmas*. Soft, almost jammy figs are stuffed with walnuts, and you can easily pick up a dozen different varieties of Turkish delight (see sidebar opposite). Prized items, such as Iranian saffron and caviar, are frequently secreted away under an owner's watchful eye at the back of each shop.

The streets twisting outward from the Spice Market merge into the alleys that pour downhill from the Grand Bazaar. Again, the shops that line this labyrinth often offer better value and are

Buying fresh grilled fish from a stall near the New Mosque

Turkish Delight

This renowned sweet, known in Turkish as *lokum*, is probably the country's most famous export. It may be urban legend, but it's said that during the late 18th century Sultan Abdulhamit I broke more than a couple of teeth crunching his way through a favorite rock candy. Without his sugary (and orthodontically destructive) fix, the sultan was inconsolable. Royal confectioner Ali Muhiddin Hacı Bekir quickly came to the rescue, and the delicate, jellyish lokum we know today was born.

Traditionally flavored with rosewater and dusted with powdered sugar, lokum is created with a blend of sugar and starch, and chances are the local varieties will far exceed anything you've tasted outside of Turkey. Try specialist varieties, including lokum made with fruit juice or sprinkled with pistachios from Gaziantep, in southeastern Turkey.

If you can't resist packing a box or two to take home with you, **Hacı Bekir**'s (İstiklal Caddesi 83A, Beyoğlu, tel 0212/245 13 75, www.hacibekir.com.tr) original confectionery, just east of the New Mosque, is hugely popular with locals. Alternatively, in the Spice Market, **Hayat**'s (Mısır Çarşısı 8, tel 0212/528 45 86) dedicated confectioner has created a divine double honey and pistachio version of the classic.

INSIDER TIP:

Find great photo opportunities and, arguably, Istanbul's best shawarma at the Egyptian Bazaar. Enter the main row from the riverside, with the New Mosque on your left, and walk about a block.

—MARLEY GIBBONS
National Geographic contributor

more interesting than the more mainstream spots within the Spice Market itself. Look out for copper *sahanda* pans, tulip-shaped tea glasses, and double-stacked Turkish teapots in the streets just behind the bazaar. To the east, the **Flower Market** (Çiçek Pazarı) is flanked by caged birds, flower bulbs, and infant vegetable plants in springtime. The teahouses in the center of this open square make for a very pleasant stop.

Along the bazaar's western exterior, merchants stock fresh and aged cheeses, olives, honeycomb, and *pastırma* (air-cured meats). Kiosks line up opposite, selling fresh fruits and vegetables, usually from the Anatolian countryside—broad beans in April, or plump cherries come June. Continue westward and you'll quickly enter a unique neighborhood selling scales, candy, and wooden handcrafted items, including a very good range of *tawula* (backgammon) sets.

New Mosque

At the southern end of the Galata Bridge, the imposing New Mosque (Yeni Camii) casts a massive shadow over the Spice Market. Although its name means "new mosque," the construction of this landmark structure was completed 350 years ago.

New Mosque

- ✉ Yenicami Meydanı Sokak, Eminönü
- ☎ (0212) 527 85 05
- 🕐 Closed Fri. a.m.
- 💲 Donation of $$ is expected

The older generation banters outside Süleymaniye Mosque.

Rüstem Paşa Mosque

✉ Hasırcılar Caddesi

☎ (0212) 526 73 50

🕐 Closed Fri. a.m.

💲 $ donation recommended

Spearheaded by Valide Sultan Safiye (mother of Sultan Mehmet III, 1566–1603), construction of the New Mosque ground to a halt when Mehmet III died in 1603 and Safiye lost her exalted position as valide. The partially completed mosque stood crumbling for six decades, until it was finally given the go ahead for completion in 1663 by Valide Sultan Turhan Hatice (mother of Mehmet IV, 1642–1693).

Both the materials used and the New Mosque's simple decor cannot rival the city's more ornate places of worship, such as nearby Rüstem Paşa Mosque or the Blue Mosque. However, it remains a popular local mosque, and at prayer time crowds pour in and out of its entrances overlooking the Golden Horn's waterfront.

Rüstem Paşa Mosque

Off the main road and up a small set of stairs, Rüstem Paşa Mosque (Rüstem Paşa Camii) is easy to miss. The petite but visually arresting octagonal mosque was built in 1561 by royal architect Sinan (see pp. 90–91), and dedicated to Sultan Süleyman the Magnificent's controversial Grand Vizier Rüstem Paşa (1505–1561).

Born in Sarajevo and raised in Constantinople, Rüstem Paşa was a great military leader who went on to marry Süleyman's favorite daughter, Mihrimah. Today he's primarily remembered for his corrupt activities, accumulation of

INSIDER TIP:

The mosque of Süleyman the Magnificent sits on a high hill, from where you can snap pictures of the city sprawling on both sides of the Bosporus and Golden Horn.

—EMILY HAMMER
National Geographic field researcher

wealth from copious bribes, and successfully conspiring with Süleyman's wife Roxelana to turn Süleyman against Mustafa, his son and heir. Mustafa's death was indeed ordered and Roxelana's son Selim "the Sot" (1524–1574) eventually took the throne instead.

Keen to impress the public with his affluence, Rüstem Paşa had the mosque—including its covered porch area—decorated with expensive, hand-painted tiles, produced in İznik during the city's artistic zenith (note the deep red tones, which only the finest artisans could achieve). The mosque is unique in that it's one of the few places where visitors can examine these precious tiles in close proximity.

Süleymaniye Mosque

This astounding mosque, completed in 1557 and the second largest in Istanbul, is one of the grandest achievements of the

Süleymaniye Mosque

- Mimar Sinan Caddesi
- (0212) 514 01 39
- Closed Fri. morning (tombs closed Mon.)
- Eminönü
- $ donation recommended

EXPERIENCE: Istanbul Eats Culinary Tours

Enthusiastic bloggers, longtime residents, and Turkish food fiends Ansel Mullins and Yigal Schleifer, along with expert photographer Jonathan Lewis, lead English-language eating excursions with **Istanbul Eats Culinary Tours** (**www.İstanbuleats.com, $$$$$**) through Istanbul's bustling backstreets.

As fluent Turkish speakers, they have established personal relationships with the city's most authentic chefs and food vendors, and offer unique insights into the history, traditions, and ongoing development of Turkish cuisine.

Three delicious itineraries get to the city's culinary heart, each one dishing up scrumptious samples, a smattering of off-the-beaten-track sightseeing, and a feast of local knowledge. Their most popular tour, looping through Sultanahmet, begins outside the Spice Market, just a fragrant whiff or two down the road from Kurukahveci Mehmet Efendi, Istanbul's oldest coffee company.

While each tour's specific route varies—it can even be adjusted for those with limited mobility—there's plenty of tasting along the way. Expect to sip a chilled glass of *boza*, a traditional drink made of fermented millet, or spoon up a mouthful of the city's weirdly renowned chicken breast pudding. Nibbles en route serve to whet the appetite, and the tour culminates with a blowout lunch: Frequently, this is Kurdish pit-roasted lamb in the little-visited neighborhood of Fatih.

An additional tour digs into the delights of European Beyoğlu, while the "Two Markets, Two Continents" tour spans Sultanahmet to the Asian shore's Kadıköy neighborhood.

The tours take about half a day and cater to small groups (tours are limited to a maximum of six people).

Renovating the Süleymaniye Mosque

In 2007 the Süleymaniye closed its doors to undergo the most thorough renovation in its 450-year history. Scaffolding covered the skyline, topping minarets until 2009, while inside a spider's web of platforms and ladders crept up to the 174-foot-high (53 m) ceiling. Temporary prayer tents were set up for patrons disturbed by the work. Much of the redecoration was both specialized and painstaking: Gold leaf was repainted on the *halil* Islamic crescents, lost tiles previously covered with plaster were exposed, and original doors were reset by hand with precious stones. By mid-2010 steeplejacks were re-leading the dome, ready for the grand opening later that year.

Ottoman age. The splendor of Süleymaniye Mosque (Süleymaniye Camii) conjures up the all-encompassing power of its patron, Sultan Süleyman the Magnificent, and the creative genius of his chief imperial architect, Mimar Sinan (see pp. 90–91).

The Ottoman Empire reached its apogee during the mosque's seven-year construction, when Süleyman's reign stretched across the Mediterranean to the Black Sea, Red Sea, and Persian Gulf. Justifiably, his architectural legacy is massive. Around the mosque, associated parks and buildings stretch for 17 acres (7 ha) and include a hospital, caravansary, *madressehs* (religious schools), a hammam, a library (now a depository of classical Islamic and Turkish texts), a kitchen (now the excellent Dârüzziyafe restaurant, see Travelwise p. 245), plus rows of shops (still shops today, with a few teahouses). At one time more than 3,000 people worked in the complex.

Sinan wove his classic clean lines and looping symmetry into the principal mosque building. Thrown into the mix was a fair amount of Süleyman symbolism and Sinan-style technology. Outside, ten balconies line the four minarets, representing Süleyman as the tenth sultan on the Ottoman throne. In the courtyard, where some of the marble and granite decoration was stripped from the former Hippodrome, Sinan chose to place ablution fountains on both sides, rather than in the center, to speed up the pre-prayer cleansing process. Inside the mosque, the main hall's four red columns were plucked from Alexandria in Egypt and Baalbek in present-day Lebanon, supposedly to placate Süleyman's mild Alexander the Great fixation by drawing upon his ancient legacy. Also inside, Sinan created a bespoke airflow system, so that fumes from the thousands of candles and oil lamps that once illuminated the interior were drawn outward, keeping the tiles and mosaics clean and soot-free.

The mesmerizing central dome (not the original decoration, but dizzying nonetheless) is held up by four elephant-leg pillars, supported by several half domes and columns. Look for the imperial balcony to the left of the mihrab. Sultans would have worshipped here, and a private entrance runs out into the courtyard. The finely carved minbar, where Friday prayers are still delivered, lies to the right.

Tombs of Sultan Süleyman & Roxelana: The resting place of Sultan Süleyman, the former caliph who doubled the size of the Ottoman Empire, attracts Turks in droves, many of whom come to utter a few solemn words by his tomb. The tomb of Roxelana (see sidebar p. 60), who died in 1558, a year after the complex was completed, is surprisingly restrained, considering her flamboyant life. A critically honest appraisal in both English and Turkish of the woman who carved a conspiratorial career out of royal marriage lies outside her tomb.

INSIDER TIP:

Visitors to Istanbul can easily wear out their shoes with the amount of walking they do. However, shoe repairs are no problem: Traditional cobblers, to be found in most neighborhoods, will renew your footwear for little cost.

—TIM HARRIS
National Geographic writer

Southern Golden Horn

Although it is the least visited part of the Old City, the southern Golden Horn is arguably its most beguiling neighborhood. Among its winding streets you will find everything from cavernous monumental mosques to small Orthodox churches filled with stunning mosaics and icons.

Behind the Sea Walls: The now crumbling sea walls—a defensive weak spot in the 1453 conquest (see p. 30)—stretch along the Golden Horn almost all the way from the Atatürk Bridge to Eyüp 3 miles (4.5 km) farther north. The promenade in front of the walls is now a favored spot for picnics and leisurely waterside walks.

Fatih, the neighborhood behind the sea walls, is dominated by the vast **Fatih Mosque** (Fatih Camii). The most interesting part of the ivory-white religious complex is the mausoleum of Mehmet the Conqueror (*fatih* in Turkish) himself. Its dome, frescoed with roses and fabulous geometric patterns, is surely one of the most exquisite in all of Istanbul. It's a very pious place, with worshippers prostrating themselves at Mehmet the Conqueror's very large tomb.

Two museums, both former churches that were transformed into mosques, lie lost in Fatih's suburban sprawl. It's no idle boast that they're home to some of the most scintillating Byzantine art and mosaics in the city, if not the world. The early 14th-century mosaics in the **Fethiye Mosque** (Fethiye Camii), formerly the Church of Pammakaristos, almost glow with religious passion. But even these gems are trumped by Byzantine mosaics in the not-so-distant **Kariye Mosque** (Fethiye Camii), formerly the Church of St. Savior in *(continued on p. 92)*

(continued on p. 92)

Fatih Municipality
 Eyüp Merkez Mh.
 (0212) 444 01 76
www.fatih.bel.tr

Fatih Mosque
✉ Fevzi Paşa Caddesi
🕐 Closed Fri. a.m
$ $ donation recommended

Fethiye Mosque
✉ Fethiye Kapısı
☎ (0212) 635 12 73
🕐 Closed Fri. a.m.
$ $ donation recommended

Kariye Mosque
✉ Küçük Ayasofya Caddesi
☎ (0212) 631 92 41
🕐 Closed Wed. & Fri. a.m.
$ $ donation recommended

The Life & Times of Mimar Sinan

The life of master builder Mimar Sinan (1490–1588) coincided with the golden age of the Ottoman Empire. The great architect's work touched every celebrity of the age, as he designed mausoleums for naval heroes, hammams for ladies of the court, and the grand Süleymaniye Mosque—his skyline-stealing masterpiece—for his principal patron, Sultan Süleyman the Magnificent (1495–1566).

The wealth and artistic freedom afforded to Sinan dwarfed even the Chicago and New York skyscraper boom in the early 20th century, or the tower fever in pre-crisis Dubai.

For a genius whose name crops up in nearly every chapter of this book, Sinan's roots were astonishingly humble. He was born to a stonemason cum carpenter father near Kayseri, in present-day Cappadocia. Originally christened Joseph, he was conscripted, converted to Islam, given the new Muslim name of Sinan (a common occurrence in early Ottoman days), meaning "spearhead," and seconded as a military engineer in the Janissary guards.

Sinan's army career took him all around the known world. From Baghdad to Belgrade and the Adriatic, he came within sight of the finest monuments of the day. As head of the Rifle Corps he targeted, bombarded, and undermined his 16th-century opponents' weakest links.

Sinan the Architect

His engineering prowess soon led him on civil commissions, albeit for mostly military means: bridges, boats, water systems, and roads. It wasn't long before Sultan Süleyman promoted Sinan to chief imperial architect in 1538. He remained in this post for more than

Statue of the Ottoman architect Mimar Sinan

50 years, his tenure ending just shy of his 100th birthday. His 70-year legacy of public works now lies scattered all over the Ottoman capital—the *Tezkiretü'l Bünyan* is the official list of his works and includes over 90 mosques, 20 mausoleums, 55 schools, more than 30 palaces, 7 primary religious schools (*madressehs*), 12 caravansaries (large inns built around a courtyard), fountains, hospitals, and nearly 50 hammams.

Luckily for those following Sinan's trail today, his buildings are neatly clustered together. Losing your way poses no problem either; simply utter the name Mimar Sinan and any proud Istanbullu will point you in the right direction for the particular madresseh or palace you're looking for.

Our visit to **Üsküdar** (see pp. 146–147) loops around several key mosques, contrasting differing works built over three decades apart. **Sultanahmet** also features strongly on any itinerary. As well as renovating the **Topkapı Palace Kitchens** and adding two minarets to the **Hagia Sophia**, Sinan's minor local works include the **Caferağa Medresesi** (see sidebar p. 64) and the **Hammam of Roxelana** (see sidebar p. 68).

His structures along European Istanbul's shore are visited by a mere handful of non-Turks. The sea all but laps the monumental **Kılıç Ali Pasha Mosque** (see p. 120) by the

Istanbul Modern, built for a grand admiral of the Ottoman Armada. The Turkish navy traditionally saluted the Sinan-designed **Tomb of Barbarossa** (see p. 125) in Beşiktaş, then prayed at his nearby **Mosque of Sinan Pasha** (Sinan Paşa Camii), dedicated to another glorious admiral.

But what would Sinan have been most proud of? Although many of his constructions are grand, most are harmonious and subtle in the extreme. Slender minarets blend with delicate domes, playfully lit mosques sit near sultry hammams, the latter featuring star-shaped windows that allow sunlight to filter in gently throughout the day.

Sinan's first truly great work was **Sehzade Mosque,** which set a pattern for his mosques with a large central dome, surrounded by four smaller half domes, which, in turn, are flanked by many smaller domes.

His masterpiece, however, is an exercise in restrained power, backed up by the wealth of an empire in its prime. Fresh from a thorough renovation, the **Süleymaniye Mosque** (see pp. 87–88) remains a place of pilgrimage for those with even a passing interest in architecture. The interior is soaring with majestic arches and a massive central dome which is ringed by 32 windows, throwing light into the white interior. Süleyman himself lies in a magnificent mausoleum in the complex, which also includes hammams, shops, madressehs, a hospital, a medical school, and stables. And in one of his most simple designs, the great Sinan, known at the end of his life as *Mimarlar Mimarı*, "architect of all architects," is buried nearby.

The lavish interior of the Süleymaniye Mosque, built by the master architect Mimar Sinan

Fish sandwich boats, lined up along the shore of the Golden Horn

Chora Museum

✉ Kariye Camii Sokak 18, Edirnekapy

☎ (0212) 631 92 41

🕒 Closed Wed.

💲 $$

www.chora museum.com

Aya Nikola Church

✉ Abdülezel Paşa Caddesi 255, Ayakapı

☎ (0212) 521 26 02

Bulgar Church

✉ Mürsel Paşa Caddesi 85–8, Balat

☎ (0212) 521 11 21

Chora, and now the city's second largest collection after the Hagia Sophia, called the **Chora Museum** (Kariye Müzesi). Scenes of the nativity, the flight to Egypt, and Joseph's journey to Bethlehem look almost as if they were painted in gold.

Fatih's Golden Horn environs were once home to Istanbul's Greek and Armenian communities. Bouts of bad blood in the 1950s, a sorry period in the city's history, led many of these residents to relocate abroad. Mass immigration from eastern Turkey has slowly turned Fatih into one of the most conservative areas of Istanbul. Black burqas for women and flowing pyjama robes for men are the norm. But the area is still studded with hidden churches and tumbling

wooden houses. For a fine remnant of local Greek history visit the early 18th-century **Aya Nikola Church** (Aya Nikola Kilisesi) down by the water. Ring the bell on the steel door to gain entry. The rows of chairs, icons, and candles all lie waiting for the congregation to return.

Around 500 yards (457 m) north of the Aya Nikola is the extraordinary **Church of St. Stephen of the Bulgars** (Bulgar Kilisesi), a towering cast-iron church that was screwed together on the banks of the Bosporus. The idea of "flat-pack churches" in the 1890s was hardly novel. The British had sent corrugated iron chapels across their empire in the preceding decades, while easy-assemble versions designed by Gustave Eiffel (of tower fame) ended up in Peru and the Philippines. But Istanbul's Bulgarian church was different. Stretching 130 feet (40 m) high with a richly decorated second-floor balcony, it weighed in at a mighty 500 tons. Made in Vienna, it was floated down the Danube through Hungary and Romania, over the Black Sea, then up the Golden Horn. It took 18 months to reassemble.

Eyüp Sultan Mosque Complex: Founded on the burial site of Ebū Eyyūb el-Ensari, standard-bearer to the Prophet Muhammad, Eyüp Sultan Mosque Complex is Istanbul's holiest site. Pilgrims flock here from all over Turkey and beyond, particularly on days of religious celebration.

During the first Arab siege on the city (A.D. 674–678), Ebū Eyyūb el-Ensari spearheaded the invasion and was killed during battle. His martyred body was buried here, and a small shrine established. When Mehmet the Conqueror (1432–1481) succeeded in taking control of Constantinople in 1453, he instructed an elaborate new shrine to be built, along with a mosque, school, and kitchens. The complex deteriorated over the centuries and was eventu-

(continued on p. 96)

Eyüp Sultan Mosque Complex

⊠ Camii Kebir Sokak, Eyüp

🕒 Closed Fri. a.m.

🅂 $ donation recommended

EXPERIENCE: A Boat Trip Up the Golden Horn

Up to 14 boats with **Istanbul Deniz Otobüsleri** (*tel 0212/444 44 36, www.ido .com.tr*) run daily from Üsküdar to Eyüp, crossing the Bosporus and Ping-Ponging their way up the Golden Horn. Hop aboard at the European shore's first stop, Eminönü Haliç İskelesi: a small, elusive ferry station just north of Zinhan Kebab Restaurant, also signposted "Storks" (*Ragıpgümüşpala Caddesi 54–6, tel 0212/512 42 75*), west of Eminönü's string of fish sandwich boats.

Following the curve of the Golden Horn, the ferry bends northward, heading across to Kasımpaşa and stopping at **Cezayirli Hasan Paşa Park,** named in honor of Hasan Paşa (1713–1790), grand vizier and founder of the Turkish Naval Academy. On the opposite shore, the ferry slips into Fener pier. There's a ribbon of green manicured parkland along the water's edge, and fantastic views of St. Stephen of the Bulgars Church (see opposite).

Swiveling northward, the boat makes a beeline for **Hasköy** (see pp. 112–113),

dropping passengers just a five-minute walk from the excellent **Rahmi M. Koç Museum** (see p. 112). Be sure to keep an eye out for the museum's submarine, visible from the left-hand side of the ferry.

The boat bounces across the Golden Horn again, stopping at the white wooden Ayvansaray pier, then chugs north to Sütlüce, passing **Feshane,** a former fez factory on the Golden Horn's western banks. The large rosy structure was built in 1839 under Sultan Abdül-mecit I (1823–1861), and today functions as an international conference center.

The boat's final stop is the Eyüp ferry landing. Step ashore to visit **Eyüp Sultan Mosque Complex** (Eyüp Sultan Camii Külliyesi, see above), or explore the neighborhood by foot (see pp. 94–95).

With some variation later in the afternoon, boats from Eminönü pick up at 45 minutes after the hour and return from Eyüp at half past the hour (*$, journey time 35 mins*).

Walk: Around Eyüp & Pierre Loti

Visitors to this neighborhood around Eyüp and Pierre Loti include a blend of religious pilgrims and boisterous tourists. The following walk takes in sights and sounds that appeal to both.

View from Café Pierre Loti toward the historic center of Istanbul

Begin at Eyüp İskelesi, the **Eyüp ferry landing** ❶. Turn left and walk along busy Yavedut Caddesi, passing the roundabout, for 150 yards (140 m). On the right, a small gateway leads to **Zal Mahmud Paşa Mosque** (Zal Mahmud Paşa Camii) ❷. Constructed by royal architect Sinan in 1540, it was built in honor of Mahmud Paşa (d. 1474), Sultan Süleyman the Magnificent's teacher and brother-in-law, buried here with his wife, Şah Sultan. The lower, palm-dotted courtyard makes a peaceful stop for a glass of tea.

Step back out of the same complex gate, make a left onto pedestrianized Feshane Caddesi, then continue straight, crossing the major road Hazreti Halit Bulvarı. Pastel-colored wooden houses line the street, and the compact **Çeribaşı Mosque** (Çeribaşı Cami) on the left is postcard-perfect.

Turn left at the **police station** and plunge into the street market that lines Cami Kebir Sokak. Stalls are piled high with headscarves and religious baubles, as well as strings of "evil eye" beads. The market opens onto **Eyüp Square** (Eyüp Meydanı) ❸, with its central, arching fountain. Look for families towing young boys, each clad in a flamboyant satin outfit—it's traditional to visit Eyüp Sultan Mosque just before circumcision.

NOT TO BE MISSED:

Zal Mahmud Paşa Mosque
• Eyüp Sultan Mosque Complex
• Piyerloti Teleferik • Pierre
Loti Café

Dip into the **Eyüp Sultan Mosque Complex** (Eyüp Sultan Camii Külliyesi, see pp. 93, 96) ❹, which includes Ebū Eyyūb el-Ensari's *türbe*, or tomb, just opposite. After exiting via the complex's westernmost gate, make a right, then another sharp right. This road—Balaban Yolu Sokak—leads straight for about 273 yards (250 m) to **Pierre Loti cable car** (Piyerloti Teleferik, $) ❺. Each double cable car seats a total of 16 passengers, and although the lines to get on can be long, the steep 90-second ride offers some impressive vistas.

Outside the upper cable car station, there's a viewing platform to the left, and the lovely **Pierre Loti Café** ❻, both perfect vantage points over the Golden Horn. Stop for a cool drink, then amble on downhill through Eyüp's cemetery. The sloping cobblestone path is wide and straight. Flashes of Golden Horn views alternate with fig trees and patches of dappled sunlight.

At the bottom of the hill, make your way back to the Eyüp pier either by turning left and heading straight to the Golden Horn, or looping back around Eyüp Sultan Mosque to the right. This walk makes a perfect addition to a boat trip along the Golden Horn (see sidebar p. 93).

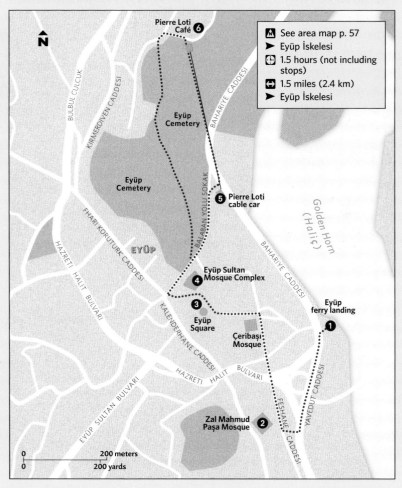

See area map p. 57
► Eyüp İskelesi
🕐 1.5 hours (not including stops)
↔ 1.5 miles (2.4 km)
► Eyüp İskelesi

Museum of Turkish Calligraphic Art

- ⊠ Beyazıt Meydanı, Eminönü
- ☎ (0212) 527 58 51
- 🕒 Closed Sun.–Mon.
- 💲 $

Vakiflar Carpet Museum

- ⊠ Imrahor Caddesi, Sütlüce
- ☎ (0212) 518 13 19
- 🕒 Closed Mon.
- 💲 $

Grand Palace Mosaics Museum

- ⊠ Torun Sokak
- ☎ (0212) 518 12 05
- 🕒 Closed Mon.
- 💲 $

ally reconstructed in its entirety in 1800 under Sultan Selim III (1761–1808) .

Passing through one of the complex's two large gates, visitors will head to an internal courtyard, where a central, tree-dotted area is fenced in. It was here that each royal "inauguration," during which the new sultan would be presented with Osman I's (see p. 25) sword, took place. To the right is Eyüp Sultan Mosque, while Ebū Eyyūb el-Ensari's *türbe* (tomb) sits opposite. The türbe's exterior wall is decorated with a patchwork of hand-painted İznik tiles. Inside, the dazzling tiles continue, making a brilliant backdrop to the crowds of devout pilgrims filing past Ebū Eyyūb el-Ensari's sarcophagus. In a corner to the left, the prophet Muhammad's sacred marble footprint is exhibited behind glass.

Remove your shoes before entering the türbe, as you would a mosque. Cover bare legs; women must also cover their heads. Scarves can be borrowed from a basket at the entrance.

INSIDER TIP:

Trace the development of Turkish humor since the first local cartoon appeared in an 1876 newspaper at the Caricature and Humor Arts Museum in Fatih.

—ANASTASIA ASHMAN
National Geographic Traveler *magazine writer*

Specialist Museums: Like any great city, Istanbul has many museums showcasing the achievements of the civilizations that have flourished within its confines. Some, like the **Museum of Turkish Calligraphic Art,** cater to a small subject area but are of general interest. There are also a number of museums that appeal mainly to particular interests.

While the Museum of Turkish and Islamic Arts (see pp. 78–79) displays the finest examples of carpets, there is also a specialist carpet museum, the **Vakiflar Carpet Museum** (Vakiflar Hali Müsezi) in

Pierre Loti

Pierre Loti was the nom de plume of 19th-century French author and naval officer Julien Viaud. Travels with the navy brought him to Istanbul in 1876–1877, and Loti was quickly enamored with the city. He learned Turkish and studied the local culture with enthusiasm. Afternoons were spent in his adopted neighborhood, atop Eyüp's hill sipping glasses of tea and gazing out over the Golden Horn.

Loti's first novel, the love story entitled *Aziyadé* (named for a girl from Salonika—then Turkish—with whom Loti was apparently smitten), was published in 1879. Later works, including *Pêcheur d'Islande* (*An Iceland Fisherman,* 1886), went on to earn him further acclaim, with Turkey featuring prominently in many of his novels.

Loti returned frequently to the city over the next 35 years. As a token of local affection, today both Eyüp's cable car and the shady café atop the neighborhood's hill bear Pierre Loti's name.

the outer courtyard of the Sultanah-met complex. Housed in this former imperial pavilion is a collection of magnificent old carpets that, until recently, adorned the floors of working mosques in the city. The carpets are undoubtedly beautiful, but the display does not match that of the Museum of Turkish and Islamic Arts—it's a must-see mainly for Turkish carpet fans.

Located behind the Sultanah-met Mosque, the **Grand Palace Mosaic Museum** (Büyüksaray Mozaik Müsezi) features a fine mosaic uncovered in situ by archaeologists in the 1950s. A palace of the sixth-century Byzantine emperor Justinian stood on the spot. What has been unearthed is only part of a huge mosaic pavement, the rest of which still lies under the great mosque and buildings along the opposite side of the street. Nevertheless, what there is to see is memorable. Within the lovely leafy border of the mosaic are depictions of gods and goddesses, hunting scenes, and animals. The signs and information boards are helpful, and the imagery is fun. Look out for the portrayal of a bad-tempered donkey throwing its rider and load off its back.

The **Caricature and Humor Arts Museum** (Karikatur ve mizah Muzesi), located in the Fatih district just west of Süleymaniye, houses a substantial collection of editorial cartoons, caricatures, and newspaper illustrations. Most are from Turkey, but there are many others from around the world. The museum is operated by the Association of Cartoonists, whose offices are nearby. When

Drying carpets the traditional way in the Fatih district

the museum first opened in 1975, drawing cartoons and caricatures was a dangerous way to make a living. Neither the fiercely nationalistic military nor Istanbul's array of armed communist cadres were known for their ability to take a joke. After being forced to close for most of the 1980s (and having its old home demolished) the museum is now thriving. In addition to its permanent collection, the museum often hosts temporary exhibitions of cartoons from a particular country or artist. ■

Caricature and Humor Arts Museum

✉ Atatürk Bulvarı, Kovacılar Sokak 12, Fatih
☎ (0212) 521 12 64

A wealthy area with a blend of shops, art galleries, museums, riverside restaurants, and palaces inspired by the final sultans

European Istanbul

Introduction & Map   100-101

Galata & Around   102-109

Experience: Tasting *Balık Ekmek*   104

Bosporus Boat Tour   106-107

Experience: Touring the Bosporus   106

İstiklal Caddesi: Walking the Old Grande Rue de Pera   110-111

The Northern Golden Horn   112-115

Experience: How to Ride a Dolmuş   113

Taksim Square & Nişantaşı   116-119

Tophane, Çukurcuma, & Cihangir   120-123

Experience: Smoking a *Nargile*   121

Beşiktaş & Ortaköy   124-129

Experience: Exploring Ortaköy's Nightlife   129

North of the Bosporus Bridge   130-135

Feature: A Day Out in Belgrade Forest   132-133

Experience: Hit the Shopping Malls   134

Hotels & Restaurants   246-251

European Istanbul's main street, İstiklal Caddesi, features bakeries, bookstores, art galleries, cafés, and other elegant businesses.

European Istanbul

North of Sultanahmet and across the Golden Horn, European Istanbul—also known as Beyoğlu—is mainly a residential area subdivided into 45 neighborhoods. Here, wealth and high fashion are neatly juxtaposed with traditional nargile cafés and flea markets.

Shop lights gleam in the twilight along pedestrianized İstiklal Caddesi.

Most visitors approach European Istanbul—or Beyoğlu—via the Galata Bridge, crossing over the water from Sultanahmet into Karaköy and Galata. Until the 15th century, this area was the Genoese heart of Constantinople, and its landmark Galata Tower still pokes above the rooftops. The Golden Horn flows at the neighborhood's feet. Working-class districts wind westward, with some patches under slow gentrification—old dockyards have been converted into the Rahmi M. Koç Museum, a treasure trove for toy and transport aficionados, and the former Silahtarağa Power Plant now houses the contemporary art museum, Santralistanbul.

Like a long, vital cord, the street of İstiklal Caddesi is etched atop Beyoğlu's central ridge. Known during the 19th century as the Grande Rue de Pera, it still buzzes with energy today. Antique trams slide among shopping crowds and restored mansions, making their way north to Taksim Square. Nearby neighborhoods are diverse, complementing each other: upscale, wealthy Nişantaşı, eclectic, colorful Çukurcuma, and bohemian Cihangir. Each of these areas rivals the Old City's Grand Bazaar as the city's principal place to shop, a key Turkish pastime if ever there was one. All bases are covered from antiques to bric-a-brac, organic markets to high fashion. Serious shopaholics will revel in Europe's largest mall, Cevahir, or its even cooler counterpart, Kanyon.

Skirting the Bosporus shore are enclaves of contrast. Tophane is home both to impressive mosques and the Istanbul Modern contemporary art museum, a must-see for modern art fans. Beşiktaş' İnönü Football Stadium sits opposite the rococo splendor of Dolmabahçe Palace (Dolmabahçe Sarayı). In fashionable Ortaköy, catch a glimpse of the city's dynamic mix of past and present—Büyük Mecidiye Camii contrasted against the towering Bosporus Bridge.

Istanbul's expanding boundaries mean that many villages north of the city, formerly discrete towns, have been slowly absorbed. But hopping on a bus and heading up the Bosporus to the seaside settlements of Arnavutköy, Bebek, Emirgan, Yeniköy, Tarabya, Büyükdere or Sarıyer will give any visitor a taste of times past. Traditional Ottoman *yalıs* (wooden mansions) are edged by wide Bosporus promenades. Tucked in among them is Rumeli Hisarı, a 15th-century Ottoman fortress. Crisscrossed by towers and gates, with steep staircases and stunning views over the Bosporus, this old fort is a joy to explore. And when Istanbul's action becomes just a little too urban, the alpine hills of the Belgrade Forest make for a perfect escape. ∎

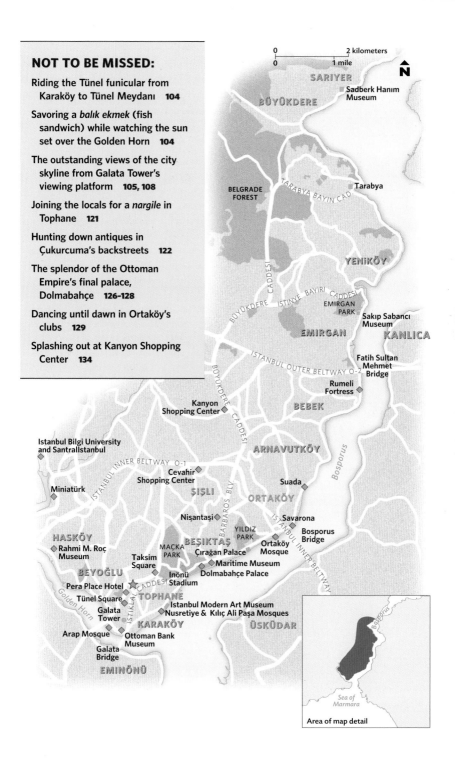

NOT TO BE MISSED:

Riding the Tünel funicular from Karaköy to Tünel Meydanı **104**

Savoring a *balık ekmek* (fish sandwich) while watching the sun set over the Golden Horn **104**

The outstanding views of the city skyline from Galata Tower's viewing platform **105, 108**

Joining the locals for a *nargile* in Tophane **121**

Hunting down antiques in Çukurcuma's backstreets **122**

The splendor of the Ottoman Empire's final palace, Dolmabahçe **126–128**

Dancing until dawn in Ortaköy's clubs **129**

Splashing out at Kanyon Shopping Center **134**

0   2 kilometers
0   1 mile

N

SARIYER
BÜYÜKDERE
Sadberk Hanım Museum

BELGRADE FOREST
TARABYA BAYIN CAD
Tarabya

YENIKÖY

BÜYÜKDERE CADDESI
ISTINYE BAYIRI CADDESI
EMIRGAN PARK
Sakıp Sabancı Museum
EMIRGAN
KANLICA

ISTANBUL OUTER BELTWAY O-2
Fatih Sultan Mehmet Bridge
Rumeli Fortress
BEBEK

Kanyon Shopping Center

BÜYÜKDERE CADDESI

Istanbul Bilgi University and Santralİstanbul

ISTANBUL INNER BELTWAY O-1
Cevahir Shopping Center
ARNAVUTKÖY
Bosporus

Miniatürk

ŞİŞLI
Suada
BARBAROS BLV
ORTAKÖY

Nişantaşı
YILDIZ PARK
Savarona
Bosporus Bridge

HASKÖY
Rahmi M. Roç Museum
MAÇKA PARK
BEŞİKTAŞ
Ortaköy Mosque
ISTANBUL INNER BELTWAY
Taksim Square
Çırağan Palace
Maritime Museum

BEYOĞLU
Inönü Stadium
Dolmabahçe Palace

Pera Place Hotel
Tünel Square
TOPHANE
Galata Tower
Istanbul Modern Art Museum
Nusretiye & Kılıç Ali Paşa Mosques
ÜSKÜDAR

Arap Mosque
KARAKÖY
Ottoman Bank Museum
Galata Bridge

Golden Horn
EMINÖNÜ

Bosporus

Sea of Marmara

Area of map detail

Galata & Around

The Galata Köprüsü (Galata Bridge) links the Old City's ancient Sultanahmet quarter with Beyoğlu (European Istanbul). It has long been considered as much an ideological bridge, spanning old and new, East and West, as a physical one, crossing the Golden Horn.

The medieval Galata Tower dominates the Beyoğlu skyline.

The area directly north of the Galata Bridge is **Karaköy,** a ferry hub and home to a score of simple seafood restaurants. Heading up the hill (preferably on the Tünel funicular railway, one of the world's first subways; see p. 104) is the suburb of **Galata,** the city's first European settlement with its landmark Galata Tower. **İstiklal Caddesi** (İstiklal Street, see pp. 110–111) runs from Galata into the heart of European Istanbul's buzzing center, past boutiques, galleries, and plenty of good restaurants.

Galata Bridge

Over the past 500 years, the Galata Bridge (Galata Köprüsü) has taken various forms. A temporary structure was put in place in 1453, when boats lined up side by side, forming a long, makeshift walkway. If not able to sail or row, travelers could hop from boat to boat to traverse the watery expanse.

During the early 16th century, Sultan Bayezit II made the first moves to install a permanent bridge. Italian artist and inventor Leonardo da Vinci drafted plans, which the sultan promptly rejected, then solicited Italian artist Michelangelo—who was uninterested in the project—for drawings instead. The bridge project was then abandoned for more than 300 years.

INSIDER TIP:

When on İstiklal Street, stop at Hacı Bekir sweet shop (open since 1777) for *kaymaklı lokum*—Turkish delight with clotted cream— and *bergamutlu akide şekeri*—bergamot-flavored hard candy.

—RÜYA KÖSAL KUDU,
National Geographic Expeditions

Valide Sultan Bezmiâlem, the mother of Sultan Abdülmecit, finally successfully raised the first Galata Bridge in 1845, which was traversed by travelers from all over the world. Due to necessary modernizations and one devastating fire, the bridge was replaced three times over the next century and a half.

The bridge's fifth and present incarnation (built between 1992 and 1994) has two action-packed levels. On the lower, restaurants, bars, and cafés face eastward across the Bosporus toward Asia, as well as up the Golden Horn, their west-facing terraces a rosy delight at sunset. Local fishermen drape lines from the bridge's upper level, as vendors pace back and forth with tea, snacks, and extra bait for sale. The city's Zeytinburnu-Kabataş tram shuttles across the bridge, escorted by a constant stream of cars and buses.

Karaköy

This neighborhood, just north of the Galata Bridge, belonged to the Genoese until the 15th century. **Yanık Kapı** (Burned Gate) is the single remaining gate from the old Genoese city walls. A daily fish market takes place on the shore west of the Galata

Ali Muhiddin Hacı Bekir
- ✉ İstiklal Caddesi 83A, Beyoğlu
- ☎ (0212) 244 28 04
- **www.hacibekir.com.tr**

Yanık Kapı
- ✉ Yanık Kapı Sokak, Karaköy

Karaköy
- Ⓜ 101 1A
- 🚊 Karaköy–Galata

Beyoğlu's Galleries

Over the past decade, numerous contemporary art galleries have sprung up around Beyoğlu, with a particularly high concentration along İstiklal Caddesi and in the Galata neighborhood. Following are a few (free) favorites:
Borusan Center for Culture and Arts *(Borusan Sanat Kültür, corner of İstiklal Caddesi & Orhan Adli Apaydın Sokak, tel 0212/336 32 80, www.borusansanat .com/_box/Popup23-09-2010_EN.htm)* opened in 2010. Contemporary Turkish exhibitions are shown over four floors; evening concerts take place here, too.
Yapı Kredi Kültür Sanat has been organizing contemporary art exhibitions

at **Yapı Kredi Kazım Taşkent Galerisi** *(Yapı Kredi Kültür Merkezi, İstiklal Caddesi 161A, tel 0212/252 47 00, www.ykykultur .com.tr)* since 1964. Also located at Yapı Kredi Kazım Taşkent Galerisi, **Yapı Kredi Sermet Çifter Hall** features excellent photography shows. In addition, the building houses a small archaeology museum showcasing coins and ancient treasures from the Yapı Kredi Bank's permanent collection.
The **Fransız Kültür Merkez** *(French Cultural Center, French Consulate, İstiklal Caddesi 4, tel 0212/393 81 11, www.infist .org)* exhibits Turkish-French photography and artworks.

Ottoman Bank Museum

⊠ Mete Caddesi 32 K:1, Taksim

☎ (0212) 292 76 05

$ $

www.obmuze.com/ eng/eldem.asp

Arap Mosque

⊠ Galata Mahkemesi Sokak, Galata

Galata Tower

⊠ Büyük Hendek Sokak 2, Şişhane

☎ (0212) 293 81 80

🚋 Tünel

$ $$$

www.galata tower.net/english/

Bridge, backed by a smattering of simple fish restaurants under nearby trees. Frequent ferries depart from the terminal east of the bridge, heading for Istanbul's Asian train station, Haydarpaşa, and its nearby neighborhood of Kadıköy (see pp. 140–142).

The **Tünel** (underground funicular connecting the Karaköy and Beyoğlu districts) departs from just over the road from the Karaköy tram stop. Designed by French engineer Henri Gavand, the Tünel was completed in 1875 and is the world's second oldest underground urban rail line, after the London Underground. It rises the 65 yards (60 m) from Karaköy to Tünel Square (Tünel Meydanı, in Beyoğlu) in just one-and-a-half-minutes, transporting around 15,000 passengers every day. Buy a *jeton* (token, $) for your journey at machines, kiosks, bus stops, or the ferry dock.

Galata

Between Karaköy and the top end of the Tünel funicular lies

this action-packed neighborhood. During the 19th and much of the 20th centuries, Galata was the city's financial district, with the aptly named Bankalar Caddesi (Bank Street) at its heart. The Ottoman Bank, former central bank for the Ottoman Empire and now owned by Garanti Bank (Turkey's third largest private bank), houses the **Ottoman Bank Museum** (Osmanlı Bankası Müzesi; *closed for extensive restoration at time of writing; call or visit website for more details*). As well as a walk-in steel vault and examples of old currency, the museum's lower level displays provide a patchwork of last century's daily life, including photographs, files, and loan agreements. There is also a temporary exhibition space upstairs.

Nearby, the hexagonal **Kamondo Staircase** (Kamondo Merdivenleri) twists uphill from Bankalar Caddesi. Jewish banker Abraham Kamondo designed the unique staircase in 1860. Its hexagonal shape was apparently

---

EXPERIENCE: Tasting *Balık Ekmek*

Hot, seared mackerel, pressed into half a loaf of fluffy white bread and topped with a handful of onions and lettuce—these *balık ekmek*, or fish sandwiches, are sold along the Bosporus from Anadolu Kavağı to Yenikapı. But it's at Galata Bridge and the mouth of the Golden Horn that traditional wooden fishing boats serve up some of the tastiest ones on offer. Follow the Turkish tourists who flock to **Deniz Yıldızı** restaurant *(tel 0216/414 76 43,*

www.denizyildizikadikoy.com, $), a rocking boat just west of the bridge on the Eminönü shore. Order—there's only one option—pay, and pick up your sandwiches at the boat, then head to one of the low tables. Waiters in flamboyant black and gold outfits serve drinks. No alcohol is available, so you may want to opt instead for traditional *turşu* (pickled vegetables in brine), then—like the locals—wash down your balık ekmek with the salty sour pickle juice!

A street vendor sells pickled vegetables.

intended to prevent the possibility of his young children tumbling down them for more than a short distance. The staircase caught the eye of the famous photographer Henri Cartier-Bresson, who featured it in one of his well-known photographs. The nearby 13th-century **Arap Mosque** (Arap Camii) was formerly the area's most important church.

The neighborhood's most prominent landmark is the **Galata Tower** (Galata Kulesi). This stone tower, coined "Christea Turris" (Tower of Christ), was built by the Genoese in 1348, sitting snugly at the center of their walled city. In bringing Constantinople under unified rule, possession of the tower passed to Mehmet the Conqueror in 1453. Perhaps the most famous story associated with the tower occurred two (continued on p. 108)

Bosporus Boat Tour

The Bosporus is central to Istanbul's history, and most of its major sites are right on the water. For a leisurely taste of this city that straddles two continents, it's best to take to the sea. Tours range from 30 minutes to a full day, and a sunset cruise is a beautiful way to see the city from the water.

View over the Bosporus and Sultanahmet from the Galata Tower

As the boat pulls out from the Golden Horn and turns north into the Bosporus, the first major sight on the left is the soaring 14th-century **Galata Tower ❶** (see pp. 105, 108), used as a fire-spotting tower until the 1970s. The gray building on the water, the **Istanbul Modern ❷** (see pp. 121–122), is the city's premier contemporary art museum. Note the ritzy café-restaurant on the building's right—it's a great place to eat.

Slightly farther up, look for Beşiktaş football club's **İnönü Stadium ❸** on the left. The Black Eagles, as they're known, were Atatürk's favorite soccer club. Little wonder, as Turkey's first president spent his later years in the **Dolmabahçe Palace ❹** (see pp. 126–128) right across from the stadium. The palace played host to U.S. President Barack Obama in April 2009.

Next on the left are two magnificent hotels, the pink-hued **Four Seasons** and the ornate **Çırağan Palace.** The latter was the home of Turkey's nascent parliament before it burned down in 1910. It remained a wreck for 80 years, before being converted into a luxury hotel. Farther on is the prestigious **Galatasaray University ❺** with a student café right on the water. Standing proud on the horizon before the **Bosporus Bridge** (1973) is the **Ortaköy Mosque ❻** built by the Balyan family, designers of the Dolmabahçe Palace.

The grand white boat normally docked after the bridge is the **Savarona ❼**, Atatürk's private yacht. Gutted by fire, it was renovated during the 1990s and can now be hired for several hundred thousand dollars a week (previous passengers include Princess Diana and actor Tom Cruise). The

---

EXPERIENCE: Touring the Bosporus

Bosporus boat tours are available from various companies. **Istanbul Deniz Otobüsleri A.S.,** or IDO *(Kennedy Caddesi, Yenikapi Feribot Iskelesi, Fatih, tel 0212/455 69 00, www.ido.com.tr)* offers short round-trip cruises from 2:30 p.m. to 4:30 p.m., or long round-trip cruises from 10:35 a.m. to 6:30 p.m., stopping for lunch at Anadolu Kavağı. Other companies offering half- or whole-day

tours are **Turkey & Istanbul Tour Company** *(Gelinlik Sokak, Sultanahmet, tel 0533/350 73 00, www.istanbultour24.com)*, **City of Sultans** *(Barbaros Bulvarı Dörtyüzlüçeşme Sokak, Güneş Apt. 2 Kat: 5, Beşiktaş, tel 0212/327 23 93, www.cityof sultans.com)*, and **One Nation** *(Binbirdirek Mahallesi, Klodfarer Caddesi 3/7, Sultanahmet, tel 0212/516 53 00, www.allistanbultours.com)*.

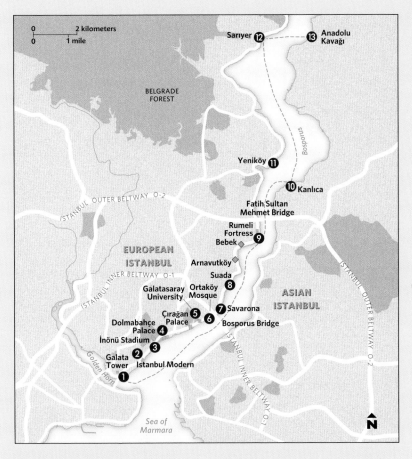

0   2 kilometers
0   1 mile

BELGRADE FOREST

Sarıyer 12 --- 13 Anadolu Kavağı

ISTANBUL OUTER BELTWAY O-2

Bosporus

Yeniköy 11

10 Kanlıca

Fatih Sultan Mehmet Bridge

Rumeli Fortress 9
Bebek

EUROPEAN ISTANBUL

ISTANBUL INNER BELTWAY O-1

Arnavutköy

Suada

Galatasaray University   Ortaköy Mosque 8

ASIAN ISTANBUL

ISTANBUL OUTER BELTWAY O-2

Çırağan 5
Dolmabahçe Palace 4   6   7 Savarona

İnönü Stadium 3   Bosporus Bridge

Galata Tower 2

1   Istanbul Modern

Golden Horn

ISTANBUL INNER BELTWAY O-1

Sea of Marmara

N

floating island nearby, replete with Olympic-size swimming pool and restaurants, is the ultra-trendy **Suada** 8.

The next stretch of the boat tour is extraordinarily pretty. The wealthy villages of **Arnavutköy** and **Bebek** slip by on the left, both lined with *yalis* and waterside promenades. It's hard to miss the two grand turrets of **Rumeli Fortress** up next 9. This massive fort was constructed in four months in 1452, as Mehmet II prepared his final assault on Constantinople's city walls the following year.

After the **Fatih Sultan Mehmet Bridge** (1988), the boat crosses over to the Asian shore, one of Istanbul's wealthiest areas. Many of the seaside mansions have ladders dipping directly

into the Bosporus. The tour frequently pulls up at charming **Kanlıca** 10, a town famed for its yogurt. Often the boat's waiters will leap off and grab a few pots to sell on board.

Back on the other side of the Bosporus is **Yeniköy** 11, a suburb so rich that each house (many are former embassies) attempts to outdo the other in terms of size and splendor.

The seafront fish restaurants of **Sarıyer** 12 appear ten minutes farther up the Bosporus. Sturdy-looking boats belonging to Turkey's Black Sea fishing fleets moor along this upper European shore, as the Asian side is given over to a vast military zone. Note the towering Genoese castle above **Anadolu Kavağı** 13 (see pp. 150–151), the tour's final destination—and a great place for lunch.

Galata Whirling Dervish Hall and Museum of Divan Literature

- Galip Dede Caddesi 15
- (0212) 245 41 41
- Closed Tues.
- $$
- Tünel

centuries later, around 1630, when local boy Hezarfen Ahmet Çelebi donned large, homemade wings and launched himself from its roof, soaring over the Bosporus to eventually land in the Asian town of Üsküdar, 2 miles (3.4 km) away. Fearing his power, Sultan Murad IV forced Çelebi out of Constantinople and into Algerian exile. Over the course of the following century, the tower was used primarily as a lookout for the city's all too frequent fires.

The Galata Tower is 200 feet (61 m) tall, and its curved walls measure 12 feet (3.75 m) thick. Over the years, the tower has lost its conical roof, been restored and modified, and had its conical roof replaced again. Visitors can hop into the tower's elevator to the upper floors and have refreshments in the tower's restaurant or café (be aware that the stunning views from here make it very popular with visitors and locals and therefore difficult to get a table). A nightclub on the top floor presents traditional Turkish entertainment. For an extra fee *($)*, after you exit the elevator you can walk up the two remaining flights of stairs to the ninth floor, where there is a slender balcony that rings the tower. This platform, open from 9 a.m. to 5 p.m. (to 7 p.m. in summer) offers some of the city's most spectacular panoramas, with clear views over the Bosporus, Topkapı Palace, the Blue Mosque, and the Golden Horn.

The **Galata Whirling Dervish Hall** (Galata Mevlevihanesi) is farther up the hill, just around the corner and south of **Tünel Square** (Tünel Meydanı). This *tekke,* or religious hall, was built in 1491 under

Muhammed Semai Sultan Divani, a direct descendant of Mevlana Celaleddin Rumi, founder of the Mevlevi Order in 1273. Seeking union with God through music, the *mevlevi* (whirling derviches) perform a spinning, trance-inducing dance called *sema.* The order was banned, along with other orders, in 1925 by Atatürk, and the tekke closed. The lodge was used for various ventures from 1934, including serving as an ethnographical museum from 1975 to 2000. Following a two-year revamp, the museum reopened in 2002 as the **Museum of Divan Literature** (Divan Edebiyatı Müzesi), also known as Galata Mevlevihane (Mevlevi Lodge), displaying traditional instruments, literary works, and calligraphy. On the left side of the courtyard is the tomb of the 17th-century poet and tekke leader, Galip Dede. Sema performances *($$$$)* take place weekly, usually on Fridays between 5 p.m. and 7 p.m., in a special room known as the *semahane,* located on the far side of the courtyard. These shows are popular and tickets are limited, so you will need to book in advance. For other spots around town to see the mevlevi in action, see sidebar p. 48.

İstiklal Caddesi

This grand, pedestrianized avenue extends northward from the Tünel line's top end to Taksim Square. To İstiklal's west, the Tepebaşı neighborhood is home to the **Pera Palace Hotel** (see sidebar below) and the **Palazzo Corpi** (*Meşrutiyet Caddesi 104-108),* built by Genoese shipowner Ignazio Corpi in the 1870s with the finest materials imported from Italy. The latter was used as the U.S. diplomatic premises from 1882, then the U.S. Embassy from 1907, then the U.S. Consulate 1937-2003, when it moved in the interests of security. Its gloriously opulent features include marble from Carrara, rosewood from Piemonte, and frescoes depicting scenes from mythology by Italian artists commissioned by the building's architect, Giacomo Leoni. Plans are now afoot to turn the vacant edifice into a five-star hotel.

Opened by the Suna and İnan Kıraç Foundation in 2005, the **Pera Museum** (Pera Müzesi) is located northeast of the palazzo in the former Bristol Hotel. The first two floors showcase the museum's permanent collection of Kütahya ceramic tiles, Anatolian weights and measures, and Orientalist art, including Ottoman artist Osman Hamdi Bey's acclaimed *Tortoise Trainer* (1906). The top three floors host temporary exhibitions, largely displaying modern art. The museum also hosts film festivals of everything from Japanese animated films to experimental art movies. ■

Pera Museum

- ✉ Meşrutiyet Caddesi 65, Tepebaşı
- ☎ (0212) 334 99 00
- 🕐 Closed Mon.
- 💲 $$
- 🚇 Tünel

http://en.pera muzesi.org.tr

Pera Palace Hotel

Designed by French-Turkish architect Alexander Vallaury and inaugurated in 1892, the legendary Pera Palace Hotel *(Pera Palas Oteli; 52 Meş rutiyet Caddesi 52, Tepebaşi, Beyoğlu, tel 0212/377 40 00, www.perapalace.com;* see Travelwise p. 246) was created to be a sumptuous final destination for Orient Express passengers upon their arrival in Istanbul. For these affluent travelers, no comfort was spared—the hotel was home to the city's first elevator and the bathrooms boasted Istanbul's only hot running water.

Occupied by the Allies during World War I, the hotel's roster of former regular visitors is very illustrious: Queen Elizabeth II; Kaiser Wilhelm II of Germany; Emperor Franz Joseph I of Austria-Hungary; American author Ernest Hemingway; Swedish movie star Greta Garbo; film director Alfred Hitchcock; French actress Sarah Bernhardt; and Dutch exotic dancer and spy Mata Hari were all guests here. Turkey's first president, Mustafa Kemal Atatürk, stayed frequently in Room 101, beginning in 1917, and the room has been transformed into a small museum in his honor.

English mystery author Agatha Christie stayed here when she visited Istanbul and she is believed to have written much of *Murder on the Orient Express* from Room 411. Serious fans can opt to stay in Christie's room, and the hotel's main restaurant, Agatha, has been named in her honor.

İstiklal Caddesi: Walking the Old Grande Rue de Pera

The heart of 19th-century Istanbul, İstiklal Caddesi is studded with former embassies, ornate art nouveau masterpieces and wiggling passageways. With its restored "Nostalgic Tram" and a smattering of churches, the pedestrianized avenue has a distinct European flavor—note that the addresses refer to the red (new) numbers outside each building.

An ice cream shop on İstiklal Caddesi

Start at **Tünel Square** ❶ (Tünel Meydanı), at the southern end of İstiklal Caddesi (see p. 109) by the Tünel underground funicular (see p. 104) entrance. Opposite, colored lights dangle from the trees marking the entranceway to pretty Tünel Geçidi, a small passageway filled with bars and restaurants. The Nostalgic Tram—restored 19th-century tramcars that cruise the length of İstiklal Caddesi—also departs from here.

Around 50 yards (45 m) to the right (east), **Galata Whirling Dervish Hall** ❷ (see p. 108) sits at the top of Galip Dede Caddesi. Visit the museum, or poke around the shady, cat-filled courtyard.

Return to İstiklal Caddesi, head north and on the right at number 235 is the seven-story art nouveau masterpiece **Botter House** ❸, currently in a state of disrepair. Italian architect

Raimondo D'Aronco designed the resplendent edifice in 1900 for Sultan Abdülhamit II's private tailor, Jean Botter.

Over the road at number 172, the budget eatery Yemek Kulübü sits on the site of the old **Markiz Patisserie**. Opened in 1940, Markiz was a hugely popular café in its heyday. As well as the sign above the passageway, French artist J. A. Arnoux's Spring and Autumn panels still adorn the café's interior.

Walking on, tall wrought-iron gates mark the entrance to Istanbul's **Russian Consulate** (İstiklal Caddesi 219). The vast building, its massive columns best seen from the Bosporus shore below, was built under the Fossati brothers in 1845.

Santa Maria Draperis Church ❹ (İstiklal Caddesi 215, tel 0212/244 02 43, www.istan coreofm.org.engindex.php) is easy to miss: Look out for the steep stairs that lead down to the entrance, underneath a golden mosaic of the Virgin Mary. Established during the late 16th century by Genoese resident Clara Bartola Draperis, the Catholic church was moved to this spot a hundred years later.

Next door, the **Borusan Culture and Arts Center Music Library** ❺ (Borusan Sanat Kültür ve Merkezi's Müzik Kütüphane; İstiklal Caddesi 213, closed Sun.) houses the country's largest collection of Turkish music. Across the street, Borusan launched their brand new, contemporary exhibition space, **Müzik Evi** in February 2010.

Strolling north again, on the right, the **Netherlands Consulate** (İstiklal Caddesi 197) was also designed by the Fossati brothers and completed

NOT TO BE MISSED:

Galata Whirling Dervish Hall • St. Anthony of Padua • Balik Pazari • Hüseyin Ağa Mosque

in 1855. Another 50 yards (45 m) along, the alley Perukar Çikmazi leads left to **Holy Trinity Church ⑥** (Surp Yerrortutyun Kilisesi; *tel 0212/244 13 82*). This Armenian Catholic church has been serving Beyoğlu since the 17th century, although the numbers attending Mass today are low, and the church often organizes mixed religious services.

About 80 yards (75 m) north, the redbrick **St. Anthony of Padua Church ⑦** (*İstiklal Caddesi 182, tel 0212/244 09 35*), the largest Catholic church in Istanbul, is visible on the right, dating from 1913. The next-door **Mısır Apartmanı building** (*İstiklal Caddesi 163*) was built for the Khedive of Egypt in 1910. Today, trendy bar 360 occupies its top floor.

Continue for another 80 yards (75 m) to **Haco Pulo Cafe ⑧** on the left. A kiosk-cluttered entrance leads to a courtyard hemmed in by old buildings. In the first decade of the 20th century, the Young Turks, including future president Mustafa Kemal Atatürk, used to meet

here. Pop through the opposite exit for a peek at the **British Consulate** (*Meşrutiyet Caddesi 34*), completed in 1855.

Galatasaray Square ⑨ is İstiklal Caddesi's approximate midway point. Artist Sadi Calik's abstract sculpture sits at its center, installed in 1973 on the 50th anniversary of the Turkish Republic. The bright white marble building over the road is the former central post office, now a museum dedicated to Galatasaray high school, established in the 15th century, and its offshoot soccer club.

Turn left onto Yeni Çarşı Caddesi. After 10 yards (9 m), make a right into **European Passage** (Avrupa Pasajı) ⑩. Designed in 1874 by Austrian architect Pulgher, this long store-lined passageway is decorated with small, detailed statues above each doorway. Exit onto Sahne Sokak, home of Galatasaray's daily **Fish Market** (Balık Pazarı), which extends downhill to the left. Turn right and walk back to İstiklal Caddesi, passing **Flower Passage** (Çiçek Pasajı) ⑪ on the left-hand corner. Previously a flower market, raucous *meyhanes* (tavernas) replaced the fragrant stalls 50 years ago.

Follow İstiklal Caddesi on its kink eastward keeping an eye out for the beautifully ornate 1920s facade of Alkazar Sineması (*İstiklal Caddesi 111*) on the right. Another 130 yards (120 m) and the white walls of **Hüseyin Ağa Mosque ⑫** (Hüseyin Ağa Camii), İstiklal's only mosque, appear on the left.

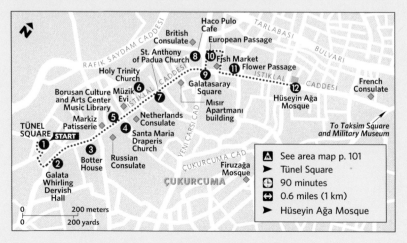

🅰	See area map p. 101
▶	Tünel Square
🕐	90 minutes
↔	0.6 miles (1 km)
▶	Hüseyin Ağa Mosque

The Northern Golden Horn

From the Jewish enclave of Hasköy and the eclectic and exciting industrial collection donated by the prestigious Koç family to the university area of Silahtarağa, with its excellent art and technology museums, and Miniatürk—with its miniature representations of Turkish landmarks—the northern Golden Horn area is packed with treats for visitors.

Hasköy Synagogue is one of many synogogues in Hasköy, long a small Jewish village.

Rahmi M. Koç Museum

- ✉ Hasköy Caddesi 27, Hasköy
- ☎ (0212) 369 66 00
- 🕐 Closed Mon.
- 💲 $$-$$$
- 🚍 Hasköy Parkı
- 🚌 Hasköy

www.rmk-museum.org.tr

Hasköy

West of Beyoğlu proper and on the eastern banks of the Golden Horn, Hasköy is mostly residential, with the pretty Hasköy Park at its center. For hundreds of years, Hasköy was a small Jewish village, tacked on to the outskirts of Constantinople. It is still dotted with synagogues and its northern section is home to the city's large Jewish cemetery, today sadly sliced by one of Istanbul's highways. On a hill to the north of the highway is the ornate mausoleum of Abraham Kamondo, creator of Karaköy's Kamondo Staircase (see p. 104). Other cemeteries in Hasköy include Greek, Muslim, Turkish Karaite (a form of Judaism), and Armenian.

Of primary interest to visitors is Hasköy's vast **Rahmi M. Koç Museum** (Rahmi M. Koç Müzesi). This excellent museum was originally housed in the former Lengerhane, a foundry that created anchors for the Ottoman army. Its

INSIDER TIP:

At sunset, the small rooftop terrace at Mikla, one of the city's most luxurious restaurants, offers stunning views over the Sultanahmet and the Golden Horn—but for a high price tag.

—JONI RENDON
National Geographic contributor

collection of model ships and trains, cars, tractors, and toys, assembled by the rich industrialist Rahmi M. Koç (see sidebar p. 114) is fascinating. As Koç's collection expanded, the old Hasköy Dockyards across the street were purchased and renovated, opening to the public in 2001. A final expansion took place in 2007, to the west of the dockyards, which includes the Hasköy-Sütlüce train station and sidings. (A sister museum is located in Ankara; see p. 172.) Exhibits tracing the industrialization and development of modern Istanbul include Turkish cars of various ages, the elaborate railroad carriage of the Ottoman sultans, an amphicar (which is part auto, part boat), relics of early Bosporus ferries, a horse-drawn tram, and a large display of electric goods. Highlights of the museum include the U.S.-built Turkish submarine *TCG Uluçalireis,* docked on the banks of the Golden Horn (from which children under age eight are barred and entrance to which is by an additional small fee, $), and a Douglas DC-3 Dakota airplane, perched outside midair and accessible via steep stairs. Signs are in English as well as Turkish, and regular demonstrations of machinery, and plenty of buttons to push on exhibits, make this an amusing and instructive visit.

Mikla Restaurant

✉ Marmara Pera Hotel, Meşrutiyet Caddesi 15, Beyoğlu

☎ (0212) 293 56 56

🕐 Closed Sun.

www.mikla restaurant.com

EXPERIENCE: How to Ride a *Dolmuş*

A wonderfully practical compromise between a bus and a taxi, in Istanbul *dolmuşes* connect just about everywhere. They have no fixed schedule—they simply depart when they are full (dolmuş means "full" or "stuffed") —although their routes and prices are regulated by the government.

Dolmuşes are usually minibuses, many of which are ex-school buses imported en masse from Germany. A dolmuş' terminus is fixed: For example, dolmuşes stopping at the Rahmi M. Koç Museum depart from Şişhane, the station itself marked by a large letter "D." The dolmuş will also display a sign in the front window stating its final destination, in this case Alibeyköy. Depending on the driver, and within reason, you can normally flag down a dolmuş at any point along its route in addition to fixed stops, and likewise, ask to hop off anywhere (shout out *"inecek var"*).

When you get on, the driver will let you know how much you'll need to pay. In Istanbul, it will never be more than TL 3.5, and the fee is the same no matter where you get off en route. Along various routes and during particular times of day dolmuşes can be packed, but normally their frequency means they're a more comfortable mode of transport than buses.

Santralistanbul

✉ Eski Silahtarağa Elektrik Santralı, Kazım Karabekir Caddesi 1, Silahtarağa

☎ (0212) 311 78 09

🕐 Closed Mon.

www.santral istanbul.org

Silahtarağa

At the northern end of the Golden Horn, the Silahtarağa neighborhood is home to **Bilgi Üniversitesi** (Istanbul Bilgi University; www.bilgi.edu.tr). Much like an Ivy League college, Bilgi's leafy green campus is neatly trimmed; its grass is sprinkled with fashionably rumpled students, snacking, chatting, or just lying around in the sunshine.

At the heart of the campus is **santralistanbul**, an art and technology museum housed within

INSIDER TIP:

To see Turks socializing away from the tourist circuit, visit a *meyhane*, a popular type of tapas bar, many of which lie near Taksim Square and Nevizade Caddesi (see *www.meyhane.com*).

—CLIVE CARPENTER
National Geographic contributor

the city's former Silahtarağa Power Plant. Built in 1911 at the junction of the Kağıthane and Alibeyköy Rivers, from 1914 to 1952, the power plant provided Istanbul with all of its electricity, and continued to serve the city until its closure in 1983. Today, two of the power station's former engine rooms have been refurbished and now house the **Museum of Energy** (Enerji Müzesi). The control room looks like something a James Bond villain would use to take over the world—a giant, arched wall of retro-futuristic levers and buttons.

The opposite wing of the museum is home to an excellent range of temporary exhibitions, including the works of contemporary Turkish artists, international projects, science and history exhibitions, and students' creations; artworks are frequently interactive installations or video-based. The center also organizes concerts, theater and dance performances, film viewings, children's programs, and weekend workshops.

There are free shuttles between Taksim Square (Taksim

The Koç Family

Along with the Sabancıs family, the Koçs are one of Turkey's most affluent and powerful families. Ankara-born patriarch Vehbi Koç (1901–1998) may have started out humbly working in his father's grocery store, but by the 1940s, his career was becoming truly illustrious. From making light bulbs to producing Turkey's first cars, refrigerators, and washing machines, Koç Holding grew to became a major international presence by the 1960s. It expanded substantially under Vehbi's son Rahmi, and today the founder's grandson Mustafa heads up the wealthy industrial dynasty.

The Koç family is also an enthusiastic patron of the arts; Vehbi's wife Sadberk opened the **Sadberk Hanım Museum** (see pp. 134–135) in 1980, while the **Rahmi M. Koç Museum** (see pp. 112–113) opened in 1994. Among other projects, the family's Vehbi Koç Foundation established a high school in Istanbul, funds a university outside the city in Rumeli Feneri and donated millions of dollars to New York's Metropolitan Museum for the creation of two new Ottoman art galleries. The foundation was awarded the Carnegie Medal of Philanthropy in 2009.

Scale models of Turkey's most famous buildings in the Miniatürk park

Meydandı), departing from in front of the Atatürk Cultural Center (see p. 117) and Bilgi University.

Miniatürk

Miniatürk celebrates all of Turkey's most popular monuments—its religious sites, geological features, and architectural structures—by re-creating them in miniature. The park opened in 2003 and contains close to one hundred models, including perfectly scaled-down versions of the ancient Library of Ephesus, Topkapı Palace, Atatürk's Mausoleum in Ankara, and Istanbul's modern airport, all set on carefully manicured lawns interspersed by artificial rocks. If you're looking to try before you actually commit to that trip

to Cappadocia or Ephesus, for instance, or you run out of time on your vacation to see everything you wanted, then this is an excellent taster. This is a place young tourists, in particular, will enjoy, especially the rides on a miniature railroad.

The park also contains the **Victory Museum** (Zafer Müzesi), detailing the Gallipoli battles of 1915–1916 and the **Kristal Istanbul Müzesi** (Istanbul Crystal Museum), where 16 of the city's monuments have been re-created in crystal. For more fun, head to the playground, giant chess set, and go-kart track next door.

Miniatürk can be reached via bus 54HT from Taksim Square, bus 47 from Eminönü or a 15-minute walk south from santralistanbul. ■

Miniatürk

 İmrahor Caddesi, Borsa Durağı Mevkii, Sütlüce

☎ (0212) 222 28 82

💲 $$$

🚋 Sütlüce

www.miniaturk.com.tr

Victory Museum

✉ Miniatürk

☎ (0272) 212 09 16

🕐 Closed Mon.

💲 $$$

Istanbul Crystal Museum

 Miniatürk

☎ (0212) 222 28 82

💲 $$$

Taksim Square & Nişantaşı

Beyoğlu's most important transport hub, Taksim Square (Taksim Meydanı) is crowded with buses running up the Bosporus shoreline and *dolmuşes* zipping around inland. Particularly during morning and evening rush hours, thousands of commuters make use of Istanbul's rapidly expanding metro line and the short Tünel funicular that connects Taksim to Kabataş, the port that links European Istanbul to the Asian side of the city and the Princes Islands.

At the modern subway station of Taksim Square

Republic Museum
✉ Taksim Square

Taksim Square

Taksim Square (Taksim Meydanı) takes its name from the octagonal-shaped Water Distribution Station on the square's west side, called Taksim Maksemi (*taksim* translates as "distribution"). Built under Sultan Mahmut I in 1732, the structure collected water funneled south from Belgrade Forest (see pp. 132–133). This water was then distributed out through the notoriously dry Beyoğlu neighbor-hood. Today, Taksim Maksemi has been given over to the **Republic Museum** (Cumhuriyet Müzesi). The spacious museum hosts temporary exhibitions that explore the history of the city, such as tulip imagery during Ottoman times, or Istanbul's soccer clubs over the course of the 20th century. The displays are well labeled in both Turkish and English.

Just south of Taksim Maksemi, **İstiklal Caddesi**—formerly Grande

Rue de Pera—angles westward to Tünel Square. Sıraselviler Caddesi branches off to the south, leading on toward the trendy **Cihangir** neighborhood (see pp. 122–123).

On the north side of the square, busy **Cumhuriyet Caddesi** heads up to the **Nişantaşı** (see p. 119) and **Şişli** neighborhoods, while İnönü Caddesi dips downhill from the square's eastern corner, through the Gümüşsuyu area and Istanbul's tiny Chinatown en route to **Beşiktaş' İnönü soccer stadium** (see sidebar p. 125).

INSIDER TIP:

If you happen to be in Istanbul at 9:05 a.m. on November 10, don't be surprised if everything suddenly stands stock still for a minute, as sirens and foghorns sound eerily. This is how Istanbullus honor their revered leader Mustafa Kemal Atatürk each year on the day he died.

—SALLY MCFALL
National Geographic contributor

Between these two major streets, **Taksim Park** (Taksim Gezi Parkı) sprawls northward. It was home to Ottoman artillery barracks and then, during the 1920s and '30s, Taksim Stadium. Since the 1950s, this green expanse has been dotted with high-end hotels, such as the Conrad and the Divan. If

you've been out for a long period shopping or seeing the sights on İstiklal Caddesi, the park's benches positioned along the paths and the outside tea gardens offer a welcome opportunity to rest your feet on a nice day (note that some areas of the park can be sketchy after dark).

The recently restored **Atatürk Cultural Center** (Atatürk Kültür Merkezi or AKM) is southeast of the park. Concerts, ballet, theater, and opera performances take place here, as well as some international festivals.

Italian sculptor Pietro Canonica designed the **Monument of the Republic** (Cumhuriyet Anıtı), located in the western half of the square's center. Installed in 1928 and fully restored in 2010, the sculpture portrays Atatürk with soldiers, as well as the republic's first political leaders. Crowds congregate at the base of the sculpture on important commemorative days, such as November 10, the anniversary of Atatürk's death.

On the southwest corner of Taksim Square is the **French Consulate.** Constructed in 1719, it also contains a café, bookstore, and exhibition space.

If you walk west of Taksim Square on İstiklal Caddesi and turn left, you'll see the huge domed roof of the **Holy Trinity Orthodox Church** (Aya Triada Rum Ortodoks Kilisesi) come looming into view on the left. This Greek Orthodox church was built in 1882; to its left, the L-shaped **Hacı Baba** (see Travelwise p. 250) is the city's oldest restaurant, and was founded in 1921.

Monument of the Republic

 Taksim Maksemi, Taksim Meydanı

 Taksim

French Consulate

 İstiklal Caddesi 4

 (0212) 233 27 20

 Taksim

Holy Trinity Orthodox Church

 Meşelik Sokak 11/1

 (0212) 244 13 58

 By appointment only

 Taksim

Atatürk Cultural Center

 İnönü Mahallesi, Kultür Sokak, Taksim

 (0212) 251 56 00

 Closed Sun.

Orhan Pamuk

Author and Nobel Prize-winner Orhan Pamuk, born in 1952, was raised in Nişantaşı. He attended Istanbul's (American) Robert College and tried his hand at architecture and journalism, before eventually settling down to a career as a hugely successful novelist. His first book, *Cevdet Bey ve Oğulları (Mr. Cevdet and His Sons,* 1982), was published when Pamuk was 30 years old. Like many of his works, it was set in and around Nişantaşı. But it was really *Beyaz Kale (The White Castle),* published in English in 1990, which catapulted Pamuk to international fame. Later books, such as the novel *Benim Adım Kırmızı (My Name Is Red,* 2003) and *Istanbul: Memories and a City* (2005) established Pamuk as Turkey's most famous author.

Although Pamuk spent his career studiously avoiding political controversy, during an interview with Swiss *Das*

Magazin in 2005, Pamuk publicly stated that one million Armenians (in 1915) and 30,000 Kurds (in recent years) had been killed in Turkey. Issues of alleged Armenian genocide (see p. 32) and Kurdish separatism (see p. 16) are tense and much contested topics in Turkey and the government responded by promptly introducing a new law: Insulting Turkishness is a crime for any Turk. Pamuk was retroactively charged, although the case against him was dropped later that year.

Today, Pamuk is known as much for his fraught relationship with his beloved, *hüzün* (melancholy)-steeped home country as his deeply successful novels. His explorations of East and West, individual and community, culminated in the Nobel Prize in literature in 2006, and the author currently divides his time between his studio in Beyoğlu and temporary writing residences abroad.

Military Museum

Vali Konagi Caddesi, Harbiye, Şişli

(0212) 233 27 20

Closed Mon.–Tues.

$

Osmanbey

www.tsk.tr/muze_internet/askeri_muze.htm

Military Museum

Given the extensive role of the military in Turkey's Ottoman and modern history, it is no surprise that Istanbul's **Military Museum** (Askeri Müze), just a half a mile (1 km) north of Taksim Square, is jam-packed with displays from early Islamic daggers to rail-mounted cannon. One of the key exhibits is the building itself. Formerly the Harbiye Military Academy, it was the Ottoman Empire's answer to the United States Military Academy at West Point, and Atatürk himself was a student here from 1899 to 1905.

The various salons house weaponry from savage medieval maces and broad swords to flintlock rifles and sophisticated

body armor. Of special note is the chain used by the Byzantines to bar Mehmet II's ships from entering the Golden Horn during the conquest in 1453 (it didn't work; the Muslim invaders simply pushed the boats over the hill). One room is dedicated to Turkey's UN peacekeeping work in Bosnia, Somalia, and Kosovo.

A traditional Mehter band, the kettledrum-bashing soldiers widely considered as the original military bandsmen, perform outside the museum at 3 p.m. from Wednesday to Sunday.

A tiny cable car (*$*) runs over the northern end of Maçka Demokrasi Parkı, providing a shortcut on the walk between Taksim and Nişantaşı. While the ride lasts little more than a couple of minutes, passengers enjoy wonderful views over the Bosporus and İnönü Stadium.

Nişantaşı

Nişantaşı is the European heart of European Istanbul. Located within the wider suburb of Şişli, it's a choice neighborhood for Istanbul's affluent residents and expats, including some of the city's most famous actors, designers, and television presenters.

Nişantaşı is also Istanbul's luxury shopping headquarters, with high-end international brands clustered along Abdi İpekçi Caddesi: Cartier, Louis Vuitton, and Prada are all located here. The city's only organic produce market is just a short walk away.

Cultural sights are limited, but **Atatürk Museum** (Atatürk Müzesi) is well worth a visit. Mustafa Kemal Atatürk, his mother, and his sister rented this pink, three-storied home from December 1918 through May 1919. Purchased by the Istanbul municipality in 1928, it was inaugurated as a museum in June 1942.

The museum contains a wealth of photographs, clothes, and personal effects, as well as portraits of Turkey's first president and a small lock of his hair. While most information is described in Turkish only, the rear ground-floor room presents a interesting bilingual exhibition of stamps, ranging from the early days of the Turkish Republic to the present. Various stamps act as a chronicle of modern Turkish history, commemorating such major events as Turkey's move to use the Latin alphabet (1928), or the surname law (1934), in which every citizen was forced to adopt a family name. ∎

Atatürk Museum
- ✉ Meşrutiyet Mahallesi, Halaskargazi Caddesi 250, Şişli
- ☎ (0212) 240 63 19
- 🕐 Closed Sun.–Mon.
- 🚇 Osmanbey

Exquisite shoes for sale in the luxury shopping quarter of Nişantaşı

Tophane, Çukurcuma, & Cihangir

The neighborhoods of Tophane, Çukurcuma, and Cihangir are all part of Istanbul's Beyoğlu district, cradled between İstiklal Caddesi to the northwest and the Bosporus shoreline to the southeast. A mix of traditional enclaves and trendy bars, this area is home to restaurants, stellar stores, and excellent sites, including the Istanbul Modern art gallery.

At a *nargile* bar in Tophane, Istanbul

Nusretiye Mosque
✉ Necatibey Caddesi, Tophane
🕐 Closed Fri. a.m.
🚇 Tophane

Kılıç Ali Paşa Mosque
✉ Just off Necatibey Caddesi, Tophane
🕐 Closed Fri. a.m.
🚇 Tophane

Tophane

Tophane's most noticeable sight, aside from the string of *nargile* cafés (see sidebar opposite) is the 19th-century **Nusretiye Mosque** (Nusretiye Camii, or Victory Mosque, 1826), designed by Armenian architect Krikor Balyan. Created to commemorate Sultan Mahmud II's suppression of the wild Janissary troops and their replacement with a trained, organized army, the mosque

is flanked by the mint-green **Tophane Kasrı** (Tophane Royal Pavilion, 1852) and **Tophane Saat Kulesi** (Tophane Clocktower, 1848).

Just south of here along Meclis-i Mebusan Caddesi, Sinan's **Kılıç Ali Paşa Mosque** (Kılıç Ali Paşa Camii, 1580) was named for an Italian slave who converted to Islam and became an Ottoman admiral. The mosque, its cemetery, and Kılıç Ali Paşa's large octagonal tomb are ringed by a stone wall. Out front, the **Tophane Fountain** (Tophane Çeşmesi, 1732), built by Sultan Mahmut I, is Istanbul's third largest fountain.

Istanbul Modern: This fantastic contemporary art gallery, opened in 2004, occupies a former 1950s cargo warehouse on the Tophane waterfront, just by the Nusretiye Mosque.

On the entrance floor, the museum's permanent collection presents a comprehensive range of Turkish artworks from the early 20th century to the present day. Pieces range from works by the "1914 Generation," artists sponsored by the Turkish government to train in Paris, to Serkan Özkaya's playful sculpture *Baker's Apprentice* (2006), complete with eggs suspended from the ceiling. The space is periodically rearranged to showcase different items from the Istanbul Modern's collection. This floor is also home to the Istanbul Modern Café.

Downstairs, the museum houses an art house cinema, library, and two exhibition spaces, as well as

Istanbul Modern

 Meclis-i Mebusan Caddesi, Liman İşletmeleri Sahası Antrepo 4, Karaköy

 (0212) 334 73 00 (café: 0212/ 292 26 12).

🕐 Closed Sun.

💲 $$, free on Thurs.

🚋 Tophane

www.istanbul modern.org

EXPERIENCE: Smoking a *Nargile*

Called hookah or *shisha* in other cultures, the *nargile* water pipe has been a tradition in Turkey since the early 17th century, when it gained popularity during the reign of Sultan Murat IV (1612–1640).

Arriving in the Ottoman Empire from Iran, water pipes quickly passed from a cultural craze to an artistic obsession. Specific types of tobacco and charcoal were sought out. Specialist craftsmen created different parts of the nargile, with *lüle* workshops—the upper portion of the pipe—concentrated primarily in Tophane.

Like the classic game of *tavla* (Turkish backgammon), water pipes were considered antiquated and unstylish through much of the late 20th century. However, over the past decade, the nargile has experienced a huge resurgence in popularity. Perhaps unsurprisingly,

Tophane is now home to a buzzing strip of nargile bars, each one's terrace boasting beanbags or giant, colored cushions. Young adults jostle for room, smoking, drinking endless cups of tea, and using the free Wi-Fi. Popular nargile bars include: **Erzurum Çay Evi** (*Sali Pazari Sira Mağazalari, Nusretiye Camii Arkasi 75, Tophane, tel 0212/252 24 69*), **Nargilem Kahvesi** (*Sali Pazari Sira Magazalar 101, Tophane, Karaköy*), **Café des Anj** (*Ayhan Isik Sokak 36, Çukurcuma*), and **Firuz Aga Cami Çay Bahçesi** (*Italyan Yokusu*).

If you'd like to join in, pick your preferred locale and settle in. A waiter will bring you a menu—choose from plain, fruit-, or herb-flavored tobaccos, such as apple, cherry, or mint. Your nargile (*$$$*) will arrive, along with a couple of packaged, sterilized mouthpieces for the pipe. Inhale gently or smoke it as you would a cigar. As coals are piled onto the foil-covered tobacco, fit the mouthpiece onto the pipe, then puff away to get the pipe going. One waiter will be in charge of passing through the bar to check your coals are glowing and adjust them accordingly. Order a glass of tea or ask to borrow a tavla board and enjoy!

Note that most nargile bars do not serve alcohol.

Richard Wentworth's permanent installation of suspended books, *False Ceiling* (2005). The Istanbul Modern's temporary shows include photography, video, and contemporary art, with exhibitions from international artists. The easiest way to reach the museum is by taxi or tram, or walk from the Nusretiye Mosque.

Turkish Pickles

Long attributed with beneficial digestive properties, Turkish *turşu* (pickles) are everywhere. Pickled cucumbers and turnips are popped into *balık ekmek* (fish sandwiches; see sidebar p. 104), while miniature spicy peppers are served alongside Black Sea *fasuli* (haricot beans). Tangy bowls of pickled green plums accompany the cocktails at 360 Restaurant (*İstiklal Caddesi, K8 11, Beyoğlu, tel 0212/251 10 42, www.360istanbul.com, closed Sun.*) and *şalgam suyu* (fermented black carrot juice, often called "turnip juice") is believed to counter the effects of excess *rakı* consumption.

Made with salt, vinegar, or lemon juice and often garlic, *turşu* were originally prepared during spring and autumn. Pickling fresh fruits and vegetables provided a means of preserving the abundant produce for the lean winter months. Today, *turşu* are available year round.

Fancy taking a pack of pickled peppers home with you? Each neighborhood has its own *turşucu* (pickle maker), but two of Istanbul's finest are Petek Turşuları (*Duduodaları Sokak 1D, Balıkpazarı, tel 0212/249 13 24, closed Sun. Sept.-Apr.*), just behind Galatasaray's Balık Pazarı and Cihangir's Asri Turşucu (*Ağahamam Cad. 9/A, tel 0212/244 47 24*), in business since 1913. And don't be shy about asking to try before you buy!

INSIDER TIP:

The backstreets of Çukurcuma satisfy both antiques treasure-hunters and fashionistas. Rummage high and low in this Beyoğlu quarter of crumbling Italian palazzos.

—ANASTASIA ASHMAN
National Geographic Traveler
magazine writer

Çukurcuma

This artsy, bohemian zone, situated northeast of Tophane and west of Cihangir, is great for antiques. A vibrant neighborhood stretched among high-end shops, art galleries, and abandoned buildings, Çukurcuma is changing quickly as it attracts both foreigners and middle-class Istanbullus. On the sidewalks, treasure troves of hand-carved furniture, ceramics, chandeliers, and vintage clothing spill out of shop entrances. For those willing to dig—there's a fair amount of bric-a-brac—there are plenty of bargains, often quirkier than the standard Grand Bazaar finds (see pp. 79–84). Well worth seeking out is picturesque **French Street** (Fransız Sokağı, formerly known as Algerian Street), which is flanked by buzzing bars, restaurants, and local designer stores.

Cihangir

Like Çukurcuma to its west, the Cihangir neighborhood is quickly becoming gentrified. Cute wooden town houses have been

Browsing in an antiques shop in the Çukurcuma district of Istanbul

bought and tastefully renovated by foreigners. A branch of French superstore Carrefour and a large wine shop flank the **Firuzağa Mosque** (Firuzağa Camii).

But Cihangir retains its charm: Explore the narrow roads that snake around Sıraselviler Caddesi, each one dotted with tiny café terraces and sprinkled with independent boutiques.

Orhan Kemal Museum:

Dedicated to the Adana-born novelist Mehmet Raşit Öğütçü (who wrote under the pen name "Orhan Kemal"), the **Orhan Kemal Museum** (Orhan Kemal Müzesi) on Cihangir's main street, Akarsu Caddesi, provides a brief cultural foil to Cihangir's shopping and snacking.

A manual laborer, Kemal (1914–1970) was imprisoned for five years (from 1943) for his apparently communist leanings. It was there that he met his hero,

the poet Nazım Hikmet. The two shared a cell, and Hikmet went on to influence and encourage Kemal's creative aspirations. After his release, Kemal moved to Istanbul and devoted himself to writing full-time. Many of his novels, including his famous *Avare Yıllar (The Idle Years)*, depict ordinary characters and everyday life in Turkey during the mid-20th century.

The museum is located in Kemal's former home. Small but packed, it includes a wealth of photographs, books, and personal knickknacks. The back room has also been re-created as it was when Kemal lived here, complete with his bed, bookshelves, notes, and typewriter. Explanations are in Turkish only, although there's a short leaflet available in English. To access the museum, pop into the bookstore to the left of the museum entrance, where staff will unlock the building's doors and guide you in. ∎

Firuzağa Mosque

✉ Firuzağa Mah. Agahaman Caddesi 1, Cihangir

☎ (0212) 293 83 75

🕐 Closed Fri. a.m.

🚇 Taksim

Orhan Kemal Museum

✉ Akarsu Caddesi 30, Cihangir

☎ (0212) 292 92 45

🕐 Closed Sun.

🚇 Taksim

www.orhan kemal.org/v05/ index_menu_en.htm

Beşiktaş & Ortaköy

Beşiktaş is a large, busy neighborhood that hugs the Bosporus shore. It spans Kabataş in the south, the end of the tram line, to the charming village of Ortaköy in the north, and is ideally suited to the city's many commuters, with a busy ferry terminal at its center. Blocks of residential neighborhoods sit just inland from Dolmabahçe Caddesi, and are packed with local shops, lively restaurants, flower vendors, and a buzzing fish market.

Fans sport the Beşiktaş soccer team's scarf.

Museum of Painting and Sculpture

✉ Hayrettin Paşa, Iskelesi Sokak, Beşiktaş

☎ (0212) 261 42 98

🕐 Closed Sun.-Mon.

🚇 Beşiktaş

Beşiktaş

Istanbul's **Museum of Painting and Sculpture** (Resim ve Heykel Müzesi) is situated in the easternmost section of Dolmabahçe Palace, which is accessed through a separate entrance a ten-minute walk down the road. Formerly Veliaht Dairesi, the apartments reserved for the sultan crown prince, Atatürk ordered the rooms to be turned into a museum, which opened in 1937, initially displaying only paintings and sculpture from Dolmabahçe Palace. The museum now owns more than 7,000 Turkish artworks from the 19th and 20th centuries, plus a smattering of international paintings by the likes of French artists Henri Matisse and Pierre Bonnard.

Renovated in 2009, portraits of old Istanbul and models of great Turkish battleships give the **Maritime Museum** (Deniz Müzesi), just down Dolmabahçe Caddesi to the east, a classic feel. The collection is split between two buildings, the one nearest the water displaying seagoing vessels and the other showing exhibits of topical artifacts, including logbooks, ship's charts, and telescopes. The Atatürk room shows handwritten letters from the former president to his naval commanders, suggesting names for Turkey's latest battleships. There's also a mock-up of Atatürk's bedroom on the vast, luxurious presidential yacht, *Savarona* (see p. 106).

INSIDER TIP:

If you're near Beşiktaş' Çırağan Palace, try lunch at secluded Malta Köşkü [see p. 126], a 19th-century royal pavilion nestled in the woods behind it.

—ANASTASIA ASHMAN
National Geographic Traveler
magazine writer

To the east of the Maritime Museum lies **Barbaros Park,** an open square in front of the attractively tiled Beşiktaş İskelesi (the ferry station). The square was named for Ottoman admiral Barbaros Hayrettin Paşa (1478–1546), more commonly known as Barbarossa, and is home to his domed, octagonal tomb, designed by Sinan (see pp. 90–91) and completed in 1542. Nearby, there's also a grand and imposing sculpture of Barbarossa (1946), installed in the square on the 400th anniversary of his death.

Continuing northeast for just under a half mile (0.7 km) up Çırağa Caddesi, the elegant **Çırağan Palace** (Çırağan Sarayı, 1874) was designed by Nigoğos Balyan, architect of the nearby Dolmabahçe Palace. It

Beşiktaş Soccer Club

Established in 1903, backed by Atatürk, and probably the city's most consistently popular soccer team, Beşiktaş Jimnastik Kulübü (Beşiktaş Gymnastic, or Soccer Club) was the first Turkish team to compete in the UEFA Champions League, and finished as winners of the Turkish Süper Lig in 2009. Their home ground, İnönü Stadium, sits just opposite the Dolmabahçe Palace. Head to the stadium to attend a soccer match or simply stop at the team's museum, where photos, memorabilia, and numerous trophies are neatly displayed.

was seemingly built under a bad cloud though—Sultan Abdülaziz died here less than two years after moving into his dream of a palace. His heir, the mentally unstable Murat V, ruled the empire from this palace for a brief three months before being replaced by his brother, Abdülhamid II. The Çırağan Palace then went on to serve as the new Turkish Parliament, until a huge fire destroyed most of its interior in 1910—yet another stroke of bad luck. Abandoned for much of the 20th century, it has now been renovated and turned into the luxurious **Çırağan Palace Kempinski Hotel** (see Travelwise p. 246), a great place either to stay or just visit for lunch or a drink by the Bosporus. The hotel also has a swimming pool in a beautiful garden setting which is open to the public, but for a rather extravagant fee ($$).

Detour about a quarter mile (0.5 km) along Çırağa Caddesi and hit a left turn to lead you to **Küçük Mecidiye Mosque** (Küçük Mecidiye Camii, 1848).

Maritime Museum
- ⊠ Barbaros Hayrettin Paşa, Beşiktaş Caddesi, Beşiktaş
- ☎ (0212) 327 43 45
- 🕐 Closed Mon.–Tues.
- 🚹 $$
- 🚇 🚌 Beşiktaş

Beşiktaş Jimnastik Kulübü Museum
- ⊠ Beşiktaş İnönü Stadyumu, Dolmabahçe Caddesi
- ☎ (0212) 236 72 01
- 🕐 Closed Sun. & match days
- 🚇 🚌 Kabataş
- www.bjk.com.tr

Küçük Mecidiye Mosque
- ⊠ Yahya Efendi Sokak
- 🕐 Closed Fri. a.m.

Schoolchildren stroll past the Sultan's Gate at Dolmabahçe Palace.

Malta Kiosk

- ✉ Yıldız Parkı
- ☎ (0212) 258 94 93
- 🚇 Beşiktaş

Chalet Kiosk

- ✉ Palanga Caddesi, Yıldız Parkı
- ☎ (0212) 259 45 70
- 🕐 Closed Mon. & Thurs.
- 💲 $
- 🚇 Beşiktaş

Yıldız Palace Museum

- ✉ Yıldız Caddesi, Yıldız Park
- ☎ (0212) 258 30 80
- 🕐 Closed Tues.
- 💲 $

Back across from Çırağan Palace is the entrance for **Yıldız Park.** A sprawling 600,000 square yards (500,000 sq m), the park is dotted with attractive wooden pavilions. The best include **Malta Kiosk** (Malta Köşkü), which now houses a plush restaurant, and the **Chalet Kiosk** (Şale Köşkü)—its name derived from the fact that it was built to resemble a Swiss chalet—the former residence of Sultan Abdülhamid II (available for viewing by guided tour only). The **Yıldız Palace Museum** (Yıldız Sarayi Müzesi), also in Yıldız Parkı, is a former carpentry workshop owned by Sultan Abdulhamit II that now displays furniture and household articles from his home.

During the spring and early summer months, the cool slopes within the park make a welcome respite from the city heat.

Dolmabahçe Palace: Sculpted swirls of ivory marble trail along the Bosporus waterfront, backed by the smoothest of walkways and pale, fairy-tale facades. Tourist-laden ferries slow down to a snail's pace when they pass, cameras hum and snap. One of Istanbul's most impressive sights, Dolmabahçe Palace (Dolmabahçe Sarayı, 1843-1856) boasts close to 300 rooms—many of them sumptuously decorated in gold and precious materials—six hammams, and 68 bathrooms.

If you want to see the stunning inside of Dolmabahçe Palace, and particularly the separate harem, make sure you get there early, as only a certain number of visitors are allowed in each day.

—SALLY MCFALL
National Geographic contributor

Dolmabahçe literally means "filled garden." The area was coined as such when Sultans Ahmet I and Osman II ordered all ships passing to drop stones off shore, extending the coastline by 400 yards (365 m). The location is steeped in legend, claiming to be the site where Jason and the Argonauts landed on their search for the Golden Fleece. Various palaces were built on this site, but it was for Sultan Abdülmecit I that architects Nigoğos Balyan and his father Karabet designed the current elaborate complex. Looking to distance himself from "outdated" Topkapı Palace, Abdülmecit moved the empire's royal headquarters to the more European-style palace of Dolmabahçe upon its completion. Virtually all of the later sultans followed suit.

Dolmabahçe Palace is divided into three main areas. The central section is the Muayede Hall, a grand hall whose 120-foot (36 m) ceilings are supported by 56 columns. It was Britain's Queen Victoria who gifted the four-and-a half-ton crystal chandelier that hangs heavily at the room's center, glowing brightly over the intricate, 1,335-square-foot (124 sq m) silk Hereke carpet. The reception of foreign leaders and important ceremonies took place here.

The Muayede is flanked by the Selamlık (men's quarters, including offices and reception halls) and the Harem (women's quarters), each with their own private gardens. The former is home to an opulent double staircase with crystal banisters, while the latter includes the sultan's mother's apartment and the rooms Atatürk lived in during

Dolmabahçe Palace

✉ Dolmabahçe Caddesi

☎ (0212) 236 90 00

⊖ Closed Mon. & Thurs.

💲 Selamlık & Muayede only $$$, Harem only $$$, all areas $$$$, camera $$

🚋 🚢 Kabataş

www.dolmabahce .gov.tr

The End of an Era: Atatürk's Final Days

In 1924, ownership of Dolmabahçe Palace passed to the new Turkish Republic. Turkey's first president, Mustafa Kemal Atatürk, used the palace to entertain visiting dignitaries and government officials. Suffering from failing health, Atatürk lived here full-time toward the end of his life until his death on November 10, 1938.

Today, visitors can see the former leader's bedroom: as only fitting for the founder of a republic, his bed is dressed with a special bright red coverlet, embroidered with the Turkish flag. For a peek at Atatürk in action over the course of his career, large weather-protected black-and-white photos adorn the long stone wall along Dolmabahçe Caddesi opposite the palace.

It is hard to imagine the magnitude that Atatürk—the man who proved so important in Turkish politics and progress—has in the minds and hearts of the Turks until you witness it firsthand.

Büyük Mecidiye Camii (Ortaköy Mosque)

✉ İskele Meydanı, Ortaköy

🕐 Closed Fri. a.m.

his final years (see sidebar p. 127).

Note that although visitors are allowed to wander through the gardens, access to all indoor areas requires joining one of Dolmabahçe's frequent English tours (included in the ticket price). Set aside two to three hours if you'd like to visit all parts of the palace.

Over the road and along Süleyman Seba Caddesi, the palace's former stables and servants' quarters have been neatly renovated to house upscale boutiques (including Marc Jacobs and Etro) and the stylish W Hotel (see Travelwise p. 247).

Ortaköy

Tucked into the shadow of the Bosporus Bridge, Ortaköy has leapt effortlessly from forgotten fishing village to hip seaside suburb with cafés, bars, and restaurants. The town has always attracted foreigners, as is evident in its combination of mosques, churches, and a synagogue (stroll along Muallim Naci Caddesi, the principle road bisecting Ortaköy, to see examples of the latter two). However, in recent years, its attractive alleys have become home to fashionable boutiques, Asian restaurants, art galleries, and a buzzing nightlife.

Ortaköy's narrow streets cluster around the waterfront square, **İskele Meydanı.** Ferries shuttle past, picking up passengers headed up the Bosporus, or south to Eminönü. The town's central mosque, **Büyük Mecidiye Camii** (Grand Imperial Mosque), is located here, and it couldn't be more picturesque. Standing under the western corner of the Bosporus Bridge, its neo-Baroque architecture contrasts appealingly with the sleek modern structure behind it. Nigoğos Balyan, architect of Dolmabahçe Palace, designed the mosque, which was completed in 1856. Inside are displays of calligraphy by Sultan

A belly dancer performs in a club in Ortaköy.

EXPERIENCE: Exploring Ortaköy's Nightlife

Lining the Bosporus shoreline just north of Ortaköy is the sweaty summertime heart of Istanbul's nightlife scene. Clubs flank both sides of the waterfront road, and come Friday and Saturday evenings, it's bumper-to-bumper traffic of swanky SUVs, Bentleys, and Alfa Romeos (valet parking is the norm here). Entrance fees (minimum $$$$) and drinks are not cheap, but the music can be excellent, and a glimpse at Istanbul's super-moneyed set in a state of dishevelled decadence is often worth it.

Celeb-seekers should head to **Reina** (tel 0212/259 59 19, www.reina.com.tr), a sprawling complex with six restaurants and a massive club; nearby **Sortie** (see Travelwise p. 263) ups the ante with nine restaurants and a dance floor. Ultra-

fashionable **Crystal** (Muallim Neci Caddesi 65, tel 0212/229 71 52), is known for its international DJs, electro-techno tunes, and late partying. Nearby, **Anjelique** (see Travelwise p. 263) dishes up sushi and sublime views of the Bosporus.

Also well worth checking out is stylish **Suada** (Galatasaray Adasi, Kuruçeşme, tel 0212/263 73 00, http://suadaclub.com.tr): A man-made "floating" island suspended in the Bosporus just south of Arnavutköy, it is home to three restaurants, a bar, and an Olympic-sized swimming pool. From Kuruçeşme's waterfront (Kuruçeşme Suada İskelesi), frequent free ferries zip back and forth to the island.

Note that clubs have a dress code: No jeans and sneakers. Also, large groups of single men are discouraged.

INSIDER TIP:

If you want to visit one of Ortaköy's many fashionable nightclubs, be prepared to pay a mighty expensive fee at the entrance, and make sure that you dress smart, as a number of these clubs impose dress codes.

—TIM HARRIS
National Geographic writer

Abdülmecit I, the Ottoman ruler at the time of its construction.

To the left of the mosque is a docking area with boats plying the Bosporus offering return cruises to see the Bosporus Bridge ($). Just behind İskele Meydanı, a string of

permanent stalls sell *kumpir,* plump baked potatoes loaded with an overwhelming choice of toppings (cheese, olives, pickles, bulgur, corn, and more). The stalls are interspersed with vendors of the *kumpir*'s sweet equivalent, waffles, again piled high with jam, cream, chocolate, and candied fruits. Either option makes for a filling snack or picnic lunch.

On Sundays, crowds flock to Ortaköy's Iskele Meydanı for the town's popular **craft market.** Stalls set up on every corner, stacking out a mix of unusual artworks, handmade clothing, and jewelry, as well as a good chunk of imported trinkets. If you're up for a bargain, set aside a couple of hours to rummage through the stalls. Or simply while away a relaxing afternoon, browsing and snacking at the town's food stands. ■

North of the Bosporus Bridge

The Boğaziçi Köprüsü (Bosporus Bridge) became the fourth largest suspension bridge in the world at the time it opened in 1973, linking Europe and Asia by road for the first time. It creates a stunning landmark for the area to its north, which includes the pretty seaside towns and resorts of Arnavutköy, Bebek, Emirgan, Yeniköy, Büyükdere, Sarıyer, Kilyos, and Rumeli Kavağı, full of excellent cafés and seafood restaurants.

Strolling amid the tulips at Emirgan Korusu in Istanbul

Bridging the Bosporus

Stretching from Ortaköy across to Beylerbeyi on the Asian shore, the Boğaziçi Köprüsü was inaugurated in 1973. It linked Europe and Asia by road for the first time, so it's no surprise that a record-breaking 28,000 cars sped across the bridge the first 24 hours after it opened. A second bridge, the **Fatih Sultan Mehmet Bridge** (Fatih Sultan Mehmet Köprüsü), was completed in 1988. It crosses the Bosporus from Rumeli Fortress to Kavacık. Istanbul is still plagued by severe traffic, and there are currently plans afoot to open a third bridge across the Bosporus, although the exact location has been kept under wraps for fear of escalating local property prices. Sadly, such a bridge is expected to have a devastating environmental impact on the city's nearby forests, and it's generally hoped that the completed Marmaray Tunnel Project (see sidebar p. 36) will stymie these plans.

INSIDER TIP:

One of the best seaside walks in all of European Istanbul, with good views of the Asian side, is from Arnavutköy to Rumeli Fortress. You'll pass fishermen casting their lines in the bay and an excellent assortment of cafés.

—SALLY MCFALL
National Geographic contributor

Arnavutköy to Tarabya

Heading northward from the Bosporus Bridge, **Arnavutköy** is the prettiest town on the European shores. Its waterfront is lined with wooden Ottoman mansions, called *yalıs,* many of them with even prettier canal-type front gardens. Meaning "Albanian village," thanks to its original contingent of Ottoman-Albanian residents, Arnavutköy has always been home to a large foreign contingency, particularly Jewish and Greek communities. Today, the town boasts quiet streets, pastel facades, and a premium selection of fish restaurants.

Fashionable **Bebek,** just north of Arnavutköy, clusters around a central park and short waterside promenade. At the town's southern end, the **Hidiv Kasrı** (Khedive's Palace), now the Egyptian Consulate, was the former residence of the mother of Egyptian Khedive Abbas II Hilmi. The palace shed its swathes of scaffolding in late 2010 after extensive renovations.

Constructed by 3,000 workers over just four months in 1452, **Rumeli Fortress** (Rumeli Hisarı) sits just north of Bebek at the Bosporus' narrowest point, overlooking the strait and the Fatih Sultan Mehmet Bridge. The fortress was built under Mehmet the Conqueror in preparation for his siege on Constantinople, and along with Anatolian Fortress (Anadolu Hisarı; see p. 150) opposite, it served to effectively cut off the city from outside assistance. The well-maintained fortress walls are dotted with five gates and multiple towers, and a leafy central amphitheater hosts outdoor concerts in June and July.

Traveling 1.5 miles (2.5 km) north of the Rumelian Fortress, you reach the attractive town of **Emirgan,** with first-rate restaurants and a gorgeous park, **Emirgan Korusu,** (continued on p. 134)

Rumeli Fortress

- ✉ Yahya Kemal Caddesi 42, Bebek
- ☎ (0212) 263 53 05
- 🕐 Closed Wed.
- 💲 $
- 🚌 🚏 Rumeli Hisarı

Getting Around

With the exception of Rumeli Kavağı, all the towns north of the Bosporus Bridge can be accessed via bus 25E (Kabataş-Sarıyer). Bus 40B (Beşiktaş-Sarıyer) cuts immediately inland from Beşiktaş, dropping back down to the coast at İstinye, then stopping at Yeniköy, Tarabya, and Büyükdere, before terminating in Sarıyer. *Dolmuşes* run from Sarıyer to Rumeli Kavağı, and ferries run between Rumeli Kavağı and Anadolu Kavağı on the Asian shore year-round.

A Day Out in Belgrade Forest

Hugging the city limits in a huge green curve, it's hard to believe that this vast 13,690-acre (5,500 ha) forest exists at all. Like New York's Central Park or London's Regent's Park, Istanbul's Belgrade Forest (Belgrade Ormani) has resisted generations of acquisitive property developers and acts as the city's green lung.

The Roman aqueduct in Belgrade Forest

Now a great escape from the city bustle, the Belgrade Forest's reservoirs (known as *bents* in Turkish) have been Istanbul's principal water supply since Roman times. In the sixth century, Emperor Justinian funneled water from the forest's many springs and streams into his burgeoning capital with a series of aqueducts that ran into the cistern (see pp. 73, 76–77) below the city—a huge engineering feat.

Over the following millennium the revolving fortunes of the Byzantine Empire ushered in a period of structural disrepair. The water supply was even snipped by besieging Avars in the seventh century, and remained cut off from the city for over a hundred years. It was left to the phenomenally energetic Sultan Mehmet II, not to mention the phenomenally wealthy Süleyman the Magnificent, to revive this vital artery in the 15th and 16th centuries.

Supplying Istanbul with Water

Süleyman turned to his royal architect, Sinan (see pp. 90–91), who upgraded the huge stone aqueducts, dams, and canals, many of which can still be seen today. The work was undertaken with the "help" of many Serbian prisoners of war taken after Süleyman's capture of Belgrade, which gave the forest its name. The woods were also used for army maneuvers and as a hunting ground (now, however, hunting is strictly forbidden here); boar and deer are still common, as are snakes, weasels, and a dozen other mammals.

By 1732, the forest's waters were channeled to a distribution point in Taksim Square and stored in the thick stone Taksim Maksemi (see p. 116), then dispersed throughout the city. Any remaining Serbians were forcibly removed a century and a half later by the paranoid Sultan

Abdulhamit II, who feared these Christians were poisoning his water supply.

A Leafy Haven

Now the forest provides a leafy haven for modern-day Istanbullus. Oak trees, oriental birch, Anatolian chestnut, hornbeam, pine, and spruce delight visitors year round. The early greens of spring and the autumn shades are particularly beautiful.

Although deserted on weekdays, the forest fills up on weekends, especially in the summer, with groups of locals and inner-city Istanbullus escaping from their work-a-day lives. In 1956, the government created the first picnic areas and there are now seven of these. Each visitor appears to tote an unfeasibly large Turkish-style 20-dish picnic—the attraction of a family feast blessed by the sound of running water, rustling leaves, chirping birds, and frogs croaking in the distance is clear. The picnic areas also provide barbecue facilities. If you use these, however, be sure you are very careful with your matches. You wouldn't want to start a forest fire that would ravage this beautiful and irreplaceable area of Istanbul.

The forest's proximity to several modern housing developments also attracts a self-consciously middle-class crowd. Some sport outdoor hiking gear, while others come to do

what no self-respecting Turk would have done a decade or two ago: wear Lycra and jog. A well-used 4-mile (6.5 km) running and mountain bike track circles Büyük Bent, where there is also a café selling drinks and snacks.

For your own taste of the country in Belgrade Forest, jump on a bus from either Taksim Square (one-hour journey) or from 4.Levent Metro station (a half-hour journey) to Bahçeköy. From Bahçeköy's tiny bus station, retrace your steps 100 yards (90 m) to the main road, head right, then walk 200 yards (180 m) to the park entrance. Even a taxi from 4.Levent Metro station is feasible if there are a few of you. There is a fee ($) to enter the forest on foot and for car parking ($$) too.

INSIDER TIP:

If you visit Belgrade Forest in summer, listen for nightingales in those areas with big, deciduous trees—they do sing in the day as well as at night. There are also plenty of woodpeckers and flycatchers in the forest.

—TIM HARRIS
National Geographic writer

Lady Mary Wortley Montagu

In centuries past, escaping the incessant summer heat and unhealthy mugginess was a prime concern—bordering on an obsession—for Istanbul's foreign residents. Many of the city's diplomatic personnel decamped to the Belgrade Forest, and none more famous than the English, serial letter-writer Lady Mary Wortley Montagu (1689–1762), whose husband was English ambassador to the Sublime Porte from 1716 to 1717.

Lady Mary's letter, collected in the book *Turkish Embassy Letters*, are still in print and capture aristocratic picnics in the park and scenes of palace life. Lady Mary used her experiences as an English woman in an elite Ottoman world to enlighten the uninformed about the different roles of women in the empire. Aristocratic society meant power for women, while those lower down the social ladder endured slavery. Particularly illuminating, especially for her sexually stifled readers in Britain, were vivid descriptions from the ladies' hammam. She is still recognized as a hugely influential female writer.

Sakıp Sabancı Museum

Sakıp Sabancı Caddesi 42, Emirgan

(0212) 277 22 00

Closed Mon.

$$$

Emirgan

muze.sabanci
univ.edu

Sadberk Hanım Museum

Büyükdere Piyasa Caddesi 27–29, Sarıyer

(0212) 242 38 13

Closed Wed.

$$

Sarıyer

www.sadberk
hanimmuzesi.org.tr

particularly beautiful during the city's April Tulip Festival. Emirgan is best known for its exceptional **Sakıp Sabancı Museum** (Sakıp Sabancı Müzesi). Opened in the Sabancı family's former summer home, and also known as Atlı Köşk, the museum has an extensive permanent collection of calligraphy and Ottoman art. However, it's the museum's temporary shows, which highlight some of the 20th century's greatest artists, that truly stand out. Past exhibitions have been dedicated to Spanish artists Pablo Picasso and Salvador Dalí, as well as French sculptor Auguste Rodin. The museum is also home to the experimental fusion restaurant Müzedechanga (see Travelwise p. 249).

About 1 mile (1.5 km) north, ultra-affluent **Yeniköy** sits directly on the waterfront, with each home backed by its own private security guard. Between here and Tarabya, former embassies turned consul-

ates or summer residences (including German, Austrian, Brazilian, Cambodian, and Iraqi) abound. **Tarabya** itself is simpler but also popular, sitting around a deep bay filled with fishing boats.

Büyükdere to Sarıyer

About 3 miles (5 km) north of Tarabya is the low-key town of **Büyükdere**. Its wide promenade runs alongs the Bosporus and makes for a pleasant stroll; the town is set just inland.

On the left-hand side of the road between Büyükdere and Sarıyer (and an easy walk from either) is the stunning **Sadberk Hanım Museum** (Sadberk Hanım Müzesi), housed in the late 19th-century Azeryan Yalısı. This traditional wooden yalı was formerly the Koç family's (see sidebar p. 114) summer home. Turkey's first privately owned museum, it was opened in 1980 by Sadberk Koç (wife of Vehbi Koç) to exhibit

---

EXPERIENCE: Hit the Shopping Malls

It seems impossible that this city could improve on what is arguably the world's finest shopping emporium—the Grand Bazaar—or even be interested in trying. But while the former may be true, the latter is not. In recent years and to hugely popular local reception, two major malls have opened in Istanbul.

Making the claim as Europe's largest mall is **Cevahir Alışveriş Merkezi** (*Cevahir Shopping Center, Büyükdere Caddesi 2 2/A, Şişli, tel 0212/368 69 00, www.istanbulcevahir.com/english.index,html*). Opened in 2005, Cevahir houses close to 350 shops over ten floors, ten cinema screens, and a light dusting of coin-fed

massage chairs. Its plunging central atrium offers shoppers a good peek at couples heading to the massive food court for a romantic frozen yogurt à deux.

Kanyon Alışveriş Merkezi (*Kanyon Shopping Center, Büyükdere Caddesi 185, Levent, tel 0212/317 53 00, www.kanyon.com.tr/#/en/homepage/*) may be Europe's coolest shopping mall. Teamed alongside an office block and apartments of the same name, Kanyon embodies experimental architecture as well as exclusive style. Escada, Max Mara, and Harvey Nichols all have stores here. Nibbles tend to be more high-end: sushi, croissants, and gourmet burgers.

The innovative, mix-use Kanyon Shopping Center on Büyükdere Caddesi

her extensive antiques collection. In 1983, as the museum expanded, the run-down yalı next door was also purchased and restored. To the left upon entering, the **Sevgi Gönül Wing** houses an overwhelming archaeological collection. Neolithic mother goddesses give way to Hittite deities; Urartian bronze belts are etched with ancient Egyptian-looking figurines. Terracotta oil lamps sit alongside Roman cameos and sixth-century B.C. glass perfume flasks. There are a number of truly standout finds, such as the 400 B.C. dancing satyr candelabra.

Next door, the exhibition continues in the **Azeryan Wing,** with traditional Ottoman wedding dresses, 16th– through 19th-century embroidery, and various dioramas, including a henna party and a circumcision room with a photo of Rahmi Koç in his circumcision bed (1939). Downstairs, there's a small gift store and a nice garden café.

Just a half mile (1 km) farther north is **Sarıyer.** Best known for its small but lively fish market, Sarıyer is the last of the European shore's easily accessible towns. It's a bustling spot, more friendly than picturesque, and its quayside fish restaurants make for a pleasant lunch. Dolmuşes leave from here for both the popular beach resort of **Kilyos** (see p. 156) and the village of **Rumeli Kavağı.**

Two miles (3 km) to Sarıyer's north, Rumeli Kavağı's **old fortress** was a strategic defensive bookend to Asia's Anadolu Kavağı (see p. 151). Today home to a cluster of popular fish restaurants, the little port offers visitors a peek north to the Black Sea and a beach. ■

Encompassing Ottoman palaces, Üsküdar's mosques, and the city's largest street market

Asian Istanbul

Introduction & Map   138-139

Kadıköy & Around   140-143

Experience: A Museum Visit, Under
   High Security   142

Boat Trip & Walk: Europe & Asia in Half
   a Day   144-145

Üsküdar & the Asian Bosporus Shore   146-151

Feature: Ottoman Palaces in Asian
   Istanbul   148-149

Hotels & Restaurants   251-253

Women shop for traditional skirts at the Salı Pazarı, or Tuesday market.

Asian Istanbul

Asian Istanbul, by far the least visited of the city's three "sides," is just a short boat ride from old Sultanahmet (or European Istanbul). Here you can admire sumptuous Ottoman palaces, haggle at huge markets or window-shop along Bağdat Caddesi, sample world-famous yogurt in Kanlıca, and dine at some of the best restaurants in the city.

The Bosporus, with Sultanahmet to the left and Üsküdar to the right

A common perception is that Istanbul's Asian shores are poorer and more religiously conservative than its European sectors. This is not so. Centuries of pashas, Ottoman administrators, and more modern, middle-class professionals have turned the right bank of the Bosporus into Istanbul's richest. Rococo summer palaces and wooden villas known as yalıs line the shores around charming Çengelköy and Kanlıca. In the latter, they frequently change hands for millions of dollars.

An exception to this moneyed trend is Üsküdar, a traditional neighborhood and the scene of our Europe-to-Asia walk and boat rides. It contains scores of mosques, five or six of jaw-dropping beauty. So rare are foreigners here that your reception will be warm and hassle-free.

Southern Suburb

The suburb of Kadıköy, at the southern tip of Asian Istanbul, is one of the most alluring destinations in the city. It offers a real taste of Asia with a few additional surprises thrown in. Every corner offers a lesson in Turkish history from the huge Haydarpaşa train station—once Europe's main link with all points east—to remnants of Florence Nightingale's Crimean War, in the form of her museum plus the moving Haydarpaşa war cemetery built on the banks of the Bosporus for the British casualties of that 19th-century conflict.

The tree-lined boulevard of Bağdat Caddesi, just over 1 mile (1.6 km) south, provides a glamorous picture of Turkey's possible future. A buzzing scene of pavement cafés and wealthy liberalism, it's the country at its most sophisticated, an image that Turkey is keen to present to the West.

NOT TO BE MISSED:

A culinary pilgrimage to Kadıköy's Çiya Sofrasi 140

Florence Nightingale's hospital inside the Selimiye barracks 142

Shopping along Bağdat Caddesi, Istanbul's ritziest street 143

Seeing where the sultans vacationed in Beylerbeyi Palace 148-149

Dipping a spoon into Kanlıca's world-famous yogurt 150

A glimpse of the Black Sea from the heights of Yoros Castle 151

Getting Around

Traveling up and down the main road running along the eastern coast of the Bosporus is easy. Just jump onto any city bus marked with the destinations Beykoz, Paşabahçe, or Çengelköy to head northward, or take a bus marked Üsküdar, Kadıköy or Taksim to head back south again.

Those on a Bosporus boat tour have the chance to see part of the coast from the water, and to alight at the route's final stop, the eerie hilltop castle of Anadolu Kavağı. A short boat hop is also required to reach one of Istanbul's most enduring sights, the Maiden's Tower, a tiny castle cum lighthouse on its own island midway between Europe and Asia. ■

To Yoros Castle

PAŞABAHÇE

BOSPORUS

PIRI REIS CADDESI

Khedive's Palace

KANLICA

Fatih Sultan Mehmet Bridge

ISTANBUL OUTER BELTWAY O.2

Anatolian Fortress (Anadolu Hisarı)

Rumeli Fortress (Rumeli Hisarı)

Küçüksu Palace

Göksu Deresi

BEŞIKTAŞ

Bosporus

KALDIRIM CADDESI

ÇENGELKÖY

Bosporus

Sea of Marmara

Area of map detail

Beylerbeyi Palace

ÜMRANIYE

Kabataş Ferry Terminal

Şemsi Paşa Mosque

Mihrimah Sultan Mosque

Çamlıca Tepesi

Yeni Valide Mosque

ÜSKÜDAR

Atik Valide Mosque

ISTANBUL INNER BELTWAY O.1

Maiden's Tower

Şakirin Mosque

Selimiye Barracks & Florence Nightingale Museum

ATAŞEHIR

Haydarpaşa War Cemetery

N

Haydarpaşa Train Station

Salı Pazarı

Ayia Efimia Ortodoks Kilisesı

KADIKÖY

ISTANBUL INNER BELTWAY O.1

Süreyya Opera House

0   2 kilometers
0   1 mile

Kadıköy & Around

Kadıköy, a residential and commercial district of Istanbul located on the Asian shore of the Bosporus, has a fabulous Tuesday market and is not overwhelmed by tourists. By contrast, the beautiful seaside suburb of Moda on the Anatolian side of Istanbul has a certain romantic *je ne sais quoi*, popular with locals and visitors alike.

Trying out an unlit water pipe—*nargile*—in a Kadıköy store (smoking indoors is banned)

Kadıköy
🅰 139

Kadıköy

Dating back to the Copper Age, 7,000 years ago, and thus centuries older than the settlements of central Istanbul, Kadıköy has nevertheless been its western neighbor's shadow for some time. Nevertheless, this cosmopolitan district has much to offer. A maze of inexpensive stores starts on **Muvakkıthane Caddesi,** with rows of bakers, designer-shoe knock-offs, a fish market, and spice shops. More sophisticated is **Güneşli Bahçe Sokak,** which contains honey salesmen (see Eta Bal p. 261), secondhand shops, pastry makers (see Baklavaci Güllüoglu p. 261), and the notable restaurant **Çiya Sofrasi** *(Guneslibahce Sokak 43, Kadıköy, tel 0216/330 31 90, $–$$$).* For antiques, it's amazing to see what treasures of Ottoman Istanbul (vases, packing trunks, candelabras) and European

INSIDER TIP:

Catch a commuter ferry to Kadıköy for priceless views of the historic quarter, or drift on the upper Bosporus past Mehmet the Conqueror's 15th-century fortress.

—ANASTASIA ASHMAN
National Geographic Traveler
magazine writer

objets d'art have landed up along **Kazasker Sokak.**

A few blocks farther east, heading away from the Bosporus, bustling **Bahariye Caddesi** is bisected by a vintage tram. Contemporary fashion outlets line this boulevard, and prices are ridiculously cheap. the **Süreyya Opera House**

(Süreyya Operası), designed by Süreyya İlmen Pasha and opened in 1927, and the beautiful Greek Orthodox church **Ayia Efimia Ortodoks Kilisesi**—rainbows of light filter through the dome's stained glass windows—hint of Kadıköy's cosmopolitan past, when Turks, Greeks, Armenians, and Jews traded with the world at this once eminent port.

Haydarpaşa Cemetery: This leafy cemetery is Kadıköy's most moving sight. Created for the British soldiers who lost their lives in the Crimean War (1853–1856), its location overlooking the Bosporus only adds to the poignancy. The tombstones in the farther of the cemetery's two large sections are the oldest, most remembering the dead of Balaclava, the British forward base in Crimea,

Süreyya Opera House
- ⊠ Bahariye Caddesi, Kadıköy
- ☎ (0216) 346 15 31
- $ $$-$$$
- www.sureyya operasi.org

Ayia Efimia Ortodoks Kilisesi
- ⊠ Yasa Caddesi 27, Kadıköy

Haydarpaşa Cemetery
- ⊠ Tibbiye Caddesi, Haydarpaşa

Salı Pazarı

Istanbul's Salı Pazarı *(Hasanpaşa, Kadıköy, every Tues. & Fri., bus 8A from Kadıköy bus station opposite Kadıköy ferry port, or taxi)*, or Tuesday market, is so grand that it draws in organized shopping tours from neighboring cities.

The bazaar overgrew its downtown location in late 2008, and the 2,000 stalls now reside 1 mile (1.6 km) east of the Kadıköy ferry terminal, just past the landmark stadium of the Fenerbahçe soccer team. Foreign visitors are very much a novelty. Much of the produce is trucked in from central Anatolia. Aside from the prices, of interest to foreigners may be the sight of "Europeanized" Turks haggling with head-scarved farm girls from the rural interior.

Some stalls are dedicated to one crop only, be it parsley, plums, or one of the many unidentifiable vegetables. Others keep shoppers' spirits up by supplying tasty kebabs, ayran (a yogurt drink), and savory *gözleme* pastries. Other vendors here are simply locals moving home, who pile all manner of flea market trinkets into a blanket, which they spread out on the ground when they reach the bazaar.

Turkish traders are known for their mercantile savvy, and one can now purchase DVDs, iPhone covers, and video games at Salı Pazarı alongside more traditional produce. Some stalls even boast portable credit card terminals. The market opens up in a slightly smaller form each Friday.

Haydarpaşa Station

✉ Haydarpaşa Gar sk, Haydarpaşa

☎ (0216) 336 20 63

www.tcdd.gov.tr

and Sevastapol, the Russian naval city that was besieged by the joint British, French, and Ottoman forces. Other epitaphs tell more futile stories, such as the marines swept overboard into the Bosporus as they transported equipment through Istanbul heading for the Crimean Front. Thousands more soldiers died at the nearby Selimiye barracks, which was the British headquarters and hospital during the campaign (see sidebar this page).

From 1867, civilians of all flags were buried at the cemetery, although most were British who resided on the Princes Islands (known as Adalar) or along the European shore. These graves accompany the neat rows of 414 Commonwealth soldiers—most

of them World War I prisoners of war. A stone memorial remembers soldiers of the Indian Army who died during the same period—some simply marked as "a musulman [Muslim] soldier of the Great War"—and whose remains were re-interred here in 1961, as their original burial spots in European Istanbul could not be maintained.

To reach the cemetery, cross over Haydarpaşa's railway tracks by walking up Tibbiye Caddesi, then take a left 220 yards (200 m) down Burhan Felek Caddesi. The cemetery, known locally as the Ingiliz Mezarligi, is 220 yards (200 m) on the left, just after the entrance to the Gata military hospital.

Haydarpaşa Station: Directly south of Haydarpaşa Cemetery,

EXPERIENCE: A Museum Visit, Under High Security

Kadıköy's **Florence Nightingale Museum** *(Haydarpaşa Ingiliz Mezarligi, Birinci Ordu Komutanligi, Selimiye Barracks, Burhan Felek Caddesi, tel 0216/343 73 10, bus or ferry from Kadıköy)* is housed in the magnificent Selimiye Barracks, headquarters of the Turkish First Army. Just getting permission to enter is an experience in itself, and few places so evoke the carnage of one of the world's first industrial wars.

Perhaps aptly, arranging a tour is a Byzantine process by modern standards. Fax a copy of your passport, a cover letter, and a contact phone number in Istanbul to the barracks office at least two days before your visit *(fax 0216/310 79 29).*

Visitors are processed through the barracks' mysterious sounding Harem Gate. On arrival, your bags are searched and cameras placed in a storage box. Do

not be alarmed by the level of security; this process is more playful than daunting, as conscripts fuss over the visitors who provide a welcome break to their military service. Visitors are then trucked into the imposing barracks.

The museum of the pioneering British nurse is contained in one of the towers. Selimiye was a British base during the Crimean War (1853–1856) and became a bedlam of wounded. In less than a year, the strict hygiene standards introduced there by Nightingale cut mortality rates from 60–70 percent to just 6 percent.

Downstairs is an exhibition dedicated to the Turkish First Army, especially their role in the Gallipoli campaign of 1915. A statue portrays a heroic Turkish strongman who single-handedly loaded the 280-pound (127 kg) shells that were fired at British ships.

Moda's sun-drenched promenade

you won't be able to miss the majestic sight of Haydarpaşa Station looming over the banks of the Bosporus. This huge train terminal was built by German architects in a Teutonic neoclassical style and opened in 1908. Its features include circular turrets with conical roofs, embellished cornices, and carved balconies. Trains run to destinations in Asian Turkey and the Middle East from here. The station's restaurant—a favorite with locals—offers good Turkish cuisine at a reasonable price.

Moda & Bağdat Caddesi:

The suburban enclave of **Moda** occupies the streets just south of **Bağdat Caddesi** (Baghdad Street). Wealthy pashas and empire functionaries planted wooden villas here at the turn of the 20th century.

Improvements in the ferry network, and the construction of the Bosporus Bridge in 1973 brought in a new wave of wealthy Istanbullus several decades later, some of whom used Bağdat Caddesi as an illegal nighttime racetrack for their high-octane cars. This leafy zone is now much quieter and great for a gentle wander, and is bordered a few blocks south by a marina and seaside promenade along the Bosporus. *Dolmuşes* run between Kadıköy and Bağdat Caddesi every minute. The street will come as a shock to those who dreamed of wailing muezzins, spice markets, and, well, "Asian" Istanbul. This tree-edged boulevard is lined with very high-end stores, reminiscent of Paris's Champs-Élysées, New York's Fifth Avenue, or London's Bond Street. ■

Boat Trip & Walk:
Europe & Asia in Half a Day

A trip to Asia is a must for any visitor. Combining a tour of the Maiden's Tower (Kız Kulesi), one of Istanbul's most famous monuments, with a wander around some of Üsküdar's mosques and markets makes for a compelling day out.

Ferries stop at the Maiden's Tower.

From Beyoğlu, on the European side of the Bosporus, boats leave every hour, on the hour (12 a.m.–6:45 p.m. weekdays & 9 a.m.–6 p.m. weekends, tel 0212/444 44 36), from the **Kabataş ferry terminal ❶** to the Maiden's Tower. The price ($$) includes the onward trip to Salacak harbor in Üsküdar.

NOT TO BE MISSED:

Maiden's Tower • Yeni Valide Mosque • Tea on Üsküdar's promenade

The **Maiden's Tower ❷** (Kiz Kulesi), commanding the Bosporus strait from its own little island, is intensely photogenic. It's been used variously as a customhouse, quarantine station, lighthouse, home for retired seamen, and a set for a James Bond movie, *The World Is Not Enough* (1999). The tower offers brilliant views from the top-floor café (12 p.m.–7 p.m., tel 0216/ 342 47 47). Ferries head over to Üsküdar on the Asian shore every ten minutes (www. ido.com.tr).

After visiting the tower, turn left and wander past the fishermen along the promenade for ten minutes to Şemsipaşa Çay Bahçesi (see Travelwise p. 253), a relaxing waterside tea room. Next door is the small **Şemsi Paşa Mosque ❸**, built in 1580 by Mimar Sinan (ca. 1490–1588, see pp. 90–91) for the grand vizier

---

The Legend of the Maiden's Tower

Two tragic legends are associated with the tower. The first tells of a sultan who installed his daughter there to keep her from being poisoned by a snake, a fate predicted by an oracle. Destiny proved unavoidable, however, as the girl was bitten by a serpent that snuck onto the island hidden in a basket of fruit. The second legend is based on the love story of Hero and Leandros. Hero, a priestess, was sequestered on the island in the tower away from the attentions of men, but she fell in love with Leandros during a brief escape from captivity. He drowned while swimming out to the tower, and Hero threw herself from the top in despair.

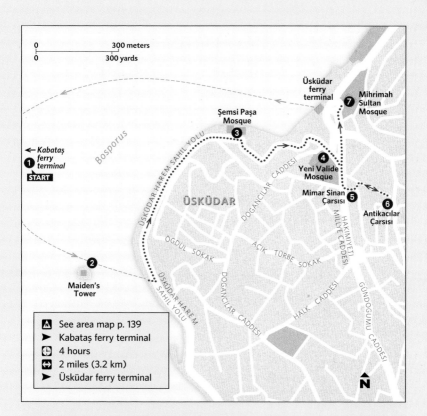

0   300 meters
0   300 yards

Üsküdar
ferry
terminal

Mihrimah
Sultan
Mosque   **7**

Şemsi Paşa
Mosque   **3**

← Kabataş
ferry
terminal   **1**

START

Bosporus

ÜSKÜDAR HAREM SAHIL YOLU

Yeni Valide
Mosque   **4**

Mimar Sinan
Çarsısı   **5**

6
Antikacılar
Çarsısı

DOĞANCILAR CADDESİ

ÜSKÜDAR

OĞDUL SOKAK

AÇIK TÜRBE SOKAK

ÜSKÜDAR HAREM SAHIL YOLU

DOĞANCILAR CADDESİ

HALK CADDESİ

HAKİMİYETİ MİLLİYE CADDESİ

GÜNDOĞUMU CADDESİ

2
Maiden's
Tower

🔺 See area map p. 139
▶ Kabataş ferry terminal
🕐 4 hours
↔ 2 miles (3.2 km)
▶ Üsküdar ferry terminal

N

Şemsi Paşa. The mosque will be closed until 2013 as work continues—literally underfoot—on the Marmaray Tunnel project. Don't miss the lines of balloons strung up in the trees: You can pay (*$*) to attempt to pop them with an air pistol.

Follow the shoreside road on from Şemsi Paşa Mosque for 200 yards (180 m). The road twists right into a huge stone archway, the gateway to the **Yeni Valide Mosque 4** (*Güfemhatun Mahallesi, Eminönü Meydan*) complex. The lovely, tree-dappled courtyards span out from a central fountain and hold many places to rest and soak up the atmosphere.

Exit the mosque from its eastern doorway onto Hakimiyeti Milliye Caddesi and turn to the right. Around 110 yards (100 m) on the left is the remains of a hammam next to a fountain, the design of which is attributed to Mimar

Sinan. This has now been re-invented as a shopping arcade known as the **Mimar Sinan Çarsısı 5**. Notice the tiny bulbous bathhouse windows on the outside, and light filtering through star-shaped holes on the inside.

Walk for another 110 yards (100 m) due east down Büyük Hamam Sokak, passing a hospital parking lot on your left, to the seldom-visited **Antikacılar Çarsısı 6**. This antiques market boasts two floors of vases, art deco clocks, 1920s soda siphons, and many other assorted treasures. Retrace your steps back to Hakimiyeti Milliye Caddesi and continue for 110 yards (100 m) to the **Mihrimah Sultan Mosque 7** (*Hakimiyeti Milliye Caddesi, Üsküdar Meydan*). Look around the mosque's moody interior and hop on a ferry to Eminönü, Karaköy, or Kabataş from the Üsküdar ferry terminal over the road.

Üsküdar & the Asian Bosporus Shore

The Bosporus' northern shore is the most diverse—and least visited—area of Istanbul. Conservative Üsküdar rewards visitors with a glimpse of its fine mosques and millennium of history. The 15 miles (24 km) of coast northward provide a fabulous vision of East meets West. A zone of magnificent villas and seaside dining, it's been the exclusive retreat of Istanbul's moneyed classes for several centuries.

Fishing on the Üsküdar waterfront

Üsküdar

🗺 139

Visitor Information

✉ Hakimiyeti Milliye Caddesi, Atlas Çıkmazı 69

☎ (0216) 531 30 00

Atik Valide Mosque

✉ Fahri Atabey Caddesi, Valideakik Mahallesi

🕐 Closed Fri. a.m.

Most visitors' first taste of Üsküdar will be as they step off the ferry from either Sultanahmet or European Istanbul. The local population is more reserved here—both in terms of dress and volubility—but they are no less friendly for it. Complexions are noticeably more swarthy, too, which is perhaps unsurprising, as many of Üsküdar's residents originally hail from Anatolia, while most Turks on the European shore trace their routes back to the Ottoman Empire's European possessions.

Üsküdar's Mosques: The proximity of Üsküdar's mosques to each other, their differing styles of architecture, and the absence of tourists—both Turkish and foreign—make visiting them a delight. Of the 20 or so in the vicinity, it's the **Atik Valide Mosque** (Atik Valide Camii) that dominates the skyline. It was built by Mimar Sinan in 1583 for Nurbana Sultan, the wife of Selim II and mother of—and later co-regent with—Murad III (not bad for a girl abducted by the Turks as a teenager and raised in the royal harem). Aside from the Süleymaniye Mosque (see pp. 87–88) in Sultanahmet, this structure is arguably Sinan's finest work. Few of Turkey's religious buildings are surrounded by such lovely grounds, with scores of park benches dotted under trees and porticoes and around the fountains. Inside, six finely

INSIDER TIP:

Kanlıca's yogurt, made from a secret blend of sheep's and cow's milk, is lip-smackingly good. Sample a bowl of yogurt, sweetened with powdered sugar, on a summer's evening in the village's square.

—CLIVE CARPENTER
National Geographic contributor

frescoed semi-domes support the magnificent central dome, itself a blaze of light and color. Fine İznik tiles portraying Islamic inscriptions face toward Mecca (in the east) from behind the minbar (pulpit).

The **Mihrimah Sultan Mosque** (Mihrimah Sultan Camii) opposite Üsküdar's ferry terminal was built by a much younger and less experienced Sinan in 1548. It was commissioned by Mihrimah Sultana, the daughter of Süleyman the Magnificent, herself a power

behind the Ottoman throne for several decades. It's interesting to see how the architect's style developed from this massive and ornate—if a little gloomy—creation, to later, light-filled edifices.

Unmissable across the road is the green-tinted **Yeni Valide Mosque** (Yeni Valide Camii, also known as the New Mosque, built in 1710), its soaring interior frescoed with flowers. The lovely courtyards, containing a gazebo-like *türbe* (tomb) plus several trees and tombstones, have remained unchanged for many decades. If you are lucky, you may even be able to savor a cup of *çay*, purchased from a passing tea boy.

For a completely different experience, visit the **Çinili Mosque** (Çinili Camii, built in 1640), 550 yards (500 m) east of the Atik Valide. The complex, with its little tea room, may look simple from the outside, but step inside for a wild cornucopia of İznik tiles. The highly regarded **Çinili Hammam** almost next door retains its original marble slabs and is split into male and female baths. Patrons bring their own towels, soap, and slippers.

North to Kanlıca: North of Üsküdar, past the pretty village of Kuzguncuk, the first main attraction is the **Beylerbeyi Palace** (Beylerbeyi Sarayı, see pp. 148–149), just north of the Bosporus Bridge. This summer residence of the later sultans has its own seaside landing jetty set in marble and stone and is a must-see sight on anyone's Asian itinerary.

(continued on p. 150)

Mihrimah Sultan Mosque
- ✉ Hakimiyeti Milliye Caddesi, Üsküdar
- 🕐 Closed Fri. a.m.

Yeni Valide Mosque
- ✉ Balaban Caddesi, Üsküdar
- 🕐 Closed Fri. a.m.

Çinili Mosque
- ✉ Çinili Camii Sokak
- 🕐 Closed Fri. a.m.

Çinili Hammam
- ✉ Murat Reis, Mahallesi, Camii, Cavusere Caddesi 204
- ☎ (0216) 553 15 93 (men), (0216) 334 97 10 (women)
- 💲 $$$–$$$$

Beylerbeyi Palace
- 🅰 139
- ✉ Abdullahağa Caddesi
- ☎ (0216) 321 93 20
- 🕐 Closed Mon. & Thurs.
- 💲 $$

Ottoman Palaces in Asian Istanbul

Two former palaces on Istanbul's Asian shore are seldom visited by foreigners, yet are both architecturally unique and riddled with interesting stories. As you walk around, marvel at the wealth that swirled about Istanbul a century or so ago.

The sumptuous interior of Beylerbeyi Palace

Beylerbeyi Palace (Beylerbeyi Sarayı)

A seaside settlement for the Ottoman Empire's rulers has stood in this spot for centuries. A certain Mehmet Paşa built the first mansion here during the late 16th century. It was his immodest salutation of Beylerbeyi (which translates as "lord of lords") that lends the settlement its current name.

After yet another wooden incarnation of Mehmet Paşa's original mansion burned down, Sultan Abdülaziz commissioned the current stone palace. It was designed by the Balyan family of Armenian architects and built 1861–1865, this time by brothers Sarkis and Hagop (their

father Karabet and elder brother Nigoğos were responsible for the Dolmabahçe Palace, see pp. 126–128). The result is fabulously ostentatious.

Neoclassical style gives way to showy Arabesque touches both inside and out. The six great halls and 24 giant rooms inside leave no doubt that this place was an official palace of the sultans, albeit just a summer residence. Chandeliers of Bohemian crystal and porcelain from Sèvres meld with splendid Moorish arches and smoking dens. Other Ottoman touches include a harem and a room for the all-powerful valide sultan, the ruler's mother. In these modern times, it's difficult to imagine these two elements co-existing peacefully, or not to cringe at the thought of the sultan going about his harem business with his mother in the vicinity.

Visiting royalty from the Austrian Emperor Franz Joseph to Shah Nasireddin of Iran were entertained at the palace with much pomp. Empress Eugenie of France once entered the palace on Abdülaziz's arm, only to be slapped on the face for such impropriety by the sultan's aforementioned mother. Nevertheless, Eugenie took full advantage of the magnificent gardens and kiosks in the grounds, three of which (including one that was once used as a stable for the sultan's horses) can be wandered around today. The rococo stone landing platform, where guests would have arrived by boat, still boasts the separate men's and women's bathing cabins where summertime guests would have changed.

The last long-term guest of Beylerbeyi Palace was Sultan Abdulhamit II, who was deposed by the Young Turks and lived here under house arrest from 1912 to 1918. He used his carpentry skills, and no doubt legions of spare time, to craft several pieces of furniture on display inside. (*Beylerbeyi Sarayı, Abdullahağa Caddesi, Üsküdar, tel 0216/321 93 20, closed Mon. & Thurs., $$, camera fee $$$$*)

Khedive's Palace (Hıdiv Kasrı)

The towering Khedive's Palace, or Hıdiv Kasrı as it's locally known, must have stuck out like a sore thumb when it was built on a once green hillside back in 1907. Italian Delfo Seminati designed the mansion as an art nouveau masterpiece. In doing so, he pushed Istanbul's idea of architectural modernity to the very limits with stained-glass skylights, soaring marble columns, and a steam-powered internal elevator that scoots up the central tower to a balcony and a terrace offering stunning river views over the Bosporus.

The palace was just what Seminati's client, Abbas II Hilmi, the last khedive (or hereditary ruler of Egypt) wanted. The khedive was wealthy, well traveled, and had modern tastes, which extended to divorcing his first wife, a Crimean-

INSIDER TIP:

The terraced gardens at Beylerbeyi Palace, with pretty ornamental pools surrounded by magnolia blossoms, are a particularly pleasant place to relax on a nice day. Its prime location on the banks of the Bosporus makes it a perfect spot to take photos of the river sights and the elegant span of the Bosporus Bridge.

—SALLY MCFALL
National Geographic contributor

born former slave, and remarrying (and quickly divorcing) a Hungarian noblewoman. But in the palace's interior, Arabic and Ottoman touches abound, from the ornate fountain surrounded by marble columns in the circular entrance hallway to the frescoed flowers decorating the ceiling. The extensive grounds, which are covered with wooded walkways and boast fine Bosporus views, contain a mini-Versailles arrangement of marble waterfalls. Back indoors, an incongruous addition—still in use inside the men's restroom—is a giant porcelain toilet fit for a sultan, manufactured by Jennings of Lambeth, London.

When the khedive died in 1914 most of his supposed subjects back in Egypt were already living under de facto British rule. The palace fell into disrepair until Atatürk demanded that it be purchased for the nation in 1937. Formerly a classy hotel, it now draws in Turkish visitors to its wonderfully ornate tea room and rather off-the-wall restaurant (see Travelwise p. 252).

To reach the palace on foot, cross over the road from Kanlıca ferry terminal, walk up Kasamahmet Sokağı for 20 yards (18 m), turn left at the Türk Telekom call box onto Hacı Muhittin Sokak, and climb 15 minutes up the hill. (*Hıdiv Kasrı, Çubuklu Yolu 32, Kanlıca, tel 0216/ 413 92 53*)

Küçüksu Palace

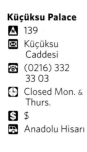

- 139
- Küçüksu Caddesi
- (0216) 332 33 03
- Closed Mon. & Thurs.
- $
- Anadolu Hisarı

One mile (1.6 km) farther north, Çengelköy is a delightful destination. Teahouses and fish restaurants pan out from its tree-dappled town square. Despite its obvious wealth—easily seen in the line of magnificent wooden *yalıs* that line the seafront—it retains a lively village atmosphere. Çengelköy is so called because Mehmet II, The Conqueror, found a cache of Byzantine anchors during the conquest of Constantinople in 1453; *Çengel* is derived from the Persian for "hook," while *köy* means "village" in Turkish.

Çengelköy Cucumbers

As far as the sweet, crunchy cucumbers from the village of Çengelköy are concerned, size isn't everything. From early April through summer, these diminutive green fingers are sold to passing traffic from huge open-air stalls: a healthy version of a drive-through if ever there was one. If you can't make a detour—although many Istanbullus will make sure they do—Çengelköy cucumbers can be found in many upscale restaurants, particularly in Asian Istanbul's main square.

Head north along the coast for 2.5 miles (4 km) and you pass **Küçüksu Palace** on the left. This splendid seafront mansion was built in 1856, again as a summer home for the Ottoman rulers. It was designed by Nigoğos Balyan, who helped his father, Karabet Balyan, design the similarly ornate **Dolmabahçe Palace** (see pp. 126–128) on the other side of the strait. About 577 yards (500 m) north is a medieval, Anatolian fortress, or castle, called **Anadolu Hisarı** (1394–1395), built by Sultan Bayezit I. Although

the Anadolu Hisarı has been extensively restored by the Ministry of Culture, there are no current plans to open it to the public.

A sister fort to this small castle, named Rumeli Hisarı (see p. 131), was built by Mehmet II in 1452, and is visible across the water. With this extra fort, Mehmet's armies could command traffic coming up and down the Bosporus. (Think how fearful the Christian residents of old Constantinople, which broadly occupies today's Sultanahmet district, would have been as two huge enemy forts sprung into action almost overnight, and right on their doorstep—the conquest of their city was not long in coming.)

Two miles (3 km) north of Anadolu Hisarı—past the Fatih Bridge, the second Bosporus crossing—lies **Kanlıca**, particularly famous for its creamy local yogurt with its thick, cheesy skin topping. The town is also the gateway to **Khedive's Palace** (Hıdiv Kasrı; see p. 149), up the hill.

To Yoros Castle: The 5-mile (8 km) route north along the Asian Bosporus past Paşabahçe—a town once famous for its glass production—and Beykoz is simply pretty. But the following 5 miles (8 km) to the village of **Anadolu Kavağı** is a road less traveled. The route skirts inland past a vast military installation on the shore, where cold winds force frequent mists across craggy hills and virgin forest. Roadside stalls sell nuts, eggs, pickles, and honey, a world away from hip European Istanbul.

The Bosporus coastal town of Kanlıca

Kanlıca
139

Khedive's Palace
139
Hidiv Youl
32, Çubuklu
Mahallesi,
Çubuklu
(0216) 413
96 44

Anadolu Kavağı
139

Yoros Castle
Anadolu Kavaği
Yolu, near
Akbaba

Anadolu Kavağı's castle, **Yoros Castle** (Yoros Kalesi), is a 20-minute uphill scramble from the seaside village of the same name. The Black Sea can be glimpsed from this strategically important point. Little wonder, then, that it has been occupied since Byzantine times, evidence of which lies not only in the castle's layered construction, but also in the imperial motif of the Paleologus dynasty on the fortification walls, whose self-confident inscription means "King of Kings, who kings it over Kings." A chain could be stretched from Anadolu Kavağı to Rumeli Kavağı across the Bosporus in times of conflict, a defensive measure replicated downstream between the Maiden's Tower and the Topkapı Palace, and also across the Golden Horn. ■

The famous waters of the Bosporus strait, and father afield to the beautiful Princes Islands, Bursa, or beyond

Istanbul Excursions

Introduction & Map   154-155

Black Sea Beaches   156-157

Feature: The Bosporus—A Strait History   158-159

Princes Islands   160-163

Experience: Five Don't-Miss Island Activities   162

Walks: Burgazada & Heybeliada   164-165

Bursa & Uludağ   166-169

Experience: Swim in a Termal Spa   169

Ankara   170-175

Experience: Visiting the Atatürk Mausoleum   171

Hotels & Restaurants   253-255

Cycling on Princes Islands

Istanbul Excursions

Escaping from such a culturally rich city as Istanbul may sound like madness, but the surrounding islands, spas, and seaside retreats are also steeped in local history and culture. Although all of these spots can be visited in a single day, some are definitely best treated as an overnight escape.

A relaxed afternoon at a Bursa café

For a taste of the real Turkey, Bursa is a town seldom visited by Western tourists. Its historic status as an important trading center on the Silk Route, coupled with its youthful student population, make this attractive ancient capital of the Ottoman Empire a great place to lose yourself for a weekend. Just an hour away, the resort of Termal has been a spa pilgrimage spot since Emperor Constantine built baths here in the fourth century A.D. Hot springs bubble to the earth's surface, their rich waters claimed to cure pretty much any ailment from arthritis to infertility. A blast in the steamy hammam and a plunge in the outdoor pool will leave you fit for another bout of haggling back in Istanbul's bazaars.

Traveling outside Istanbul reveals a calmer more restful side to modern Turkey. Conversations with locals tend to be longer and more probing than those with their city-based cousins. Feel the wind in your hair on one of the boats that steam around the Bosporus or while clipping around the Princes Islands on a horse-drawn carriage or bicycle, the principal modes of transport on this car-free archipelago. Vintage cable cars grind up the mountain of Uludağ, Turkey's principal ski resort, while the train is the best way to reach Ankara, whether on the cozy night sleeper or on the high-speed express that will bring the capital within three hours of Istanbul by 2013.

In terms of accessibility, the easiest day trip is a Bosporus cruise: This vast waterway has given travelers their first taste of the city for over two millennia. The ever popular boat tour lends a sense of scale to the city's history, geography, and, judging by the ritzy wooden mansions (*yalıs*) lining the strait, abundant wealth.

NOT TO BE MISSED:

Spending a summer afternoon at one of the Black Sea's beach clubs **156–157**

Hopping aboard a Bosporus boat tour to explore Istanbul from the water **161**

Seeing the Princes Islands from a horse-drawn *fayton* **162**

Haggling for bargains at Bursa's Koza Han (silk market) **167**

Hitting the ski slopes in the winter resort of Uludağ **168–169**

Termal's rich mineral springs **169**

Coming face-to-face with 10,000 years of history at Ankara's Museum of Anatolian Civilizations **172–173**

And although Ankara gets only a trickle of tourists, it boasts two wonderful sites that are key to understanding Turkish history—the Atatürk Mausoleum, where millions of Turks pay their respects to modern Turkey's first leader each year, and the Museum of Anatolian Civilizations, tracing the area's history back to cave paintings and cuneiform writing. ■

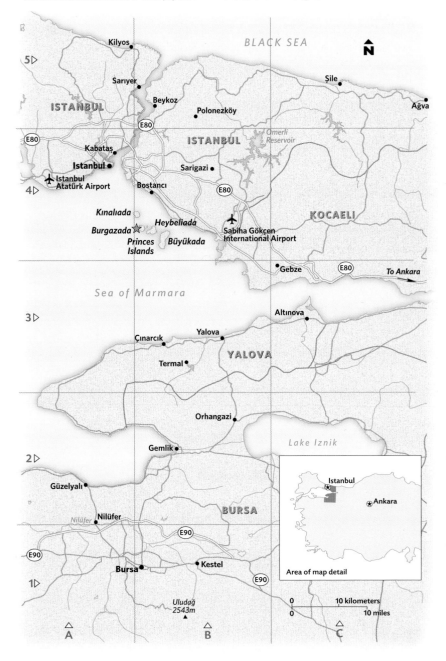

Black Sea Beaches

While the Princes Islands may be the traditional escape for well-to-do Istanbullus fleeing the city's smog, their quaint villages and seaside cafés can get seriously packed in high summer and on sunny weekends. Quieter, and more popular with Istanbul's more budget-conscious visitors, is the arc of beaches along the Black Sea coast north of Istanbul. And you can top off your urban escape with a night in the charming village of Polonezköy.

Şile's beautiful beaches are firm favorites with Istanbullus.

Kilyos

🅰 155 A5

A string of great beaches runs along the Black Sea north of Istanbul, from Kilyos due north of Istanbul to Ağva in the northeast corner of the province of Istanbul.

Kilyos

Perhaps the pick of Istanbul's Black Sea beaches, Kilyos has fine sand, cheap hotels, and a stack of cafés and restaurants. The water is generally clean and long, sweeping waves provide excellent entertainment—

although beware of the strong undercurrents here. A line of trendy beach clubs hems in the main part of the beach, each of which has a bar, beanbags, parasols, and sun loungers. The trendiest—try **Solar** (*Eski Turban Yolu 4, Kilyos, tel 0212/201 26 12*) to scope out Istanbul's coolest crowd at play—boast a backdrop of ear-poppingly loud music.

A *dolmuş* service runs to and from Sarıyer (see p. 135) to Kilyos until the early evening.

If you choose to swim at one of Turkey's Black Sea beaches, be sure to stay close to the shore, as the strong and unpredictable under-currents along this stretch of coast can be extremely treacherous.

—SALLY MCFALL
National Geographic contributor

Şile

Şile's ever popular **Kumbaba Beach** is the closest stretch of sand on Istanbul's Asian side, 40 miles (65 km) northeast of the city. While you won't be the only one visiting Şile on a sunny summer afternoon, the off-season feel is that of an overgrown fishing village. Indeed, the seafood restaurants in the village—with their scenic views of the harbor and ruined Genoese castle perched high up on a small rock island just off the mainland— are something special, although most locals tend to bring a picnic or barbecue directly on the beach. A stroll away from the crowds along the headland is recommended, as is a visit to the 19th-century black-and-white-striped **lighthouse** *(feneri)*, which houses a small museum next to a café and is surrounded by a pretty park.

Şile is a 90-minute bus ride from Üsküdar's Doğancılar Caddesi bus station *(tel 0216/391 13 47)*.

Ağva Plajı

A more tranquil seaside option is Ağva Beach (Ağva Plajı), 25 miles (40 km) east of Şile. Here, there are longer sandy beaches and several simple accommodation options. Like Şile and Kilyos, the undertow can be very dangerous, as water funnels into the Bosporus just down the coast. Although little is left of Ağva's tumultuous past, it was a powerful trading town in the first millennium before being switched between Seljuk Turks, Crusaders, Byzantines, and Ottomans over the last thousand years.

Ağva is about an hour farther along from Şile on the same bus. ∎

Şile
◭ 155 C5

Şile Feneri
✉ Şile port
🕐 Closed Sun.
💲 $

Polonezköy
◭ 155 B5

Ağva
◭ 155 C5

Polonezköy

Just 6 miles (10 km) east of the Asian shore's Istanbul suburb of Beykoz is Polonezköy, a village founded by Polish dissidents in 1842. The countryside setting could pass for rural Poland and there is a Catholic church and a cemetery. Attracting such luminaries as former Polish president Lech Walesa, the charming village is now frequented by wealthy Istanbullus in search of peace and a plate of pork chops. Pork may be frowned upon by Islam, but it's a ubiquitous menu item here. Other highlights include local liqueurs, Polish pies, and the annual cherry festival in June. The pretty drive can be made by private vehicle only.

The Bosporus—A Strait History

Stretching for 20 miles (32 km) from the Sea of Marmara to the Black Sea, the Bosporus is a constant companion to Istanbul's hectic history. Although it physically splits the city in two, it's also the symbolic meeting point of Europe and Asia and has been criss-crossed by boats, pontoons, bridges, and—most recently—a tunnel, in the pursuit of trade, conflict, and human migration.

The Bosporus is key to the history of Istanbul and Turkey.

Ancient History

Emperor Constantine was wise to move the Roman capital to Istanbul, then known as the Greek city of Byzantium before it was renamed Constantinople in A.D. 330. Protected on one side by the unpredictable currents of the Bosporus strait, the city proved impregnable to attack for over a thousand years. Further-more, the imperial armies could sail down the Bosporus to Europe, Africa, and Asia Minor to fight and return with the spoils of war.

But as any visitor to the city will know, Bosporus traffic is seldom one way. The expand-ing Ottoman Empire wanted the strategic strait for themselves, and in 1452, at the narrowest section of the Bosporus, the fortress at **Rumeli** Hisarı (see p. 131) was built on the European side across from **Anadolu Hisarı** (see p. 150) on the Asian side, and together the two served to control the passage. Istanbul fell a year later, and it was then the Turkish Sultan who sat in the **Topkapı Palace** (see pp. 58–64) to watch treasure ships, victorious armies, and foreign ambassadors pour in. Sections of the riverbanks were even filled in with soil so that future palaces could be built along the Bosporus, all of which would boast tranquil waterside gardens and landing jetties jutting out to sea.

The Bosporus at War

Although the decisive Turkish defense at **Gallipoli** (see pp. 182–185) in 1915 saved Istanbul the indignity of another seaborne invasion, the post-World War I Treaty of Sèvres turned the strait into a peaceful international waterway. In the 1920s, from his Dolmabahçe Palace residence, Atatürk would take dips in the Bosporus and occasionally swim across it.

The Montreux Convention in 1936 curtailed passage for military traffic, in particular Soviet aircraft carriers. After World War II, smaller Russian battleships would enter the Mediterranean via the Bosporus, but each boat would cruise through the strait with only a skeleton command; the rest of the crew was locked below lest they glimpse the growing prosperity of the NATO alliance's largest city. And despite restrictions, Soviet submarines would sneak through the strait at night. As Cold War antagonism melted, the gargantuan Ukrainian aircraft carrier *Varyag* was auctioned off to the Chinese government in 1998. It took a Chinese ministerial delegation, plus a 20-vessel support group, to persuade Turkey to open the Bosporus to this 1,000-foot-long (305 m) ship.

Balance of Trade

The Bosporus is a chokepoint for the world's cargo and energy industry, but navigating it is a treacherous affair. In places it is only 700 yards (645 m) wide and has several 45-degree turns skewed by seven-knot crosscurrents. Occasionally, thick fog reduces visibility to just 100 yards (91 m), and pilots must use radar to weave around scores of tugs, fishing boats, and ferries that clutter the route.

The calamitous collision of the M/T *Independenţa* oil transporter with a Greek freighter in 1979, which blew out the Haydarpaşa train station windows and left 43 dead, shows how dangerous the passage can be. Merchant ships now travel in one direction at a time, switching direction every 12 hours, and tankers can travel during daylight hours only. Accidents are still a seasonal occurrence, however, and in March 2010 the 945-foot-long (288 m) *Giant Pescadores* lost power, collided with another

vessel, and drifted toward the historic seafront at Rumeli Fortress. A motley crew of passenger ferries and tugs threw lines around the stricken vessel, and skillfully towed it to safety.

As the world cargo trade begins to rebound after the recent financial crisis, pressure on the strait grows. The undersea **Marmara Tunnel** (see p. 36) and a planned third Bosporus bridge promise to relieve a portion of the Bosporus' daily crossing, but maritime traffic funneling through the strait is so concentrated that passages can still be subject to delays of up to a month.

The Bosporus is a particularly important artery for the oil industry, with a steady stream of tankers leaving Russian ports such as Novorossyisk on their way to the United States and Europe.

Jason & the Argonauts

In the Greek legend of Jason, the young voyager passes through the Bosporus on his way to retrieve the Golden Fleece from Colchis, in modern-day Georgia. The strait was then known as the Symplegades, or the Clashing Rocks, and it was assumed that any ship that attempted the route would be crushed to smithereens.

However, Jason was given some insider knowledge. If he released a dove through the strait and it survived, so would his vessel, the *Argo*. With the loss of a few tail feathers, the dove just made it, although it took the combined might of Jason's 50 fellow Argonauts, among them Telamon, Castor, and Pollux, to row north, losing just a piece of the ship's stern in the process.

As recounted in his 1986 book *The Jason Voyage*, British explorer Tim Severin attempted the same route in a replica of the *Argo*. He barely lived to tell the tale, but managed to identify many of the legend's landmarks on the way.

Princes Islands

These nine small islands, clearly visible at the southern end of the Bosporus, are located 9 to 18 miles (15–30 km) from Istanbul's center and make an ideal escape from the city bustle. Called the Prens Adaları, or simply Adalar ("the Islands") by locals, their name derives from Byzantine times, when constant power struggles meant princes and patriarchs were frequently exiled here out of harm's way.

Making and selling daisy chains and garlands on Büyükada

Kınalıada

🔼 155 B4

Of the islands, only Kınalıada (Henna Island), Burgazada, Heybeliada (Saddlebag Island), and Büyükada (Big Island) are accessible via public ferries. Sedef Adasi (Mother-of-Pearl Island) can be reached by private boat only; Yassıada (Flat Island), Sivriada (Sharp Island), and Tavşanada (Rabbit Island) are uninhabited; and Kaşık Adası (Spoon Island) is privately owned.

Kınalıada

The closest island to Istanbul, Kınalıada (Henna Island) gets its name from the reddish color of its soil—a result of the iron and copper mining that once took place here. The island has been home to a slew of exiled Byzantine emperors, from the 9th century's Michael I through Romanus IV Diogenes during the 11th century. Over recent decades, it has been heavily developed, but most of the beaches are public and easily accessible.

Yassıada

British ambassador Sir Henry Bulwer purchased this barren island during the mid-19th century, and built himself a miniature, self-sufficient empire complete with castle. Possession of Yassıada (Flat Island) passed to the Turkish Navy. The island is most famous as the site of imprisonment of former Prime Minister Adnan Menderes, deposed in the military coup of 1960 and hanged the following year.

Sivriada

Various royal and religious figures have been banished to this conical speck. But locals' favorite Sivriada (Sharp Island) story tells of Istanbul's stray dogs, rounded up in 1911 and dumped on the island to starve. An earthquake, which occurred immediately after the dogs were deposited, was perceived as divine disapproval. The dogs were promptly herded on board another ship and brought back to Istanbul.

Burgazada

Formerly known as Antigone, this sleepy island is host to a blend of year-round residents and affluent Istanbullus at leisure. Although little visited by tourists, it is laced with secluded trails and pleasant scenery (see p. 164). Forest fires in 2003 destroyed much of its woodland, but the island is rapidly recovering. **Aya Yani**

Rum Ortodoks Kilisesi (St. John the Baptist's Greek Orthodox Church, open for services only) is visible from much of Burgazada's eastern side. Originally built in A.D. 876 (though its current form is 19th century), the church's foundations lie on a dungeon where ninth-century Patriarch of Constantinople Methodius was imprisoned for close to a decade.

Kaşik Adası

Sitting enticingly between Burgazada and Heybeliada, the long, spoon-shaped Kaşık Adası (Spoon Island) is—and has always been—privately owned.

Heybeliada

A mix of hilltop monasteries, 19th-century mansions, and acres of pristine countryside, Heybeliada (Saddlebag Island), this archipelago's second largest island, is a fascinating place to explore (see pp. 164–165).

Heybeliada
◭ 155 B4
Visitor Information
✉ Altinnordu Caddesi 21, Büyükada
☎ (0216) 382 78 50

Princes Islands Ferries

IDO (Kennedy Cd. Yenikapi Feribot Iskelesi, Eminönü, tel 0212/444 44 36, www.ido.com.tr) runs ferries to Kabataş, Kınalıada, Burgazada, Heybeliada, and Büyükada, with many stopping at Bostancı en route. On a clear day, there's no better way to see Sultanahmet's sights than from these ferries, skirting the peninsula. Boats also run between the islands themselves.

EXPERIENCE: Five Don't-Miss Island Activities

1) Take an island tour in a traditional *fayton* (phaeton, or horse-drawn carriage). A fayton not only serves as transport, but also makes for effortless access to country lanes and island vistas. Standard, fixed-price tours offered are the shorter *küçük* (small, *$$$$*) or *büyük* (big, *$$$$$*), normally looping the island.

2) Rent a bike. All the islands have plenty of bicycle rental stands (*$/hour, $$$/day*). If you're reasonably fit, cycling around each island allows you to explore at your own pace, stopping for lunch, a swim, or the perfect photo opportunity.

3) Hike on Heybeliada, the second largest of the Princes Islands (see pp. 164–165).

4) Visit a monastery. Crowning peaks throughout the archipelago, any island monastery makes for an energetic morning climb. And, other than offering fascinating history, each one boasts stunning panoramas over rocky outcrops and nearby private islands.

5) Kick back at a beach club. With free speedboat access to and from the island's ferry terminal, the Princes Islands summer beach clubs (*day entry $$$–$$$$*) are popular with sun-seekers of every age. All offer cushioned lounge chairs, shady umbrellas, and colorful beanbags, as well as changing rooms, showers, lively music, and a bar.

Greek Orthodox School of Theology

⊠ Ümit Tepesi

☎ (0216) 351 84 17

⊕ Groups by appointment only

İnönü Evi Museum

⊠ Refah Şehitleri Caddesi 73

☎ (0216) 351 84 49

⊕ Closed Mon.

Büyükada

▲ 155 B4

Visitor Information

⊠ Ferry Terminal, Iskele Square, Büyükada

The Holy Trinity Monastery (Aya Triada Manastırı) was built on the island's northern peak during the ninth century under Patriarch Photius, an important catalyst for Christianity's split into Eastern Orthodox and Roman Catholic. This spot is now the site of the Halki Seminary, or **Greek Orthodox School of Theology.** As well as a 19th-century monastery, this religious complex includes an important library and an opulent chapel housing a 720-year-old, double-sided icon of Virgin Mary and the Crucifixion, recently showcased in a Byzantine exhibition at the New York Metropolitan Museum. The monastery's former theological school was closed in 1971 by the Turkish government: Walking around it now is like stepping into a Victorian schoolroom.

During the 19th century, the island's population slowly grew,

as students of both the island's prestigious Naval Academy (now the Naval High School, located near the island's ferry terminal) and the monastery's theological school made Heybeliada their permanent home. Today, intricately carved wooden homes are dotted around town, and excellent fish restaurants line the wide waterfront promenade. Well worth a visit is the **İnönü Evi Museum** (İnönü Evi Müzesi): Formerly the home of Turkey's second president, İsmet İnönü, the small museum showcases personal photographs and a selection of furniture given to İnönü as a gift from Atatürk.

Büyükada

The largest of the Princes Islands, Büyükada (Big Island) is also the most populated and attracts the most tourists. And for good reason—the town is littered with

INSIDER TIP:

Opt for the slow boat to Büyükada, a bucolic island where cars are banned and the only transport is by horse and carriage.

—JONI RENDON
National Geographic contributor

art nouveau masterpieces, restaurants, bars, and beach clubs, and is expansive enough for a vigorous day of discovery.

Büyükada was originally the site of four monasteries, plus a sixth-century convent built by Emperor Justinian, to which Empresses Irene (8th century), Theophano (10th century), Zoe (11th century), Euphrosyne (12th–13th century), and Augusta (Anna Dalassene, 13th century) were exiled. More recently, Leon Trotsky (1879–1940) lived in the Izzet Paşa Köşkü from 1929 to 1933, while nearby the ornate Villa John Paşa (under renovation at time of writing) was built by the founder of the islands' first ferry service in 1880.

Visitors who trek their way up Büyükada's steep southern hill, Yüce Tepe (660 feet/202 m), will be amply rewarded. Not only are the vistas from **Aya Yorgi Manastırı** (St. George Monastery) stunning, but the attached open-air restaurant is a top spot for lunch or a cold beer.

Sedef Adasi

During the ninth century, Emperor Michael III exiled Con-

stantinople's Patriarch Ignatius to Sedef Adasi (Mother-of-Pearl Island) for a decade. During this time Ignatius established a monastery where he was later buried. Today, the island is the site of numerous summer villas, and is accessible by private boat only.

Tavşan Adası

Although it may not actually boast rabbits, **Tavşan Adası** (Rabbit Island) is home to the windswept ruins of a convent, also founded by Patriarch Ignatius during the ninth century. ∎

Aya Yorgi Monastırı

✉ Sanatoryum Yolu Sokak, Büyükada

🕓 Closed Sun.

A traditional *fayton* in Burgazada

Walks: Burgazada & Heybeliada

Part of the appeal of the Princes Islands is escaping the crowds. For a bucolic amble through fields of bluebells or a clamber around the rocks of a secluded cove, visit the quieter islands of Burgazada or Heybeliada. Each makes for an enjoyable afternoon ramble, or combine the two for an active day out.

Burgazada

From Burgazada's ferry terminal, head to the town's main seafront square. Bear immediately left, then right toward the domed **Aya Yani Rum Ortodoks Kilisesi ❶** (see p. 161).

Cross the square and follow the road on the right uphill. Turn right at the top and continue on between the ornate 19th-century wooden houses until the road splits. Take the left-hand turn, which leads out of town and, during springtime, bisects fields of wildflowers. Stop at the solitary **bench ❷** at the road's peak, perfectly positioned to admire the captivating views over **Kaşık Adası** (Spoon Island, named for its spoon-like shape, see p. 161) and **Heybeliada** (Saddlebag Island; see pp. 161–162) beyond.

A quick dip into the sea at Burgazada island

NOT TO BE MISSED:

Stunning views of the islands
• **Terki Dünya Manastırı** • **Ornate 19th-century wooden villas**

Backtrack 5 yards (4.5 m) and take the unpaved trail leading to the right. Continue uphill to the crossroads—you'll likely pass a horse or two grazing en route—and take a right. The path slopes downhill, soon ducking among shady trees. Twisting along another 200 yards (180 m), the road becomes paved shortly before a bench marks a T-intersection. Turn right, then immediately left, following the ribbon of a road along Burgazada's northern shore. On the western horizon, you can see **Yassıada** (Flat Island; see p. 161) and **Sivriada** (Sharp Island; see p. 161).

The road meanders past a Muslim **cemetery ❸** (look for the pre-20th-century tombs, marked with Islamic calendar dates) and various sheltered beaches as it continues the half-mile (1 km) route back to Burgazada's town center.

Heybeliada

Descending from the ferry at Heybeliada, take in the impressive **Naval High School ❶** (Deniz Harp Okulul, formerly the Turkish Naval Academy), then turn right and walk along Saddlebag Island's (Heybeliada) seafront. Upon reaching the golden **Atatürk statue ❷**, turn left and begin heading inland.

İşgüzar Sokak threads between bike rental spots and antiques stores, eventually feeding into Refah Şehitleri Caddesi. Restored and crumbling 19th-century wooden homes flank this street,

Sea of Marmara

N

cemetery

3

bench

2

Aya Yani Rum
Ortodoks Kilisesi
Burgazada Ferry Terminal

1 START

Burgazada

*Kaşik
Adası*

Merit Halki
Palace
Hotel

wide public path

4

İnönü Evi
Museum

3

Atatürk
statue

2

Naval
High
School

1

START

Heybeliada
Ferry
Terminal

Heybeliada

7

5

stables

6

Terki
Dünya
Manastırı

*Çam
Limanı*

Sea of Marmara

| 0 | 1 kilometer |
| 0 | 0.5 miles |

Burgazada

- 🗺 See area map p. 155
- ▶ Burgazada ferry terminal
- 🕐 1.25 hours (not including stops)
- ↔ 1.8 miles (3 km)
- ▶ Burgazada ferry terminal

Heybeliada

- 🗺 See area map p. 155
- ▶ Heybeliada ferry terminal
- 🕐 2 hours (not including stops)
- ↔ 3 miles (5 km)
- ▶ Heybeliada ferry terminal

INSIDER TIP:

**Stay at the Merit Halki
Palace Hotel [see Travelwise
p. 254] in Heybeliada and
enjoy the breathtaking
sunset over the other Princes
Islands from your room.**

—ITIR ERHART
Assistant Professor, Istanbul Bilgi University

including **İnönü Evi Museum 3** (see p. 162).

Continue westward for another 650 yards (600 m), passing the blocky outpost of the island's naval school. The road veers to the right, becoming Alp Görüngen Yolu. Look for the hand-painted "Plaj" (beach) signs on your right, and descend the gentle slope downhill toward the waterfront. From here, a **wide public path 4** sits around 65 feet (20 m) above the shoreline. Easily navigated, it winds its way past casual summer cafés, petite coves, and moored yachts for about a mile (1.6 km), before veering steeply to the left and rejoining Alp Görüngen Yolu.

At the southwest tip of the island, you'll pass Saddlebag Island's *fayton* **stables 5**, with their own dedicated pastures, and the turn-off for **Terki Dünya Manastırı 6**, a Greek Orthodox monastery perched scenically on an isolated promontory. The road quickly dips down to **Çam Limanı 7**, a perfect arc-shaped bay favored by locals during the busy summer months.

Follow Çam Limanı Caddesi for another two-thirds of a mile (1 km) eastward back to Heybeliada's town center.

Bursa & Uludağ

The Ottoman Empire's first capital, Bursa, located 150 miles/240 km south of Istanbul (reachable also by ferry), stands in the shadow of Uludağ Mountain—a national park and Turkey's most popular ski resort, located 25 miles (40 km) southeast of Bursa.

Winter trekking in Bursa

Bursa

🏔 155 B1

Visitor Information

✉ Ulucami Parki Orhangazi Alt Geçidi 1, Heykel, Bursa

☎ (0224) 220 18 48

Bursa

Patronized by the Romans, who flocked to the town for its mineral-rich hot springs (which still draw visitors to this day), Bursa achieved equal fame during the sixth century as a center of silk trading. Its economy flourished over the years, and in the early 14th century Osman Gazi (1258–1325), leader of the Osmanlı Turks (and whose genetic lineage was passed through successive sultans until the early 20th century), besieged the city for close to two decades with dreams of making it his prize. Command then passed to Osman's son, Orhan Gazi (1281–1362), who finally succeeded in conquering Bursa in 1326 and proceeded to crown it the capital of the Ottoman Empire.

Try some of Bursa's traditional culinary delights, such as the famous İskander kebab (thinly cut grilled lamb or beef covered with tomato sauce and served on *pide* bread slices with yogurt) and a succulent dessert of candied chestnuts called *kestane şekeri.*

—SALLY MCFALL
National Geographic contributor

Green Mosque & Mausoleum:

East of the city center and across the artisan-lined, 15th-century **Setbaşı Bridge** (Setbaşı Köprüsü), the Yıldırım quarter is home to Bursa's most famous sight: Green Mosque (Yeşil Cami, 1424). Although it was never fully completed, the mosque's interior is overwhelming, lined entirely with deep, emerald green, hexagonal tiles. The natural light filtering into the building heightens their hue, making them shimmer a cobalt color. Opposite, the recently restored, turquoise **Green Mausoleum** (Yeşil Türbe, 1421) houses the tomb of Sultan Mehmet Çelebi (1382–1421), his two sons, and his daughter.

Atatürk Caddesi & Around:

Bursa's most appealing area is the pedestrianized streets and market alleyways that lace their way from Pirinç Han, a 16th-century trading center now packed with *nargile* bars, to the **Great Mosque** (Ulu Camii), which was built under Sultan Yıldırım Beyazıt (1360–1403) in 1399 and boasts 20 massive domes and an interior of grand columns, soaring arches, and a finely carved wood pulpit. In between the two, **Ipek Han** (clothing market), 15th-century **Bedesten** (jewelry market), 14th-century **Emir Han,** and splendid **Koza Han** (silk market) make for a dedicated shopper's paradise. Like Istanbul's Grand Bazaar (see pp. 79–84), much of this area is covered. Absolutely unmissable is Koza Han, Bursa's center of all things silk. Merchants line the two stories around a central courtyard and small mosque, and the city's famous silk cocoon auction is held here every year in June.

Green Mosque & Green Mausoleum

⊠ Yeşil Caddesi, Yıldırım
🕑 Closed Fri. a.m.

Great Mosque

⊠ Atatürk Caddesi
🕑 Closed Fri. a.m.

Koza Han

⊠ Off Koza Park, Atatürk Caddesi
www.kozahan.org

Getting to Bursa

Two to three daily ferries (www.ido.com.tr, $$$$) service the route between Istanbul's Yenikapı terminal in Eminönü and Bursa *(1 hr 20 mins.).* One to two daily ferries run between Istanbul's Kabataş and Bursa *(2 hrs.),* stopping at Kadıköy en route. Upon arrival at Bursa's ferry terminal at Güzelyalı, hop on a *dolmuş ($)* to Organize Sanayi, the final stop on the local metro line. Trains *($)* zip between here and Şehreküstü, a ten-minute walk from the city center.

Osman Gazi & Orhan Gazi Türbesi
✉ Tophane Park, Hisar

Muradiye Külliyesi
✉ Murat Caddesi, Muradiye

Eski Kaplıca
✉ At intersection of Zübeyde Hanim Cd. & Çekirge Cd., Çekirge
☎ (0224) 233 93 00
💲 $$-$$$
www.kervansaray hotels.com

Citadel (Hisar): Ringed with ramparts, five gates, and 14 towers, Hisar is Bursa's ancient quarter, dating back to Roman and Byzantine times. Today, the citadel is a peaceful neighborhood full of houses from the Ottoman era and offering spectacular panoramas over the city from Tophane Park's terraces, which flank the town's prominent clock tower (1906). Nearby, two mausoleums, **Osman Gazi** and **Orhan Gazi Türbesi,** house the revered remains of the founders of the Ottoman Empire.

Muradiye: Although Bursa remained the empire's capital for less than 50 years, it was long

Interior of Bursa's Muradiye Külliyesi Mosque

considered the spiritual home of the sultans. In Muradiye, west of Hisar, lies **Muradiye Külliyesi,** a religious complex built by Sultan Murat II (1404–1451). It's best known for its 13 imposing imperial tombs and 40 sarcophagi, including those of Mehmet the Conqueror's midwife, Şehzade Mustafa (son of Süleyman the Magnificent), and Murat II himself. Behind the mosque, there's a **cemetery** where Bursa's most affluent citizens were buried until the early 20th century. Visit Murat II's hammam, still functioning and open to the public, or one of two house museums: the 17th-century **Osmanli Evi Müzesi,** across the park in front of the mosque, and **Hüsnu Züber Evi,** an uphill climb behind the hammam.

Çekirge: At Bursa's western tip, the neighborhood of Çekirge is famed for its thermal baths; various spa hotels take advantage of these steamy springs. If you want an afternoon's soak, the 700-year-old **Eski Kaplıca** (Old Baths, run by the Kervansaray Hotel next door) is the most atmospheric.

Uludağ

Casting a massive shadow over Bursa's town center, Uludağ mountain towers at a sky-scraping 8,343 feet (2,543 m). Much of the summit was declared a national park in 1961, but Uludağ is best known as Turkey's premier skiing destination. From December through mid-March, **Oteller,** the cluster of hotels and restaurants at the base of Uludağ's ski slopes, is packed.

EXPERIENCE: Swim in a Termal Spa

Emperor Constantine may have started a day-spa trend in the 4th century, but it was during the 19th and early 20th centuries that Termal's mineral springs morphed into the great healing complex that it is today.

Valide Sultan Bezm-i Alem (1807–1853), mother of Sultan Abdülmecit (1823–1861), credited the waters of Termal with the disappearance of her debilitating rheumatism; two decades later, Sultan Abdulhamit II (1842–1918) erected the ornate buildings visitors make use of today. In 1929, Atatürk too joined the devoted. He had a summer home, the **Atatürk Köşkü,** constructed just across from the baths, and spent vacations here.

The most popular of Termal's baths is **Kurşunlu Hotel & Spa (Çavundur Beldesi, Kurşunlu, Çankırı, tel 0376/485 51 60, www.kursunlutermal.com, $$),** its foundations laid by Emperor Justinian during the sixth century. Inside are two thermal pools, a sauna, Turkish bath, masseurs, changing rooms, a café, and more. Outdoors, the vast swimming pool

steams away at a constant 100°F (38°C). Nearby, and also within the Kurşunlu complex, private *aile* (family) hammams can be rented by the hour. Note that both sexes can use all areas of Kurşunlu at any time. Be sure to bring your bathing suit, and you'll be allotted a towel and a pair of rubber slippers.

Five daily ferries *(1 hr., $$$)* run between Istanbul's Yenikapı terminal and Yalova (8 miles/21 km NW of Termal). Frequent *dolmuş* services *($)* depart from just outside Yalova terminal for Termal, about a half-hour meander through the countryside to Kaplıcalar, the complex of thermal springs located just after Termal's town center. Numerous buses also run between Bursa *(Terminal Otobüs Durağı)* and Yalova bus stations *(Yalova Otogarı, 1 hr., $).*

Snow bunnies from İzmir vie with designer-clad Istanbullus for café tables, chairlifts, and space on the ski runs. Heli-skiing is also available. Midweek, the scene is much quieter. Cycling, hiking, and bird-spotting aficionados flock to this lively area in the summer.

By far the most delightful way to reach Uludağ is via the chunky red *teleferik,* or 1960s cable car *($$ round-trip).* Departing from the lower station of Teferrüç *(accessible via dolmuş services, $, departing from just outside the Bursa City Museum, behind the Atatürk statue on Atatürk Caddesi),* daily cable cars run every 40 minutes in winter *(8:30 a.m.–8 p.m.)* and every 10 minutes during summertime *(8:30*

a.m.–10 p.m.). The journey takes around 30 minutes in total, as the mountain must be scaled via two separate 8-minute rides. When you exit at Sarıalan, at the top, you'll need to take another dolmuş to reach Oteller *(10-min. journey, $).*

Renting Gear & Ski Passes: In Uludağ you can rent any and all the ski gear you need. Expect to pay around $$$ for a half day's rental of ski jacket, waterproof trousers and gloves, boots, skis, or snowboard. A one-day, unlimited chairlift pass costs $$$$. Hourly or daily lessons are available for all levels of skiing abilities, as is snowmobile rental. ∎

Uludağ
☎ (0224) 285 21 11
www.snow-forecast .com/resorts/Uludag

Uludağ Oteller
☎ (0212) 518 87 34
www.uludag otelleri.com

Ankara

In a firm dismissal of the Ottoman ancien régime, Atatürk declared this central Anatolian village—280 miles/451 km southeast of Istanbul and once famed for angora wool—as the new Turkish Republic capital in 1923. The plan was to create a modern European city with wide boulevards and leafy parks; the reality was brutalist and heavy architecture. Today, its major museums, park, and mosques make it an interesting place to visit.

The memorial to Kemal Atatürk, founder of the Turkish Republic

Ankara

⚑ Inside front cover

Visitor Information

✉ Esenboga Havalimani Dis Hatlar Yolcu Çikisi

☎ (0312) 231 55 72

www.ankara.com

This hard-working city of five million people has much to offer visitors. Like most capitals, it has an excellent selection of must-see sights including the Museum of Anatolian Civilizations, the citadel, and the Atatürk Mausoleum, where Turkey's heroic first leader now lies in peace.

Ulus

Most of the capital's museums, parks, and attractions are located in the old suburb of Ulus, which radiates out from Ankara's three-story art deco railroad station. The station itself has a great little **train museum** displaying plans of Turkey's railroad tracks, vintage costumes, whistles, model trains, and Atatürk's own private rail coach. **Gençlik Park,** on the station's doorstep, is a flower-filled home of courting couples, al fresco cafés, a summertime boating lake and an amusement park.

Cumhuriyet Bulvarı, which hems in the park to the north, boasts the excellent **Republic Museum** (*Cumhuriyet Müzesi 22, tel 0312/310 53 61, closed Mon., $*). This grand building was home to Turkey's second parliament and was overhauled in 2008. Audio guides escort visitors around the Atatürk-heavy exhibits. A selection of the leader's hats, including a dapper Panama and a woolly Astrakhan, date from after his nationwide fez ban in 1925, when he sought to sweep away any old empire traditions. The freshly renovated **Ankara Palas** building across the road is a guesthouse for government guests. Its ballroom was used by Atatürk for many a glamorous fête.

Ankara's pre-republic sights all lie across Atatürk Bulvari, just north and south of Hisarparki Caddesi. The towering 15th-century **Haci Bayram Mosque** (*Hükümet Caddesi, Ulus, closed Fri. a.m.*) contains the tomb of Ankara's most famous Muslim saint, and was built on the Roman **Temple of Augustus**, dating back to circa 25–20 B.C. The temple's walls can be peeked at from behind a barrier and are the capital's most important ancient ruin. Ulus' nearby **bazaar** area is a bargain-basement maze of dried

Ankara Railway Station Museum
- ✉ Gar Ulus, 19 Mayis Caddesi, Ankara
- ☎ (0312) 388 56 03
- 🕐 Closed Sun.–Mon.
- 💲 $$

www.mymerhaba.com

Atatürk Mausoleum
- ✉ Anit Caddesi Tandogan
- ☎ (0312) 231 79 75
- 🕐 Museums closed Mon.

EXPERIENCE: Visiting the Atatürk Mausoleum

The *anıtkabir*, or mausoleum, of Turkey's founding father dominates the Ankara skyline. It's also a place for foreign dignitaries to pay their respects to the Turkish state: U.S. President Barack Obama laid a wreath here in 2009. For visitors to Ankara, this monumental memorial and collection of mini-museums is a must-see sight.

Visiting the Site

Security at the mausoleum is tight, so bring your passport with you. Visitors are also expected to maintain a state of reserved respect at all times. Once inside, it's a 15-minute hike through several acres of pristine parkland to a grand, colonnaded piazza. The views over Ankara make this a very photogenic spot. Follow the example of the locals and snap the ceremoniously dressed soldiers on guard—there's no need to ask permission as they're forbidden to speak to visitors!

Hall of Honor

Silence is generally observed on the walk up the steps into the Hall of Honor. Hats should be removed as a mark of respect. The mausoleum rises to 56 feet (17 m), and with its gilded ceilings and dense hush, it's awe inspiring. Atatürk's tomb is hewn from a solid block of stone.

Symbolically, materials from all over the country were used to build the complex as a whole. Although Atatürk died in 1938, work did not begin until 1944, near the end of World War II—a conflict that the former Turkish leader had carefully steered a path of neutrality toward—and was crowned with the Hall of Honor in September 1953.

The Museums

The small museums in a row around the monumental square contain items from the beloved leader's wardrobe, which lend little doubt as to his sartorial elegance. One room has photographic portraits of Atatürk through the ages, another houses his private library, and another his lovingly preserved official cars—two vintage Cadillacs and a Lincoln.

Rahmi M. Koç Museum

✉ Depo Sokak Güzergahı 1, Tarihi Ankjara, Kalesi, Ulus, Ankara

☎ (0312) 309 68 00

🕐 Closed Mon.

💲 $$

www.rmk-museum .org.tr

Museum of Anatolian Civilizations

✉ Gözcü Sokak 2, Ulus, Ankara

☎ (0312) 324 31 60

🕐 Closed Mon.

💲 $$$

fruit, clothes, water pipes, and shoes, all piled high. Follow Hisarparki Caddesi uphill to Ankara's best site, the citadel.

Ankara Citadel & Rahmi M. Koç Museum

Fortified by every occupier from the Romans through the Seljuks, Ankara's towering citadel is now steeped with visions of 1950s Anatolia. Tiered wooden houses, each with its door left wide open to all visitors, hang precipitously over ancient alleys, Roman columns, and Byzantine archways. The centerpiece is a ruined **castle,** which can be explored freely. The entire citadel has been spruced up in recent years, and crafts such as weaving, knitting, metalwork, and pottery are sold on the streets around the Rahmi M. Koç

Angora Wool

Blame the harsh winter climate, but Ankara's animals are mostly white, fluffy, and impossibly cute. The angora cat, angora goat (from which mohair is derived), and angora rabbit all take their name from the Turkish capital's ancient name: Angora. It's the soft, silky hair from the floppy-eared angora rabbit that has spread so widely, and this once-localized breed even reached the United States early last century. Animals are sheared three or four times yearly to produce the feathery wool.

Museum. The museum's collection of vintage cars, bicycles, and engineering equipment—all housed in a 16th-century caravansary (caravan train warehouse)—will elicit a squeal of schoolboy delight from transport enthusiasts and children alike.

Museum of Anatolian Civilizations

This former *bedestan,* or marketplace, sits under ten huge domes and revels in its status as a former "European Museum of the Year" (1997). Its catalog of ancient artifacts is so rich that even the statues and pillars in the tree-dappled gardens would be prize relics in any other museum. Better yet, exhibits follow a timeline, logically illuminating periods of history piece by piece.

The 10,000-year-old Paleolithic collection with its flints, arrowheads, and rudimentary axes is first up. The Bronze Age artifacts were mostly found around Ankara: delicate female sculptures, chalices, statues of wild Anatolian beasts, and exquisite jewelry. Pre-Christian trade with ancient Turkey's trading partners is epitomized by the introduction of cuneiform text and imperial seals—note the clay tablets that are inscribed with ancient trade agreements.

In a final piece of drama, the dimly lit center atrium is lined with life-size friezes of lions, bulls, crocodiles, and warriors excavated from all over Anatolia. Lining the walls are black-and-white photos of huge statues being unearthed; any one of them could be a still from an Indiana Jones movie.

Kızılay & Kavaklıdere

These two upmarket suburbs, strung along the western side of Atatürk Bulvarı, are a shopper's delight. Underground malls, multifloored stores, and street markets are mixed with restaurants and cafés. For the most high-end enclave, take a taxi to **Tunalı Hilmi Caddesi** and wander north to the **Kocatepe Mosque** (Kocatepe Camii, 1967–1987), the city's grandest. About 2.5 miles (4 km) farther south is the **Atakule**, a 410-foot (125 m) observation tower (*kule* means "tower") with a shopping mall at the bottom and revolving restaurant on top: a little overpriced, but great fun.

Cer Modern

While it's hard to outdo Istanbul in the modernity stakes, especially where contemporary art is concerned, Ankara tried to do just that by opening the **Cer Modern** in 2010. This vast modern art space has indoor and outdoor photo galleries, an

A statue of mother goddess, the Museum of Anatolian Civilizations, Ankara

artists' residency program, a sculpture park, and an exhibition hall (Turkey's largest) for temporary shows. All is housed within redeveloped railroad sidings and a locomotive repair factory, just south of Ankara's train station.

Ankara Transport

As the nation's capital, Ankara has excellent transport links to all corners of the country. The most frequently served route is from Turkey's diplomatic capital, Ankara, to its cultural capital, Istanbul. Four comfortable high-speed **trains** (see sidebar p. 39) connect the two cities four times daily. The current 5.5 hour journey will be slashed to just 3 hours in 2013. Several extremely snug night trains ply the route, too. **Buses** take between five and six hours. Hourly **flights** from

Kocatepe Mosque
✉ Kültür Mh., Atatürk Bulvari, Ankara
🕐 Closed Fri. a.m.

Atakule
✉ Cinnah Caddesi, Atakule Sokak, Çankaya
☎ (0312) 438 98 61
💲 $$
www.atakule.com

Cer Modern
✉ Altınsoy Caddesi 3
☎ (0312) 310 00 00
🕐 Closed Mon.
💲 $
www.cermodern.org

Turkish women in an Ankara market take a break from shopping.

Sabiha Göçken Airport

✉ ISG Yönetim, Binasi Pendik, Kurtköy, Istanbul

☎ (0216) 585 50 00

www.sgairport.com

Atatürk Airport

✉ Havalimani Basmüdürlügü, Istanbul

☎ (0212) 463 30 00

www.ataturkairport.com/eng

Esenboga Airport

✉ Havalimani Basmüdürlügü, Esenboga, Ankara

☎ (0312) 398 01 00

www.esenbogaairport.com

Ankara to Istanbul's Atatürk and Sabiha Gökçen airports have a flight time of one hour. A Havas airport bus service runs every 30 minutes from the suburb of Ulus to Esenboga Airport (Ankara).

Aside from the ubiquitous yellow taxis, buses run up and down the main Atatürk Bulvari thoroughfare and connect most of Ankara's sights. Select an Ulus bus to head north, or a Kızılay or Kavaklıdere bus to head south. Ankara's efficient **Metro system** also runs to Ulus, Tandoğan (for the Atatürk Mausoleum), and Aşti for the *otogar* (bus station).

Around Ankara

There are several minor archaeological sites around Ankara, although most of their artifacts now reside in the Museum of Anatolian Civilizations (see pp. 172–173). Furthermore, none of these locations are nearly as impressive as the sprawling ancient Greek and Roman ruins in Istanbul or along Turkey's Aegean coast.

The site that has remained most true to its original form is the ancient Phrygian city of **Górdion** (Gordium), near the town of Polatlı, 58 miles (94 km) southwest of Ankara, by the modern town of Yassıhüyük. Here, several ancient *tumuli* (burial mounds) lie in the dusty steppe. It was here in 333 B.C. that a passing Alexander the Great "undid" the impossibly complex Górdion knot by, in typical Alexander fashion, slicing through it with his sword.

Gölbaşı Lake and dam, 15 miles (24 km) south of Ankara are a popular picnic and walking spot for local residents.

The thermal springs around **Haymana** 40 miles (64 km) south of Ankara have several accommodation options plus mineral-rich waters steaming to the surface. The waters of the Turkish baths of Haymana are volcanically heated and are said to have healing properties to treat arthritis and rheumatism. Weekend health spa visitors come from Ankara.

North of Haymana is the **Fortress of the Infidels** (Gavur Kalesi), a site of Hittite, Phrygian, and Roman settlement. Partially surrounded by ancient walls, the ruins of the ancient city are approached along a paved processional way. At the center of Gavur Kalesi is a large underground Hittite tomb with a vaulted ceiling. Look out for rock carvings dating from the Hittites.

The quiet appearance of the market town of **Beypazari** belies its former importance. It was the city of Anastasiopolis in the time of the Byzantine Empire and grew along the Silk Road from Constantinople to Baghdad. Today, Beypazari is a popular destination for day-trippers from Ankara, some 60 miles (100 km) to the east. View Beypazari from the top of rocky Hirdirlik hill or walk the cobbled streets of the old town between period Ottoman Empire buildings. So authentic is the historic vision that Turkish moviemakers often use the ancient streets as a film location. The food market is a colorful place to wander through and the ideal spot to buy a local delicacy, *sucuk,* a sticky walnut and fruit candy.

Beypazari is famous for its carrots. Enterprising citizens make carrot-flavored ice cream, and the vegetables even feature in the lively annual festival held in early June, showcasing local crafts, Beypazari's old wooden houses, and the hearty cuisine of the district.

Just north of Beypazari is the **Inözü Valley,** a favorite short excursion from the town. The valley is a dramatic, rocky, steep-sided canyon whose walls are lined with strangely shaped rocks that have been eroded by the stream flowing through the gorge. Caves penetrate the cliff face, and there are the remains of churches and tombs carved into the rock to explore. With shady vegetation in places, the valley is an ideal place for a leisurely walk and a picnic. ∎

Górdion Archaeological Site

⊠ Yassıhüyük

sites.museum.upenn .edu/gordion

Fortress of the Infidels

⊠ Gavur Kalesi, Haymana

$ $

Why Move Turkey's Capital?

By moving the capital from Istanbul to Ankara in 1923, Atatürk took Turkey on another step toward modernization. As well as changing the Turkish alphabet from the Arabic to Latin script, he believed that constructing a new European-style capital would prove to the world that the new Turkish Republic was both bold and forward thinking. Strategically, the move was a smart one. Like Constantine the Great, who relocated his imperial capital from Rome to Constantinople 1,700 years earlier, Atatürk's Ankara was physically detached from historic elites or power brokers back in Istanbul. And by placing the capital of the nascent republic in the center of the land, Turkey's rulers could keep a watchful eye over the young country and its borders.

western turkey

Troy & Gallipoli 178-191 ■ **Ephesus & Roman Turkey** 192-205
The Turquoise Coast 206-219 ■ **Cappadocia** 220-231

The surging Dardanelles strait, haunting Gallipoli Peninsula, and the nearby archaeological site of Troy—a history lover's paradise

Troy & Gallipoli

Introduction & Map 180-181

Gallipoli 182-185

Experience: Exploring Gallipoli's Sites & Memorials 183

Troy, Çanakkale, & Bozcaada 186-190

Experience: Exploring Bozcaada Island 189

Experience: Wine-tasting on Bozcaada 191

Hotels & Restaurants 255-256

Anzac Cove, peaceful and quiet today, was the scene of intense carnage during the 1915 Allied invasion of Gallipoli.

Troy & Gallipoli

Like the Bosporus 125 miles (200 km) to its northeast, the Dardanelles strait (38 miles/60 km) forms part of the passage between the Black Sea and the Mediterranean. The waterway's surface current flows southward but has a teeming undercurrent that pushes in the opposite direction—a phenomenon that armies advancing in ships on ancient Troy and on 20th-century Gallipoli both had to contend with.

Also like the Bosporus, the Dardanelles strait forms a strategic split between Europe and Asia and has witnessed the passage, and often humiliation, of several empires.

The Persian king Xerxes I had a pontoon bridge constructed over the channel—known in antiquity as the Hellespont—in 482 B.C. on his way to battle the Greeks. When a storm destroyed his handiwork, he maniacally decreed the Dardanelles be whipped in punishment. Xerxes' campaign was not without success nonetheless, and included a victory at the Battle of Thermopylae in 480 B.C., in spite of the now legendary suicidal last stand of 300 Spartans there. However, the Dardanelles witnessed a reversal in regional power in 334 B.C., when Greek conqueror Alexander the Great crossed with his army in the other direction on his way to give the Persians a taste of their own medicine.

Fast-forward to World War I, when an Anglo-French flotilla tried to push through the Dardanelles to reach Istanbul. The Allied plan in March 1915 was to bombard the Turkish capital by sea, delivering a hammer blow to the teetering Ottoman Empire and knocking it out of World War I. But the attack was a failure: Naval retreat was followed soon after by a disastrous land invasion of the nearby Gallipoli Peninsula. A century later, this pastoral peninsula is set with orchards, forests, and beaches, with few scars of battle aside from the scores of memorials to the fallen.

Just south of here, another titanic battle took place a thousand years earlier. The Trojan War—surely the only conflict to involve a wooden horse with 30 soldiers hidden inside—featured an historical cast that included Odysseus, Agamemnon, Achilles, and Helen. Declared a UNESCO World Heritage site in 1998, the ruins of Troy are actually those of several empires, rebuilt and destroyed by fire, earthquake, and battle for three millennia. Ironically, the controversial 19th-century German explorer, Heinrich Schliemann, who rediscovered the site, ended up robbing the ruins blind.

Beyond the Battlefields

And for those who've overdosed on history, Bozcaada makes the perfect antidote. On a

---

NOT TO BE MISSED:

Driving or hiking the bucolic battlefields of the Gallipoli Peninsula 182-184

Soldiers' heartrending letters in the Kabatepe War Museum 185

Three thousand years of ruins at Troy 186-187

Strolling or sipping a glass of çay on Çanakkale's waterfront promenade 187-188

Renting a bike and cycling around Bozcaada, Turkey's wine island 189

Sampling half a dozen red wines on Bozcaada at one of the island's renowned wineries 191

warm Aegean Sea dotted with neighboring Greek islands, it offers beaches, vineyards, innovative cuisine, and boutique accommodations; everything, in fact, to help one forget about the swords, arrows, cannon, and gunboats of the warfare millennia before.

One of the few mainland settlements in this part of Turkey is the lively port of Çanakkale. Along with providing a base from which to explore these sites, it has its own attractions, from medieval castles and war museums to shops displaying its traditional homemade pottery. From here, ferries run across the Dardanelles from the Ezine Yükyeri Wharf to the Gallipoli Peninsula, Gökçeada, and Bozcaada, while frequent *dolmuş* services run south to Troy, Assos, and Alexandreia. Çanakkale's helpful tourist bureau on the main square offers maps of the battlefield sites, Trojan history leaflets, ferry timetables, and much else. ■

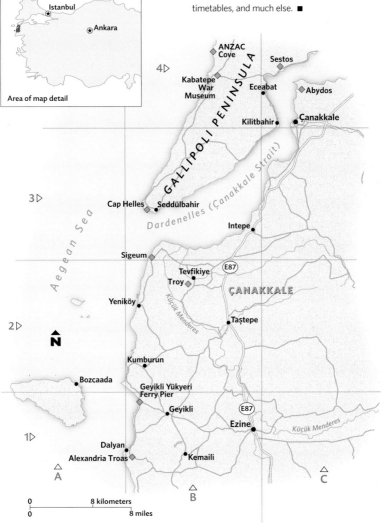

Istanbul
Ankara
Area of map detail

ANZAC Cove
4▷
Kabatepe War Museum
Sestos
Eceabat
Abydos
GALLIPOLI PENINSULA
Kilitbahir
Çanakkale
3▷
Cap Helles
Seddülbahir
Dardenelles (Çanakkale Strait)
Intepe
Aegean Sea
Sigeum
Tevfikiye
E87
Troy
ÇANAKKALE
Yeniköy
Küçük Menderes
Taştepe
2▷
N
Kumburun
Bozcaada
Geyikli Yükyeri Ferry Pier
Geyikli
E87
Ezine
Küçük Menderes
1▷
Dalyan
Alexandria Troas
Kemaili
△
A
△
B
△
C

0   8 kilometers
0   8 miles

Gallipoli

The Gallipoli Peninsula, which juts 40 miles (64 km) into the Aegean Sea, is bucolic. Wildflowers take over from the winter frosts each spring as orchards and fishing villages bounce back to life. In summer, Turkish tourists delight at the often deserted beaches, eventually replaced by autumn shades along the peninsula's ridge of forests. The sadder side of Gallipoli is demonstrated by the 31 war cemeteries found here.

Many shoreline war cemeteries dot the Gallipoli Peninsula.

Gallipoli

 181 B4

Visitor Information

✉ Iskele Meydani 6, Çanakkale

☎ (0286) 217 11 87

The name Gallipoli means "beautiful city"—a particular irony considering the death and misery the place has seen. A century ago, tens of thousands of soldiers from all corners of the world lost their lives at Gallipoli. The legacy of the battle here, one of World War I's bloodiest, is well maintained with a set of very poignant memorials dedicated to the heroes of the nine-month campaign.

Battlefields

The 70,000-strong Mediterranean Expeditionary Force that attempted to seize the Gallipoli Peninsula was a multinational one. It consisted primarily of British, Australian, and New Zealand troops. Additional contingents included Irish, Indian, Gurkha, Senegalese, and Jewish regiments from Palestine, backed up by a significant French naval and infantry force. The opposing

INSIDER TIP:

To experience the spirit of Gallipoli, visit on April 25, Anzac Day, when thousands of New Zealanders and Australians go to pay their respects.

—TOM JACKSON
National Geographic contributor

defenders were led by German commander Otto Liman von Sanders, with a Turkish division headed by Mustafa Kemal Atatürk, who was familiar with the local topography from an earlier Balkan campaign.

After a diversionary attack by the French navy on the Turkey mainland, the mighty Allied force landed on the peninsula at dawn on April 25, 1915. It was grouped in two main areas: Cap Helles on the southern tip, and Anzac Cove and Suvla Bay, around 20 miles (32 km) north, on Gallipoli's western edge.

But the campaign's planning was terribly disorganized. Continual mismanagement, combined with a supposed lack of concern by Allied officers for their troops arguably doomed the landings from the start. It was widely presumed that the Turks would crumble in the face of attack. But, unexpectedly, they fought back with tenacity, particularly those on the front under Atatürk's personal command. As trench warfare set in, unhygienic conditions and heat claimed as many lives as the sniping defenders.

At **Anzac Cove** and **Sulva Bay,** the story was even more tragic. Thanks to a drifting marker

---

EXPERIENCE: Exploring Gallipoli's Sites & Memorials

With sturdy shoes and a map—preferably the Commonwealth War Graves Commission map available from Çanakkale's tourist bureau (see p. 187)—you can see many of the Gallipoli frontlines on foot. Before you set off from the Gallipoli port of Eceabat *(ferries run from Çanakkale every hour 7 a.m.–12 a.m., every 30 mins. in summer, tel 0286/814 10 33)*, get the cell-phone number of a local taxi driver, should the going get too tough. Then jump on a *dolmuş* to the Kabatepe War Museum (see p. 185). From here, the road runs down to the Allied landing beaches. Anzac Cove is some 2 miles (3 km) along the shore.

Signposts lead from Anzac Cove (see pp. 183–184) along to the Shrapnel Valley and Shell Green cemeteries, and uphill to the Australian Lone Pine Memorial. Continue north along the former frontlines to more cemeteries and the New Zealand War Memorial at Chunuk Bair, or walk south for 3 miles (4.5 km) back to the Kabatepe War Museum.

If you don't want to walk, to take in the most of the sights—including the Kabatepe museum, Anzac Cove, Cap Helles, and the national war memorials—you'll need your own wheels, or to join a guided tour. In Istanbul, **Travel Planet** *(tel 0212/511 48 69, www.traveltoplanet.com)* and **Trooper Tours** *(tel 0212/516 90 24, www.troopertours.com)* run excursions. In Çanakkale, try **Hassle Free Tours** *(tel 0286/213 59 69, www.nzachouse.com).*

buoy, the predominantly Australian and New Zealand force, referred to as the Anzac corps, landed not on the long, sandy Kabatepe beach as planned, but 1.5 miles (2 km) north, against a muddy cliff face. This small bay, now officially renamed Anzac Cove by the Turkish government, was the scene of horrific losses as the Allies fought the defenders to an eventual standstill just half a mile (1 km) inland.

War Cemeteries

There are 21 cemeteries containing some 22,000 graves placed along the former Anzac frontline (there are 10 more on other parts of the peninsula). Most of them face the sea and are landscaped with trees and flowers. Historical markers detail the individual battles, from **Shrapnel Valley** and **Shell Green cemeteries** on the coast road, to **The Nek** (where soldiers of the famous cavalry charge depicted in Australian director Peter Weir's film *Gallipoli* are buried), **Quinn's Post,** and **Johnston's Jolly** farther inland. The Australian War Memorial at **Lone Pine** cemetery—perched on a plateau at the top of Victoria Gully and

A Turkish memorial on the Gallipoli Peninsula shows a Turkish infantry soldier—a "Mehmet" —advancing on the enemy, known by the Turks as "Johnnies."

named after the lone pine tree on the site that was cut down by Turkish soldiers to cover their trenches—and the New Zealand memorial at **Chunuk Bair cemetery** are popular pilgrimage sites for travelers from those two nations.

The majority of the British and French cemeteries lie near **Cap Helles.** These include the **V Beach cemetery,** located on the site of a landing beach between Cap Helles and the village of Seddülbahir, where disembarking troops suffered 70 percent casualty rates on the first day of the conflict.

Memorials: The **Helles Memorial,** located on the very tip of the Gallipoli Peninsula, is dedicated to the 18,985 British, 248 Australian, and 1,530 Indian servicemen who fell in the Gallipoli Campaign and have no known grave or who were lost at sea. The immense **Turkish war memorial** is also here, on the southern tip of the peninsula at Cap Helles; it commemorates the estimated 66,000 Turkish soldiers who lost their lives defending Gallipoli—some put the losses nearer 80,000. Most organized tours do not cover Cap Helles. You can hire a tour guide to take you or go by your own (or rented) transport to get there. For car rentals, try **Gezgin Oto** (Kemalpasa Mahallesi, Tekke Sokak 2, Çanakkale, tel 0286/212 83 92) or **Rumeli Oto** (tel 0286/ 213 29 42), both located in Çanakkale.

Despite the tens of thousands of Turkish lives lost at Gallipoli,

WWI Battles for the Dardanelles

Next to Çanakkale's naval museum (see pp. 188–189) is a replica of the Ottoman navy's minelaying warship *Nusrat (www .nusratmayingemisi.com)*. The vessel may seem tiny, but its mark on history is indelible. Under Winston Churchill's instruction (then British First Lord of the Admiralty) in February 1915, a naval attack was launched on the Dardanelles, hoping to access Istanbul (capital of the Ottoman Empire)—an ally of Germany. However, as the Allied navy cleared the Dardanelles of mines by day in early March 1915, the plucky *Nusrat* surreptitiously laid them back at night, often in fog, under enemy fire, and without radar.

Little surprise, then, that on March 18, when the Allied fleet pushed confidently through the strait on its way to level Istanbul, H.M.S. *Ocean*, H.M.S. *Irresistible*, and the French battleship *Bouvet* were quickly lost, while another quarter of the flotilla was seriously damaged, mostly by mines but also by cannon fire from the shore. These naval losses were deemed unacceptable by the Anglo-French high command and a retreat was ordered.

Some would call the ensuing decision to secure the Dardanelles by land invasion tenacious; the less charitable would call it foolhardy. It took six weeks to assemble an infantry force, which included a newly created ANZAC corps of Australian and New Zealand troops. These volunteers were training in Egypt before they were launched on the Western Front between France, Belgium, and Germany. By the time the soldiers ran ashore on April 25, 1915, the Turks— along with their German advisers—had secured the peninsula with barbed wire and machine-gun nests perched on high ground overlooking the beaches, and were ready for battle.

---

local people are proud to welcome any foreign visitor who comes to pay respects. Their sympathetic attitude is summed up by a 1934 quote from Atatürk, once a Gallipoli commander and by then the leader of the Turkish nation. His words are set in stone near Anzac Cove:

"Those heroes that shed their blood and lost their lives . . . you are now lying in the soil of a friendly country. Therefore rest in peace. There is no difference between the Johnnies and the Mehmets to us, where they lie side by side.

"You, the mothers, who sent their sons from far away countries . . . wipe away your tears. Your sons are now lying in our bosom and are in peace. After having lost their lives on this land they have become our sons as well."

Kabatepe War Museum

This must-see history museum (Kabatepe Müzesi, also known as the Gallipoli War Museum) in the grounds of the **Gallipoli Historic National Park,** contains hundreds of artifacts from the Gallipoli conflict, from uniforms, weapons, and ammunition to more ghoulish exhibits, such as the skull of a Turkish soldier with the bullet hole in it. The most moving items here are eyewitness accounts, letters sent home, and portraits of grinning soldiers on their way to the front. The diagrams of the battlefield sites, plus the views to the Anzac beaches and Lone Pine Memorial on the hill, are useful for understanding the layout of the conflict. ■

Kabatepe War Museum

✉ Gallipoli Historic National Park

☎ (0286) 814 12 97

🕐 Closed Mon.

💲 $

www.canakkale.gov.tr

Troy, Çanakkale, & Bozcaada

A good dose of imagination is necessary when visiting the ancient city of Troy. Unlike the Roman ruins in western Turkey, with their soaring columns and amphitheaters seating thousands, Troy is much older, and what remains has been scarred by fires, earthquakes, and fierce battles. Nearby is Çanakkale—home to 15th-century castles, interesting museums, and homemade ceramics—and the beaches and vineyards of Bozcaada Island.

The wooden horse at Troy recalls the famous tale from the Trojan War.

Troy

The ruins of Troy, set over acres of leafy pasture, are key to understanding ancient Western history, not least the calamitous Trojan War.

Having been permanently occupied from around 3000 B.C. until the fourth century A.D., Troy is actually nine cities piled on top of one another. Remains from each period (referred to as Troy I to Troy IX) are coupled with information boards placed around the several acres of grounds. These clearly explain the period and purpose

of each stone, wall, or pillar. The site is further brought to life by an excavation information center, with vivid reconstructions and detailed descriptions of the city. Kids will love the life-size mock-up of the **Trojan Horse:** Climb into the horse's belly for a photo.

Following the self-guided tour of the ruins past stone archways, columns, an amphitheater, and trees is good fun. The most impressive ruin is perhaps the carved marble **Temple of Athena,** which was built upon the remains of several other temples around

The ancient site of Troy is close to Çanakkale, near a village called Tevfikiye. The wooden Trojan horse from the 2004 movie *Troy* is exhibited in Çanakkale and has become the city's symbol.

— KEMAL NURYADIN
Executive Editor, National Geographic Turkey

the first century A.D. Its original layout can be traced on the ground by the remains of the foundations.

The walls dating from Troy VII

ring much of the site, and make it easy to imagine Troy as a fortified citadel, as most important settlements were in those war-torn days. The redbrick remains of the **Megaron building**—a covered palatial hall dating from the early Bronze Age (ca 3000 B.C.)—plus the natural spring set in a tranquil area dotted with park benches are both of particular interest.

The archaeological site of Troy is easily accessed by minibus from Çanakkale, a town 20 miles (32 km) north of Troy.

Çanakkale

Not only does Çanakkale make a great base midway between Gallipoli and Troy, but it is also of interest to travelers in its own

Troy
- Teşikiye Köyü Truva, Çanakkale
- (0286) 283 05 36
- $$$$

Çanakkale
- 181 C4

Visitor Information
- Iskele Meydani, 67, Çanakkale
- (0286) 217 11 87

Interpreting Troy

It may be entertaining to see Brad Pitt as Achilles parading around in a skirt, but if you're keen to truly understand Troy, the eponymous 2004 movie probably isn't the best place to start. In actuality, much of what we know about the settlement today—and particularly the ten-year-long siege of the city during the Trojan War—is derived from Homer's epic poem, *The Iliad.* (His other great work, *The Odyssey,* traces the eventful journey back home of Odysseus, one of the Greek victors at Troy.)

Greek historians, including the great Herodotus (ca 484 B.C.–425 B.C.), describe the Homeric city as existing in the 13th century B.C. In around 333 B.C., Alexander the Great visited Troy to pay homage to the tomb of Achilles, whom he presumptuously claimed as an ancestor. The tale of Troy was jazzed up by Virgil during the first century B.C. in his wordy

epic, *The Aeneid,* allegedly to add a Roman dimension to this Greek legend.

In contemporary times, a nod must be given to the British amateur archaeologist Frank Calvert (1828–1908), who began excavations at Hisarlik (Troy), and then to German archaeologist Heinrich Schliemann (see sidebar p. 188) for continuing his work and rediscovering the site. However, it was the excavations from 1932 to 1938 by University of Cincinnati professor Carl Blegen (1887–1971) that really shed light on the timeline of different settlements at Troy. In 1988, German archaeologist Manfred Korfmann (1942–2005)—again with the University of Cincinnati's backing—was given license to excavate the site. His finely illustrated book *Troia* is the most modern work on the ruins currently available. His passion for Troy was rewarded with Turkish citizenship in 2004.

The Real Heinrich Schliemann

German-born businessman Heinrich Schliemann (1822–1890) dedicated his life to the discovery and excavation of Troy. He even called his two children Andromache and Agamemnon in honor of figures from the Trojan War, while his servants were renamed after Greek mythological characters.

But his obsessive nature, combined with a lack of formal archaeological training, has ever tarnished his reputation. Schliemann's excavations at Troy were audaciously haphazard, with workmen (up to 150 employed daily) slicing down through the stratified periods of remains.

The gross pilfering of artifacts also colored his name. Following an early dig, a relief of the sun god, Apollo, ended up in Schliemann's garden, despite a promise to share all finds with the Ottoman government. His most famous haul was Priam's Treasure: millennia-old gold bottles, silver vases, and fine jewelry, which his young Greek wife models in a famous photograph. These treasures were smuggled to Germany and then into Berlin's Imperial Museum. The Soviet Union's Red Army in turn captured the hoard in 1945, and it now resides in Moscow's Pushkin Museum.

Naval Museum

- ✉ Fevzipasa Mahallesi, Çimenlik Sokak,
- ☎ (0286) 213 17 30
- 🕐 Closed Mon, Thurs. (park open daily)
- 💲 $

right thanks to its pottery. Visitors will find colorful ceramics on sale all over town. It's worth seeking out **Fetvane Sokak** one block back from the seafront—once a street lined with imposing mansions, it's now a tidy avenue dotted with cafés and bookshops. The best place to purchase gifts is in the **Aynalı Bazaar,** a covered market four or five blocks farther south again.

Naval Museum (Deniz Müzesi): The main attraction of the Çanakkale Strait Command Naval Museum (Deniz Müzesi) is the replica of the *Nusrat* minelayer (see sidebar p. 185), whose work re-laying bombs in the Dardanelles strait caused such huge losses on that fateful day in March 1915. However, the park around the museum complex is a great place for a stroll by the shores of the Dardanelles. Home to scores of mines, torpedoes, and cannon—the likes of which

defeated the British, French, and ANZAC forces in World War I—the park is an open-air museum in its own right.

It's well worth paying for access to the Gallipoli gallery, located within an old wooden mansion in the park, as diagrams, weapons, army uniforms, and captured provisions tell the story of Gallipoli from a Turkish perspective. This angle is significant, as these battles through 1915 gave rise to the legend of Atatürk, the key commander of the Ottoman forces, who created the modern state of Turkey in 1923.

The same ticket grants access to **Çimenlik Castle,** also on the museum grounds and the edifice that lends Çanakkale its turreted logo. Mehmet the Conqueror constructed this mammoth defensive fortress in 1461 along with the Kilitbahir castle across the strait, thus controlling the southern approach to Istanbul. Sultan Süleyman the Magnificent enhanced the castle further. Once inside, note the network of ramps along the outer walls enabling ordnance to be swiftly pushed up to the ramparts when needed. The main feature of the courtyard is a massive fortified keep and drawbridge, which would have rendered the castle almost impregnable. Çanakkale's **Military Museum** (Askeri Müzesi) now occupies the interior of Çimenlik castle and is dedicated to Turkish history and the Gallipoli Campaign. Greeting you at the start of your visit are the holes in the fortress walls, made during the Gallipoli Campaign, and extracts from nearby battleground memorials.

Archaeology Across Millennia: Çanakkale's **Archaeology Museum** (Arkeoloji Müzesi) is spread across five halls. Among other exhibits, Hall 1 contains ancient ceramics and the locations of ancient settlements in the area on a wall-hung board; Hall 2 boasts Çanakkale's oldest collections, including Troy artworks, Stone Age weapons, fossils, and prehistoric ruins; Hall 3 offers Hellenistic art, including some excavated at Bozcaada; Hall 4 contains excavated bronze pieces, textiles, jewelry, and more, found at the Dardanus

Tumulus, just south of Çanakkale. Finally, Hall 5 displays art, coins, and glass articles from Assos (Behramkale, 47 miles/75 km south of Çanakkale) and Gülpınar (Apollon Smintheion Holy Area, 60 miles/96 km southwest of Çanakkale). Various sarcophagi and large sculptures are dotted throughout the museum gardens.

Bozcaada

The small island of Bozcaada (also known as Tenedos) is only 15 square miles (39 sq km) in area and has a population of just 2,500. Like the Greek islands of

Military Museum
✉ Çimenlik Sokak
☎ (0286) 213 17 30
🕐 Closed Mon., Thurs.
💲 $

Archaeology Museum
✉ Barbaros Mahallesi, 100 Yıl Caddesi
☎ (0286) 217 65 65
🕐 Closed Mon.
💲 $

Riding through the pretty island town of Bozcaada

thousands of years of attacks from Romans, Venetians, Genoese, and imperial Russians is a magnificent castle and a woefully low population, even given the island's size. Recent tussles between Greece and Turkey made the island off-limits to foreigners until the mid-1990s when the diplomatic temperature cooled, thus preserving its tranquil coastline for generations to come.

Bozcaada Castle (*$*) draws the eye of each new arrival. Bigger than might be expected for such a small town, this castle is actually one of the best preserved in all of Turkey. By night it's illuminated, forming a backdrop to al fresco dinners along the harbor. The grand fortifications are testament to the island's frontline seat in Mediterranean history, although it has been rejigged and augmented many times; its current incarnation dates from 1815. Inside are tombstones, pillars, amphorae, and stunning views out to sea.

Bozcaada town is still very "undiscovered" and overseas visitors remain a novelty. A few liberal Istanbullus have added shabby-chic bars and boutiques and the odd hip guesthouse to the row of superb seafood restaurants around the main square. The island's action centers around this piazza, which plays host to cafés, and several cobbled streets each leading off into the backstreets of the tiny town. The square's colorful **morning market** overflows with fresh produce, olive oil, seafood, flowers, and delicious preserves, including tomato jam—a fruity speciality only available on this island. Look for the "Salto" sign to find it. ■

Bozcaada Castle

✉ Bozcaada Harbor

$ $

Lesbos and Limnos that shimmer just a few miles across the water, this herb-scented rock is famed for its fine seafood (for proof, just take a peek at any of its restaurants' display cabinets). Yet it differs from its Greek neighbors in that there's no airport, no crowds, and no euro currency, the last ensuring the island is a cut-price Eden, lapped by limpid waters.

History along this stretch of the Mediterranean has long been turbulent. And Bozcaada, strategically placed at the foot of the Dardanelles, has only recently come up smelling of roses (or rather of grapes). The local legacy of

EXPERIENCE: Wine-tasting on Bozcaada

If there's one thing those who enjoy a glass of *sarap* (wine) shouldn't neglect on a visit to Bozcaada Island, it's tasting the delectable local wines. Wine production has been intrinsic to life here for five long millennia, and Bozcaada's excellent vintages have been famous for centuries. With four major wine producers offering wine tastings and tours, as well as a Vintage Festival in June, visitors are spoiled for choice.

What all of the island's invaders have had in common was a strong appreciation for Bozcaada's wine. Viticulture is a 5,000-year-old tradition here, and today the island is carpeted with hundreds of tiny vineyards. Bozcaada supplies about 10 percent of Turkey's wine, and the scores of varieties on offer promise to befuddle even the most ardent wine buff, and that's even before drinking any! Best of all, the wine here is always both reasonably priced and absolutely delicious.

A favorite producer—and one of the island's largest wineries, producing 23 different wines of their own— is **Talay** (*Lale Sokak 5, tel 0286/697 80 80, www.talay .com.tr*). It has an excellent store and tasting salon in the village, where samples of six to eight bottles are laid out with local cheeses and fruit. Look out for the traditional wines of **Yunatçılar Camlibag** (*Cumhuriyet Mahallesi, Emniyet Sokak, 24, tel 0286/697 80 55*) and the newer, more boutique producer, **Corvus** (*Tuzburnu Mevkii, tel 0286/697 58 80, www.corvus.com.tr*), in restaurants around town. The fourth major producer on the island is **Gülerada** (*Tekirbahçe Mevkii, tel 0286/ 697 01 77, www.gulerada .com*).

During harvest time, Talay runs the "Tasting Wine Tour" and the "Vintage Tour." During these tours, you can observe the stages the grapes have to go through on their way to becoming wine or even help the workers in the vineyards.

Wines to seek out at the Bozcaada wineries include white wines made from the crisp Vasilaki and sweet Çavus grapes, and the hefty red wines made from the Karasakiz, Karalahna, and Kuntra grapes.

Try to visit Bozcaada during the annual three-day **Vintage Festival,** usually in the last weekend of June. Concerts of Gypsy music, with dancing, and classical music are held amid a lot of wine tasting, and general merriment. There is also a contest for the tastiest sweet white grape found on the island.

Local children proudly show off the grape harvest in a vineyard in Bozcaada.

Golden beaches, water sports, and ancient temples—a sunny slice of western Turkey

Ephesus & Roman Turkey

Introduction & Map   194–195

Çeşme Peninsula   196–197

Experience: Water Sports in Alaçatı   197

Ephesus & Around   198–201

Experience: Visiting Ephesus   199

Experience: Splashing Around   201

Feature: Hellenistic & Roman Turkey   202–203

Pamukkale & Hierapolis   204–205

Experience: Visiting Cleopatra's Pool   205

Hotels & Restaurants   256–257

An ancient sculpted head from the Sebastion at Aphrodisias

Ephesus & Roman Turkey

Like seeds flung over a vast and fertile field, ancient Greek and Roman settlements fleck western Turkey. On the coast, İzmir is the region's largest city. Here, ethnic Greeks, Italians, and Levantines mix with eastern Anatolian immigrants, creating a multicultural community. Nearby, the adjacent Çeşme Peninsula, ringed with golden beaches, pokes 50 miles (85 km) westward into the Aegean Sea.

One of Ephesus' best sights is the ruins of the Library of Celsus, with a monumental facade.

This region is home to Turkey's most famous ancient city—Ephesus was founded around 1000 B.C., although shifting sea levels mean the archaeological site's ruins date from the fourth century B.C. The city boasted the Temple of Artemis, one of the Seven Wonders of the Ancient World, and was the Aegean's most important port. Under Roman rule, glorious buildings were constructed, such as the Library of Celsus, and Ephesus was cultivated as a regional capital. The settlement was also an early adopter of Christianity, and hosted St. Paul and St. John the Evangelist (and some say the Virgin Mary) during the first century A.D.

The remains of other ancient cities radiate outward from Ephesus in all directions: hilltop Priene, Miletus with its nearby temple at Didyma, Pergamum, Laodicea, and Aphrodisias. Farther east, much of the vast ruins of Hierapolis are untouched. Hierapolis sits atop Pamukkale's travertine thermal pools. From afar, this unusual natural phenomenon could be easily mistaken for snowcapped cliffs—but the brilliant white glow is where any likeness ends. Surely one of the country's most alluring sights, Pamukkale was created by a network of 17 mineral springs, which bubbled up from the earth and deposited the soft, chalky travertine in layers.

Into the Present

Although the region's colorful history is visible at every turn, there is simply heaps to do if you're not allured by such an abundance of sarcophagi and ruins. The vibrancy of İzmir and the Çeşme Peninsula is mirrored in the bustling towns of Selçuk and Şirince, close to Ephesus. Trips to the Greek islands are a possibility, as are country walks and several aquatic theme parks. Water sports are popular all along the coast, and a World Kiteboard Championship is held in Alaçatı every summer.

Foodies take note: Seafood along the coast is fantastic, as is *tulum peyniri,* a white İzmir cheese. Inland, vines have been cultivated on these former Roman lands for centuries—look out for Şirince's fruit wine, too. The most popular snack is the ubiquitous *gözleme,* a griddled pastry filled with spinach, feta, or potatoes. ■

NOT TO BE MISSED:

Spending a sunny afternoon at one of Altınkum's beaches **197**

Kite- or windsurfing in Alaçatı, one of Turkey's premier spots for water sports **197**

Exploring the ancient ruins of Ephesus, including the town's stunning terraced houses **198–200**

Losing the crowds at the little-visited archaeological sites of Aphrodisias or Priene **202–203**

The sculpted Medusa head at Didyma **203**

Watching the sun set over Pamukkale's white travertine terraces and mineral pools **204**

A swim around the ancient ruins in the warm waters of Hierapolis' Cleopatra's Pool **205**

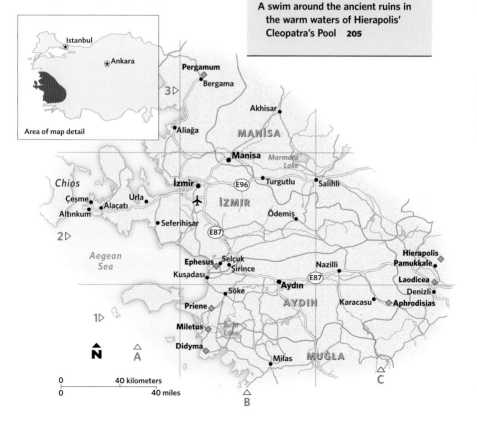

Çeşme Peninsula

Situated along Turkey's Aegean coast, west of İzmir, the Çeşme Peninsula offers golden sands and water sports, ancient ruins, quality dining, and local charm. Visitors approaching from the busy, historic port city of İzmir, will proceed past olive groves and rocky outcrops, and lust after the azure waters of the Aegean Sea. Whether you are a beach lover, keen historian, or simply want to relax, the Çeşme Peninsula caters to all.

Kitesurfing is becoming a popular water sport in Alaçatı.

İzmir

⚑ 195 B2

Visitor Information

✉ Akdeniz Mahallesi 1344 Sokak 2 Pasaport, İzmir

☎ (0232) 483 62 16

www.tourism turkey.org

İzmir

İzmir is Turkey's third most populous city and the gateway to the Çeşme Peninsula. Its architectural mix of Ottoman stone and art nouveau swirls reflect the city's colorful past as a world-renowned trading city, where even the average inhabitant could command three or four languages. Known as Smyrna until 1930, İzmir is still a bastion of multiethnic diversity, despite being the site of huge battles between Greeks and Turks nearly a century ago. The

city offers a handful of interesting museums and a buzzing nightlife, particularly in the northern neighborhood of Alsancak. Don't miss the excavated Roman artifacts at İzmir's **Archaeology Museum** (Arkeoloji Müzesi), some of which were found at the city's agora, lying in the center of İzmir.

Çeşme

Perched on the peninsula's tip, Çeşme is a relaxed, seaside resort. A wide promenade faces the Greek island of Chios, to which Erturk Lines provides daily

INSIDER TIP:

Windsurfers should not bypass Alaçatı, with its consistent winds and crystal clear waters.

— KEMAL NURYADIN
Executive Editor, National Geographic Turkey

ferries (*Beyazit Cad. 6–7. Çeşme-İzmir, tel 0232/712 67 68, www.erturk.com.tr*). A 16th-century castle, which houses the superb **Çeşme Archaeology Museum** (Çeşme Müzesi), sits at the town's heart. Originally a gun museum, it now houses artifacts excavated at Ildiri. Exhibits include sculptures, coins, and amphorae. Çeşme makes a good base for exploring the peninsula and beyond. Weekly ferries also connect the town with Ancona in Italy from May through October.

Alaçatı

Just over 5 miles (9 km) southeast of Çeşme, this picturesque village is rapidly becoming summertime's Istanbul-on-sea. Alaçatı's narrow, cobblestone streets are lined with perfectly restored pale stone houses and some top-quality restaurants. It's an enchanting place to eat, snooze, and even surf your way through a long weekend—indeed, the World Kiteboard Championship is held here. Most of the town's guesthouses dish up cheesey *gözleme* pastries for breakfast within their walled gardens and, while Alaçatı's vibrant nightlife attracts a young,

affluent crowd, others are drawn by the ruins of the Ionian city of **Ildiri** (ancient Erythrai), built in the 11th century B.C., and located within the borders of Alaçatı.

Altınkum

A few miles south of Çeşme, the coastal stretch known as Altınkum ("golden sand") is tucked into the peninsula's southwest corner, rocky outcrops and silky sand. With umbrella-shaded bars and plenty of towel space, the beaches here are more than ideal. Note that chilly currents mean the water remains bracingly cool most of the summer. *Dolmuş* services run to and from Çeşme, or you can hire a scooter for the day. ■

İzmir Archaeology Museum

✉ Bahri Baba Park, İzmir

☎ (0232) 484 83 24

🕐 Closed Mon.

💲 $

Çeşme

🅰 195 A2

Visitor Information

✉ Kale Sokak No 1

☎ (0232) 484 21 48

Çeşme Archaeology Museum

✉ İnkılap Caddesi, Çeşme

☎ (0232) 712 66 09

🕐 Closed Mon.

💲 $

EXPERIENCE:
Water Sports in Alaçatı

With proper training, kitesurfing is a safe and thrilling sport. Kite-Turkey (*Progressive Boardsports, Myga Surf City, Çark Yolu 39, Alaçatı, tel 0538/381 56 86, www.kite-turkey.com*) offers courses for beginners and experts alike and also has a center in Urla, 18.5 miles (30 km) east of Alaçatı.

Alaçatı's bay is ideal for windsurfing, particularly around its sheltered and shallow northwestern corner. Both Myga Surf City (*Çark Mevkii, 8011 Sokak 4, Alaçatı, tel 0232/716 64 68, www.myga.com.tr*) and Alaçatı Surf Paradise Club (*1 Alaçatı Liman Mevkii, Alaçatı, tel 0232/716 66 11, www.alacati.info/ecms*) offer lessons, courses, board rentals, and storage.

Alaçatı's water sports centers are all located around 2 miles (3 km) south of the town center. Frequent *dolmuş* services connect the two areas, or you can stay nearby at one of the bay's many hotels.

Ephesus & Around

Outside of Istanbul's historical sights, the ruins of ancient Ephesus attract the highest number of Turkey's visitors. Just 2 miles (3 km) west of Selçuk and 52 miles (84 km) south of İzmir, the site dates from the fourth century B.C., when the harborside city relocated to take advantage of the Aegean's shifting coastline. Its perfectly preserved temples, merchants' houses, and theaters are breathtaking.

The ruins of the Roman theater in Ephesus

Ephesus
 195 B2
✉ 2 miles (3 km) from Selçuk
 $$$$; terraced houses additional $$$

Ephesus

Entering from the **Upper Gate,** the path heads straight toward the upper **agora** (market), passing the **Baths of Varius** on the right before reaching the **Odeon,** or parliament. Clamber up the tiered rows, which seated 1,500 in the second century A.D., for views over the **Prytaneum** (Palace of Council) and two **temples** next door. Two statues of Artemis (exhibited in Selçuk's Efes Müzesi, see pp. 200–201), originally housed in the nearby **Temple of Artemis,** were discovered here.

The central colonnaded road dips downhill, before opening out onto the **Pollio Fountain** and **Domitian Temple** (both first century A.D.) on the left, and the first-century B.C. **Tomb of Memmius** and **Monumental Fountain** (first through fourth centuries A.D.) on the right. Keep an eye out for the **Gate of Hercules,** which flanks the start of **Curetes Street.** During Ephesus' heyday, this street was lined with shops, each vendor positioned between two columns.

Passing the first-century A.D. **Temple of Trajan** (its sculptures now in Selçuk's Efes Müzesi), the stunning **Temple of Hadrian,** built on the occasion of Emperor Hadrian's second-century A.D. visit to the city, was restored during the fourth century. Behind it are the public **latrines** and the **Baths of Skolasticia.** The bathing complex—built during the second century A.D. and extensively remodeled by the eponymous Skolastica during the fourth century—was originally three stories, but only the top floor is currently visible.

The **terraced houses** sit on the opposite side of Curetes Street. Although there is a supplemental charge, Terrace House 2—a warren of six first- and second-century A.D. luxury dwellings still undergoing restorations—is absolutely unmissable. The homes were abandoned after a series of severe earthquakes during the third century A.D., and their treasures have remained relatively undisturbed. Painstaking reassembly of the banquet hall's marble-lined walls (discovered shattered into 120,000 pieces) takes place in Unit 6, while Units 2 and 3 boast superb wall murals and mosaic floors.

Back in the brilliant sunshine, the impressive **Library of Celsus** is one of the site's highlights. Consul Gaius Julius Aquila (A.D. 110) had the library constructed in honor of his father, the proconsul of the province of Asia; it was completed in A.D. 135. Copies of the four sculptures representing intellectual virtues (the originals are in Vienna's Ephesus Museum) sit in niches on the library's facade. The building once held thousands of texts, but these were burned and

EXPERIENCE: Visiting Ephesus

Few ancient sites have the impact of a day at Ephesus. As you step slowly through the numerous areas of ruins, you begin to feel a connection with the departed life of this once great city. Set out early to avoid the crowds and enter from the Upper Gate, in order to proceed slowly downhill as the heat of the day increases. There's nowhere to buy drinks or snacks within the ruins, so pack a large bottle of water, no matter what the season. Although all major points of interest are labeled in Turkish and English, there are no detailed explanations save the lengthy descriptions posted within the terraced houses. History buffs may choose to hire an audio guide ($$$) or one of the many multilingual guides ($$$$$ per group, 2 hours) lingering near the site's entrance. Note that most of the hotels in Selçuk (2 miles/3 km east) will shuttle you to and from the ruins for free.

destroyed by invading Goths during the third century A.D.

To the right of the library's entrance, the **Mazeus & Mithriadates Gate** marks the entrance to the lower agora. Funded by former slaves Mazeus and Mithriadates, this 52-foot (16 m) triple archway was erected in imperial gratitude for freedom bestowed upon them.

Back up on **Marble Street** and heading northeast, visitors will pass the town's **brothel** on the right—note the etched footprint and female figure, an ancient advertisement for the world's oldest profession, on a left-hand paving stone. Ephesus' massive 25,000-seat **theater** (first through second centuries A.D.) towers up to

Selçuk

195 B2

Visitor Information

Atatürk Mah. Agora Çarşısı 35, Selçuk

(0232) 892 69 45

www.selcukephesus .gen.tr

Efes Müzesi

Atatürk Caddesi, Uğur Mumcu Sevgi Yolu 28, Selçuk

(0232) 892 60 10

Closed Mon.

$$

the right. From its upper tiers, there are excellent views over the town's **theater gymnasium** and **Harbor Street** (also referred to as the Arcadian Way), funneling visitors north and then east toward the **Lower Gate's** exit.

Selçuk

For many visitors, Selçuk is purely a dormitory for the nights before and after a day at Ephesus. However, there are reasons to linger.

Efes Müzesi: Selçuk's dedicated museum, located just opposite the visitor information office, displays ancient objects from nearby archaeological sites. Look for the diorama re-creating Roman daily life in a terraced house, the Pollio Fountain statues, and the tiny, perfect Eros-engraved oil lamps in

the Eros Room. The real stars, however, are housed in the **Artemis Room:** Three stunning sculptures of Artemis (first to second centuries A.D.), as well as a small model of the **Temple of Artemis** (Artemision). The

Visitors write notes on fabric or paper to add to the wishing wall at Meryemana.

EXPERIENCE: Splashing Around

When the kids are squirming at the mere mention of yet another Roman ruin, **Aqua Fantasy AquaPark**'s *(Ephesus Beach, Selçuk, tel 0232/89 31 11, www .aquafantasy.com)* 45 acres (18 ha) of slippery slides, wave pools, and giant plastic sea creatures could be just the antidote. The park's central pool is packed with rides for little ones, including the gentle Pirates' Slide; tubes bump along Adventure River, which loops around it. Older kids will enjoy the snake-themed slides, as well as X-Treme, a vertiginous drop boasting seven seconds of gut-wrenching, 50 miles per hour (80 km/h) speed. And when the games get a little too giddy, parents can retire to the Adults' Pool or enjoy a Turkish bath and spa treatment. The park is a great place for tourists to mix with local families.

remains of the actual temple are about a ten-minute walk west of the museum. One of the Seven Wonders of the Ancient World, today the site is almost empty, dotted with just a few large stones and one column.

St. Jean Bazilikası: St. John the Evangelist was buried on Selçuk's Ayasoluk hilltop in the first century A.D. Three hundred years later, Emperor Constantine built a huge basilica over the tomb, with Emperor Justinian expanding it further during the sixth century. Today, St. John's central tomb is well marked, as are the approximate church outlines. At sunset, the ruins offer rosy vistas over Selçuk's mosque, **İsa Bey Camii** (14th century).

Meryemana

A site of both Christian and Muslim pilgrimage, this woodland chapel, atop Mount Koressos, near Ephesus, is believed to be where the Virgin Mary spent her last years. She is said to have traveled here with St. John the Evangelist. The house appeared in a vision to German nun Sister Anne Catherine Emmerich during the early 19th century, and was officially "discovered" by Christian clergy in 1891.

Şirince

The picturesque 19th-century Greek town of Şirince is located 5 miles (8 km) from Selçuk. Serene out of season, in spring and summer Şirince is a popular destination for *köy kahvaltısı* (village breakfast) or an al fresco lunch. On its main streets, shops and kiosks sell handmade clothes and the town's tasty fruit wines.

Getting Around

There are *dolmuş* services to all of these towns and sites, but some run only once a day. Driving yourself or joining an organized tour will be easier. Try **Ephesus Tours** *(Liman Caddesi Belediye Çarşısı 17 Kuşadası/Aydın, tel 0256/618 32 68, www.ephesustours.org)* or **Meander Travel** *(Kibris Caddesi 1/A Kuşadası/Aydın, tel 0256/ 614 38 59, www.ephesustours.net)* for private tours with English-speaking guides. ∎

Meryemana
 5 miles (8 km) from Selçuk
$ $$$

Şirince
▲ 195 B2
✉ 5 miles (8 km) from Selçuk

Hellenistic & Roman Turkey

Excavations have uncovered ancient Greek settlements all across Turkey, particularly in the Anatolian area. The following are some of western Turkey's most prominent ancient sites open to explore. Find ancient Greek coins at Miletus, the Great Altar of Zeus at Pergamum, and imposing, sculpted stone heads at Didyma and Aphrodisias.

Aphrodisias is named after its Temple of Aphrodite.

Pergamum

Around 62 miles (100 km) north of İzmir, the hilltop city of Pergamum reached its zenith under the reign of King Eumenes II, who ruled 197–159 B.C. Its **library** was one of the greatest of the era, housing 200,000 precious texts. The sprawling site's most famous structure, the **Great Altar of Zeus,** is permanently located at the Pergamum Museum in Berlin, although the local museum, **Bergama Müzesi** (*Zafer Mahallesi, Cumhuriyet Caddesi 6, tel 0232/631 2883, closed Mon., $*), exhibits a scale model.

Priene, Miletus, & Didyma

Even during summer's peak, you can expect to ramble around the ancient Greek ruins of **Priene,** around 22 miles (35 km) south of Ephesus, in relative solitude. At first an ancient harbor city built at the foot of a cliff, Priene is believed to have been moved around 10 miles (16 km) away from the sea during the fourth century B.C. when it looked possible that silt from the Meander River might bury it. The city was excavated in the 19th century; of particular interest are the **Temple of Athena,** built under the auspices of Alexander the Great, and the site's small but well-preserved **theater.** Also found here are an **agora,** a **Prytaneion** (seat of government), and a **Bouleterion** (council house).

Like Priene, 14 miles (22 km) to its north, **Miletus,** too, was an affluent port, although its origins long predate those of its neighbor: Over two-and-a-half millennia ago—from around 700 B.C.—the city was thriving. An expansive site perfect for roaming around, today Miletus consists of ancient Greek ruins (its still intact and enormous **theater**), Roman ruins (the town's impressive **harbor**), Byzantine ruins (the **fortress** that flanks the theater) and medieval ones (the alluring, crumbling mosque, **İlyas Bey Camii**).

Didyma's marble **temple** (fourth century B.C.) was a shrine to its much consulted oracle, Apollo. The renowned spot was under the ownership of nearby Miletus, and a 10-mile (17 km) **Sacred Way,** no longer visible, connected the two. Look for the temple's famous sculpted **Medusa head** (see photograph right).

Aphrodisias

Set 124 miles (200 km) east of Didyma, the Roman city of Aphrodisias enjoyed far-reaching fame due to skilled local artisans and their exquisite marble sculptures. Today, a good number of these impressive artworks

can be viewed at the site's excellent **museum** *(Geyre, Aydın, tel 0256/448 80 86, closed Mon.),* which was renovated and expanded in 2009. Of particular note are the 80 sculptures excavated from the **Sebastion** (Temple of the Emperors, A.D. 20–60), and a large, detailed depiction of Aphrodite.

The ancient city's most important structure is the **Temple of Aphrodite** (late first and second centuries A.D.): It was here that the local goddess Aphrodite of Aphrodisias was worshipped. However, Aphrodisias' **stadium** is surely the most breathtaking of the site's ruins. Its long, slender ring of 22 rows (30,000 seats), patchy but entirely intact, measures a grandiose 860 by 194 feet (262 x 59 m), larger even than the original Olympic stadium in Greece.

The famous head of Medusa at Didyma dates from the fourth century B.C.

Dr. Kenan Tefvik Erim (1929–1990)

Although its archaeological digs have been ongoing since the start of the 20th century, Aphrodisias owes its careful excavation almost exclusively to one man: Dr. Kenan Tefvik Erim. Istanbul-born, but raised in Switzerland and the United States, Erim came across the site in 1959—it was then partially covered by the modern town of Geyre, which has since relocated—and was instantly enchanted. Over the next 30 years, the dedicated archaeologist oversaw all of the site's precise digs.

Upon his death in 1990 in Ankara, Erim was buried at Aphrodisias as he had requested. His neatly tended grave sits near the site's double-gated Tören Kapısı (A.D. 200).

Pamukkale & Hierapolis

The town of Pamukkale, located 12 miles (20 km) outside of the region's major city, Denizli, is situated at the base of the travertine cliffs that have become one of Turkey's top sites. Another major attraction on the hill above is the ancient site of Hierapolis, which translates as "sacred city." The thermal waters of this site are deemed healing, and consequently attract thousands of international tourists and locals alike.

Limestone terraces with travertine pools in Pamukkale

Pamukkale & Hierapolis

 195 C2

Visitor Information

✉ Örenyeri Pamukkale

☎ (0258) 272 20 77

www.pamukkale .gov.tr

Pamukkale

Translated as "cotton castle," Pamukkale has been attracting visitors, plus more permanent residents, for thousands of years. The ancient city of Hierapolis was built on the plateau atop these snow-white, travertine (solidified calcium carbonate) cliffs to make use of its 17 healing springs. More recently, particularly during the 1980s, tourists mobbed the unique site. Five hotels were actually built on its precious slopes (and since demolished) before it

was declared a UNESCO World Heritage site in 1988.

Today, the luminescent pools are heavily protected. Gushing streams are artificially redirected, allowing the natural chalky deposits to slowly rebuild areas damaged in the past. It is possible to hike up though the travertine pools, keeping to a wide, well-marked path. However, shoes are not allowed (which makes the normally toe-tingling trek a chilly one in winter). You can also swim (no additional ticket necessary) in the pools along this central route. Alternatively,

EXPERIENCE: Visiting Cleopatra's Pool

Swimming below the warm bubbling waters of Cleopatra's Pool is like being an aquatic explorer visiting a sunken city. The mineral-rich waters steam away at a constant 96.8°F (36°C) at the heart of Hierapolis. The pool is open daily, its turquoise waters shimmering over ancient columns that tumbled down during a seventh-century earthquake. Be sure to bring your bathing suit, a towel, and goggles to get a good view underwater. Taking a dip in the healing springs is idyllic, particularly early in the morning or during the late afternoon. Buy your ticket (valid for two hours) from the desk on the left as you enter the complex, then head to the low yellow building on the far right, which houses changing rooms. You can store your belongings in the nearby lockers for free before heading for a swim in the central Cleopatra's Pool (*$$$$; 6-12 years old, $$$; under 6 free*).

INSIDER TIP:

Photographers should note that travertine is reflective, and that Pamukkale's pools take on a stunning rose or golden glow early in the morning and at dusk.

—TOM JACKSON
National Geographic contributor

access is possible from the top, via the ruins of Hierapolis.

Hierapolis

Pergamum's Eumenes II (see p. 202) laid the foundations of this Hellenistic city during the second century B.C. However, it was when Hierapolis came under Roman rule, around a century later, that it became a renowned urban center, its sprawling ruins still standing today.

Past the Antique Pool Complex is where Hierapolis' oracle, Apollo Kareios, conversed with priestesses through the toxic gases emitted from the **Plutonium,** next to the

Sanctuary of Apollo, dating from the first through third centuries A.D. Just beyond, the impressive third-century **theater** offers towering vistas over the entire site. The **Martyrion of St. Philip** (fifth century A.D.), a ten-minute stroll northeastward, marks the site where St. Philip was stoned to death in A.D. 80. The **agora** (second century), colonnaded **Frontinus Street** (first through sixth centuries A.D.), and the **necropolis** (first through third centuries A.D.) are all en route to the Northern Gate.

In three vaulted rooms within the central Roman Baths, the **Hierapolis Archaeology Museum** offers a clear, bilingual display that includes statues of gods, gladiator reliefs, coins, tools, and sarcophagi. Finds come both from Hierapolis and nearby archaeological digs, like **Laodicea,** 6 miles (10 km) south of Hierapolis—an important religious site during the Byzantine era.

Shuttles (*$*) run from outside the Antique Pool Complex to the theater, necropolis, and South Gate. Shuttles to the North Gate are free. ∎

Hierapolis Archaeology Museum

- ✉ Hierapolis
- ☎ (0258) 272 20 34
- ⏱ Closed Mon.
- $ $

Cleopatra's Pool

- ✉ Pamukkale
- ☎ (0258) 272 20 24
- $ $$$$
- www.pamukkale thermal.com

Untouched ancient ruins, deserted coves, stunning beaches: the hidden treasures dotted along Turkey's incredible Turquoise Coast

The Turquoise Coast

Introduction & Map   208-209

Göcek to Kaş   210-211

Experience: Taking a Blue Cruise   211

Walking the Lycian Way   212-215

Kekova to Antalya   216-219

Experience: Sea Kayaking Around Kekova   218

Restaurants & Hotels   257-259

The beach of Kaputas, Kalkan, on the Turquoise Coast

The Turquoise Coast

Twisting from the southern Aegean Sea eastward into the Mediterranean, this stretch of coast is a world away from brassy Aegean resorts like Bodrum farther north. In fact, this dramatic coastline has plenty of areas where you're more likely to spot a dolphin, sea turtle, or egret than a fellow human being.

A day at sea on the Mediterranean waters near Kekova

Beginning with the yachting center of Göcek and stretching to Antalya, the length of Turkey's Mediterranean coast, known as the Turquoise Coast, takes in crumbling ruins, beaches and seaside resorts, fishing villages, and some of the country's best water sports. Get off the mainland—either by sailboat, a traditional *gulet,* or kayak—and you'll discover plenty more superb spots that the main roads don't yet reach.

Most of this region was Lycia, an ancient group of cities that historians date back as far as the 13th century B.C. Mentioned both by Homer and Herodotus, and ruled by both the Persians and Alexander the Great, these cities formed the Lycian Federation at the start of the

second century B.C., history's first documented democracy. In A.D. 46 it was absorbed into the all-consuming Roman Empire.

Today the Lycians are perhaps best remembered locally for their unique rock-cut tombs, such as those at Myra, and the Lycian Way (Likya Yolu in Turkish). The latter is a combination footpath and mule track that traces 316 miles (509 km) of coastline from Fethiye to Antalya. The route was unmarked, forgotten, or remembered by word of mouth only until the late 1990s, when it was reestablished and way-marked by keen trekkers Kate Clow (b. 1947) and Terry Richardson (b. 1957).

Antalya, marking the Turquoise Coast's eastern edge, is the sun-kissed southern coast's largest city. As an urban center, it's often overlooked in favor of surrounding resorts, but its superb Ethnographic Museum and Archaeological Museum, teamed with the Kaleiçi, its attractive old town, make it a buzzing base for exploring the region.

Inexpensive flights to both Dalaman and Antalya airports, both from Istanbul and farther afield, combined with a bus service that essentially runs on a coastal loop, make the Turquoise Coast easily accessible even without your own wheels. The region is best visited in spring or autumn. During the summertime it can become crowded and uncomfortably hot.

Best of all, this fragrant strip of coastline is sprinkled with equal parts sleepy fishing villages, such as Çıralı and Ulupınar, and overgrown ancient ruins, such as Letöon and Xanthos, or Olympos and Phaselis farther west. Whether you're a budding archaeologist or just looking to splash around with the kids, the Turquoise Coast makes an idyllic escape. ■

NOT TO BE MISSED:

Relaxing on Ölüdeniz, one of the best beaches in Turkey 210–211

A week or two on an enchanting Blue Cruise 211

Spotting loggerhead turtles on the protected Patara or Çıralı beaches 211, 217

Hiking a solitary stretch of the Lycian Way 212–215

Kayaking around the submerged ruins at Kekova 218

Exploring the ancient sites of Olympos or Phaselis 217–219

The treasures on display at Antalya's archaeological museum 219

Göcek to Kaş

Boasting world-class yachting and water sports, ancient ruins, pristine beaches, and myriad cruise options, the coastal region between Göcek—with its superb natural harbor—and the lively diving center of Kaş borders the southernmost slice of the Aegean. Adventurous types can try kayaking at Antalya or paragliding at Fethiye, while others may prefer to relax at Patara beach.

A diver meets a branching sponge off the coastline of Kaş.

Göcek to Ölüdeniz

Having evolved from a lonely port famed for its citrus fruit into a world-class marina complex, **Göcek** is a popular starting point for many a Blue Cruise (see sidebar opposite) or private sailing course.

Farther south, **Fethiye** has also outgrown its fishing village roots and is extremely popular with holidaying Brits, despite the cement architecture burying what culture remains. The **Fethiye Müzesi** (Fethiye Museum; *Kesikkapı Mahallesi, tel 0252/614 11 50, closed Mon, $*) doesn't disappoint. Look for the Trilingual Stele, a tablet carved in Greek, Lycian, and Aramaic that served as a linguistic key to Turkey's ancient tongues.

Six miles (10 km) south of Fethiye is a hauntingly picturesque spot: **Kayaköy,** a ghost town abandoned by its Anatolian Greek residents in 1923 during the Greco-Turkish population exchanges (see sidebar p. 32). Some 13 miles (20 km) farther south of Fethiye, the sandy spit of **Ölüdeniz** beach (*www.oludenizbeach.com*) jutting out into a turquoise bay has featured on a thousand tourist posters. Busy it may be, but as a water-sports and nightlife center, combined with **paragliding** opportunities from the towering Mount Babadağ (*Skysports*

Turkey, Carsi Caddesi, Tonoz otel alti, Ölüdeniz, Fethiye, tel 0252/617 05 11) and hiking opportunities (www.altitudeaction.com), it's an unbeatable lively destination.

Kalkan & Kaş

Both Kalkan and Kaş are former Greek fishing ports blessed with narrow, bougainvillea-strewn streets and a distinct, relaxed attitude. **Kalkan** (www.kalkanturkey.com) is the best base for exploring the UNESCO World Heritage sites of **Xanthos** (Lycia's former capital) and **Letöon,** plus the amphitheater and 10-mile-long (17 km) beach at **Patara,** one of Turkey's finest,

INSIDER TIP:

Kaş is one of the best diving spots in the Mediterranean, with many shipwrecks and rich underwater life.

—KEMAL NURYADIN
Executive Editor, National
Geographic Turkey

and a nesting site for endangered loggerhead turtles. Down the coast, **Kaş** is a watersports hub. It is also the starting point for tours of the ruins at Kekova (see p. 216) or Myra (see pp. 216–217) farther east. ∎

Göcek
🄰 209 A2
Visitor Information
✉ Skopea Marina, Göcek, Fethiye
☎ (0532) 363 30 80
www.gocek.info

Kaş
🄰 209 B1
Visitor Information
✉ Cumhuryet Meydani, 5
☎ (0242) 836 12 38

Patara
🄰 209 A1

EXPERIENCE: Taking a Blue Cruise

Lapped by crystal clear waters and dotted with colorful fishing villages—some only accessible by sea—the Turquoise Coast is perfect for a cruise. Boat trips along the coast are styled as "Blue Cruises," and can stretch from a few days to a fortnight, and can be joined from most of the Turkish Mediterranean's major towns, including Göcek, Fethiye, Kalkan, Kaş, and Antalya.

Most voyages take place aboard a *gulet,* a traditional Turkish, two-masted sailing vessel with wooden decks and bucketloads of charm. These boats sleep between about 12 and 20 guests, along with a crew of three or four who sail the boat and prepare three delicious meals a day. Passengers have little to do other than play cards, lounge in the hammocks dangling over the water, or use the snorkels, dinghy, or occasional Windsurfer strapped aboard. Itineraries are up to the charter organizer; the tranquil islands in Göcek Bay, historic Kekova

Island, and the ancient ruins near Çıralı are highlights.

Visitors to any of the coastal centers will see lines of gulets moored up awaiting charter. Short trips can be negotiated on the spot and paid for in cash. A three-day trip, often inclusive of local tipples like *rakı* and Efes beer, will set a group of ten back between $270–$400 per person, depending on the boat size and season.

Week-long trips hover around $660–$990 per person and are best organized a few months in advance. Reputable family-run firms include **Turkish Gulet** (tel 0252/645 11 31, www.turkishgulet.com), with offices in Göcek, and **Turhan Yachting** (tel 0252/417 46 50, www.bluevoyagegulet.com). For an upscale gulet journey accompanied by acclaimed archaeologist and historian Peter Sommer, try **Peter Sommer Travels** (tel +44 1600 888 220, www.petersommer.com), based in the United Kingdom.

Walking the Lycian Way

The ancient Lycian Way winds along the coast from Ovacik, near Fethiye, to Antalya for 316 miles (509 km). It is best trekked between September and May, as strong sunshine and searing temperatures render the path unsuitable during Turkey's scorching summer months.

The lighthouse near the town of Fethiye

The Lycian Way route is waymarked every 100 yards (90 m) or so with clear, horizontal slashes of red and white. When there's a confusing crossroad, a red "x" serves to indicate which of the forks not to follow. Main junctions are marked with yellow "Likya Yolu" (Lycian Way) signs, and distances are indicated in kilometers (1 km = 0.6 miles). If you plan to hike more of the Lycian Way, see Kate Clow's very useful website (*www.lycianway .com*) or purchase her book, *The Lycian Way: Turkey's First Long Distance Walking Route* (Upcountry Ltd, 2009), which includes maps and detailed directions.

Note that the following walks are by far the most challenging of those outlined in this guidebook. You'll need to pack adequate food and water, as there are no kiosks to stock up en route and public fountains can, and do, run dry. Suitable hiking shoes are strongly advised, as

NOT TO BE MISSED:

Ancient ruins of Olympos • A picnic at the small shepherd's hut overlooking Adrasan • Morning views of Mount Tahtalı • Secluded, sandy coves • Maden Beach and its ghostly abandoned mining machinery

the ground along the route is rocky and uneven.

Both of these walks begin in Çıralı (*www.cirali .org*), making this tranquil seaside town an ideal place to base yourself, but at the end of each walk, you'll need to jump in a taxi in order to return to Çıralı.

Çıralı to Adrasan

Beginning with an easy stroll along the beach, this walk then entails a steep clamber upward, reaching heights of around 2,300 feet (700 m), which is then followed by a long, medium-grade descent.

Start your walk in **Çıralı,** heading south along the main road. Look for the **yellow "Likya Yolu" sign ❶**, as well as the horizontal red-and-white waymarks, which you'll be following for the duration of the walk. Head eastward along the riverbank, crossing over the water when you reach the stepping stones. Cut across **Olympos Merhaba's restaurant garden** and onto the beach. Walk south along the pebble beach shoreline to the ruins of **Olympos ❷** (see p. 217), where you'll need to pay the admission fee (*$*) in order traverse the archaeological site. Although it may be tempting a clamber around

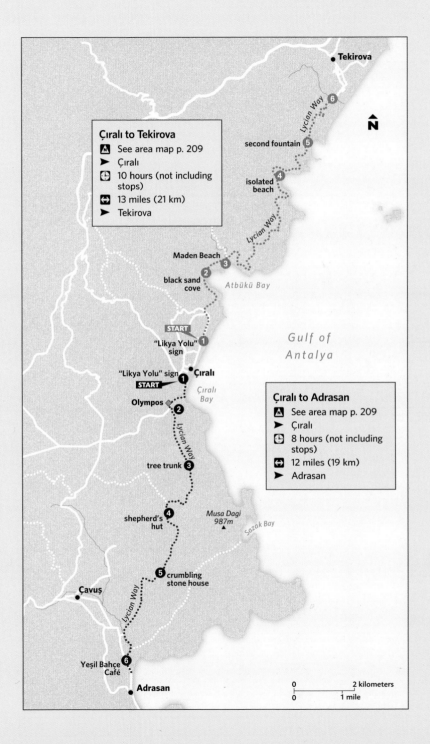

Tekirova

Lycian Way

⑥

N̂

second fountain ⑤

isolated
beach ④

Lycian Way

Maden Beach
② ③
black sand
cove

Atbükü Bay

START
①
"Likya Yolu"
sign

*Gulf of
Antalya*

"Likya Yolu" sign ① **Çıralı**
START
*Çıralı
Bay*

Olympos ◇ ②

Lycian Way

tree trunk ③

*Musa Dagi
987m* ▲

Sazak Bay

shepherd's ④
hut

⑤ crumbling
stone house

Çavuş

Lycian Way

⑥
Yeşil Bahçe
Café

Adrasan

Çıralı to Tekirova
- ⛰ See area map p. 209
- ► Çıralı
- 🕐 10 hours (not including stops)
- ↔ 13 miles (21 km)
- ► Tekirova

Çıralı to Adrasan
- ⛰ See area map p. 209
- ► Çıralı
- 🕐 8 hours (not including stops)
- ↔ 12 miles (19 km)
- ► Adrasan

0   2 kilometers
0   1 mile

the site's Roman remains, it's best to save the exploring for another day—this walk is long and relatively strenuous.

Head 500 yards (450 m) straight along the park's main path until you reach the fenced-in parking lot. Scale the rocky riverbank and skirt the stream until you reach the **stepping stones,** which can be found directly opposite the sign for the South Necropolis.

To the right of the "Nekropol" sign, you'll spot a red-and-white waymarking. Begin climbing uphill, keeping an eye out for the additional red-and-white waymarkings and piles of rocks. During this initial 150 yards (140 m) of the ascent, the trail is unclear and careful attention is needed.

You'll soon reach a rough but evident forest path, as the trail follows a dry riverbed uphill, crossing back and forth over it as you continue the tough climb. An eventual plateau, its trees scarred by recent fires but the forest floor thick with new growth, marks a welcome change in the terrain.

The path dips downhill, and a massive fallen **tree trunk ❸** bisects your route. Climb around it, following the slim but clear path leading again uphill. In the distance to your right, you'll be able to see the cluster of islands almost directly opposite Tekirova.

The trail winds its way through a treeless, recently logged area, and then bears left into soft, golden meadows, between a small well and a stream. The path can be tricky to follow at this point, so look out for the small **shepherd's hut**

❹ on the hill's crest. The shady area just behind the hut makes a cool picnic spot, with views over the town of Adrasan. Hikers trekking the whole of the Lycian Way often use this hut as an overnight shelter. Inside, it's not uncommon to find a few nonperishable food items, or wild delights such as recently foraged spring garlic. Remember to replace in kind whatever you may eat or take with you.

From this point onward, the trail slowly descends, again following a dry riverbed. The terrain is relatively open, sunny, and dotted with pines. You'll cross a small stream, after which the path arcs to the left around a **crumbling stone house ❺**. Turn left again and loop back down to the stream. A wide logging road has eradicated this portion of the Lycian Way's markings, however the flat walkway easily covers the remaining 2.5 miles (4 km) to Adrasan.

Just before the town, look for the **Yeşil Bahçe Café ❻**, where you'll have to wade across the shallow river. Turn left and follow the paved road past the riverside restaurants to the taxi stand, or on to the town's sandy bay. Adrasan itself is a pleasant and relaxed riverside town and, if you arrive there on a Sunday and have any energy left after your trek, you might want to visit its excellent Sunday market.

Çıralı to Tekirova

This walk, although never exceeding a height of 1,000 feet (280 m), involves numerous short, steep climbs and descents to sea level.

Short Walks

Limited time? Not keen on quite such an adventurous adventure? No need to fret, as both of these walks can be just as magical even if abbreviated.

Çıralı to Adrasan: Follow the walk's directions to **Olympos**. Explore the ruins, including the overgrown and often missed hammam on the stream's south side. Take a leisurely dip in the sea before heading back to Çıralı. Allow two hours to

walk to Olympos and back, plus time for exploration of the ruins, swimming, and lunch on the beach.

Çıralı to Tekirova: Pack a picnic lunch and follow the walk's directions to the **black sand cove**. Spend a couple of hours swimming, sunbathing, and generally lazing around before setting off back to Çıralı. Allow four hours to walk to the cove and back.

Tourists at the site of the eternal flames of the Chimaera in Olympos (see sidebar p. 217).

Pack your bathing suit: The trail crosses some of the area's most beautiful deserted beaches.

Beginning in Çıralı, head north along the main road. At the open valley's northern end, look out for the **yellow "Likya Yolu" sign** ①, as well as the horizontal red-and-white waymarks, which you'll be following for the duration of the walk. Head up the rocky slope. At the top, vistas pan all the way back to the ruins of Olympos.

The trail begins to dip up and down, skirting the edges of two bays, with towering Mount Tahtalı (see p. 219) on the northwest horizon. Depending on the season, you may catch a glimpse of sea turtles poking their heads above the turquoise waters; some hikers report spotting pods of dolphins or even the occasional seal. The path soon descends to a **black sand cove** ②, idyllic for a picnic or a paddle. Head inland, away from the water. Waymarkings at the beach's north end lead uphill, before dipping down to **Atbükü Bay,** an open beach backed by shady pines. Walk along the water to the end of the beach, following the dry riverbed inland before veering right and again uphill.

The path's next descent will bring you to grassy, tree-dotted **Maden Beach** ③. At its

eastern end, friendly Mustafa has been farming sea bass in open pens in the bay for six years. A solitary life means he's keen to chat, and will happily regale you with stories as you explore the former **chromium mines** and 200-year-old Swedish drilling machines nearby.

From this point onward, the pathway is clear and wide, undulating steeply up and down. You'll pass a fountain, then head uphill again, before crossing a wide and **isolated beach** ④. This breezy beach is an idyllic spot to relax for an hour or more, gathering a final burst of energy before pushing on to Tekirova. Note that along much of the second half of this walk, waymarkings drop off for large chunks of the route, but you should stay on the main (unpaved) road.

When the pathway reaches a **second fountain** ⑤, turn left and skirt the edge of a fenced section of private property. The trail finishes on the **main road** ⑥, 2 miles (3 km) outside of Tekirova's town center. Turn left to continue on foot, or hop on a *dolmuş,* to this quiet harbor town for refreshment in a restaurant or café. The truly energetic can extend the day's adventure with a trip to Phaselis (see p. 218), also served by dolmuş from the main road's closest bus stop.

Kekova to Antalya

The heart of ancient Lycia is where Turkey's Aegean coast gives way to the Mediterranean proper. From uninhabited Kekova Island to isolated strips of the Lycian Way (see pp. 212–215), this territory is a stomping ground for real explorers and sun worshippers alike.

The ruins of the Lycian tombs in Myra (Demre)

Kekova

Eastward, around the corner from Kaş, the Kekova region encompasses protected Kekova Island and the mainland shores opposite. The area is best known for its proliferation of ruins and translucent waters, and is still insulated from mass tourism; boat trips from Kaş, Kalkan, and Demre remain the easiest way to access most of Kekova. **Üçağız,** a pretty port 12 miles (19 km) off the main highway, retains its village feel. **Sea kayaking excursions** (see sidebar p. 218) depart from here, exploring the submerged ruins off Kekova Island, known as **Batık Şehir** (Sunken City). The necropolis ruins of nearby **Teimiussa** and **Simena** (see sidebar p. 218), outside the town of Kale, and **Aperlae,** farther west, make for a pleasant afternoon's exploring.

Demre (Myra)

Demre—the ancient town of Myra, and today also referred to as Kale—lies 13 miles (20 km) east of Üçağız. It is famous as the long-term residence of Saint Nicholas, perhaps better known as Santa Claus (A.D. 270–346). Built atop the saint's tomb, the town's former Church of St. Nicholas has now been transformed into the **Noel Baba Müzesi** (Santa Claus Museum).

INSIDER TIP:

Stay in a tree house in the middle of Olympos's historic national park and enjoy stunning scenery and a bird's-eye view of the Lycian ruins.

—KEMAL NURYADAIN
Executive Editor, National Geographic Turkey

It draws thousands of visitors every year, particularly during the annual Feast of St. Nicholas (first week of December). One mile (1.6 km) north of the modern city, the ancient ruins of **Myra** cascade down a mountainside, and include an impressive rock-cut necropolis and an amphitheater.

Olympos & Çıralı

Continuing eastward, the ancient ruins of **Olympos,** 50 miles (80 km) south of Antalya, sit at the heart of one of the Turquoise Coast's most unspoiled havens. Originally a Lycian port in the second century B.C., Olympos was taken over by the Romans a century later. While it's true that backpackers arrive here in droves, keen to bed down in Olympos' famous tree houses, the overgrown ruins are some of the most enchanting in the country. Look for the crumbling **Mosaic Building,** fed by a tumbling canal, or visit the southern **Genoese Castle** and ruined theater.

Two miles (3 km) north along the beach (or a 15-minute drive around the hefty coastal mountains) lies sleepy seaside **Çıralı.** *Pansions* and family-run restaurants abound, and the protected, near-deserted beach is a nesting ground for loggerhead turtles. Nearby, the natural **Chimaera flames** (see sidebar this page), signposted and easily reached on foot, are particularly visible as dusk falls. West of the Chimaera, the quiet village of **Ulupınar,** lined with local trout restaurants, makes a pleasant lunchtime destination.

Phaselis

Founded in the seventh century B.C., the ruins of Phaselis sit on the border of the ancient regions of Lycia and Pamphylia. It is said

Kekova

🅰 209 B1

Myra

✉ Demre

☎ (0242) 238 56 88/89

🅂 $

Noel Baba Müzesi

✉ Müze Caddesi, Demre

☎ (0242) 871 68 20

🅂 $$$

Olympos

✉ Olympos, Kemer

☎ (0242) 892 13 25

🅂 $

Çıralı

🅰 209 C1

www.cirali.org/en

Phaselis

✉ 2 miles (3 km) N of Tekirova

☎ (0242) 824 45 06

🅂 $$

Chimaera Flames

Not alone in the ancient world to see fire as sacred, the Lycians regularly worshipped Hephaestus (Vulcan in Roman mythology), the Greek god of fire. The proximity of the Chimaera under modern-day Mount Tahtalı (one of the many mountains formerly known as Mount Olympus, Hephaestus' home until Zeus kicked him out) was undoubtedly of supreme importance to the residents of ancient Olympos.

The flames themselves are the result of the spontaneous combustion of gas as it vents from the rocks. Visitor accounts from centuries ago tell us that the flames were much more volatile then, and were even used as a rudimentary lighthouse in ancient times. Some historians claim that the original Olympic flame was once lit at the Chimaera, then passed along to Olympia in modern-day Greece, a precursor of today's Olympic flame rally.

that the town's original founders purchased the peninsula surrounded by three natural harbors for an indeterminate amount of dried fish, a enviable swap if there ever was one! Passing from Persian to Carian rule, before being stormed by Alexander the Great in 333 B.C., petite but geographically perfect Phaselis was much coveted.

Today, most of the site's ruins date from Roman and Byzantine times and flank the almost impossibly pretty main street. The large, southern gate—or **Hadrian Waterway Gate**—was erected in honor of Emperor Hadrian's visit in A.D. 129. Like nearby Olympos, visitors will feel they're truly "discovering" the site as they find pieces of sarcophagi strewn in with rocks along the beach.

Exploring Phaselis can be combined with taking the nearby

EXPERIENCE: Sea Kayaking Around Kekova

In the isolated bays east of Kaş lie a lost Roman city, Lycian rock tombs, and a striking Byzantine castle. As successive earthquakes have partly submerged many of these ruins, the best way to get up close to them is by sea kayak. This wonderful day out is suitable for ages 8 to 80. Of several firms in Kaş who offer sea-kayaking trips, **Bougainville Travel** (see Travelwise p. 265) is the most reliable.

Most day trips start with a 45-minute bus ride from Kaş to the fishing village of Üçağız. As a paved road only reached this secluded bay two decades ago, much is still blissfully unspoiled. Several carved rock tombs lie just east of Üçağız, known in pre-Roman times as Teimiussa.

Your guides will then help you select a sturdy sea kayak. Two-seater canoes are available for those with a child—or a very trusting partner! After a safety briefing, the flotilla sets off. The 20-some multi-colored kayaks make for quite a sight as they cross the channel to uninhabited Kekova Island. A safety boat follows with the fleet's luggage, and will gladly lend a tow to any stragglers.

Following a swim in Kekova's Ter-shane Bay—home to a ruined church, rock-carved steps, and graves—the kayaks paddle past the haunting **Batık Şehir,** or "sunken city." Once a thriving Roman town, earthquakes left the settlement half underwater, half tumbling into the sea. As diving and swimming are banned here, kayaking is the only way to see the ancient harbor wall, rock churches, and houses. The passage back to the mainland at Kale, ancient Simena, is short. Above lies a **medieval castle ($$)** built by the Knights of St. John. There are several 2,000-year-old sarcophagi dotted among the olive trees. After a paddle past some sunken tombs of Lycian nobles, it's back to Üçağız for a complimentary lunch.

Musicians perform in Antalya.

teleferik (cable car; *www.tahtali
.com*) to the top of the 7,760-foot-high (2,365 m) **Mount Tahtalı** (Mount Olympos). Daily cable cars run every 30 minutes *(winter 10 a.m.–5 p.m., summer 9 a.m.–7 p.m.)* and the journey takes around ten minutes. At the top there's a restaurant, and the surrounding area is the **Olympos-Bey Mountains National Park,** where there are opportunities for trekking, rock climbing, mountain biking, and sea kayaking.

Antalya & Around

The most attractive quarter of bustling Antalya is **Kaleiçi.** Its marina is often crowded with *gulets* offering day-long boat rides, and the old town, with winding, pedestrian alleys dotted with courtyard hotels, has hidden gardens and excellent boutiques.

Although Antalya is not renowned for its sights, the city's **Hadrian Kapısı** (Hadrian's

Gate; *Atatürk Caddesi*)—a triple archway gate built when the emperor visited—must be seen. Tucked into a nearby backstreet, the ethnographic museum **Suna-İnan Kıraç Kaleiçi Müzesi** (Suna-İnan Kıraç Kaleiçi Museum), located within an adapted Antalyan home, showcases Kütahya ceramics and a fascinating selection of mid-19th-century photographs taken by the Abdullah brothers, the Ottoman Empire's official photographic chroniclers. West of Kaleiçi, the excellent **Antalya Müzesi** (Antalya Archaeological Museum) houses a range of artifacts from Paleolithic to Ottoman times, including coins, mosaics, and musical instruments, as well as a children's section.

Outside of the city, interesting day trips include the ancient ruins at **Perge** (11 miles/18 km northeast), **Aspendos** (30 miles/48 km east), and **Termessos** (20 miles/33 km northeast), the **Düden Waterfalls** (6 miles/10 km southeast), or the seaside resort of **Side.** ∎

Antalya
 209 C2
Visitor Information
✉ Cumhuriyet mah., Ozel Idare ishani. Alti 2
☎ (0242) 241 17 47

Antalya Müzesi
✉ Konyaaltı Caddesi
☎ (0242) 238 56 88
🕐 Closed Mon.
💲 $$$

Suna-İnan Kıraç Kaleiçi Müzesi
✉ Barbaros Mahallesi, Kocatepe Sokak 25
☎ (0242) 243 42 74
🕐 Closed Wed.
💲 $
www.kaleici muzesi.com

An otherworldly landscape of naturally formed fairy chimneys, frescoed churches, entire subterranean cities, and rose-hued valleys

Cappadocia

Introduction & Map   222-223

Walk: The Rose Valley   224-225

Göreme & Around   226-231

Experience: Hot-air Ballooning   227

Feature: History & Architecture—Cave Dwellings   228-229

Restaurants & Hotels   258-259

Cave houses are carved out of the fairy chimneys near Zelve.

Cappadocia

South of Ankara, east of Konya, and hours inland from the sea, the UNESCO World Heritage site of Cappadocia is laced with some of the world's most stunning geological anomalies—large, mushroom-shaped "fairy-chimney" cones made from solidified ash spewn from volcanoes 8,000 years ago.

The old town of Göreme was built by carving cave dwellings out of volcanic tufa.

Once a violently volcanic region, the mountains of Göllü Dağ, Hasan Dağı, and Erciyes Dağı—the last a heady 12,848 feet (3,926 m)—spewed ash over the Anatolian plain until 8,000 years ago. This matter solidified into a soft, ashy sort of limestone rock known as tufa. In places where hardier basalt rock fell, rain ate away the tufa below, leaving a mushroom-like fairy-chimney cone with a thick, rock cap.

Cappadocia's history is unique. Its location on the lucrative Silk Road made the region wealthy in the Middle Ages, and in turn its riches were coveted by looters from outside the region. The area's soft tufa was ideal for carving out homes, stables, and places of worship—all of which could be easily concealed with a cleverly placed bolder or two.

As time passed and dangers grew, particularly for Christians under religious persecution, the single-family dwellings morphed into the region's famed underground cities. A few of these multistory complexes sheltered up to 20,000 (some even estimate 50,000) people at their peak, as well as schools, hospitals, and churches. Visitors strolling through the Rose, Red, or Ihlara Valleys today will stumble across scores of churches and thousands of dwellings, many with a fireplace, chimney, rock-hewn shelves, and steps leading deep into the ground.

But it's not all ancient history in Cappadocia. Between Göreme and Avanos lie eight massive, permanent time and land sculptures (2007–2009), created by Australian artist Andrew Rogers, with plenty of local assistance. The land sculptures (or geoglyphs), which include a giant horse and the Tree of Life, are visible from space, but are perhaps best admired from a hot-air balloon ride at dawn.

Many of Cappadocia's towns feature lots of secondhand bookshops, bicycle and scooter rental shops, and travel agents organizing tours to all of Cappadocia's major highlights. Every hotel also has established relationships with guides, drivers, and tour companies, as most visitors arrange their itinerary upon arrival in the region. And although locals moved above ground in the 1950s—the threat of continuing rock falls, plus the pull of modern apartments, are obvious rationale—sleeping in one of Cappadocia's cave hotels is a unique delight. ∎

NOT TO BE MISSED:

Hiking through Cappadocia's otherworldly Rose, Red, or Ihlara Valleys 224–225, 231

A night in one of Cappadocia's atmospheric cave hotels 226

Viewing haunting frescoes in the Göreme Open-air Museum's Dark Church 226–227

Floating above the region in a hot-air balloon at dawn 227

The jaw-dropping vistas from atop Çavuşin's ancient village 230

Visiting the underground cities of Derinkuyu and Kaymaklı 231

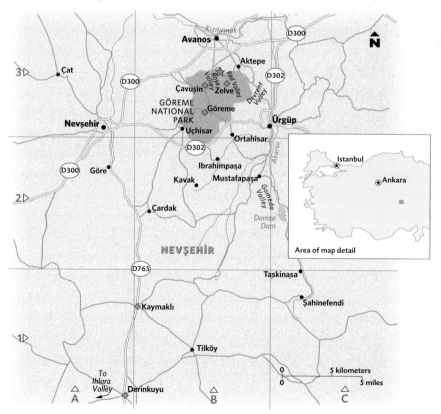

Walk: The Rose Valley

In years to come, this path may be waymarked and its sights crowded with walkers, but for now it's a voyage of discovery, sprinkled with "fairy-chimney" frescoed churches and stunning panoramic views. Although only moderately difficult (if exceptionally poorly marked), it has two short, arduous sections.

A local farmer walks across dramatic rock formations near the Rose Valley.

Start at **Panorama restaurant** ❶ in Çavuşin's village center, a short uphill walk from the **Church of St. John the Baptist** ❷ (see p. 230)—masterfully hewn out of the rock and set precariously on a cliff face. One of the few maps of the valleys is printed on the restaurant wall. Turning right out of the restaurant's entrance, the asphalt road becomes a gravel track. It leads into the valley, passing a graveyard on the left. Some of the headstones chart lives that stretched well into their nineties.

Carry straight on, ignoring the left-hand turn off, but do turn around to peek at the conical fairy-chimney church at the graveyard's edge; it has handholds used by ancient worshippers to clamber up into the raised entrance hole. After some 200 yards (183 m), bear left at the fork.

Following a scrubby start, the path becomes

NOT TO BE MISSED:

Church of St. John the Baptist
• dovecotes • Haçli Church

---

a serene mix of grapevines, olives, and birch, with more fairy chimneys off to the left. After 200 yards (183 m) turn onto the narrow track signposted **Ayvalı Kulesi** (Ayvalı Cave Church) ❸. A further 200 yards (183 m) along, take the sandy trail left to several rudimentary cave churches, their frescoes battered but not destroyed.

Back on the main path, carry on for 50 yards (46 m), then follow the right-hand fork signposted **Rose Valley** ❹. This narrow path leads uphill for 200 yards (183 m), the first of the two slightly arduous sections of the walk. Take in the vistas, as the earth gets pinker and pinker and the panorama over this fairy-tale kingdom becomes ever more enchanting.

At the top of this hill, the path bends right along the ridge. Carry on, noting the **dovecotes** ❺ (see sidebar p. 231) carved on the right, and the windows carved high into the red-rock face far on the left—what a view those cave-dwellers had! It's a 1,000-yard (0.9 km) hike to the 11th-century red-rock **Haçli Church** ❻. Inside, the church's ceiling has a huge carved Celtic cross and the nave is decorated with some faded yet fabulous frescoes. The path here is worn away in parts, but undulates around countless breathtakingly beautiful fairy chimneys. Next to this stunning cave church is a simple teahouse, improbably named **Flintstone's Café** ❼.

Take the left path downhill from the tea-house (i.e., not the way you arrived), then fork right, again downhill, after 20 yards (18 m). This trail leads you into the shaded valley floor. Keep an eye out for several more frescoed churches high up on the right.

After 200 yards (183 m), turn right at the T-junction and follow the path 100 yards (91 m) to a clearing. Here you can peep through the grates into yet another **frescoed church** ❽; there's an additional cave church around the corner that is worth a visit.

From the clearing, carry on downhill for 1,000 yards (0.9 km), cutting under two huge stone arches. You'll cross over the old Çavuşin–Göreme main road, where another simple teahouse dispenses drinks to weary walkers. Head directly over this main road, then follow the steep path straight up and over the hill—the second slightly arduous part of this walk. At the top, look back: The entire Rose Valley opens up behind you. Ahead of you, the red rooftops of Göreme village poke up in the distance.

From here, a mile and a half (2.4 km) of track weaves toward **Göreme** ❾. You're in rural Anatolia, not on the Appalachian Trail, so the path is unmarked. The adventurous can veer left along the ridge to find an alternative route home, always keeping Göreme in their sight.

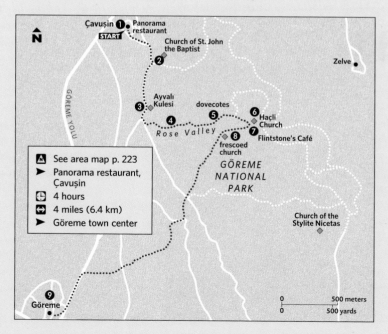

Göreme & Around

Göreme, at Cappadocia's core, is full of religious and geological importance, captured in its fairy chimneys, caves, abandoned villages, and lunarlike rocky outcrops. For a little escapism, take a tour of the underground cities and try to imagine living there.

Göreme

🅰 223 B3

Visitor Information

✉ Teminal Meydani, Göreme

☎ (0384) 271 11 11

www.goreme.org

Göreme

Göreme has retained its village feel and is the best base for exploring the region. Rock-cut homes are interspersed with more modern accommodation, while pavement cafés and out-

Hot-air ballooning over the fairy chimneys of Cappadocia

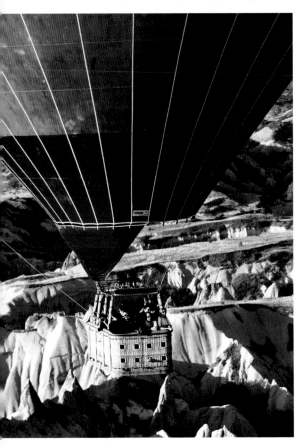

door restaurants lend the town real color. To the north, **Avanos** sits on the banks of Turkey's longest river, the Kızılırmak, and is best known for handcrafted pottery and earthenware. Small vineyards surround **Ürgüp,** home to several upscale cave hotels (see Travelwise p. 259), a whole-sale wine outlet, and an annual wine festival (early September). Nearby, the two hilltop citadels, **Ortahisar** and **Uçhisar** (the highest point in Cappadocia), offer unparalleled panoramas over the unique, pock-marked Cappadocian landscape.

Christian Cappadocia

A group of former churches, chapels, and monasteries sits just a mile (1.6 km) east of Göreme in the **Göreme National Park** (*Göreme Milli Parklar, Avanos Nevşehir, tel 0384/213 36 59*), a UNESCO World Heritage site (listed in 1985) often referred to as the Valley of the Fairy Chimneys. The **Göreme Open-air Museum** here is a must on every tourist's itinerary. Go either early in the morning or late afternoon to avoid the crowds.

Grouped together in the center of the museum complex, St. Basil's Chapel, Apple Church, and St. Barbara's Chapel each dates from the 11th century and has its own independent entrance. In **St. Basil's**

Chapel (Aziz Basil Şapeli), the apse is adorned with images of the Virgin Mary and infant Jesus, with St. Theodore on the chapel's north wall and St. George on the south. **Apple Church** (Elmalı Kilise)—believed to take its name from a long-gone apple orchard nearby—is the most interesting of the three, with superbly detailed and colorful 11th- and 12th-century frescoes. Decorated with red geometrical patterns, **St. Barbara's Chapel** (Azize Barbara Şapeli) also has richly colored frescoes of St. Barbara and St. George, as well as a depiction of Christ Pantocrator.

Dedicated to St. Onuphrius, **Church of the Snake** (Yılanlı Kilise) was never completed. It includes frescoes of this hermit-saint, as well as Emperor Constantine the Great. The church's name derives from the serpentlike depiction of St. George's dragon.

Beyond the **refectory** (with its remains of a kitchen and larder), the **Dark Church** (Karanlık Kilise, 12th and 13th centuries) is the museum's highlight. This church was used as a pigeon house until the 1950s, and centuries of pigeon droppings preserved its vibrant frescoes almost perfectly. Colorful scenes depict the life of Jesus, as well as Old Testament stories. Note that the small additional fee to visit this church is well worth the price.

Continuing back toward the museum's entrance, the path loops past the 11th-century **St. Catherine Church** (Azize Catherine Şapeli), followed by the **Sandal Church** (Çarıklı Kilise; 12th–13th centuries). The latter is stunningly frescoed,

and takes its name from the two footprints just below the depiction of the Ascension.

Keep your entrance ticket handy, as you'll need it to visit the four-chambered **Buckle Church** (Tokalı Kilise), slightly downhill about 55 yards (50 m) toward Göreme and outside of the museum. It's believed to be the oldest church in the area (early tenth century), with many of the frescoes depicting scenes from the life of Christ in deep blue hues.

The region was an important area for early Christianity, as made clear by the one thousand rock churches and monastic ruins dating from the 5th to the 13th century.

(continued on p. 230)

EXPERIENCE:
Hot-air Ballooning

The most thrilling way to take in the magical region of Cappadocia is undoubtedly from the suspended basket of a hot-air balloon. As the sun rises, the sky above Göreme is filled with multicolored flecks, floating silently above the stunning landscape. Sound enticing? Book at least a day or two in advance, as it's hugely popular. Most flights set off at dawn, last about an hour, and finish with a glass of champagne upon landing. The number of passengers per flight can vary, so if you're keen on a more intimate experience, be sure to read the small print. Note that the experience doesn't come cheap ($$$$$, children often half price or free), although booking through your hotel can often get you a discount of around 10–15 percent. Otherwise, try Kapadokya Balloons (www.kapadokyaballoons.com), Göreme Balloons (www.goremeballoons.com), or Anatolian Balloons (www.anatolianballoons.com).

Avanos
 223 B3
Visitor Information
✉ Atatürk Caddesi Avanos, Nevsehir
☎ (0384) 511 43 60

Ürgüp
▲ 223 B3
Visitor Information
✉ Park Ici, Ürgüp
☎ (0384) 341 40 59

Göreme Open-air Museum
✉ Göreme National Park, Göreme
☎ (0384) 271 21 67
§ $$$

History & Architecture: Cave Dwellings

Need another bedroom for your expanding family? Simply dig one out! Since the middle of the first millennium B.C., Cappadocia's cave dwellers have been carving out hospitals and schools—and, more recently, churches and mosques—developing underground cities that subsist more than ten stories below the earth's surface.

Visitors marvel at detailed frescoes inside Dark Church in the Göreme Open-air Museum.

Although impossibly picturesque, who would want to live in a hollowed-out cave? Dwelling deep inside "houses" people carved from the "fairy chimneys" was advantageous in Cappadocia for three main reasons. The first is simply geological: Just as tectonic activity pushed the Taurus mountain range to over 10,000 feet (3,048 m) high, it thrust the surrounding plain to 3,000 feet (914 m), making the climate a mix of cold, snowy winters and searing continental summers. However, temperatures inside the breathable tufa are regulated, hovering at a constant 60°F (15°C).

Safe from Harm

The second reason is for defense: Living in these camouflaged, rock-hewn homes makes sense from a defensive point of view. Trading routes, including the Silk Road, swept across Cappadocia, making the region particularly wealthy. Visit the underground cities of Derinkuyu or Kaymaklı (see p. 231) to witness how tens of thousands of people could take refuge below the earth's surface for months at a time. Moreover, the tunneling advance of any invader who pushed past the sliding stone entrance would be slowed to a crawl.

The third, and perhaps the most integral, reason for the existence of these underground dwellings was respite from religious persecution. Christianity came to the region early thanks to the first of several missionary journeys through the Cappadocian region by St. Paul the Apostle. This new religion only truly flourished a few centuries later, partly because of the reforming edicts of Constantine the Great

(A.D. 272–337), the first Christian ruler of the Roman Empire. The teachings of locally born St. Basil (A.D. 330–379), who later became one of the so-called Cappadocian Fathers, helped to cement the faith here.

Persecuted Christians

Tufa caves may have been used during early Christian times either as places of monastic retreat, or as clandestine places of worship for this still sect-riven religion, when Arab raiders in the seventh and eighth centuries pushed early Christians deeper below ground. Massive rocks were rolled in front of the unassuming entrances to their caves.

During the same period, an iconoclastic debate ravaged the Byzantine Empire as Emperor Leo III (685–741) prohibited worship of what he saw to be graven images, forcing many who valued and reverenced icons into the wilds of Cappadocia. Their arrival ushered in a golden age of fresco painting that lasted for several

An abandoned Cappadocian village

INSIDER TIP:

Cave hotels in the area range from simple affairs to five-star hotels. Cappadocia Turkey can help you find your ideal dwelling (www.cappadociaturkey.net).

—TIM HARRIS
National Geographic writer

centuries. The rock churches are home to some of the world's most beautiful frescoes, including several representations of St. Paul and St. Basil. Some of the earliest lie in the alluring **Church of St. John the Baptist** (see p. 230), a key ancient pilgrimage site. Those in the nearby **Nicephorus Phocas Church** (see p. 230) commemorate this Byzantine emperor's passage through Cappadocia in around A.D. 964. Some sites, such as Göreme's **St. Barbara's Chapel** (see p. 227), are decorated with simple geometric patterns, the only adornment permitted by earlier iconoclasts.

Subterranean Architecture

The architectural features of the underground cave communities, which were accessed by camouflaged entrances, include waste and air shafts, chimneys, wells, and houses, all connected by subterranean passages. The houses' lower levels were used as chapels for worship, storage rooms, or workrooms for grinding flour or making wine, while the upper levels were living quarters. Many of these cave dwellings are still inhabited, benefiting from electricity, telephones, and even satellite TV.

In fact, one of the most exciting attractions for visitors to the region—adults and children alike—is to stay in a cave dwelling. Options vary from Turkish families offering accommodation in two- or three-room cave houses to luxury five-star cave hotels. One of the very first cave hotels was **Esbelli Evi** (see Travelwise p. 259) in Ürgüp. Its owner bought some traditional cave houses, including a stable and wine-pressing room, and turned them into a hotel of stylish suites.

Apart from their practical origins, the cave dwellings today create a fantastical, otherworldly environment that continues to attract visitors from all over the world.

Çavuşin
 223 B3

Nicephorus Phocas Kilise
 Çavuşin
 $$

Zelve
 223 B3

Zelve Open-air Museum
✉ Zelve, Ürgüp in Göreme National Park
☎ (0384) 411 25 25
$ $$
www.goreme.com/zelve-open-air-museum.php

Çavuşin

Just over a mile (1.6 km) north-east of Göreme, Çavuşin is home to two extraordinary churches. And they are, for the most part, delightfully tourist free. **Nicephorus Phocas Church** (963–969) is one of the few places of worship in the area that can be specifically dated. It contains a fresco depicting Byzantine emperor Nicephorus Phocas, born in Cappadocia and known to have passed through the region on his travels east.

Çavuşin's uninhabited ancient village sits to the modern town's east, an abandoned terrace of elegant facades and rock-hewn homes. Be sure to watch your step, as the delicate tufa is worn thin in places, rendering the path to the top uneven. The walk to the ruined

INSIDER TIP:

At sunset, watch the soft light over the pinkish rock formations in the Rose Valley.

—ATIL ULAŞ CÜCE
Nature guide, Cappadocia

fifth-century **Church of St. John the Baptist** is a precipitous voyage of discovery. One entire side, open to the elements, peers over the plunging valleys below.

Zelve

A key center of monastic life from the 9th through the 13th centuries, the settlement of Zelve was inhabited until 1952. The network of rosy-hued, abandoned homes, churches, dovecotes (pigeon houses, see sidebar opposite),

Hikers in Çavusin take a break to admire the dramatic valleys.

Cappadocia's Pigeon Houses

The entire Cappadocian plain is littered with dovecotes—or pigeon houses—carved into the soft tufa stone. Some are simple, others surrounded by complex, geometric frescoes. Pigeon breeding was encouraged in ancient times as the birds were used to courier messages to distant towns. Moreover, their guano was considered the perfect accompaniment to the fertile volcanic soil, adding a sweet taste to locally grown fruit. Pigeon eggs were also an essential component in local paint manufacture, used to fresco Cappadocia's scores of cave churches. The famed Dark Church (see p. 227)—the highlight of the Göreme Open-air Museum—was once used as a giant pigeon coop. Remarkably, it was the bird droppings that kept the frescoes in perfect condition for nearly a thousand years.

and mosques covers four valleys, and makes a more tranquil alternative to the Göreme Open-Air Museum. Three of these narrow ravines can be explored at the **Zelve Open-air Museum** (Zelve Açık Hava Müzesi); **Turkish Heritage Travel** in Göreme conducts tours. Highlights include the early painted Christian symbols at the **Church with the Deer** (Geyikli Kilise), **Church with Grapes,** and **Church with Fishes** (Baliki Kilise). To Zelve's west, the **Monks' Valley** (Paşabağları) chapel, dedicated to St. Simeon, and smooth, almost bubbly rock formations can be explored for free.

Cappadocia's Valleys

Invisible until you're almost falling into it, **Ihlara Valley** (Ihlara Vadisi) is the most visually arresting of Cappadocia's valleys, and a popular excursion for hikers. The **Melendiz River,** tumbling along the valley floor, carved this 9-mile (14 km) canyon. It's dotted with scores of ancient dwellings, some dating back to the fourth century A.D., and around 60 Byzantine churches (11th–13th centuries). Nearby, the

well-preserved, formerly Greek town of **Güzelyurt** sits between Ihlara Valley and the underground cities of Derinkuyu and Kaymaklı.

Crisscrossing the countryside around Göreme, **Devrent Valley** (Devrent Vadisi) is a maze of mushroom-topped fairy chimneys, while **Rose Valley** (Güllüdere, see pp. 224–225) and **Red Valley** (Kizilcukur) are perfect for poking around on foot.

Underground Cities

Numbering nearly a hundred in total, though not all are open to visitors, Cappadocia's underground cities served as a hiding place for persecuted Christians. Each self-sufficient city had its own water source, school, hospital, and place of worship. The most famous underground cities are **Derinkuyu** and **Kaymaklı.** These warrens, connected by subterranean passages, housed tens of thousands of people at their peak between the fifth and tenth centuries A.D. Narrow corridors and steep stairs spiral deep underground before opening out into larger halls. ■

Ihlara Valley
 223 A1

Derinkuyu
 223 A1
✉ 31 miles (50 km) S of Zelve
☎ (0384) 213 42 60
$ $$

Kaymaklı
 223 B1
✉ Nevsihir, 25 miles (41 km) S of Zelve
$ $$
www.kaymakli.net

Rose Valley
 223 B3

Red Valley
 223 B3

TRAVELWISE

Planning Your Trip 232–234 • Further Reading 234 • How to Get to Istanbul 234–236 • Getting Around 236–237 • Practical Advice 237–241 • Emergencies 241 • Hotels & Restaurants 242–259 • Shopping 260–261 • Entertainment 262–263 • Activities 264–265

A carriage driver waits for a fare in Sultanahmet, Istanbul.

PLANNING YOUR TRIP

When to Go

Istanbul is a city of extremes. It can be hot and crowded in summer, with biting winds and snowy skies in winter. The ideal time to visit Istanbul is spring (April–June) and fall (Sept.–Nov.). During these temperate months, cafés and restaurants spill out onto the city streets, Istanbullus haven't yet decamped to their holiday homes, and there's a general buzzy feel to the city.

Cappadocia (see pp. 220–231), Troy and Gallipoli (see pp. 178–191), and the excursions outlined in Chapter 5 (see pp. 152–175) generally share Istanbul's same climatic rhythms. Travelers to the sunny Turquoise Coast (see pp. 206–219) will find warm, sunny weather from March to November. If you're planning to hike the Lycian Way (see pp. 212–215), this ancient footpath is best trekked between September and May. The ruins of Ephesus (see pp. 198–203) are also exposed to the summer sun, and visits during peak summer months should be made at dawn or dusk.

Be sure to keep public and religious holidays (see pp. 239–240) in mind when scheduling your trip, as both accommodation and transport throughout the country can be pricey and congested.

What to Take

Be sure to bring along any personal items you can't do without. Take extra prescription medications, and be sure to pack them in your carry-on luggage. Imported items, such as disposable contacts and solution, tend to be heavily taxed in Turkey, and therefore more expensive than at home. Any special equipment, such as hiking, cycling, or snorkeling gear, should be purchased and put to the test well before your trip.

If you do find you've forgotten anything, it's likely you'll be able to replace it easily in Istanbul. Many big international brands have factories in Turkey, with discounted items (and brand-free) items sold along the city streets.

There are plenty of student discounts on sights throughout Turkey. To prove you qualify for these lower entry fees, be sure to get an International Student Identity Card (ISIC) before you travel.

Insurance

All visitors to Turkey should be covered by a private heath insurance policy. You'll have to pay for Turkish treatment upfront; be sure to keep evidence of your medical expenses in order to be reimbursed back home. Note that insurance companies will require a police report for any lost or stolen items when assessing a claim.

Entry Formalities
Visas

Most visitors are required to obtain a visa in order to enter Turkey. Note that your passport must be valid for a minimum of 90 days from the date you arrive in Turkey. Visas can be purchased at any point of entry, including all customs points along train and bus routes and at all airports before passport control.

U.S., U.K., EU, and Canadian citizens will be issued a multiple-entry visa. Visas are valid for 90 days, with fees as follows: U.S.A. $20 or €15; U.K. £10, €15, or $20;

Canada $60 or €45. You can apply for a longer visa (valid for one year, with multiple stays of up to 90 days each entry) by contacting the Turkish Embassy in your home country, although it won't entitle you to work in Turkey.

If you'd like to stay in Turkey longer than permitted by your visa, you can apply for an extension from within the country, although this process tends to be both lengthy and bureaucratic. An easier option is to make a short trip to either Greece or Bulgaria, purchasing a new visa when you reenter the country.

Visitors planning to stay on in Turkey should refer to the Turkish Ministry of Labour and Social Security's website (www.csgb.gov.tr) for information about applying for a work permit. Alternatively, it's possible to request a residence permit from the Foreigner's Branch of any local police department (Yabancılar Şube Müdürlüğü; yabancilar.iem.gov.tr). For additional information, see Turkey's visa website: www.konsolosluk.gov.tr

Turkish Embassies
Canada
197 Wurtemburg Street
Ottawa, Ontario K1N 8L9,
Canada
Tel (613) 789 4044
Fax (613) 789 3442
E-mail turkishottawa@mfa.gov.tr
www.ottava.be.mfa.gov.tr

United Kingdom
43 Belgrave Square,
London, SW1X 8PA, U.K.

Tel (020) 7393 0202
Fax (020) 7393 0066
Email: turkemb.london@mfa.gov.tr
www.london.emb.mfa.gov.tr

United States
2525 Massachusetts Ave. NW,
Washington, D.C. 20008,
U.S.A.
Tel (202) 612-6700
Fax (202) 612-6744
E-mail contact@turkishembassy.org
www.washington.emb.mfa.gov.tr

Customs

Visitors can import 200 cigarettes and 50 cigars, plus 200 grams of tobacco. In addition to these allowances, visitors are allowed to purchase 200 cigarettes, 100 cigars, and 500 grams of pipe tobacco in Turkish Duty Free Shops upon entering Turkey. (The official individual allowances for these goods are in metric units only.) You may also bring one (100 cl) or two (75 cl or 70 cl) bottles of wine and/or spirits into the country. Laptops, electronics, and medical and sports equipment for private use may be taken into the country duty-free.

For a more detailed breakdown of exactly what's allowed, see the Tips for Travelers page on any of the Turkish Embassy websites listed above.

Drugs & Narcotics

Drugs—marijuana, cocaine, ecstasy, and heroin included—are illegal in Turkey. Possession, sale, and drug trafficking in Turkey are punishable by both heavy fines (calculated per gram) and up to 20 years imprisonment.

Quarantine
Pets can be brought into Turkey, provided they have an internationally recognized certificate of health.

Currency Restrictions
It's illegal to export more than $5,000 worth of Turkish lira from the country. There are no restrictions as to how much currency you may bring into Turkey.

FURTHER READING
So many books have been written about Turkey that we have included an additional list of historical titles (see pp. 50–51) plus a round up of Istanbul's best bookshops (see sidebar p. 27).

Culture
The Bridge by Geert Mak (2008)
Istanbul by Ara Güler (2009)
Tales from the Expat Harem edited by Anastasia M. Ashman and Jennifer Eaton Gökmen (2006)

Guides
A Guide to Independent Istanbul Stores by Ilgin Yorulmaz (2011)
Classic Turkish Cookery by Ghillie Basan (1995)
Eat Smart in Turkey by Joan Peterson (2005)
Istanbul's Bazaar Quarter: Backstreet Walking Tours by

Ann Marie Mershon and Edda Renker Weissenbacher (2010)
Modern Mezze Anissa Helou (2007)

Fiction
The Bastard of Istanbul by Elif Shafak (2007)
Belshazzar's Daughter (2000), *Deep Waters* (2002), *Deadly Web* (2005), and *Death by Design* (2010) by Barbara Nadel
Birds without Wings by Louis De Bernieres (2004)
The Black Book (2006), *My Name is Red* (2002), *Snow* (2005), and *The Museum of Innocence* (2009) by Orhan Pamuk
Count Belisarius by Robert Graves (1938)
The Janissary Tree (2007) and *The Bellini Card* (2008) by Jason Goodwin
Memed, My Hawk by Yaşar Kemal (1955)

History & Archaeology
The Age of Sinan by Gülru Necipoglu (2007)
Atatürk by Andrew Mango (2004)
Atatürk: The Rebirth of a Nation by Patrick Kinross (2001)
Gallipoli by Alan Moorehead (1956)
Gallipoli by Les Carlyon (2003)
The New Turkey: The Quiet Revolution on the Edge of Europe by Chris Morris (2006)
The Ottoman Centuries: The Rise and Fall of the Turkish Empire by Patrick Kinross (1979)
Ottoman Turkey by Godfrey Goodwin (1977)

Twice a Stranger: How Mass Expulsion Forged Modern Greece and Turkey by Bruce Clark (2006)

Outdoors & Nature
The Lycian Way: Turkey's First Long Distance Walking Route (2000) and *The St Paul Trail: Turkey's Second Long Distance Walking Route* (2004) by Kate Clow and Terry Richardson (2000)

Travel & Memoirs
A Fez of the Heart: Travels through Turkey in Search of a Hat by Jeremy Seal (1996)
From the Holy Mountain: A Journey in the Shadow of Byzantium by William Dalrymple (1997)
Istanbul: Memories of a City by Orhan Pamuk (2006)
The Lycian Shore (1956) and *Gateways and Caravans: A Portrait of Turkey* (1971) by Freya Stark
Turkish Embassy Letters by Lady Mary Wortley Montagu (1716; reprinted 1994)

HOW TO GET TO ISTANBUL
By Airplane
From North America there are nonstop flights to Istanbul from New York. Flights from Washington, D.C., Miami, Los Angeles, Chicago, Toronto, Montreal, and Vancouver require at least one change, normally in Western Europe. From Europe, nonstop flights to Istanbul depart from almost every major city, including London, Paris, Madrid, Milan, and Berlin.

International flights land at one of the city's two airports. Major flag carriers normally use the larger Istanbul Atatürk Havalimanı (Istanbul Atatürk Airport; *Yeşilköy, tel 0212/465 55 55, www.ataturkairport.com*), located on the European side of the city, while discount carriers generally serve the Asian side's Sabiha Gökçen Havaalanı (Sabiha Gökçen Airport; *Pendik, tel 0216/585 50 00, www.sgairport.com*). Both airports have international and domestic terminals, banks, change facilities, and ATMs.

Istanbul Atatürk Airport is 17 miles (28 km) west of the city center. Taxis depart from outside the arrivals hall. A taxi downtown takes about 40 minutes and costs around TL 45. If you're traveling solo and your luggage is manageable it can be just as easy to hop aboard the tram. Follow the airport's red and blue "M" (Metro) signs to the Aksaray-Havalimanı Hafif Metrosu (Aksaray-Airport Metro). Purchase two *jeton* (tokens; TL 1.50 each): pop one into the turnstile to enter this line. Metros depart every few minutes, all of them heading to Aksaray. Descend at the sixth stop, Zeytinburnu, where you'll change lines. Look for signage pointing the way to the Zeytinburnu-Kabataş Tramvayı (Zeytinburnu-Kabataş Tramway). Insert your second jeton into the turnstile, walk down the steps to your left and board the waiting tram. This journey from Istanbul Atatürk Airport to the city center is about an hour.

The tram is convenient if you are staying in Sultanahmet, Galata, or Tophane. Be sure to check the exact location of your hotel before you set off on public transport. If your accommodation is around Taksim Square, the Havaş bus (see below) is an easier option.

On the other side of the Bosporus, Sabiha Gökçen Airport is 31 miles (50 km) east of Taksim Square. Taxis depart from outside the arrivals hall. A taxi downtown takes about an hour and costs around 70TL.

Havaş buses *(tel 0212/444 04 87, www.havas.net, 10TL per person)* ply the routes between both airports and Taksim Square, departing every 30 minutes. The journey time to Sabiha Gökçen Airport is an hour, while the trip to Istanbul Atatürk Airport takes around 45 minutes. Always allow extra time for traffic delays.

By Boat

Istanbul's largest ferry terminal is Yenikapı Hızlı Feribot Iskelesi *(Fatih, tel 0212/455 69 00, www.ido.com.tr)*. Boats arrive here from various locations around the Sea of Marmara, including Yalova, Bursa, Bandırma (for İzmir), and suburbs along the Asian shore.

During the summer months, a nonstop procession of cruise ships dock at Karaköy. Companies that serve Istanbul include MSC and Costa Cruises.

By Train

Unsurprisingly for a city that bridges two continents, Istanbul has two main train stations. Trains from Europe—including Thessaloniki, Sofia, Budapest, and Bucharest—arrive at Sirkeci Tren İstasyonu (Sirkeci Train Station; *Sirkeci Meydanı, Eminönü, tel 0212/458 88 34*). Eastbound trains—to Konya, Van, Aleppo, Ankara, and on to Tehran—depart from the Asian Haydarpaşa Tren Garı *(Kadıköy, tel 0216/348 80 20)*. Both stations are well connected by public transport. Sirkeci is on the Zeytinburnu-Kabataş tramline; frequent ferries stop just outside of Haydarpaşa. Facilities at Sirkeci include a restaurant, newspaper kiosk, a small tourist information office, and luggage lockers. In Haydarpaşa, there's a post office, restaurant and, again, luggage lockers.

By Bus

Istanbul is home to two principal bus stations. The city's main terminal is the European Büyük Istanbul Otogarı *(Bayrampaşa, tel 0212/658 05 05, www.otogaristanbul.com)*. The station is on the Aksaray-Havalimanı metro line, and a direct ride away from Istanbul Atatürk Airport. To reach the city center by public transport, take this metro to its terminus, Aksaray. From here, follow the signs out of the station to the Aksaray tram stop on the Zeytinburnu-Kabataş tramline. You'll need two transport tokens (jeton) for the complete journey. Alternatively, a taxi downtown will cost around TL 30.

Harem Otogarı is located on Istanbul's Asian shores. All Asian buses that arrive in Istanbul stop here first, before proceeding on to the European side's Büyük Istanbul Otogarı. Regular ferries run from Harem to Eminönü, and compared to traveling by road, tend to be a much faster way of reaching the city center.

GETTING AROUND
By Airplane

With the exception of a handful of routes from Ankara, all flights to anywhere in Turkey depart from Istanbul. Domestic departures are frequent and, provided you avoid holidays and peak periods of travel, they're also inexpensive. The country boasts a number of Turkish-operated airlines, including flag carrier Turkish Airlines, Pegasus Airlines, Onur Air, Atlas Jet, and Ankara-based Anadolu Jet.

Andadolu Jet
Tel (0212) 444 25 38
www.anadolujet.com
Atlas Jet
Tel (0212) 663 20 00
www.atlasjet.com
Onur Air
Tel (0212) 663 23 00
www.onurair.com.tr
Pegasus Airlines
Tel (0212) 444 07 37
www.flypgs.com
Turkish Airlines
Tel (0212) 444 08 49
www.thy.com

By Train

Train travel around Turkey is hugely enjoyable. Destinations are limited (trains do not travel along the Aegean coast) and routes can be prone to delays, but if you're not in hurry, its a great way to see the Turkish countryside. Many lines boast slick private sleepers and a dining car, carriages tend to be clean and spacious, and the high-speed Istanbul-Ankara route is the best way to travel between the country's two largest cities (see sidebar p. 39).

For specific train routes and more information, see the Turkish State Railways website (TCDD; www.tcdd.gov.tr). Tickets can be purchased at stations and from some travel agents.

By Water

Istanbul's location—on the Bosporus, Golden Horn, and Sea of Marmara—means that thousands of boats serve the city daily. Most of these vessels take the form of commuter transport, ferrying passengers (and often their cars) from Eminönü, outside the Spice Market, to the residential neighbourhood of Üsküdar; from Asian Kadıköy to the European shores of Karaköy; from bustling Kabataş to the Princes Islands. Note that most ferry services stop around 9 p.m. For ferry terminals, timetables, and ticket prices, see www.ido.com.tr

By Bus

Buses provide the bulk of transport around Turkey's vast terrain. It's a hugely popular way to travel long distances.

Reliable bus companies include Kamil Koç (www.kamil koc.com.tr), Pamukkale (www .pamukkaleturizm.com.tr), Ulusoy (www.ulusoy.com.tr), and Varan (www.varan.com.tr). All have ticket offices in Istanbul, as well as counters at each bus station. Note that unless you're traveling to a little-served destination, or during a holiday, booking a long-distance bus ticket a day or two in advance should be sufficient. Most companies operate free shuttles that run from their city offices to the bus station (available to ticket holders only).

Dolmuş services operate over shorter distances, often between major cities and smaller towns, while hundreds of buses cover urban travel within Istanbul itself.

By Car

Istanbul is hugely congested: renting or driving a car within the city limits should be avoided at all costs. However you may wish to rent a car when traveling independently in certain areas of the country that are poorly served by public transport, such as Cappadocia. Cars can be rented at all major airports.

By Metro & Tram

Istanbul's public transport system is excellent. The metro, tramway, buses, and ferries (see above) will get you anywhere you need to go. Transport tokens (TL 1.50) are valid on metro lines and trams, and can be purchased at each station.

For Istanbul transit routes and schedules, see www.iett.gov.tr. An electronic key fob known as an AKBİL is the smart way to pay for public transport in Istanbul. Credit can be stored on this little device, which is available from most newsstands or stations for a TL 6 returnable deposit. When you jump on any of the city's trams, trains, ferries, buses, and funicular lines, simply punch your AKBİL at the electronic barrier and hop on board. And AKBİL holders don't just jump the queue for tokens, they also get a small discount on each journey.

By Taxi

The Istanbul streets are filled with bright yellow taxis (taksi). They're metered and relatively inexpensive, especially if shared between three or four passengers. Taxis charge additional fees for luggage and toll roads, and there's a higher nighttime (gece) rate implemented between midnight and 6 a.m.

PRACTICAL ADVICE

Addresses

Istanbul is threaded with thousands of tiny, twisting streets, often making a particular home or business difficult to find. It's for this reason that addresses are often written with two street names. The first, larger street (usually Bulvarı, Mahallesi, or Caddesi) serves to identify the particular section of a neighborhood. The second street (normally Sokak) is the actual address. For example, "Alemdar Mahallesi, Çatalçesme Sokak 21, Sultanahmet, Istanbul" denotes the building located at number 21 Çatalçesme Sokak, just off of Alemdar Mahallesi in the neighborhood of Sultanahmet in Istanbul.

Although this guide contains an address for every listing, official addresses are frequently used as a formality. On Istanbul's steep hills the easiest route is not always the shortest. Don't be surprised if when you ask some locals for directions, you receive a few conflicting sets of directions, followed by a heated debate.

Communications

Internet Access

Internet is widely available. If you're traveling with your laptop, almost all hotels, and many cafés and restaurants offer free Wi-Fi. All of İstiklal Caddesi is blanketed with free coverage, for which you'll need to register the first time you go online. Some websites are banned in Turkey, the most prominent being YouTube.

Mail

Postal offices (PTT; www.ptt .gov.tr) are dotted throughout Istanbul, and there's at least one per major town. The main offices in Istanbul are Sirkeci PTT (Büyük Postane Caddesi, Sirkeci, tel 0212/526 12 00) and Galatasaray PTT (Yeniçarşı Caddesi 4A, Galatasaray, Beyoğlu, tel 0212/251 51 50).

If you're sending a package home, note that it's common for postal staff to open the parcel and check its contents in your presence before you pay for postage. It's prudent to close your pack loosely, adding extra tape at the post office counter.

Telephones

Public telephones are found in train stations, along major streets, and in or outside most post offices. They work with credit cards or prepaid telephone cards (telekart). You can purchase the latter at post offices, shops, and street kiosks.

Most foreign mobile phones will work in Turkey. If you have a GSM phone and plan to receive a lot of calls during your trip, you may wish to purchase a Turkish SIM card. Simply take your passport and head to any branch of Turkcell, Vodafone, or AVEA to buy one. The process is straightforward and inexpensive.

All Turkish numbers consist of 11 digits: a four-number area code (0212 or 0216 for Istanbul), then a seven-digit number. If you are calling Turkey from abroad, dial your international access code (011 from the United States and Canada, 00 from the United Kingdom), 90 for Turkey, followed by the area code—dropping the initial 0—then the telephone number. The same system applies for cell-phone numbers.

To call abroad from Turkey, dial 00, then the country code, area code, and telephone number. Should you need additional assistance, international operators can be reached on 115.

Conversions

Turkey uses the metric system. Weights are calculated in grams and kilograms (1 kg = 2.2 pounds), while liquids are usually given in liters (1 l = 0.2 gallon) or fractions of liters—it helps to remember that half a liter (500 ml) is equal to a little more than one pint. Distances are given in meters (1 m = 3.3 feet) and kilometers (1 km = 0.6 mile), while speed limits are given in kilometers per hour. Temperatures are given in degrees Celsius, a scale with a different zero point to Fahrenheit (0°C = 32°F). A quick way to convert one to the other is to double the figure in Celsius and add 30, so that, for example, 15°C converts to 60°F. This method is accurate to within a few degrees when converting the sort of temperatures you're likely to encounter in Istanbul.

Electricity

Turkey's electrical system operates on 220 volts/50 Hz. Electrical outlets accept plugs that have two round prongs, the same as those plugs used in Europe. Travelers from both North America and the United Kingdom will need adapters —these are much cheaper to purchase in your home country than in Turkey.

Etiquette & Local Customs

Although Istanbul is an international, modern-thinking place, it's still likely a more conservative city than your hometown. It is considered polite to dress modestly when out in public, especially if you're planning to visit a mosque. This means no short skirts and no plunging necklines for women and no shorts for men or women.

Women are advised to wear tops that cover their shoulders and upper arms. Women are not expected to wear headscarves, and wearing one is likely to attract more hassle than going without.

Holidays

Expect that banks, public offices, and many shops will be closed on the following holidays. See Religious Festivals, opposite, for further closures.

January 1, New Year's Day (Yılbaşı)

April 23, Independence and Children's Day (Ulusal Egemenlik ve Çocuk Bayramı)

May 1, Labor Day (Emek Günü)

May 19, Atatürk's birthday, as well as Youth and Sports Day (Atatürk'ü Anma Gençlik ve Spor Bayramı)

August 30, Victory Day (Zafer Bayramı)

October 29, Republic Day (Cumhuriyet Bayramı)

November 10, Anniversary of Atatürk's death; one minute of silence is observed at 9:05 a.m.

Liquor Laws

Efes Pilsen (plus light and dark) is the local beer. Turkey also produces an excellent, often-overlooked range of wines. Kavaklıdere and Doluca are two reputable, long-established wine houses, although there are plenty of smaller, quality vineyards too. See Bozcaada, Turkey's wine island (see pp. 190–191), for more information.

The local liquor is anise-flavored rakı, weighing in at a hefty 80–90 proof (40–45 percent abv). It's normally diluted with water and drunk while eating meze or lingering over fish-based meals.

Alcohol can be purchased at many kiosks, supermarkets, restaurants, and bars.

Media
Newspapers

Turkey has two daily English newspapers: Today's Zaman (www.todayszaman.com) and Hürriyet Daily News (formerly Turkish Daily News; www.hurriyet dailynews.com). International newspapers are widely available: each of Istanbul's neighborhoods have at least one newsstand. Tünel and Taksim Squares are both good spots to pick up the International Herald Tribune, The Guardian, and the Financial Times. Expect weekend editions to be available from around 5 p.m. on Saturdays.

Magazines

English-language magazines range from the quality publication Cornucopia (www.cornucopia .net), a Turkophile quarterly glossy packed with well-written articles about contemporary and historical Turkey, to monthly InIstanbul, useful for its detailed monthly agenda. Time Out's Istanbul magazine (www .timeoutistanbul.com) is also published monthly.

International magazines are both expensive and difficult to find. The local chain of Macro Center supermarkets (www .macrocenter.com.tr) is a sure bet.

TV

Through the satellite provider Digiturk, most hotels offer a few or all of the following English-language channels: CNN, BBC, Euronews, Eurosport, and Al Jeezera.

Money Matters

For information about the Turkish lira (Türk lirası, abbreviated TL) and its denominations, see sidebar p. 10.

Money can be changed at some—but not all—banks. In Istanbul, there are change offices in the airports and along İstiklal Caddesi; branches of Döviz (at numbers 39 and 53, and in Taksim Square) are normally open from around 9 a.m.-7.30 p.m.

In Istanbul, credit (Mastercard and Visa, less so American Express) and debit cards are generally accepted as payment in larger establishments or those places that cater to tourists. Be sure that you know your pin code. There are also plenty of banks and ATMs. The same is not always true outside of the city; it's wise to travel with a small amount of cash in hand, just in case. If your credit card should be lost or stolen, contact:

American Express
Tel (0212) 310 23 15
www.americanexpress.com
Mastercard
Tel 00 800 13 887 0903
www.mastercard.com
Visa
Tel 00 800 13 535 0900
www.visaeurope.com

Opening Times

Most banks are open Monday-Friday 9 a.m.-12 p.m. and 1:30 p.m.-5 p.m. Some are also open on Saturday mornings.

Post offices (PTT) are generally open Monday-Saturday 8:30 a.m.-5 p.m., sometimes with an hour's closure over lunchtime.

Major tourist sights are open from 8:30 a.m. or 9 a.m. until 5:30 p.m. Their weekly closure is usually on Monday or Tuesday.

Restaurants often offer continuous service, with kitchens opening for breakfast from around 8 a.m. and not closing until after dinner, often in the early morning hours. Turks eat their evening meal late by North American or British standards, and popular restaurants tend to get crowded from around 9 p.m. onward.

Shops are normally open Monday-Saturday 10 a.m.-7 p.m., with those along Istanbul's central İstiklal Caddesi staffed until 10 p.m. or later. Larger supermarkets are open 8:30 a.m.-10 p.m. Note that opening hours for neighborhood shops can vary immensely.

Pharmacies are open Monday-Saturday 9 a.m.-7 p.m. Each neighborhood also has a night pharmacy, usually rotating between different branches.

Religion

Although Turkey is a predominantly Sunni Muslim country, it is also a liberal, secular republic. Religious practices tend to be moderate, and non-Muslims are enthusiastically welcome everywhere, including mosques.

Many of the world's major organized religions are also represented in Istanbul. The Ecumenical Patriarchate of the Orthodox Christian faith resides in the city, and Istanbul is home to significant numbers of Greek Orthodox and Armenian Christian residents. A close-knit community of Jews worships at synagogues in Galata and Balat, and two prominent Catholic churches (see p. 111) sit on İstiklal Caddesi.

Religious Festivals

Islamic holidays are calculated according to the lunar Hijri calendar. One calendar year is approximately 355 days, or 11 days shorter than the 365-day Gregorian year. For this reason, the following religious festivals shift slightly earlier each year. Note that all Islamic holidays begin on the evening of the first day, and continue until the evening of the final day.

Ramadan (1-30 Aug., 2011; 20 July-18 Aug., 2012): During this month-long feast of religious reflection, devout Muslims fast from sunrise to sunset. In Istanbul, most restaurants will be open nonetheless, but it's considered polite to avoid openly snacking or drinking on the street. At dusk, there's an inclusive air of celebration as tables are laid and the ritual fast is broken. Restaurants may serve special evening menus, and it's wise to reserve at the most popular spots in advance.

Şeker Bayramı or Ramadan Bayramı (30 Aug.-2 Sept., 2011; 18-21 Aug., 2012): A joyful glut of sugar (şeker) and sweets are consumed over this three-day holiday, marking the end of Ramadan.

Kurban Bayramı (6–10 Nov., 2011; 25–29 Oct., 2012): This important four- or five-day festival marks the annual Muslim pilgrimage to Mecca (hajj). It is celebrated 70 days after the end of Ramadan. Traditionally, a sheep is sacrificed, and an exquisite, abundant meal will be prepared.

During both Şeker Bayramı and Kurban Bayramı, transport will be expensive, less frequent, and extremely crowded as residents travel to celebrate with family and friends. Museums and sights will close for the first day or two of each holiday period, while offices and businesses shut for the duration.

Restrooms

Public restrooms (*tuvalet*) are widespread, and usually cost TL 1 per person. Mosques also always have public toilets. While some restrooms you'll encounter sport Western-style toilets, many are equipped with "squat" toilets, particularly in places outside of Istanbul. Toilet paper should always be thrown into the garbage, and never into the toilet itself.

Time Differences

All of Turkey is in the Eastern European time zone. It is two hours ahead of the United Kingdom, seven hours ahead of North America's eastern standard time, and ten hours ahead of Pacific standard time. Daylight savings move the clocks forward an hour (Greenwich mean time +3) from the last Sunday in March, then back an hour to GMT+2 on the last Sunday in October.

Tipping

While tipping may not be traditional in Turkey, it has been enthusiastically embraced. Most hospitality workers now expect a small tip from foreigners, and leaving nothing is viewed as rude. In restaurants, a tip of 10 percent is generous. In all other cases (cafés, bars, taxis, porters), round the bill up, or leave a couple of lira.

Travelers with Disabilities

High-end hotels and prominent tourist sights are generally outfitted with facilities for travelers with disabilities. However, not a lot else is. Roads and sidewalks are irregular and ramps are rare; both elevators and restrooms can be tight. Turks will go out of their way to assist you in any way possible, but it's prudent to gather as much local information as you can in advance.

In the United States, you can contact The Society for Accessible Travel & Hospitality (*347 Fifth Ave., Suite 605, New York, NY 10016, tel 212/447-7284, www.sath.org*) before you travel; in the United Kingdom, RADAR (*12 City Forum, 250 City Road, London EC1V 8AF, tel 020/7250 3222, www.radar.org.uk*) can help you plan your travels.

Visitor Information
Tourist Offices

Local tourist offices tend to be very poorly stocked in Turkey. Staff are friendly, and will go out of their way to make calls or seek out information on your behalf, but there's rarely more than a very general city map and few glossy brochures to take away with you, so don't plan to rely on these places too much.

In striking contrast, the tourist board's official website (*www.kultur.gov.tr*) is packed with addresses, phone numbers, and opening hours. Google Maps (*maps.google.com*) is also handy for checking directions and exact locations before you hit the streets.

Websites

www.goturkey.com
Turkey's official tourism portal, with destination guides to links for accommodation.

www.tourismturkey.org
U.S.-based Turkish Culture and Tourist Office.

www.turkeytravelplanner.com
An excellent resource for all things Turkish, written by local expert Tom Brosnahan.

www.english.istanbul.com
A good spot to learn about goings-on around the city, plus sights, restaurants, and hotels.

www.en.istanbul2010.org
Istanbul's many projects, initiated during the city's year as European Capital of Culture 2010, are tracked and reported on here.

www.turkey-gay-travel.com
Lists gay-friendly hotels, with links to recommended bars, clubs, and tours.
For more practical pointers, see also "Istanbul blogs," p. 16.

EMERGENCIES
Crime & Police
Turkey is generally a very safe country. You should carry some form of identification at all times: driver's license or a photocopy of your passport is sufficient.

In Istanbul, be aware of pickpockets—keep your belongings close at hand, particularly in crowded areas and on public transport. Your camera should remain tucked away when you are not using it. Count your change. And, as in any big city, it's prudent to avoid poorly lit, empty streets at night. Report any problems immediately to the Tourist Police *(Yerebatan Caddesi, Sultanahmet, tel 0212/527 45 03)*.

Embassies & Consulates
Canadian Embassy
Cinnah Caddesi 58, 06690, Çankaya, Ankara
Tel (0312) 409 27 00
www.canadainternational
.gc.ca

Canadian Consulate
İstiklal Caddesi 189/5, Istanbul
Tel 0212 251 98 38
www.canadainternational.gc.ca

U.K. Embassy
Şehit Ersan Caddesi 46/A, Çankaya, Ankara
Tel (0312) 455 33 44
www.ukinturkey.fco.gov.uk

U.K. Consulate
Mesrutiyet Caddesi 34, Tepebasi, Istanbul
Tel (0212) 334 64 00
www.ukinturkey.fco.gov.uk

U.S. Embassy
110 Atatürk Bulvarı, Kavaklıdere, Ankara
Tel (0312) 455 55 55
www.turkey.usembassy.gov

U.S. Consulate
İstinye Mahallesi, Kaplıcalar Mevkii 2, İstinye, Istanbul
Tel (0212) 335 90 00
www.istanbul.usconsulate.gov

Emergency Telephone Numbers
Ambulance 112
Fire 110
Police 155
Tourist police 0212 527 4503

Lost Property
If your passport or valuable property is lost or stolen, head to the Tourist Police station in Sultanahmet, located just opposite the entrance to the Yerebatan Cisterns *(Yerebatan Caddesi, tel 0212/527 45 03)*. File an official police report here, which you'll need for a replacement passport as well as for insurance purposes.

Health
No specific vaccinations are needed to travel to Turkey. Avoid tap water, and opt instead for cheap and readily available bottled water. Note that cases of rabies are still known to exist in Istanbul. If a stray animal bites you, head directly to any hospital and you'll be given a free anti-rabies injection.

For over-the-counter medication and antibiotics, pharmacies *(eczane)* are dotted throughout the city. Hospitals with English-speaking staff include:

Amerikan Hastanesi (American Hospital)
Güzelbahçe Sokak 20, Nişantaşı
Tel (0212) 444 37 77
www.americanhospital
istanbul.com

Alman Hastanesi (German Hospital)
Sıraselviler Caddesi 119, Taksim, Beyoğlu
Tel (0212) 293 21 66
www.almanhastanesi.com.tr

Hotels & Restaurants

Hotels in Turkey are comfy and convivial places to stay. Particularly in Istanbul and the western areas of the country covered in this book, accommodation is also extremely sophisticated. After all, Turks are known to have a knack for business, and a classy hotel scene has simply been created to match their worldly, well-educated customer base.

Istanbul's hotels fit into four broad categories: luxury, boutique, historical, and budget. Each category tends to be concentrated in a particular area of the city.

Several showstopping luxury hotels have opened along the Bosporus in recent years. Some, such as the Çırağan Palace Kempinski Istanbul and the Four Seasons Istanbul at the Bosphorus, are in former palaces. Many boast their own airport transfer service—by boat—plus resident tour guides and award-winning restaurants. None of these upscale options are particularly well located: guests are expected to hop in a taxi to reach the major sights.

Less expensive are the ten or so boutique hotels, such as Witt Suites or the House Hotel, which have set up shop in the last five years. All are exclusively located in the trendy Beyoğlu or Beşiktaş areas—great for bookstores, clothes, and art galleries, but a 15-minute taxi or tram ride from the historical Old City. Some hip apartment hotels can also be found in this chic neighborhood.

For those prepared to forgo iPod docks, marble sinks, and pillow menus, Istanbul's historical hotels are similarly priced. Almost all are in the Old City—touristy, but great for sightseeing vacations. Many have quirky rooms covered

in Turkish rugs and kilims, and each one is packed with heaps of charm. Istanbul's budget hotels are tend to be dotted throughout Beyoğlu or sprinkled along the Old City's backstreets. All are clean, tidy, and sparsely furnished.

Hotels around Turkey are less expensive than those in Istanbul. The ones listed in this guide are universally charming. All but the most expensive hotels offer a complimentary Turkish breakfast of eggs, cheese, olives, toast, and tea. Many offer an airport transfer service too, although it's normally cheaper to jump in a cab. Almost all hotels in Turkey offer complimentary Wi-Fi Internet access.

With visitor numbers to Turkey growing each year, it's advisable to book accommodation before you travel. Those visitors who reserve a hotel two months or so in advance often receive a generous "early bird" discount from the hotel website in question. It's also worth looking on some hotel consolidator sites, such as Booking.com (*www.booking.com*) or Laterooms.com (*www.laterooms.com*).

Dining in Turkey is one of the greatest experiences known to humankind. Only the freshest seasonal ingredients are sourced, flavors are sublime, prices are generally low, and service—especially outside the touristy Old City

PRICES

HOTELS

An indication of the cost of a double room in the high season is given by $ signs.

$$$$$: Over TL 500
$$$$: TL 300–TL 500
$$$: TL 150–TL 300
$$: TL 100–TL 150
$: Under TL 100

RESTAURANTS

An indication of the cost of a three-course meal without drinks is given by $ signs.

$$$$$: Over TL 80
$$$$: TL 40–TL 80
$$$: TL 20–TL 40
$$: TL 10–TL 20
$: Under TL 10

—is frequently fit for a sultan.

Although Turks generally lunch at set hours and dine late, most restaurants serve from around midday to 4 p.m., and from 7 p.m. until midnight, with a good percentage also offering nonstop service. Almost all the establishments listed in this book are open every day, barring religious holidays (see pp. 239–240). In 90 percent of restaurants menus are in English as well as Turkish, and restaurant staff can usually shed light on any hard-to-translate dishes. Many locals, however, simply forgo the official menu and banter with the waiter about what fish, meat, or vegetable has just been landed, picked, and purchased—although a menu will almost always exist if you require one. Only the fanciest restaurants in European Istanbul require a reservation.

Locals start their meal with a selection of cold meze, such as stuffed vine leaves or eggplant salad, selected from a waiter's trolley. These tasty appetizers are never more than a few dollars each. Next come any hot appetizers (grilled squid and stuffed peppers among them), followed by the main course. Most meals are washed down with beer, local wine, or rakı, Turkey's aniseed-flavored spirit, although a few restaurants recommended in this guide are alcohol free. Credit cards are universally accepted in medium to large restaurants, although cash is still very useful for tips and the occasional network problem.

Most restaurants have serviceable restrooms. Tiny cafés will point you to the nearest public toilets if they lack facilities themselves. Finally, some restaurants in this book may be tricky to find. If in doubt, point out the place you'd like to go to a local shopkeeper or business person, and you'll be swiftly guided in the right direction.

Hotels and restaurants have been organized by price, then in alphabetical order.

■ THE OLD CITY

HOTELS

🏨 FOUR SEASONS
🍴 ISTANBUL AT SULTANAHMET
$$$$$
TEVKIFHANE SOKAK 1, SULTANAHMET
TEL (0212) 402 30 00
FAX (0212) 402 30 10
www.fourseasons.com/istanbul

Life at this former Ottoman prison is rosier now that hotel super-group Four Seasons is running the show. Rooms have marble bathrooms, iPod docking stations, Bose music players, and a distinct oriental flavor. The refined Seasons restaurant boasts modern world cuisine such as tiger-prawn-and-pineapple terrine, and almond-crusted lamb with sweet shallots, and is home to a famed brunch every Sunday lunchtime.

🛈 65 🍴 115 🅿 🚭 🅢
🏊 📺 🅢 🅢 All major cards
🚇 Gülhane

🏨 HOTEL EMPRESS ZOE
$$$$
AKBIYIK CADDESI, ADLIYE SOKAK 10, SULTANAHMET
TEL (0212) 581 25 04
www.emzoe.com

A true boutique hotel boasting romantic rooms, many with frescoes and antique touches. Delightful garden. Prayer call audible from the neighboring Blue Mosque. Steep, narrow staircases may be an issue.

🛈 25 🅢 🅢 All major cards
🚇 Sultanahmet

🏨 HOTEL AMIRA
$$$-$$$$
KUCUK AYASOFYA MAHALLESI, MUSTAFAPASA SOKAK 79,

SULTANAHMET
TEL (0212) 516 16 40
FAX (0212) 516 16 45
www.hotelamira.com

A new upscale spot in the heart of Istanbul's Old City. Rooms feature stylish yet cozy modern decor; bathrooms are equipped with rain showers or Jacuzzi tubs. Multinight stays can be teamed with special packages catering for families (including a visit to Miniatürk) or gently assisting guests to savor a long romantic weekend (featuring chocolate fondue and rose petals). A winter garden room can be hired for small conferences and other events.

🛈 30, plus 2 suites
🚭 📺 🅢 All major cards
🚇 Sultanahmet

🏨 WHITE HOUSE HOTEL
🍴 $$$-$$$$
ALEMDAR MAHALLESI, ÇATALÇEŞME SOKAK 21, SULTANAHMET
TEL (0212) 526 00 19
FAX (0212) 526 09 14
www.istanbulwhitehouse.com

Amid the cluster of Sultanahmet's many hotels, the welcoming White House Hotel is a distinct cut above the crowd. Staff are friendly, and the petite Ottoman-style rooms have been decorated with care. Perfectly located for all Istanbul's major sights; large discounts out of season.

🛈 22 🍴 60 🅿 🅢 🅢 All major cards 🚇 Sultanahmet

🏨 AYASOFYA PANSIYONLARI
$$$
SOĞUKÇEŞME SOKAK, SULTANAHMET
TEL (0212) 513 36 60
FAX (0212) 513 36 69
www.ayasofyapensions.com

A historical hotel set in a row of traditional wooden town houses by the Hagia Sophia, with a sumptuous private garden in the rear. This tranquil place boasts nine elegantly styled rooms, several of which hosted Queen Sophia of Spain and her family on their visit to Istanbul.

🛈 9 💳 💳 💳 All major cards 🚇 Gülhane

🏨 HOTEL IBRAHIM PASHA
$$$

TERZIHANE SOKAK 7, SULTANAHMET
TEL (0212) 518 03 94
FAX (0212) 518 44 57
www.ibrahimpasha.com
An incomparably sleek hotel that blends its 19th-century origins with open fireplaces, contemporary furniture, and a DVD and book library. Head up from the designer foyer and guest-only bar to stylish, peaceful quiet rooms. Rooftop terrace overlooks the Blue Mosque.

🛈 12 💳 💳 💳 All major cards 🚇 Sultanahmet

🏨 HOTEL POEM
$$$

ARKBIYIK CADDESI, TERBIYIK SOKAK 12, SULTANAHMET
TEL (0212) 638 97 44
FAX (0212) 517 68 36
www.hotelpoem.com
Minutes away from the Blue Mosque, rooms at this inviting boutique hotel are named after Turkish poets. Each one is richly and romantically decorated, some with sea views. All are housed in two sturdy 19th-century villas.

🛈 16 💳 💳 💳 All major cards 🚇 Sultanahmet

🏨 🍴 SIRKECI KONAK
$$$

TAYA HATUN SOKAK 5, SULTANAHMET
TEL (0212) 528 43 44
FAX (0212) 528 44 55
www.sirkecikonak.com
An award-winning hotel with on-site hammam and spa,

plus a rooftop sun terrace. Opulent rooms come with pillow menus plus tea- and coffeemaking facilities. Restaurants include rooftop Neyzade for classic Anatolian cuisine, and Sirkeci Balıkçısı for top-notch seafood.

🛈 52 🪑 120 ⬆ 💳 💳 🅿 🚇 All major cards 🚇 Sirkeci

🏨 APRICOT HOTEL
$$

AMIRAL TAFDIL SOKAK 18, SULTANAHMET
TEL (0212) 638 16 58
FAX (0212) 458 35 74
www.apricothotel.com
Fine, friendly budget hotel within striking distance of all Sultanahmet's sights. Its modern rooms may be small, but each one features satellite TV; some also boast Jacuzzi baths and views over the Bosporus.

🛈 5 ⬆ 💳 💳 💳 All major cards 🚇 Gülhane

🏨 BERCE HOTEL
$$

MUSTAFAPAŞA SOKAK 22, SULTANAHMET
TEL (0212) 518 88 83
www.bercehotel.com
Top value, just a few hundred yards from all the Old City's attractions, Blue Mosque and Hagia Sophia included. Rooms are modern, but the Berce's big pull is its panoramic terrace, where guests can breakfast and or enjoy an aperitif in view of the Bosporus.

🛈 7 💳 💳 💳 All major cards 🚇 Sultanahmet

🏨 KARIYE HOTEL
$$

KARIYE CAMII SOKAK 6, EDIRNEKAPI
TEL (0212) 534 84 14
FAX (0212) 521 66 31
www.kariyeotel.com
A great-value hotel for historians, nestled up against

the Chora Museum and the crumbling sights of Fatih. Rooms inside this renovated 19th-century villa possess old Ottoman charm, wooden bedsteads, and antique reading lamps included.

🛈 26 💳 💳 💳 All major cards 🚇 Aksaray

RESTAURANTS

🍴 KONYALI
$$$$

TOPKAPI PALACE, SULTANAHMET
TEL (0212) 513 96 96
Patrons pay a worthwhile premium to dine in these regal surroundings with Bosporus views. Foreign and domestic tourists alike lap up the traditional Ottoman cuisine, much of it slow-cooked in a tandır oven. Dishes include baked baby lamb and aubergine caviar. Former patrons include Britain's Queen Elizabeth II and American boxer Muhammad Ali.

🪑 110 💳 💳 🕐 Closed Tues. 💳 All major cards 🚇 Gülhane

🍴 PANDELI
$$$$

MISIR ÇARŞISI 1, SULTANAHMET
TEL (0212) 527 39 09
Rated one of the best restaurants in Istanbul for over a century. Little of Pandeli's décor (marble comptoirs, turquoise Ottoman tiles) has changed since the turn of the 20th century, but its traditional menu is positively 1950s. There are no help-yourself Turkish sharing platters here, only classic plates of eggplant kebab and thyme-roasted lamb shank, served by deferential waiters in white jackets.

🪑 70 💳 💳 💳 All major cards 🚇 Eminönü

ALBURA KATHISMA
$$$
CANKURTARAN MAHALLESI,
AKBIYIK CADDESI 26,
SULTANAHMET
TEL (0212) 517 90 31
Utterly congenial restaurant
and café, located in the string
of tourist-friendly eateries just
south of the Blue Mosque.
Sample Turkish cuisine, from
yogurt-laden *İskender kebab*
and earthenware-baked *testi
kebab,* or opt for international
favorites, such as saffron
chicken and Gorgonzola
steak.
🛏 100 🚭 🆒 🌊 All major
cards 🚇 Sultanahmet

ASITANE
$$$
KARIYE CAMII SOKAK 6,
EDIRNEKAPI
TEL (0212) 635 79 97
www.asitanerestaurant.com
Asitane boasts over 200
authentic Ottoman recipes
discovered in the Dolmabahçe
and Topkapı Palace kitchen
libraries. Uniquely, its menu
often cites the recipe's
archived date, such as almond
soup (1539), or vine leaves
stuffed with sour cherries
(1844). Pair your meal with
a visit to the nearby Chora
Church, famed for its stunning
mosaics.
🛏 70 🚭 🌊 All major cards
🚇 Aksaray

BALIKÇI SABAHATTIN
$$$
SEYIT HASAN KUYU SOKAK 1,
SULTANAHMET
TEL (0212) 458 18 24
Long an insider secret,
word's now out on this rustic,
atmospheric seafood res-
taurant located half inside a
crumbling 1920s villa, half on
a vine-covered outdoor ter-
race. Authentic home cooked
cuisine—try anchovy kebabs,
local turbot, or octopus salad.
Early booking is essential.

🛏 120 🚭 🆒 🌊 All major
cards 🚇 Sultanahmet

BEYTI
$$$
ORMAN SOKAK 8, FLORYA
TEL (0212) 663 29 90
The only restaurant in this
section located out of town
(close to Istanbul Atatürk Airport). Beyti's proprietor lent
his name to one of Turkey's
most famous kebabs, and his
restaurant's monumental dining rooms have hosted such
luminaries as former Turkish
presidents Süleyman Demirel
and Turgut Özal and former
French president Jacques Chi-
rac. The grills are the menu's
centerpiece: fillet steak, *döner
kebab,* and the restaurant's
signature Beyti kebab.
🛏 300 🚭 🆒 🌊 All major
cards 🚇 Florya

CAFÉ TURING
$$$
SOĞUKÇEŞME SOKAK 38,
SULTANAHMET
TEL (0212) 513 36 60
The prices for drinks and
light salady snacks at this
bourgeois wooden mansion
may be expensive, but what
a location. Seconds from
the Hagia Sophia, it also
possesses an opulent outdoor
terrace.
🛏 110 🚭 🆒 🌊 All major
cards 🚇 Gülhane

DÂRÜZZIYAFE
$$$
ŞIFAHANE SOKAK 6, FATIH
TEL (0212) 511 84 14
A tranquil-by-day, often
raucous-by-night, classic
Ottoman restaurant, set in
the expansive former kitchens
of the Süleymaniye Mosque.
Over 50 traditional Turkish
dishes are served daily, from
chicken and walnut stew to
pistachio-stuffed lamb and
Noah's pudding. The drink
menu includes sherbet,

rosehip juice, and grenadine
pressé (no alcohol).
🛏 720 🚭 🌊 All major cards
🚇 Sultanahmet

DUBB INDIAN
RESTAURANT
$$$
INCILI ÇAVUŞ SOKAK 10,
SULTANAHMET
TEL (0212) 513 73 08
Widely regarded as the
best Indian restaurant in
town, Dubb serves world-
beating Asian cuisine on its
Parisian-style outdoor terrace
and in its subtle southeast
Asian interior. Try *raita* (cool
cucumber yoghurt), *chana
chat* (chickpea curry), or
tandoori-oven baked Peshwari
kebabs. The Indian desserts
are a dream.
🛏 80 🚭 🆒 🌊 All major
cards 🚇 Sultanahmet

HAMDI
$$$
TAHMIS CADDESI, KALÇIN SOKAK
17, EMINÖNÜ
TEL (0212) 528 03 90
www.hamdi.com.tr
Decades-old kebab specialist
Hamdi is set over various
intimate dining rooms on
three vast floors, one of which
is open to the stars. Well-
presented classics include
testi kebabı (a ceramic-baked
meaty meal from Cappado-
cia), *İskender kebab* (a heart-
stoppingly heavy dish from
Bursa) and *fıstıklı kebab* (with
chewy pistachios).
🛏 320 🚽 🚭 🆒 🌊 All major
cards 🚇 Eminönü

AKDENIZ HATAY
SOFRASI
$$
ISKENDERPASA MAHALLESI,
AHMEDIYE CADDESI 44,
AKSARAY
TEL (0212) 531 33 33
By day, the manifold dishes
such as hummus, *mumbar*

dolması (intestine and rice rolls), muamara (walnut and garlic dip)—almost all hailing from Turkey's Hatay region near Syria—are worth the tram ride to Aksaray. On Sunday mornings a gastronomically intense 100-plus dishes are laid out for brunch, a meal that qualifies as perhaps the best value in Istanbul.

⊞ 120 ⊚ ⊛ ⊛ All major cards ⊠ Aksaray

🍴 CAFERAĞA MEDRESESI
$$

CAFERIYE SOKAK, SULTANAHMET

A hidden gem surrounded by the porticoes of an old religious school, just steps from the Hagia Sophia. Simple dishes such as stuffed mantı pasta and köfte meatball sandwiches are served on wooden stools in the courtyard.

⊞ 20 ⊚ ⊛ All major cards ⊠ Gülhane

🍴 HAVUZLU
$$

GANI ÇELEBI SOKAK, GRAND BAZAAR, SULTANAHMET

TEL (0212) 527 33 46

A fabulously atmospheric Grand Bazaar favorite. Fading wallpaper is dotted with yellowing newspaper clippings; the dining room is covered with ceiling fans and twinkling chandeliers. The menu is of the look-and-point variety. Steaming platters include köfte meatballs, lamb chops, and artichokes under oil, plus a solid range of syrupy Turkish desserts.

⊞ 60 ⊚ ⊕ Closed Sun. ⊛ All major cards ⊠ Beyazit

🍴 SULTANAHMET FISH HOUSE
$$

PROFESSOR ISMAIL GURKAN CADDESI 14, SULTANAHMET

TEL (0212) 527 44 41

Istanbul's European shores may be famed for their raucous seafood restaurants, but this simple Old City fish house offers fried squid, fish soup, and grilled sea bass in slightly more sanitized conditions. The handmade lamps that light up the dining room are all for sale.

⊞ 70 ⊚ ⊛ ⊛ All major cards ⊠ Gülhane

▪ EUROPEAN ISTANBUL

HOTELS

SOMETHING SPECIAL

🏨 ÇIRIĞAN PALACE
🍴 KEMPINSKI ISTANBUL
$$$$$

ÇIRAĞAN CADDESI 32, BEŞIKTAŞ

TEL (0212) 326 46 46

FAX (0212) 259 66 87

www.kempinski.com

Quite simply, this Ottoman palace situated in former home of the Turkish parliament is one of the finest hotels in Europe. The vast majority of the sumptuous rooms and suites—some palatially appointed three-bedroom affairs—overlook the adjacent Bosporus. Of its three restaurants, upscale **Tuğra** is widely regarded as the finest Ottoman dining room in the world, its dishes sourced from culinary archives across the city, all backed up by an unrivaled selection of Turkish and French wine.

① 313 ⊞ 250 🅿 ⊜ ⊚ ⊠ ⊛ ⊛ ⊕ Tuğra restaurant closed lunch ⊛ All major cards ⊠ Beşiktaş

🏨 FOUR SEASONS
🍴 ISTANBUL AT THE BOSPHORUS
$$$$$

PRICES

HOTELS

An indication of the cost of a double room in the high season is given by $ signs.

$$$$$: Over TL 500
$$$$: TL 300–TL 500
$$$: TL 150–TL 300
$$: TL 100–TL 150
$: Under TL 100

RESTAURANTS

An indication of the cost of a three-course meal without drinks is given by $ signs.

$$$$$: Over TL 80
$$$$: TL 40–TL 80
$$$: TL 20–TL 40
$$: TL 10–TL 20
$: Under TL 10

ÇIRAĞAN CADDESI 2, BEŞIKTAŞ

TEL (0212) 381 40 00

FAX (0212) 381 40 10

www.fourseasons.com/bosphorus

One of the city's most sumptuous hotels since its inception in 2008, set in a former Ottoman palace separated from the Bosporus by a vast outdoor terrace. The dreamlike spa boasts couples' hammams and Istanbul's finest indoor pool, complete with underwater music. High-end Turkish-Italian restaurant **Aqua** is on site.

① 195 ⊞ 220 🅿 ⊜ ⊚ ⊠ ⊛ ⊠ ⊛ ⊕ Agua restaurant closed Sun. ⊛ All major cards ⊠ Beşiktaş

⊞ Hotel 🍴 Restaurant ① No. of Guest Rooms ⊞ No. of Seats 🅿 Parking ⊠ Metro ⊕ Closed ⊜ Elevator

🏬 PERA PALACE
🍴 $$$$$
MEŞRUTIYET CADDESI 52,
BEYOĞLU
TEL (0212) 222 80 90
FAX (0212) 222 81 79
www.perapalace.com
Even a cocktail at the Pera
Palace will bring you face-
to-face with history. Such
luminaries as female spy
Mata Hari, British author
Agatha Christie, and the
Turkish Republic's founding
father, Atatürk, all stayed
here; the latter's favorite
room is now immortalized
as a museum (see sidebar
p. 109). This once creaking
grande dame hotel reopened,
refreshed, in September
2010. Elegant dining options
include the refined Franco-
Turkish Agatha Restaurant,
a patisserie, and the classic
Orient Bar.
🛏 115 🛏 184 🅿 ⬛ 🆂 📶
🅲 🅐 All major cards 🅦
🚇 Tünel

🏬 ANEMON GALATA HOTEL
🍴 $$$$
GALATA KULESI MEYDANI,
GALATA, BEYOĞLU
TEL (0212) 293 23 43
www.anemonhotels.com
An elegant accommoda-
tion option commanding
the square under the Galata
Tower. Non-guests are
welcome at the Anemon's
panoramic rooftop restaurant,
the Pitti Terrace, for their
excellent breakfast and
Sunday brunch, or for classic
Turkish and international
cuisine come lunch or dinner.
🛏 30 🛏 80 ⬛ 🆂 🅲
🅐 All major cards 🚇 Tünel
🚋 Karaköy

🏬 PARK HYATT
🍴 ISTANBUL-MAÇKA
PALAS
$$$$
BRONZ SOKAK 4, NIŞANTAŞI

TEL (0212) 315 12 34
FAX (0212) 315 12 35
www.istanbul.park.hyatt.com
Nişantaşı's Maçka Palas is a
magnificent art deco edifice,
constructed by Milanese
architects in 1922. Since
2008 it has been Hyatt's
coolest Istanbul offering
(although the even more
upscale Grand Hyatt lies near
Taksim Square), coupling
luxury period-style rooms
with iPod docks and lashings
of walnut wood and marble.
The stylish restaurant, Prime,
sears steaks and fresh fish on
a lava stone rock.
🛏 100 🛏 150 🅿 ⬛ 🆂 🎽
🚣 🅦 🅐 All major cards
🅐 Osmanbey

🏬 TOMTOM SUITES
$$$$
BOĞAZKESEN CADDESI,
TOMTOM KAPTAN SOKAK 18,
CIHANGIR, BEYOĞLU
TEL (0212) 292 49 49
FAX (0212) 292 42 30
www.tomtomsuites.com
What started life as an out-
building of the nearby French
Embassy is now a Nordic-
style boutique palace. This
suite-only hotel is replete
with handmade furniture, art-
covered walls, rain showers,
a vast literature and music
library, and some astounding
Bosporus views.
🛏 15 ⬛ 🆂 🅲 🅦 🅐 All
major cards 🅐 Tophane

🏬 VILLA DENISE
🍴 $$$$
BIRINCI CADDESI 50,
ARNAVUTKÖY
TEL (0212) 287 58 48
FAX (0212) 287 58 49
www.villadenise.com.tr
In the picturesque Bosporus
village of Arnavutköy,
Villa Denise is located in a
200-year-old wooden *yalı*.
Within its five rooms (three
of which face the sea),
sumptuous Ottoman fabrics

are paired with an antique
French-style decor. Owned
by Aydın Harezi, former
president of Istanbul's Classic
Automobile Club, the bed-
and-breakfast can arrange
Bosporus and city tours in
one of Mr. Harezi's collection
of classic cars. The elegant
on-site Spanish L'Ola Res-
taurante dishes up gazpacho,
tapas, and platters of paella.
🛏 5 🛏 60 🆂 🅐 All major
cards 🅐 🚋 Arnavutköy

🏬 W ISTANBUL
🍴 $$$$
SULEYMAN SEBA CADDESI 22,
BEŞIKTAŞ
TEL (0212) 381 21 21
FAX (0212) 381 21 99
www.wistanbul.com.tr
Totally unique, and easily
Istanbul's trendiest hotel
since its opening in 2008.
Rooms are lavishly cool
with 350-thread linen count
bedspreads, marble sinks,
and Ottoman loungers; some
rooms even have private
gardens, outdoor cabanas,
or their own rooftop terrace.
W Kitchen fusion restaurant
and decadently hip W Lounge
bar on site.
🛏 180 🛏 100 ⬛ 🆂 🚣 🚿
🅦 🅲 🅐 All major cards
🅐 Beşiktaş

🏬 WITT SUITES
$$$$
DEFTERDAR YOKUSU 26,
CIHANGIR, BEYOĞLU
TEL (0212) 293 15 00
www.wittistanbul.com
Seventeen mind-blowingly
luxurious rooms that have
been voted some of Istanbul's
finest by travelers and magazines alike. Rooms are giant
(at least 600 square feet/60
sq m) open-plan creations
with walk-in wetrooms,
six-headed rain showers, and
center-room kitchenettes
with just the right equipment

---

to mix a vodka martini. Jaw-dropping.

[i] 17 **[elevator] [S] [S] [S]** All major cards **[metro]** Tophane

🏨 THE HOUSE HOTEL
$$$-$$$$

FIRUZAĞA MAHALL-
ESI BOSTANBAŞI CADDESI 19,
BEYOĞLU

TEL (0212) 244 34 00

FAX (0212) 245 23 07

www.thehousehotel.com

An 1890s mansion was converted into this extraordinarily hip collection of suites in 2010 by Istanbul's leading design agency, Autoban. Parisian-style interiors—art deco sinks, parquet floors, and chandeliers—are combined with high thread-count linens and exemplary service.

[i] 25 **[elevator] [S] [S] [S] [S] [S]** All major cards **[metro]** Tophane

🏨 MIA PERA
🍴 **$$$-$$$$**

MEŞRUTIYET CADDESI 34,
KAMER HATUN

TEL (0212) 245 02 45

FAX (0212) 245 33 30

www.miaperahotel.com

This brand-new hotel is perfectly positioned, steps away from İstiklal Caddesi and adjacent to the British Consulate. Behind the hotel's 19th-century facade, decor is a blend of contemporary chic and unique early 1960s touches: mosaic-tiled bathrooms, rain showers, and a pillow menu complement the retro decor and LCD screens. The indoor swimming pool—unique in downtown Istanbul—is a refreshing bonus come summertime.

[i] 85 **[seats]** 70 **[S] [S] [S] [S]** All major cards **[metro]** Galatasaray

🏨 ISTANBUL SWEET HOME
$$$

VARIOUS LOCATIONS, BEYOĞLU

www.istanbulsweethome.com

These ten exquisite man-aged apartments are dotted around Beyoğlu's most charmingly antique areas. All are well equipped with Wi-Fi, proper kitchens, period features, and much else. Some even feature Turkish hammams, panoramic terraces, and entire libraries. All work out cheaper than a hotel if booked by the week.

[i] 10 **[S] [S]** All major cards **[metro]** Tünel

🏨 I'ZAZ
$$$

KAMER HATUN MAHALESSI,
BALIK SOKAK 12, BEYOĞLU

TEL (0212) 252 13 82

FAX (0212) 252 13 78

www.izaz.com

An ultra-hip loft living concept, with a chic one-bedroom apartment on each floor. There are designer bathrooms, flatscreen TVs, hardwood furniture, and DVD players. Guests share a rooftop terrace and a communal kitchen. Two blocks from İstiklal Caddesi.

[i] 4 **[elevator] [S] [S] [S] [S]** All major cards **[metro]** Tünel

🏨 HOTEL DEVMAN
$$

ASMALIMESCIT SOKAK 22,
BEYOĞLU

TEL (0212) 245 62 12

FAX (0212) 292 72 50

www.devmanhotel.com

Pick of the budget hotels close to the venerable Pera Palace. Recently renovated—if rather standard—rooms are quiet, although they lack a view. Clean and tidy bathrooms.

[i] 22 **[elevator] [S] [S] [S]** All major cards **[metro]** Tünel

RESTAURANTS

SOMETHING SPECIAL

🍴 BEBEK BALIKÇI
$$$$

CEVDETPAŞA CADDESI 26, BEBEK

TEL (0212) 263 34 47

Bebek Balıkçı's award-winning seafood is served with aplomb either in its maritime-themed dining room or on a terrace built on stilts over the Bosporus. It's a classic feast of cold meze (fish dumplings, shrimp, seaweed) followed by larger hors d'oeuvres (salted tuna, marinated sea bass, and tarama like you've never tasted), then harbor-fresh fish by the kilo. Excellent.

[seats] 80 **[S] [S] [S]** All major cards **[metro]** Bebek

🍴 BEYMEN BRASSERIE
$$$$

ABDI İPEKÇI CADDESI 23,
NIŞANTAŞI

TEL (0212) 343 04 43

Nestled underneath Beymen's flagship Nişantaşı store (Istanbul's answer to Macy's). This chic restaurant is a see-and-be-seen venue, where patrons sip Cosmopolitans on Turkey's premier shopping street. Reassuringly expensive pastas and salads. Great coffee.

[seats] 60 **[S] [S] [S]** All major cards **[metro]** Osmanbey

🍴 VOGUE
$$$$

SPOR CADDESI, BJK PLAZA, A
BLOK, BEŞIKTAŞ

TEL (0212) 227 44 04

As its name suggests, a resolutely chic—yet disarmingly friendly—contemporary restaurant, lording over Istanbul from an awesome rooftop location. Dip into the sushi bar, the modern Mediterranean menu, or the 100-platter Sunday brunch; the latter is one of the city's best.

[seats] 150 **[S] [S] [S]** All major cards **[metro]** Beşiktaş

🍴 ZUMA
$$$$
SALHANE SOKAK 7, ORTAKÖY
TEL (0212) 236 22 96
www.zumarestaurant.com
Istanbul branch of London
and Hong Kong's Japanese
dining gems. Zuma's menu
may be top-tier gourmet,
but its dining vibe is stylishly
izakaya (informal). Patrons
can sample sushi, nibble
char-grilled meats, or sip
exotic fresh fruit cocktails.
Decor is ultracontemporary,
playing off the floor-to-ceiling
Bosporus views.
🏠 150 🚫 🗝 All major cards
🚇 🚊 Ortaköy

🍴 HÜNKAR
$$$–$$$$
MIM KEMAL ÖKE CADDESI 9,
NIŞANTAŞI
TEL (0212) 296 38 11
While restaurants in this ritzy
neighborhood tend toward
exotic fusion, this former
Fatih neighborhood institution
proudly promotes its
outstanding Ottoman
delights. Opt for *hünkar
beğendi,* or "the sultan's
favorite," eggplant topped
with grilled beef, Hünkar's
signature dish since 1950.
🏠 70 🚫 🗝 All major cards
🚇 Osmanbey

🍴 MÜZEDECHANGA
$$$–$$$$
SAKIP SABANCI CADDESI 22,
EMIRGAN
TEL (0212) 323 09 01
www.changa-istanbul.com
The summertime outpost of
Istanbul restaurant Changa—
renowned for its trendsetting
Turkish-Mediterranean fusion
cuisine—is a streamlined
vision of blond wood, shim
mering steel, and glass.
Set in the Sakıp Sabancı
Museum gardens and privy
to jaw-dropping Bosporus
views, Müzedechanga's menu
includes zucchini flowers

stuffed with cheese and pine
nuts, artichokes with mustard
pea puree, and pistachio-
studded Changa sausage.
🏠 200 🚫 🗝 Closed Mon.
🗝 All major cards
🚇 🚊 Emirgan

🍴 ABRA CADABRA
$$$
ARNAVUTKÖY CADDESI 50,
ARNAVUTKÖY
TEL (0212) 359 60 87
www.abracadabra-ist.com
On the top floors of a traditional wooden *yalı,* chef and
food artist Dilara Erbay dishes
up flamboyant contemporary
takes on Anatolian staples.
Highlights include her *etsiz
çiğ köfte* (meatless bulgur
balls) and onions stuffed
with *gambas ceviche.* Views
from the third-floor terrace
sweep over the picturesque
ferry pier and Asian Bosporus
shore opposite.
🏠 70 🚫 🗝 All major cards
🚇 🚊 Arnavutköy

🍴 ARA KAFE
$$$
YENI ÇARŞI CADDESI, TOSBAĞA
SOKAK 8A, BEYOĞLU
TEL (0212) 245 41 05
Tucked just off Galatasaray's
main square, Ara Café is the
brainchild of famous Istanbul
photographer Ara Güler.
Walls are hung with decades
of his haunting black-and-
white shots of the city, while
outdoors there's a casual
terrace. Dining is modern
Turkish, with particularly tasty
desserts.
🏠 160 🚫 🗝 All major cards
🚇 Galatasaray

🍴 GALATA HOUSE
$$$
GALATA KULESI SOKAK 15,
GALATA, BEYOĞLU
TEL (0212) 245 18 61
Experimental diners and
lovers of Eastern European
cuisine might try this Russo-

Georgian restaurant, housed
in Galata's old British prison.
Sweet Georgian wine accom-
panies courses of spicy warm
cheeses, borscht, and other
beetroot-heavy appetizers or
stewed plums with lamb.
🏠 40 🚫 🗝 Closed Mon.
🗝 All major cards 🚇 Karaköy

🍴 GALATA KONAK
$$$
BEREKET ZADE MAHALESSI, HACI
ALI SOKAK 2, GALATA, BEYOĞLU
TEL (0212) 252 53 46
This restaurant's charm lies
in its panoramic roof terrace
and hidden gem atmosphere,
all reached via a creaky lift or
an ancient marble staircase:
both antiques. Solid standard
cuisine with omelets for
breakfast, pastas for lunch,
and skewers of lamb, beef,
and chicken for dinner. No
alcohol.
🏠 50 🚫 🗝 🗝 All major
cards 🚇 Karaköy/Tünel

🍴 KARAKÖY LOKANTASI
$$$
KEMANKES CADDESI 133,
KARAKÖY
TEL (0212) 292 44 55
A must-seek-out seafood
specialist in Karaköy's former
docklands. The polished
traditional interior is set with
several dining booths, jars full
of pickles, a mouthwatering
meze counter for diners to
point and choose from, and a
wide assortment of different
rakı: a relative rarity in Turkey.
Small outdoor terrace, too.
Specialties include grilled
octopus and fried liver.
🏠 70 🚫 🗝 🗝 All major
cards 🚇 Karaköy

🍴 KIVA HAN
$$$
GALATA KULESI MEYDANI 4,
GALATA, BEYOĞLU
TEL (0212) 292 98 98
A light, refreshingly modern

🚫 Nonsmoking 🚱 Air-conditioning 🏊 Indoor Pool 🏊 Outdoor Pool 💪 Health Club 🗝 Credit Cards

eatery in the shadow of the Galata Tower. Provides lip-smackingly good breakfasts and specialist dishes from eastern Turkey. Smartly presented bites include *imambayıldı* (stuffed eggplant), and corn soup with yogurt from the Black Sea region.

🛏 110 🅢 🕙 🅢 All major cards 🚇 ⛴ Karaköy/Tünel

🍴 MISS PIZZA
$$$

AKARSU CADDESI, HAVYAR SOKAK 7, CIHANGIR, BEYOĞLU
TEL (0212) 251 32 79
Firmly established as Istanbul's premier pizzeria, a hop away from bustling Cihangir Square, which was joined by a sister branch by the Tünel station in 2010. Outdoor seating and a trendy interior melds with a short, sweet (but pricey) wine list, plus mouthwatering oven-fired pizzas.

🛏 60 🅢 🕙 🅢 All major cards 🚇 Taksim

🍴 REJANS
$$$

İSTIKLAL CADDESI, OLIVYA GEÇIDI 7, BEYOĞLU
TEL (0212) 243 38 82
Atmosphere-laden Russian restaurant, barely touched since pre-Soviet times. Slavic specials include salmon tartare, borscht, and chicken Kiev. A former fave of Mustafa Kemal Atatürk, it's now frequented by boisterous Turks and nouveau riche Russians alike.

🛏 80 🅢 🕙 🅢 All major cards 🚇 Tünel

🍴 YAKUP 2
$$$

ASMALI MESCIT MAHALESSI 35, BEYOĞLU
TEL (0212) 249 29 25
Reliably brilliant Turkish

seafood *meyhane*. Meze from pickled anchovies to stuffed squid a delight; simply grilled bream, monkfish, and turbot are superb. Large groups can go for a set price of 30 or so Turkish dishes. Reserve on weekends.

🛏 150 🅢 🕙 🅢 All major cards 🚇 Tünel

🍴 HACI BABA
$$–$$$

İSTIKLAL CADDESI 49, BEYOĞLU
TEL (0212) 244 18 86
www.hacibabarest.com
Overlooking the courtyard of the Aya Triada Greek Orthodox Church, Hacı Baba has been dishing up delicious Ottoman cuisine since it opened its doors in 1921. Try *piliç dolma* (stuffed chicken, Topkapı Palace-style) or *beğendi kebap* (smoked, pureed eggplant kebab). Former patrons include renowned author Orhan Pamuk.

🛏 230 🅢 🅢 All major cards 🚇 Taksim

🍴 ARNAVUTKÖY SOSYAL TESISLERI
$$

ARNAVUTKÖY CADDESI 72, ARNAVUTKÖY
TEL (0212) 257 42 08
For classic Turkish meze or lip-smackingly good grilled fish, this unpretentious spot is hard to beat. Pick a table on the waterfront terrace, flanked by one of the town's picturesque canals, then squeeze in among the families and boisterous groups of students. No alcohol.

🛏 250 🅢 🚇 🅢 No credit cards ⛴ Arnavutköy

🍴 CUPPA
$$

YENI YUVA SOKAK 26, CIHANGIR, BEYOĞLU
TEL (0212) 249 57 23
An almost wholly organic

PRICES

HOTELS
An indication of the cost of a double room in the high season is given by $ signs.

$$$$$: Over TL 500
$$$$: TL 300–TL 500
$$$: TL 150–TL 300
$$: TL 100–TL 150
$: Under TL 100

RESTAURANTS
An indication of the cost of a three-course meal without drinks is given by $ signs.

$$$$$: Over TL 80
$$$$: TL 40–TL 80
$$$: TL 20–TL 40
$$: TL 10–TL 20
$: Under TL 10

juice and lunch lounge, with outdoor terrace and chic, urban interior. Juices include the self-explanatory Baby on Board, Detox, Liver Up, and Jedi Juice. Aside from the pastas and salads, try classics like the roast beef sandwich or bacon omelet.

🛏 80 🅢 🛏 🅢 All major cards 🚇 Taksim

🍴 EGE KAHVALTI YEMEKLERI
$$

CIHANGIR MEYDANI 33, CIHANGIR, BEYOĞLU
TEL (0212) 251 45 60
Traditional Aegean cuisine in the heart of trendy Cihangir. Vegetable-stuffed *mantı*, mini-meatballs in yogurt, and homemade lemonade are

served in the open-kitchen interior, or under fairy lights on the covered terrace.

🔲 20 ◎ 🕐 Closed Mon. ◎ No credit cards 🚇 Taksim

🍴 ENSTITÜ RESTORAN

$$

MESRUTIYET CADDESI 59, TEPEBASI, BEYOĞLU
TEL (0212) 251 22 14
www.istanbulculinary.com
This lunchtime café profits from its position below the city's premier professional cooking school. The stellar menu—created by chefs-in-training—features daily, weekly, and seasonal specialties. Expect experimental cuisine—try the yogurt and bulgur soup, or heirloom spring vegetables served with a powerful garlic dip. Easygoing ambience.

🔲 74 ◎ 🕐 Closed Sun. ◎ All major cards 🚇 Tünel

🍴 FURREYYA GALATA BALIKCISI

$$

SERDAR EKREM SOKAK 2, BEYOĞLU
TEL (0212) 252 48 53
Of the ring of restaurants around Galata Tower, this low-key fish house is an eminently affordable treat. Seafood snacks include *balık durum* (a sea bass and salad wrap) and fish cakes with tangy garlic sauce. No alcohol.

🔲 10 ◎ No credit cards 🚇 Tünel

🍴 KALE CAFÉ

$$

YAHYA KEMAL CADDESI 16, RUMELI HISARI
TEL (0212) 265 00 97
www.kalecafe.com
Tucked between the shadow of Rumeli Hisarı's imposing walls and the Bosporus, low-key Kale is a sunny

spot. Stop in for a lunchtime bowl of *mantı* or a leisurely weekend breakfast. The latter comprises a decadent spread of eggs, olives, and Anatolian cheeses; follow up by dunking freshly made bread into *kaymak* and honey.

🔲 90 ◎ ◎ No credit cards 🚇 Rumeli Hisarı

SOMETHING SPECIAL

🍴 KARDEŞLER

$$

PERŞEMBE PAZARI, KARAKÖY
For fresher than fresh seafood, walk straight through Karaköy's teaming fish market, where three poorly signed but packed fish restaurants vie for trade on the banks of the Golden Horn. All dish up fried bream (*çupra*), sea bass (*levrek*), squid (*kalamar*), and sardines, with platters of melon and cheese. Kardeşler is licensed to sell wine, beer and *rakı*: not so its waterside competitors.

🔲 80 ◎ No credit cards 🚇 Karaköy

SOMETHING SPECIAL

🍴 VAN KAHVALTI EVI

$$

KILIÇ ALI PAŞA, DEFTERDAR YOKUŞU 52, CIHANGIR
TEL (0212) 293 64 37
The Van Breakfast Club brings together wholesome dishes from Turkey's breakfast capital: Lake Van in the country's distant east. Bites include village cheese with herbs, *menemen* scrambled eggs, grape molasses, tahini, and *kaymak* clotted cream with honey. Stupendous.

🔲 60 ◎ 🕐 ◎ All major cards 🚇 Tophane

🍴 BY ÇORBACI SOUP BAR

$–$$

YENI ÇARŞI CADDESI 8A,

BEYOĞLU
TEL (0212) 244 51 69
www.bycorbaci.com.tr
Make like the locals and pick up a breakfast cup of tomato, or pop in at lunchtime for one of the 20 daily soups on offer; more than 600 varieties are in daily rotation. Plenty of nonmeat options are available, including four cheese and summer vegetable.

🔲 35 ◎ ◎ No credit cards 🚇 Galatasaray

🍴 MOMA

$

AKARSU YOKUŞU SOKAĞI, CIHANGIR, BEYOĞLU
TEL (0212) 245 44 74
Cool coffee stop on Cihangir Square where Beyoğlu locals sip espresso and iced lattes. Light bites can be eaten indoors on the terrace, and include local pizza, berry-filled gateaus, cakes, croissants, and specialty hamburgers.

🔲 15 ◎ 🕐 ◎ All major cards 🚇 Taksim

▪ ASIAN ISTANBUL

HOTELS

🏨 A'JIA
🍴 $$$$$

ÇUBUKLU CADDESI 27, KANLICA
TEL (0216) 413 93 00
TEL (0216) 413 93 55
www.ajiahotel.com
Sumptuous hotel inside an Ottoman mansion commanding the Kanlıca waterfront. Playful and extravagant decor; high thread-count linens, orchids, and seaview terraces abound. Upscale award-winning Mediterranean restaurant on-site.

🛏 15 🔲 80 🅿 ◎ 🕐 ◎ All major cards 🚇 Kanlıca

🏨 SUMAHAN ON THE WATER

$$$$$

KULELI CADDESI 51, ÇENGELKÖY

TEL (0216) 422 80 00

TEL (0216) 422 80 08

www.sumahan.com

Once a *rakı* distillery before its recent reincarnation as a fabulous boutique hotel, Sumahan is an elegant arrangement of suites, dining terraces, a wellness center, and even a hammam, right on the Bosporus. Its private launch lies ready to whisk you across to Europe.

🛏 20 🍴 40 🅿 🚭 🏧 🍷 🏧 All major cards 🚢 Çengelköy

RESTAURANTS

🍴 İSKELE

$$$$

İSKELE MEYDANI 10, ÇENGELKÖY

TEL (0216) 321 55 05

Formerly a fisherman's rest, then a drinking den in the 1930s, İskele is now one of Asian Istanbul's premier seafood spots. Kick off with elegantly presented shrimp wraps and seared octopus; choose from grouper to sole for mains. The double-layered terrace is open to the elements in spring and summer.

🍴 150 🚭 🏧 🏧 All major cards 🚢 Çengelköy

🍴 HIDIV KASRI

$$$

ÇUBUKLU YOLU 32, KANLICA

TEL (0216) 413 92 53

Set in the art nouveau decadence of the Khedive's Palace (see p. 149), this is palatial eating for paupers. Managed by Istanbul's tourist authority, the menu is a great value, and more than a little zany: dishes include lamb neck with spinach and pilaf, and sultan's chicken wrap with almond sauce.

🍴 80 🚭 🏧 🏧 All major cards 🚢 Kanlıca

🍴 KANAAT LOKANTASI

$$$

SELMANIPAK CADDESI 9, ÜSKÜDAR

TEL (0216) 341 54 44

Shockingly good family-run establishment that has been dishing up Turkish classics since 1933. The dessert counter boasts a dozen varieties, including Noah's pudding and *künefe*, plus an ever popular takeout service. Their meze section is twice the size: Just point at your choices, then sit down and eat.

🍴 200 🚭 🏧 🏧 All major cards 🚢 Üsküdar

🍴 KOSINITZA

$$$

CADIYE CADDESI, BEREKETLI SOKAK 2, KUZGUNCUK

TEL (0216) 334 04 00

With classical decor and a one-on-one waiting service, this spot is a little like dining in 1970s Paris. Dishes are similarly refined and structured, with traditional fish soup paired into a bouillabaisse, mussels in white wine, and seafood wraps with an aioli dip. Excellent.

🍴 25 🚭 🏧 🏧 All major cards 🚢 Kuzguncuk

🍴 ÇENGELKÖY BALIKÇI

$$

ÇENGELKÖY MEYDANI 20, ÇENGELKÖY

TEL (0216) 557 52 50

A low-key one-man establishment opposite Çengelköy's main square. The decor consists of cream walls and a solitary Atatürk portrait, but the inexpensive and simply prepared grilled fish—served with salad, French fries, and tea—is superb.

🍴 40 🚭 🏧 All major cards 🚢 Çengelköy

🍴 ÇIYA SOFRASI

$$

GÜNESLIBAHCE SOKAK 48/B, KADIKÖY

TEL (0216) 336 30 13

Site of foodie pilgrimage, where Gaziantep-born owner-chef Musa Dağdeviren painstakingly collects regional recipes and creates experimental Anatolian cuisine. Help yourself to a plate of meze (weighed before you return to your table); follow with hot daily delights like lamb-stuffed onions, or chunky saffron yogurt stew. Save room for candied walnuts served with *kaymak*. No alcohol.

🍴 70 🚭 🏧 All major cards 🏧 🚢 Kadıköy

🍴 KADI NIMET BALIKÇILIK

$$

SERASKER CADDESI 10, KADIKÖY

TEL (0216) 348 73 89

No-nonsense seafood restaurant in the heart of Kadıköy's fish market. Mouthwatering good appetizers include *levrek* (sea bass) marinated in oil and Aegean seaweed. Mains a choice of five market-fresh fish, all washed down with Efes or *rakı*. Fish sandwiches available to go.

🍴 30 🚭 🏧 All major cards 🚢 Kadıköy

🍴 MERCAN

$$

YASA CADDESI 56, KADIKÖY

TEL (0216) 346 68 73

One of several branches on Yasa Caddesi of this low-key seafood specialist. Snack on skewers of fried mussels with nutty garlic sauce on the go, or select fried fish and salads in the top-floor dining room.

🍴 120 🚭 🏧 All major cards 🚢 Kadıköy

🍴 YORUS

$$

YORUS KULESI, ANADOLU KAVAĞI

TEL (0216) 320 21 48

On the thigh-busting walk up to Anadolu Kavağı's Byzantine castle, Yorus occupies a swath of hillside with a magnificent dining terrace. Fish, soup, and set-lunch menus available.

🚪 200 🚭 🖎 All major cards 🚇 Anadolukavağı

🍴 LIMAN KAHVESI

$

KADIFE SOKAK 37, KADIKÖY

TEL (0216) 349 98 18

Friendly pub on Kadıköy's grungy Kadife Sokak with vintage furniture, wooden floors, and piles of board games from Monopoly to Jenga. Light snacks available. DJs on the weekend.

🚪 40 🚭 🖎 No credit cards 🚇 Kadıköy

🍴 ŞEMSIPAŞA ÇAY BAHÇESI

$

PAŞA LIMANI CADDESI, ÜSKÜDAR

Vast tearoom with terrace by the Bosporus. Toasted sandwiches, snacks, and nargile waterpipes also available.

🚪 250 🚭 🖎 No credit cards 🚇 Üsküdar

■ ISTANBUL EXCURSIONS

AĞVA

🏨 GUNAY HOTEL

$$$

YAKUPLU CADDESI 47, AĞVA

TEL (0212) 721 77 22

FAX (0212) 721 77 20

www.gunayhotel.com

A hop away from Ağva's beaches and pristine countryside. Surrounded by gardens and specked with balconies and wood panels, the Gunay is a peaceful retreat. Breakfast—served inside or poolside—is laden with fruit, nuts, and local cheeses.

🛏 32 🅿 🖨 🏊 🚭 🖎 🖎 All major cards

ANKARA

🏨 DIVAN ANKARA
🍴 $$$

TUNALI HILMI CADDESI, GÜNIZ SOKAK 42, KIZILAY, ANKARA

TEL (0312) 457 40 00

www.divan.com.tr

Chic urban haven on Tunalı Hilmi Caddesi, Ankara's glamorously modern shopping street. Pampering additions include pillow menu, sauna, and winter garden. Formal restaurant, brasserie and hip bar on-site.

🛏 83 🚪 100 🅿 🖨 🚭 🚭 🖎 All major cards

🏨 OTEL ATLANTA

$$

NECATIBEY CADDESI 28, KIZILAY, ANKARA

TEL (0312) 232 58 00

www.otelatlanta.com

Budget accommodation that ticks all the boxes: clean, tidy, quiet, and totally central. Rooms are basic, but the rooftop bar, where the extensive buffet breakfast is also served, is a panoramic delight.

🛏 70 🖨 🚭 🚭 🖎 All major cards

🍴 ÇENGELHAN BRASSERIE

$$$

NECATIBEY MAHALLESI, DEPO SOKAK 1, CITADEL, ANKARA

TEL (0312) 309 68 00

Highly rated brasserie in the middle of Ankara's Rahmi M. Koç Museum. The atmospheric location is backed up by a superb wine list and an offbeat fine dining menu: Try braised lamb shank, or roast veal with herbs and eggplant purée.

🚪 60 🅿 🚭 🚭 🕒 Closed Mon. 🖎 All major cards

🍴 RESTAURANT ULUDAĞ

$$$

DENIZCILER CADDESI 54, ULUS, ANKARA

TEL (0312) 309 04 00

Where wealthy Ankara locals come for a belly-busting İskender kebab. Indeed, aside from salads and sides, this calorific pile of meat, bread, and yogurt is the only thing on the menu. Foaming butter is poured over your portion as it's set down on the table. A delight.

🚪 150 🅿 🖨 🚭 🚭 🖎 All major cards

🍴 ADANA SOFRASI

$$

NECATIBEY CADDESI 28-30, KIZILAY, ANKARA

TEL (0312) 230 02 72

A traditional meze and grill on one side, an ultramodern pizza and pide joint on the other. Creations at the latter brim with pastrami, sweetcorn, broccoli, and olives. Stuffed chicken breasts and grilled racks of lamb available, too.

🚪 90 🚭 🚭 🖎 All major cards

🍴 CAFÉ ANO

$$

DEMIRFIRKA MAHALLESI 29, CITADEL, ANKARA

TEL (0312) 312 79 78

A hidden gem of a café built into Ankara's citadel walls. Vintage 1970s furniture fills the salon, while a glass-walled conservatory commands views over the entire city. Beer, wine, and gourmet sandwiches available.

🚪 60 🚭 🚭 🖎 All major cards

BURSA

🏨 KITAP EVI BUTIK OTEL
🍴 $$$-$$$$

KAVAKLIDERE CADDESI, BURÇÜSTÜ SOKAK 21, BURSA

TEL (0224) 225 41 60
www.kitapevi.com.tr
A former bookstore and café, Kitap Evi is now Bursa's only boutique hotel. Each room is unique: The Hamamli Room has its own private hammam, while the Cumba Suite's has great views from its bathtub. There's a restaurant with tables under magnolia trees in the courtyard, and a Turkish bath and spa on site.
12 50 All major cards

HOTEL ÇEŞMELI
$$
GÜMÜŞÇEKEN CADDESI 6, BURSA
TEL (0224) 224 15 11
Run by a friendly team of women, this neat hotel's baby blue bedrooms are seemingly unchanged since the 1950s. Centrally located, just off the town's many bazaars, with a very good breakfast buffet.
15 All major cards

KEBAPÇI İSKENDER
$$$
ÜNLÜ CADDESI 7, BURSA
TEL (0224) 221 46 15
www.kebapciiskender.com.tr
It was here that the famously rich *İskender kebab* was invented in 1876—lamb drenched in tomato sauce and yogurt, and topped with ladles of foaming butter. Still deliciously decadent.
140 No credit cards

BÜYÜKADA

NAYA HOTEL
$$$
YILMAZ TÜRK CADDESI 96, BÜYÜKADA, PRINCES ISLANDS
TEL (0216) 382 45 98
www.nayaistanbul.com
This once dilapidated villa was given a boutique gipsy overhaul by its German owner in 2010. Ornaments drip from the chandeliers, and writing and yoga retreats are held in the flower-filled garden where an all-natural swimming pool also resides.
7 No credit cards

SPLENDID PALAS HOTEL
$$$
23 NISAN CADDESI 53, BÜYÜKADA
TEL (0216) 382 69 50
FAX (0216) 382 67 75
www.splendidhotel.net
Opened in 1908, Splendid Palas' silver domes and red-shuttered facade dominates Büyükada's charming town center. Classically decorated rooms—many with sea views—center around the hotel's inner courtyard. An idyllic base for exploring the sleepy Princes Islands.
74 All major cards

HEYBELIADA

KARAMANYAN
$$$-$$$$
REFAH ŞEHITLERI CADDESI, HEYBELIADA
TEL 44 (0)20 7436 8009 (IN U.K.)
www.istanbulislands.com
Four chic apartments, each with their own shady, hammock-slung garden space, located within the former Grand Bretagne Hotel, built in 1875. Karamanyan's British owners have restored the mansion with an obvious eye for style. Weekly rentals.
4 All major cards

MERIT HALKI PALACE HOTEL
$$$
ISMET INÖNÜ SOKAK, HEYBELIADA
TEL (0216) 351 00 25
FAX (0216) 351 00 32
www.halkipalacehotel.com
Set among the forested hills of Heybeliada, this neat 19th-century hotel is a peaceful and relaxing island hideaway. Guests can explore the island on foot, or just spend a few days by the pool.
45 All major cards

BAŞAK ET VE BALIK RESTAURANT
$$$
AYYILDIZ CADDESI 26/A, HEYBELIADA
TEL (0216) 351 12 89
www.basakrestaurant.com
This welcoming terrace stands out from Heybeliada's string of seafront restaurants. Meze are exceptional, such as marinated mackerel, or rice-stuffed mussels. True

PRICES

HOTELS
An indication of the cost of a double room in the high season is given by **$** signs.

$$$$$: Over TL 500
$$$$: TL 300–TL 500
$$$: TL 150–TL 300
$$: TL 100–TL 150
$: Under TL 100

RESTAURANTS
An indication of the cost of a three-course meal without drinks is given by $ signs.

$$$$$: Over TL 80
$$$$: TL 40–TL 80
$$$: TL 20–TL 40
$$: TL 10–TL 20
$: Under TL 10

to its name (Başak Meat and Fish Restaurant), this spot also offers meat or fish-based set menus for groups of four diners (minimum).

🛏 140 🚭 🅰 All major cards

🍴 MELTEM PASTANESI
$

HEYBELIADA
TEL (0216) 451 26 56
Excellent spot to pick up a picnic: try the spinach börek, olive-stuffed bread, or fruit cakes. There are five tiny tables outside, perfect for people-watching, where you can also order tea.

🛏 10 🚭 🅰 No credit cards

POLONEZKÖY

🏨 POLKA COUNTRY HOTEL
🍴 $$$

CUMHURIYET YOLU 20, POLONEZKÖY
TEL (0216) 432 32 20
FAX (0216) 432 32 21
www.polkahotel.com
This wooden country inn offers the perfect Istanbul escape. Laze by the pool, play chess, hit the hotel library, or explore Polonezköy rural locale. The old-style dining room is the setting for rich organic breakfasts (home-made jam, honey) and dinnertime blowouts (chestnut pie, steaks).

🛎 15 🛏 40 🅿 🚭 🅰 🏊
🅰 All major cards

ULUDAĞ

🏨 BECEREN OTEL
🍴 $$$$

OTELLER, ULUDAĞ
TEL (0224) 285 21 11
www.beceren.com.tr
This large, Swiss-inspired chalet-hotel is positioned steps from the ski runs, at the heart of Oteller. Full board is included in room rates.

🛎 87 🛏 250 🏊 🅿 🛡 🅰 All major cards

YALOVA

🏨 ÇAMLIK HOTEL
🍴 $$$

TERMAL, YALOVA
TEL (0224) 675 74 00
FAX (0224) 675 74 08
www.yalovatermal.com
Basic rooms with large balconies, set on the hill above Termal's hot-springs complex. Rates include free access to all of Termal's facilities, including private hammam rooms. The on-site restaurant offers a good value set menu.

🛎 91 🛏 200 🏊 🅿 🛡 🅰 All major cards

🍴 ÇINAR CAFÉ
$

ÇINAR MEYDANI, TERMAL, YALOVA
A picturesque stop for tea or a toasted sandwich. Outdoor tables are tucked beneath the shady canopy of a 200-year-old plane tree.

🛏 100 🚭 🅰 No credit cards

◼ TROY & GALLIPOLI

BOZCAADA

🏨 GÜMÜŞ OTEL
$$

KURTULUŞ CADDESI, BOZCAADA
TEL (0286) 697 82 52
FAX (0286) 697 00 52
www.gumusotel.com.tr
Pure romance in an old Greek mansion, a few steps back from the seafood restaurants on Bozcaada's quay. Simple whitewashed rooms overlook a vine-covered terrace, where a mammoth buffet breakfast of preserves (including the island's specialty, sweet tomato jam), fruit, and local cheese is laid out each morning.

🛎 21 🚭 🅰 🅰 All major cards

ÇANAKKALE

🏨 HOTEL KERVANSARAY
$$$

FETVANE SOKAK 13, ÇANAKKALE
TEL (0286) 217 81 92
FAX (0286) 217 20 18
www.otelkervansaray.com
Çanakkale's single boutique offering, housed in a former Ottoman judge's residence, is a lavish treat with high ceilings, cable TV, and lots of space. Enjoy breakfast or a beer in the secluded ornamental garden.

🛎 19 🅿 🚭 🅰 🅰
🅰 All major cards

🏨 HOTEL TUSAN
🍴 $$$

GÜZELYALI 47, ÇANAKKALE
TEL (0286) 232 87 47
FAX (0286) 232 82 26
www.tusanhotel.com
Highly recommended family-run option, a short drive from the ruins of Troy. Includes all amenities including a swimming pool, tropical garden, and pool table. Its quiet beachfront location is 10 miles (14 km) from Çanakkale.

🛎 25 🛏 100 🅿 🚭 🅰 🅰
🏊 🅰 All major cards

🏨 ANZAC HOTEL
$$

SAAT KULESI MEYDANI 8, ÇANAKKALE
TEL (0286) 217 77 77
FAX (0286) 217 20 18
www.anzachotel.com
Dated but highly recommended central hotel purveying its own line of Gallipoli and Troy tours. Popular with groups and visiting Australasians (look for the Vegemite spread at breakfast).

🛎 25 🚭 🅰 🅰 🅰 All major cards

🏨 ÇANAK HOTEL
🍴 $$

CUMHURIYET MEYDANI, DIBEK
SOKAK 1, ÇANAKKALE
TEL (0286) 214 15 82
FAX (0286) 214 09 06
www.canakhotel.com
Smart new budget hotel by
Çanakkale's ferry port and
main square. Modern rooms
have kettles, TVs, and, in
most cases, small balconies.
Dinner deals available at
the panoramic top-floor
restaurant, where breakfast is
also served.
[i] 50 [seats] 80 [elevator] [closed]
[metro] [cards] All major cards

🍴 YALOVA
$$
YALI CADDESI 7, ÇANAKKALE
TEL (0286) 217 10 45
The premier restaurant in
Çanakkale dates from the
1940s and has a classic Turk-
ish seafood menu: seaweed
salad, stuffed mussels,
anchovies, cuttlefish eggs,
and lots of harbor-fresh fish.
[seats] 120 [parking] [closed] [metro] [cards] All major
cards

🍴 ALBATROS
$
ATATÜRK CADDESI 42,
ÇANAKKALE
TEL (0286) 217 81 11
Locals-only fish restaurant
famed for its delicious fish
soup, plus simple but sublime
grilled seafood. Around 200
yards (180 m) southwest of
the Otogar (bus station) over
the traffic lights, on the right.
No alcohol.
[seats] 60 [closed] [metro] [cards] No credit
cards

🍴 DONAMA ÇAY BAHÇESI
$
YALI CADDESI 10, ÇANAKKALE
TEL (0286) 217 18 64
A dawn-til-dusk teahouse—
the nearest thing Çanakkale
has to a see-and-be-seen
establishment—crowning the
seafront promenade. Menu
items stretch from espresso,

and cheese toasties, to *köfte*
meatballs.
[seats] 150 [metro] No credit cards

🍴 KAHVESI
$
HANIM SOKAK 14, ÇANAKKALE
This romantic little shop is
the only place in Çanakkale
to dose up on quality coffees,
including latte, cappuccino,
and mocha. Homemade
cakes are also served.
[seats] 15 [closed] [metro] No credit cards

ECEABAT

🍴 LIMAN RESTAURANT
$$
ISTIKLAL CADDESI 67, ECEABAT
TEL (0286) 814 27 55
Eceabat's finest eatery is a
seafood specialist with white
tablecloths inside and a leafy
terrace outside. Seasonal
menu revolves around fruits
of the sea from squid to
lobster to sea bass.
[seats] 80 [parking] [closed] [metro] [cards] All major
cards

▰ EPHESUS & ROMAN TURKEY

PAMUKKALE

🏨 HOTEL HAL-TUR
🍴 $$
MEHMET AKIF ERSOY BULVARI
71, PAMUKKALE
TEL (0258) 272 27 23
www.haltur.net
Taking its architectural
inspiration from Pamukkale's
nickname ("cotton castle"),
Hal-Tur offers superb views
over the nearby travertine
pools. The most upscale
option in town.
[i] 10 [seats] 90 [parking] [metro] [closed-full]
[closed] [cards] All major cards

🏨 HOTEL VENUS
🍴 $
HASAN TAHSIN CADDESI 16,
PAMUKKALE

TEL (0258) 272 21 52
www.venushotel.net
Welcoming, eye-catchingly
pink Hotel Venus has been
family-run for two decades.
During summertime, the new
swimming pool and outdoor
terrace (where home-cooked
meals are served) is a delight.
Day trips organized, including
trips to the ruins of Aphrodisias.
[i] 15 [seats] 40 [parking] [metro] [closed] [cards] All
major cards

🍴 MELROSE ALLGAU HOTEL
$
VALI VEKFI ERTÜRK CADDESI 8,
PAMUKKALE
TEL (0258) 272 22 50
www.allgauhotel.com
Charming owners Mehmet
and Ummu run this friendly
little hotel, complete with
garden, pool, and an excellent
restaurant. It's a short walk
to Pamukkale's travertine
terraces.
[i] 25 [seats] 40 [parking] [metro] [closed] [cards] All
major cards

SELÇUK

SOMETHING SPECIAL

🏨 HOTEL BELLA
🍴 $$
ATATURK MAHALLESI,
ST. JOHN STREET 7, SELÇUK
TEL (0232) 892 39 44
FAX (0232) 892 03 44
www.hotelbella.com
Gregarious childhood pals
Erdal and Nazmi own and
operate this charming spot.
Rooms are snug, each one
decorated with unique carpets,
carved wooden furniture, and
ceramics
from their shop (see Divan p.
260) downstairs. Congenial
rooftop restaurant with fireplace in winter, library
and Internet point.
[i] 11 [seats] 50 [parking] [closed]
[metro] [cards] All major cards

🍴 ARTEMIS RESTAURANT & ŞARAPEVI
$$-$$$
ŞIRINCE KÖYÜ, SELÇUK
TEL (0232) 898 32 40
www.artemisrestaurant.com
Built 150 years ago to house the village primary school, today Artemis is Şirince's best restaurant and wine bar. Stop to sip local fruit wines in their manicured gardens, or during winter, sample heartier fare alongside the roaring fire.
🪑 700 🚭 🌀 All major cards

🍴 AMAZON BISTRO
$$
ANTON KALLINGER CADDESI 22, SELÇUK
TEL (0232) 892 38 79
Located in a residential western neighborhood of Selçuk, the Amazon's petite terrace peeks out over the Artemision's sole column and the nearby ancient hammam. Particularly tasty grilled meat dishes and seasonal vegetables.
🪑 40 🚭 🌀 No credit cards

SIRINCE

🏨 NIŞANYAN HOUSE HOTEL
$$-$$$$
ŞIRINCE
TEL (0232) 898 32 08
www.nisanyan.com
A selection of lovingly restored village homes, newer cottages, plus a guesthouse and an inn, all dotted around the picturesque hilltop town of Sirince. Owned by Turkish travel writer and local activist Sevan Nişanyan.
🛏 19 🪑 40 🚭 🌀 All major cards

▪ THE TURQUOISE COAST

ANTALYA

🏨 OTANTIK BUTIK OTEL
$$$
HESAPÇI SOKAK 14, KALEIÇI, ANTALYA
TEL (0242) 244 85 30
FAX (0242) 244 85 31
www.otantikbutikotel.com
Gorgeous boutique hotel occupying a renovated Antalya town house. Built around a vast open terrace and "wine house," where Turkish wine can be sipped while nibbling local cheeses and fruit.
🛏 8 🪑 40 🚭 🌀 All major cards

🏨 HOTEL REUTLINGEN HOF
$$
MERMERLI BANYO SOKAK 23, KALEIÇI, ANTALYA
TEL (0242) 247 63 72
FAX (0242) 248 40 75
www.reutlingenhof.com
Little gem of a hotel inside an old Antalya town house. Perfectly located for exploring the old city and marina.
🛏 16 🚭 🌀 All major cards

🍴 SERASER
$$$$
KARANLIK SOKAK 18, KALEIÇI, ANTALYA
TEL (0242) 247 60 15
Fine-dining restaurant with impeccable service. Find stuffed squid, sea bass baked in vine leaves, and beef casseroled inside homemade puff pastry. All elegantly presented.
🪑 120 🚭 🌀 All major cards

BOZBURUN

🏨 HOTEL APHRODITE
$$$
VILLAGE, BOZBURUN
TEL (0252) 456 22 68
FAX (0252) 456 26 45
www.hotelaphrodite.net
This boutique hotel in laid-back Bozburun ranks as one of southern Turkey's ultimate escapes. Simple beach cabins hem in a hammock-strewn piazza, which fronts the crystal clear sea. The obligatory half-board meals are a staggering collection of local fruit, fish, and cheese.
🛏 15 🪑 50 🅿 🚭 🌀 All major cards

SOMETHING SPECIAL

🏨 OTEL METE
$$
VILLAGE, BOZBURUN
TEL (0252) 456 20 99
www.otelmete.com
The simple hotel on the sleepy Datça peninsula is a real find. Popular with holidaying Turkish families, it's right on the water, is a spectacular value, and hosts an obligatory half-board evening feast. Has its own sea kayaks and boat for tours around the bay.
🛏 25 🪑 40 🅿 🚭 🌀 All major cards

CIRALI

SOMETHING SPECIAL

🏨 ARCADIA
$$$$
SAHIL YOLU, ÇIRALI
TEL (0242) 825 73 40
www.arcadiaholiday.com
Sublime Thai-style beach bungalows with a touch of the 21st century: fridges full of drinks, terraces with rocking chairs, and glass roof panels for star-gazing. First-rate dining at any hour of the day. Munch through the 12-platter breakfast at midday, then order up an evening set menu, best enjoyed by the campfire on the beach.
🛏 10 🪑 40 🅿 🚭 🌀 All major cards

🏨 AZUR ÇIRALI
🍴 $$$
SAHIL YOLU, ÇIRALI
TEL (0242) 825 70 72
www.azurhotelcirali.com
Beautiful family-size
bungalows and solid timber
lodges dotted around a
vast beachside garden. The
restaurant is very authentic:
Try octopus salad, barbecue
fish, or plenty of vegetarian
options under the terrace's
ancient mulberry trees.
🚪 30 🛏 60 🅿 🚭
🎫 🦽 All major cards

🏨 MYLAND NATURE
🍴 $$$
SAHIL YOLU, ÇIRALI
TEL (0242) 825 70 44
www.mylandnature.com
Bungalows set inside an
organic haven of fruit trees
and fragrant herbs. Run by
Istanbul escapees Pinar
and Engin, Myland offers
daily yoga lessons, plus free
bikes and beach mattresses.
Cuisine locally sourced and
all organic, plus fish sourced
from the sea 100 yards (90
m) away.
🚪 13 🛏 50 🅿 🚭
🎫 🦽 All major cards

GÖCEK

🏨 A&B HOME HOTEL
$$
TURGUT ÖZAL CADDESI, GÖCEK
TEL (0252) 645 18 20
FAX (0252) 645 18 43
www.abhomehotel.com
A stone's throw from the
marinas on Göcek's seafront,
rooms at this quiet retreat
are charming if simple. Better
still is the poolside bar and
breakfast area, where an
open buffet of melon, preserves, and cheeses await.
🚪 11 🚭 🎫 🏊 🦽 All major
cards

KALKAN

🏨 ASFIYA HOTEL
🍴 $$$
YALIBOYU MAHALLESI,
CUMHURIYET CADDESI, KALKAN
TEL (0242) 844 23 28
FAX (0242) 844 23 27
www.asfiyahotel.com
There is much to rave about
the Asfiya, ten minutes on
foot from Kalkan's historic
harbor. The rooftop pool,
body treatment and massage
spa, and Mediterranean
restaurants are all sublime.
Every room boasts a balcony
or terrace, while some suites
include Jacuzzi baths and
reclining lounges.
🚪 50 🛏 120 🛗 🎫 🚭
🏊 🍸 🦽 All major cards

KAŞ

🏨 HOTEL OREO
🍴 $$
CUKURBAGLI CADDESI 10, KAŞ
TEL (0242) 836 22 20
FAX (0242) 836 16 05
www.oreohotel.com
This bougainvillea-covered
hotel has the facilities
of those normally twice
the price: a tree-dappled
swimming pool, barbecue
restaurant, and sun terrace.
Standard rooms come with
balconies, some looking
far out to sea. Popular with
hikers, mountain bikers,
divers, and other outdoor
enthusiasts.
🚪 30 🛏 60 🅿 🛗 🚭
🎫 🦽 All major cards

🍴 BAHÇE
$$$
ILKOKUL SOKAK 31, KAŞ
TEL (0242) 836 23 70
Bahçe translates as "garden,"
and it's in this cozy vine-
covered yard that delicious
meze (tarama, fish cakes)
and meaty delicacies (fillet
steak, herb-crusted lamb) are
served up with an alfresco

elegance. Seating ranges
from huge tables to romantic
couple-size nooks.
🛏 60 🚭 🎫 🦽 All major cards

SOMETHING SPECIAL

🍴 BALIK BAHÇE
$$$
SULEYMAN SANDIKCI
SOKAK 18, KAŞ
TEL (0242) 836 27 79
Combines delicious local
seafood with a romantic
candlelit atmosphere. The vast
whitewashed alfresco terrace
is hemmed by a meze counter
(choose between shrimp rolls
and marinated sea bass among
others) and a well-staffed
fish desk (pick your monkfish,
bream, or swordfish kebab for
the grill).
🛏 80 🚭 🎫 🦽 All major cards

OLYMPOS

🏨 LIMON PANSIYON
$
YAZIR KÖYÜ, OLYMPOS
TEL (0242) 892 14 05
www.olymposlemon.com
Still retains the tranquil naive
charm once standard in this
former backpacker valley. Basic
wooden tree houses (actually
rooms on stilts) combine
with open-air wooden booths
stuffed with cushions, all set
inside a fragrant lemon grove.
🚪 14 🅿 🚭 🎫 🦽 All major
cards

■ CAPPADOCIA

AYVALI VILLAGE

🏨 GAMIRASU HOTEL
$$$
AYVALI VILLAGE
TEL (0384) 354 58 15
FAX (0384) 354 58 64
www.gamirasu.com
An isolated retreat that smacks
of authenticity at every turn.
Expect kilim rugs, Ottoman

🏨 Hotel 🍴 Restaurant 🚪 No. of Guest Rooms 🛏 No. of Seats 🅿 Parking 🚇 Metro 🕐 Closed 🛗 Elevator

recliners, hollowed-out cave rooms and wooden writing desks. Beautiful rooms range up to deluxe suites with panoramic views.

ⓘ 25 ⓢ ⓐ ⛱
⚜ All major cards

ÇAVUŞIN

🏠 THE VILLAGE CAVE
🍴 $$$

ÇAVUŞIN
TEL (0384) 532 71 97
FAX (0384) 532 71 44
www.thevillagecave.com
An old stone mansion half built into the rock, and the only hotel opposite the Church of St. John the Baptist. Discreet early morning and evening access to Cappadocia's best sights after a blowout buffet breakfast or traditional Turkish dinner.

ⓘ 5 ⓢ ⓐ ⚜ All major cards

GÖREME

🏠 ANATOLIAN HOUSES
$$$$$

GAFERLI MAHALLESI, GÖREME
TEL (0384) 271 24 63
FAX (0384) 271 22 29
www.anatolianhouses.com.tr
Ultra-elegant collection of boutique cave houses, most with fireplaces and Ottoman trimmings. All are scattered around a courtyard filled with pools, bridges, and hammocks. Facilities include a Turkish bath and spa.

ⓘ 19 ⓢ ⓐ ⚜ ⚜ All major cards

🏠 LOCAL CAVE HOUSE
$$$

CEVIZLER SOKAK 11, GÖREME
TEL (0384) 271 21 71
FAX (0384) 271 24 98
www.localcavehouse.com
Basic, friendly, and very cute. Nine ornate cave rooms (some family-size) with vintage furniture form an amphitheater-like backdrop

to the large sun terrace and swimming pool. Services range from airport pickup to local guide and car hire.

ⓘ 9 ⓢ ⓐ ⛱
⚜ All major cards

🍴 LOCAL RESTAURANT
$$$

MÜZE CADDESI 38, GÖREME
TEL (0384) 271 26 29
Smart tableware and solid dishes wrapped up with an Anatolian attempt at silver service. Upscale cuisine ranges from the experimental (hummus with cumin, eight-flavor sharing platters) to the classic (roast zucchini with yogurt, grilled lamb chops).

🪑 60 ⓢ ⓐ ⚜ All major cards

🍴 SEYYAH HAN
$$$

MÜZE YOLU 56, GÖREME
TEL (0384) 271 26 62
Popular stop on the walk between Göreme and the Open-Air Museum, with a tree-dappled garden and a first-floor café terrace. Tasty Turkish cuisine—try *lahmacun* pizza, *testi* pottery bakes, and assorted meze.

🪑 200 ⓢ ⓐ ⚜ All major cards

🍴 S&S RESTAURANT
$$

BILAL EROĞLU CADDESI, GÖREME
NO PHONE
Family-run with a low-key outdoor dining terrace. Speciality is the tasty testi, where beef, lamb, chicken or vegetables are slow cooked in a ceramic pot, which diners smash with a hammer at their table. 🪑 35 ⓢ ⓐ ⚜ None

🍴 SILK ROAD KEBAB HOUSE
$$

MÜZE YOLU, GÖREME
NO PHONE

Great spot for a beer on Göreme's central square. The waiter will carve you off a chicken or lamb kebab from the revolving döner skewer. Vegetarian options include falafel wraps with hummus.

🪑 50 ⓢ ⓐ ⚜ None

ÜRGÜP

🏠 4ODA CAVE HOUSE
$$$$

ESBELLI SOKAK 46, ÜRGÜP
TEL (0384) 341 60 80
FAX (0384) 341 60 90
www.4oda.com
Intimate boutique establishment managed by a female former tour guide. Heaps of nooks and crannies in which to relax, play backgammon, or strum a guitar. Breakfast is a brunch-like volley of homemade pastries and fresh fruit.

ⓘ 5 ⓢ ⓐ ⚜ All major cards

🏠 ESBELLI EVI
$$$-$$$$

ESBELLI SOKAK, 8 (P.K. 2), ÜRGÜP
TEL (0384) 341 33 95
FAX (0384) 341 88 48
www.esbelli.com
This collection of lovingly restored cave houses provides the most atmospheric and luxurious accommodation of all the area's cave hotels. The rooms are all unique, with smooth, bare stone walls, carved doorways, and comfortable beds.

ⓘ 13 ⓢ ⚜ All major cards

🍴 SÖMINE
$$$

CUMHURIYET MEYDANI 9, ÜRGÜP
TEL (0384) 341 84 42
Offbeat dishes include carrot and lamb stuffed *börek*, local meatballs, spinach-stuffed chicken, and *testi* pottery bakes.

🪑 150 ⓢ ⓐ ⚜ All major cards

ⓢ Nonsmoking ⓐ Air-conditioning 🏊 Indoor Pool ⛱ Outdoor Pool 🏋 Health Club ⚜ Credit Cards

Shopping

Be sure to leave plenty of space in your suitcase: Istanbul is nothing short of a shopper's paradise. It's home to what is arguably the world's first shopping mall—the Grand Bazaar—and this covered market is a cornucopia of delights from stacks of hammam towels to glowing glass lamps, pashmina scarves, and finely decorated ceramics.

Fanning out from the Grand Bazaar, Sultanahmet's streets are similarly littered with treasures. It's here that exquisite hand-knotted carpets and *kilims* are concentrated.

Across the Golden Horn, European Istanbul is the city's best spot for one-off boutiques. As well as Çukurcuma's piles of antiques and art deco objets d'art, the nearby neighborhood of Nişantaşı houses unique Turkish designers and their high-end ateliers. And of course, Beyoğlu's main pedestrian thoroughfare, İstiklal Caddesi, can satisfy any whim—chocolatiers nestle alongside piles of discounted T-shirts, and brand-name outlets squeeze in among contemporary art.

Travelers outside of the country's cultural capital will have plenty of temptations, too. For honey, pistachios, and spicy dried chilies, look for local markets: Each town has a weekly bazaar. Tiny shops also ply their handmade wares, often authentic contrasts to big city finds, and always with a story behind them.

Books

Pandora Kitabevi

Büyük Parmakkapı Sokak 8, Beyoğlu, Istanbul
Tel (0212) 243 35 03
Excellent range of English-language books—from fiction and children's books to cookbooks and dictionaries—as well as many travel guides.

For additional bookshops, see sidebar p. 27.

Carpets & Kilims

Carpets are synonymous with Turkey. The best are created using silky, vegetable-dyed, lamb's neck wool with a high percentage of lanolin. A quality carpet will be made over eight to nine months, and is double-knotted by hand. Traditional patterns are unique to different villages. Turkish carpets tend to come in one of six approximate standard sizes. Although similar to carpets, kilims are woven, rather than knotted. Carpet and kilim prices depend on the piece's quality, complexity, size, and age.

Divan

Hotel Bella, Ataturk Mahallesi, St. John Street 7, Selçuk
Tel (0232) 892 39 44
www.hotelbella.com
A veritable carpet, kilim, and ceramic haven. Owners Erdal and Nazmi will patiently explain the origins (sourced from village families in eastern Turkey) and techniques used to create each piece. Traditional hand-carved wooden furniture is a delight.

Yörük

Kürkçüler Çarşısı 16, Grand Bazaar, Istanbul
Tel (0212) 527 32 11
This tiny, wonderful shop is packed with top-quality carpets and kilims from across the country. An essential Istanbul shopping stop.

Chocolate

Inci

İstiklal Caddesi 124, Istanbul
Tel (0212) 293 92 24
Long established, old-style chocolate and sweet shop. Be sure to sample a plate of their famed profiteroles.

Clothes

Ece Sukan Vintage

Ahmet Fetgari Sokak 152, Teşvikiye, Istanbul
Tel (0212) 233 54 39
www.ecesukanvintage.com
Brand-new vintage clothing shop owned by Ece Sukan, *Vogue Turkey*'s style consultant.

Umit Unal

Asmalımescit Mahallesi, Ensiz Sokak 1B, Tünel, Istanbul
Tel (0212) 245 78 86
www.umitunal.com
Owned by brother-sister team Umit and Sevtop, this combination atelier and clothes shop was one of the neighborhood's first high-end boutiques. Simply cut, flattering women's clothing, plus bags, belts, and scarves.

Zeki Triko
Valikonaği Caddesi, Akkavak Sokak, Tunaman Çarşısı 27, Nişantaşı, Istanbul
Tel (0212) 233 82 79
www.zekitriko.com.tr
Sleek, sexy swimwear and women's clothing.

Coffee
Kurukahveci Mehmet Efendi
Tahmis Sokak 66, Eminönü, Istanbul
Tel (0212) 511 42 62
www.mehmetefendi.com
Brown paper sacks of traditional Turkish coffee are stuffed by the genial staff, then sold from this legendary shop's window.

Honey
Eta Bal
Güneşli Bahçe Sokak 28/A, Kadiköy, Istanbul
Tel (0216) 414 99 77
High-quality honeys, pollen, and propolis from the Black Sea.

Interior Design
Hall
Faik Pasa Caddesi 6, Çukurcuma, Istanbul
Tel (0216) 292 95 90
www.hallİstanbul.com
An Aladdin's cave of antique Ottoman finds and uniquely designed pieces, owned by New Zealand-born collector and designer Christopher Hall.

Jewelry
Stonebul
Kavaflar Sokak 47, Grand Bazaar, Istanbul
Tel (0212) 522 23 64
www.stonebul.com
This friendly, family-run boutique sells unusual silver, gold, and precious stone jewelry; pieces can be made to order.

Pastries
Baklavacı Güllüoğlu
Yoğurtçu Sütçü Sokak 10, Kadiköy, Istanbul
Tel (0216) 330 22 16
Sticky, pistachio-laden pastries (and copious free samples!) from the eastern city of Gaziantep.

Özkonak
Akarsu Caddesi 60, Cihangir, Istanbul
Tel (0212) 249 13 07
Petite purveyor of *sütlaç* (Turkish rice pudding), *tavuk göğsü* (the bizarre chicken pudding), plus plenty of syrup-soaked sweets.

Pickles (*turşu*)
Petek Turşuları
Duduodaları Sokak 1D, Balık Pazarı, Galatasaray, Istanbul
Tel (0212) 249 13 24
This snug entranceway is impossible to miss—look out for the jars of pickled plums, artichokes, and even eggs.

Pottery & Ceramics
Avanos Anatolia Pottery
Alaettin Mah., Uluada Mevkii, Avanos
Tel (0384) 511 60 71
www.avanospottery.com
Traditional rustic terra-cotta pottery from Cappadocia, including jugs, urns, pots, and vases.

Shoes
Nr 39
Süleyman Nazif Sokak 39, Nişantaşı, Istanbul
Tel (0212) 241 40 59
www.nr39.com
Stunning, handmade women's shoes, including soft tassled boots and colorful sandals.

Spices
Kral
Hasırcılar Caddesi 6, Eminönü, Istanbul
Tel (0212) 513 88 93
Just outside of the Spice Market, Kral has been an essential stop for local shoppers for three generations. Today, the three sisters/owners stock barrels of bright candy-covered cardamon, hazelnuts, Turkish delight, saffron, pistachios, and spicy red pepper.

Turkish Delight (*lokum*)
Hacı Bekir
Hamidiye Caddesi 83, Eminönü, Istanbul
Tel (0212) 522 06 66
In business since 1777, when Turkish Delight inventor Hacı Bekir was chief confectioner to Sultan Abdulhamit I.

Wine
Kaplankaya Şarapları
Şirince Koyu
Tel (0232) 898 31 69
www.kaplankaya-sirince.com
A stellar selection of sweet fruit wines, ranging from melon to blackberry. Free tastings available.

Entertainment

Istanbul is a boisterous city of 13 million souls with live music, dancing, and concerts every night of the year. In addition, several internationally renowned music festivals take place annually, ranging from opera to jazz to classical. Turks also love the movies, with acclaimed homegrown talent on display at the city's plentiful cinemas. Most picture houses show international hits in their original language (with Turkish subtitles), and tickets are routinely purchased in person a few hours before the show.

Note that several Istanbul consulates, plus the city's bars, churches, public squares, museums, and old buildings, regularly show theater, music, and opera performances. Some of the settings are sublime. Hotels also provide their own entertainment, particularly along the coast, with traditional Turkish music and even belly dancing on display.

For local listings, check the pages of local monthly events magazine *Time Out,* or English-language daily newspapers *Today's Zaman* or *Hurriyet Daily News.*

Festivals
April
Istanbul Film c
www.iksv.org/film
International and art-house films compete for the coveted Golden Tulip award. Movies are shown at ten cinemas across the city.

June
Istanbul International Music Festival
www.iksv.org/muzik
Symphonic and classical concerts in offbeat venues, including the Hagia Eirene church and the Istanbul Archaeology Museum.

July
Aspendos Opera and Ballet Festival

Aspendos, near Antalya
Tel (0312) 231 85 15
www.aspendosfestival.gov.tr
Compelling open-air displays of powerful music and dance, against a backdrop of one the world's most fabulous Roman amphitheaters.

Istanbul Jazz Festival
www.iksv.org/caz
Jazz, blues, and gospel are performed in various Istanbul venues, including restaurants, clubs, and rooftop bars.

September
Bozcaada Wine Festival
Bozcaada
www.bozcaadarehberi.com
Free wine tastings and open-air concerts are held when harvest-time takes over this beautiful Aegean island.

October
Ürgüp International Wine and Grape Festival
Harvesttime wine sampling in Cappadocia, with free tastes plus music performances in and around Ürgüp.

Efes Pilsen Blues Festival
www.pozitif-ist.com
Nationwide blues gathering, with major international and Turkish musicians performing in a handful of the country's cities.

November
Akbank Jazz Festival
Tel (0212) 334 01 00
www.pozitif-ist.com
Istanbul-wide jazz fiesta, with a dozen nightly concerts at many of the venues listed on p. 263.

Cinemas
Alkazar
İstiklal Caddesi 179, Taksim, Istanbul
Tel (0212) 293 24 66
Multiscreen picture house. Recommended for all genres, from old art films to the latest Hollywood releases.

Atlas
Atlas Pasajı, İstiklal Caddesi 209, Taksim, Istanbul
Tel (0212) 252 85 76
Art-house flicks, foreign romance films, and mainstream Turkish movies are shown over a series of small screens.

Istanbul Modern Cinema
Meclisi Mebusan Caddesi, Liman İşletmeleri Sahası Antrepo 4, Karaköy, Istanbul
Tel (0212) 334 73 00
www.istanbulmodern.org
Boutique screening room focusing on artsy, director-led film seasons and classics from celluloid history.

Classical & Theater

Atatürk Cultural Center

Taksim Square, Taksim, Istanbul
Tel (0212) 251 56 00
www.iksv.org
Istanbul's premier music and performance venue, and home of the State Symphony Orchestra. Reopened in 2010 after lengthy renovations.

Cemal Reşit Rey Symphony Hall

Darülbedai Caddesi 1, Harbiye, Istanbul
Tel (0212) 232 98 30
This vast space holds classical performances, recitals, and symphony concerts.

Sabancı University Performing Arts Center

Orhanlı, Istanbul
Tel (0216) 483 90 00
www.sgm.sabanciuniv.edu
Home to a world-class theater, showcasing drama and the performing arts.

Süreyya Opera House

Bahariye Caddesi, Caferağa Mahallesi 29, Kadıköy, Istanbul
Tel (0216) 346 15 31
www.sureyyaoperasi.org
Kadıköy's authentically classic opera venue has a top-notch year-round schedule, plus a lovely traditional interior.

Clubs & Bars

Anjelique

B Muallim Naci Caddesi, Salhane Sokak 5, Ortaköy, Istanbul
Tel (0212) 327 28 44
www.istanbuldoors.com

Hip dancing and dining spot attracting a young, showy, well-dressed crowd. Right on the Bosporus.

Badehane

General Yazgan Sokak 1, Tünel, Istanbul
Tel (0212) 249 05 50
Cozy café-bar with gypsy music, acoustic guitar sessions, and a fantastic range of offbeat live bands.

Babylon

Seyhbender Sokak 3, Tünel, Istanbul
Tel (0212) 249 05 50
Home to some of the city's best alternative concerts, drawing international talents such as ex-Lamb's Lou Rhodes. There's also inventive electronic and rocking house music every weekend.

Dogzstar

Kartal Sokak 3, Taksim, Istanbul
Tel (0212) 244 91 47
www.dogzstar.com
Nightly show of reggae, dub, world music, and DJ beats. Action spills onto the surrounding streets.

Garajistanbul

Kaymakam Reşat Bey Sokak 11, Yeni Carsi Caddesi, Tünel, Istanbul
Tel (0212) 244 44 99
Cutting-edge music, dance, and DJ performances in an industrial-chic renovated garage.

Indigo

Akarsu Sokak 1, İstiklal Caddesi, Tünel, Istanbul

Tel (0212) 244 85 67
This intimate spot's schedule is split: Britpop, English punk, and rocking old melodies on one hand, and experimental electronic acts on the other.

Lokal Bar

Asmalı Mescit Mahalessi, Tünel, Istanbul
Tel (0212) 245 57 44
Buzzy fusion restaurant turns into hopping nightspot after hours.

Nardis Jazz Club

B Kuledibi Sokak 14, Tünel, Istanbul
Tel (0212) 244 63 27
www.nardisjazz.com
Respected jazz and blues club with near-nightly piano, brass or vocal performances. Near the foot of the Galata Tower.

Sortie

Muallim Naci Caddesi 54, Kuruçeşme, Istanbul
Tel (0212) 327 85 85
www.sortie.com.tr
Chic waterside drinking and dancing spot with fabulous outdoor terrace. Dress to impress.

Sultanas Nights

Cumhuriyet Caddesi, Taksim, Istanbul
Tel (0212) 219 39 04
www.sultanas-nights.com
Loud, unashamedly cheesy, and bags of fun. Belly and traditional dancing, audience participation, and belly dancing lessons.

Activities

Turkey is an action-packed nation with scores of things to do and places to see. Most of the listings on these pages are broken down into three general areas: guided tours in specific destinations such as Cappadocia or Gallipoli; English-language courses covering niche activities, primarily in Istanbul, such as artisanal crafts or cooking classes; and finally travel agencies, which are useful for booking sleeper compartments on train, ferries to the Greek islands, and air tickets around the country.

It's worth noting that in Turkey your hotel often acts as a reliable travel agency, and is often your best bet for local tours and even car hire and airport transfers.

Most activities in Turkey are well organized, with kits ready on-site, or not arduous enough to require much equipment.

ISTANBUL

Cooking Courses

Cooking Alaturka
Akbiyik Caddesi 72,
Sultanahmet
www.cookingalaturka.com
Tel (0212) 458 59 19
Group courses covering classic Turkish menus, from Michelin-trained Dutch tutor Eveline Zoutendijk and Turkish master chef Feyzi Yıldırım.

Culinary Arts Academy
Meydan Sokak, Beybi Giz Plaza B Block, Maslak
Tel (0212) 290 35 50
www.msa.tc
This professional academy runs courses in cakes, cocktails, and terrines and classic Turkish one-day and week-long lessons.

Culinary Tours

Anissa Helou
www.anissas.com
Tel 44 (0)20 7739 0600 (in U.K.)
With roots in neighboring Leba-

non and Syria, it's no surprise British-based cookbook author Anissa Helou puts together stellar culinary expeditions. Her annual ten-day Turkish tours begin in Istanbul and head east to foodie havens like Gaziantep or the Black Sea coast.

Istanbul Eats
www.İstanbuleats.com;
İstanbuleats@gmail.com
Long-time Anglo-American residents Yiğal, Ansel, and Jonathan mix little known foodie spots with off-the-beaten-track sightseeing. Various tours take in Istanbul's Old City, European neighborhood, and Asian shores.

Dance

Whirling Dervishes

Istanbul Dervishes
Hodjapasha Culture Center,
Hocapaşa Hamam Sokak 5,
Sirkeci
Tel (0212) 511 46 26
www.istanbuldervishes.com
In this ancient hammam, awesome whirling dervish *sema* ceremonies take place five times weekly; Turkish dancing on alternate evenings.

Silivrikapı Mevlana Cultural Center
Mevlânakapı Mahalessi, Yeni Tavanlı Çeşme Sokak 8, Fatih
Tel (0542) 422 15 44

www.emav.org
Sema ceremonies take place every Thursday night. Performances tend to be lengthier and more spiritual, with visitors welcomed in religious discussions.

Outfitters

Atlas Outdoor

Karaköy Meydanı 4, Karaköy
Tel (0212) 252 32 82
Positioned not far from the Galata Bridge, this establishment offers a huge range of tents, sandals, fishing rods, outdoor pants, and jackets.

Decathlon

Forum Istanbul, Kocatepe Mahallesi, Bayrampaşa
Tel (0212) 640 05 12
Possibly Istanbul's largest and most varied selection of outdoor gear, from diving watches to hiking poles and energy bars. Excellent value for money.

Travel Agencies

Fez Travel

Akbiyik Caddesi 17, Sultanahmet
Tel (0212) 516 90 24
www.feztravel.com
Organizes everything from hop-on hop-off buses to Greek island ferries and Cappadocia flights.

Hotel Marble Travel Agency

Siraselviler Caddesi 41, Taksim
Tel (0212) 252 24 48

www.marblehotel.com
This petite agency can book and print long-distance rail tickets on the spot.

Istanbul Walks
İstiklal Caddesi 53, Floor 5, Beyoğlu
Tel (0212) 292 28 74
www.istanbulwalks.net
Join group city walks around the sights, or let them plan your own tailored trip around town.

One Nation Travel
Binbirdirek Mahalessi, Klodfarer Caddesi 3, Sultanahmet
Tel (0212) 516 53 00
www.onenationtravel.net
Services range from Istanbul city tours to escorted trips around Turkey; can also set up car hire.

WESTERN TURKEY
Travel Agencies
Anker Travel
İnönü Bulvarı 14, Kuşadası
Tel (0256) 612 45 98
www.ankertravel.net
Known for their highly regarded, private Ephesus tours, and organized trips to other Roman sites or Greek island boat tickets.

Bougainville Travel
Çukurbağlı Caddesi 10, Kaş
Tel (0242) 836 37 37
www.bt-turkey.com
The Turquoise Coast's premier travel agency for hiking, biking, diving, and kayaking.

Cappadocia Tours & Travel Turkey
İstiklal Caddesi 59, Ürgüp,

Cappadocia
Tel (0384) 341 74 85
www.cappadociatours.com
Reputable firm for Cappadocia hotels, car hire, transfers, and private tours.

Context Walking Tours
Tel (800) 691-6036 (in U.S.)
www.contexttravel.com/city/Istanbul
Walks in architecture, cuisine, and Byzantine history, led by a network of researchers living in Istanbul.

Hassle Free Tours
Cumhuriyet Meydani 59, Çanakkale
Tel (0286) 213 59 69
www.anzachouse.com
Specialist in Gallipoli battlefield tours, plus trips to Troy and local accommodation.

Meander Travel
Kibris Caddesi 1, Kuşadası
Tel (0256) 612 88 88
www.meandertravel.com
Private tours for visitors and cruise-ship passengers around Ephesus, the House of Virgin Mary, and Şirince.

Walking Mehmet
Cappadocia
Tel (0384) 271 20 64
www.walkingmehmet.com
Private walking tours among the fairy chimneys and valleys of Cappadocia with experienced guide Mehmet Güngör.

Water Sports & Yachting
Budget Sailing
Harbor, Göcek
Tel (0252) 645 13 23

www.budgetsailingturkey.com
Highly recommended Turquoise Coast yacht hire and sailing flotilla specialist.

Kite-Turkey
Progressive Boardsports, Çark Yolu 39, Alaçatı
Tel (0538) 381 56 86,
www.kite-turkey.com
Respected British-run kite-surfing outfit, with advanced-level tuition and beginner's courses.

Mavi Diving
Kucuk Cakil, Kaş
Tel (0242) 836 31 41
www.mavidiving.com
Professional scuba and free-diving specialists.

Turhan Yachting
Adnan Menderes Bulvari 15, Marmaris
Tel (0252) 417 46 50
www.bluevoyagegulet.com
Hire one of these three traditional Turkish gullets, with fine food and luxury interiors.

Turkish Gulet
Turgut Özal Caddesi, Göcek
Tel (0252) 645 11 31
www.turkishgulet.com
Gullet charter, cabin rental, and yacht hire, with reps in Marmaris, Göcek, and Bodrum.

Myga Surf City
B Çark Mevkii, 8011 Sokak 4, Alaçatı
C 0232 716 6468
www.myga.com.tr
Everything a windsurfer needs to kick off an adventure in Turkey's premier surfing spot.

INDEX

Bold page numbers indicate
illustrations
CAPS indicates thematic categories

A
Abdulhamit I 85
Abdulhamit II 25, 32, 149
Abdullah Brothers 47-48, 219
Abdülmecit I 25, 32
Addresses, Turkish 237
Adrasan 212, 214
Aegean Sea 43, 194, 196-198, 208, 210
Ağa, Sedefhar Mehmet 70
Agriculture 43
Ağva 156, 157
Ahmet I, the Pious 56, 70, 71
Ahmet III 32
AKBİL travel card 10
Alaçatı 15, 195, **196**, 197
Alexander the Great 22, 65, 88, 174,
   180, 187, 202, 208, 218
Alexander Sarcophagus **65**, 65
Alexandreia 181
Alexius Comnenus 68
Alkazar Sineması 111
Altınkum 197
Amicis, Edmondo de 51, 77
Anatolian Fortress 131, 150, 158
Anadolu Kavağı 107, 131, 135, 150-151
Anastasiopolis 175
Anatolia 22, 23, 24, 36, 38-39, 222
Angora wool 172
Ankara 10, 28, 38, 154, 155, 170-175,
   174
   Atakule 171
   Atatürk Mausoleum 155, **170**, 170, 171
   bazaar 171-172
   Cer Modern 173
   Citadel 172
   Gençlik Park 170
   Haci Bayram Mosque 171
   Kavaklıdere 173
   Kocatepe Mosque 173
   Kızılay 173
   Museum of Anatolian Civilizations
      155, 170, 172-173, **173**
   Palas 171
   Rahmi M. Koç Museum 93, 100,
      112-113, 172
   Republic Museum 171
   Temple of Augustus 171
   Train Museum 170
   Tunalı Hilmi Caddesi 173
   Ulus 170-172
Ankara, Battle of 25
Antalya 48, 208-209, 210, 211, 212,
   219, 219
Antikacılar Çarsısı 145
Anzac Cove **178**, 183, 184, 185
Aphrodisias 44, **192**, 194, **202**, 202,
   203
Apollo Kareios 205
Aqueducts 76, **132**
Arabs 27, 32, 93, 229
Arap Mosque 105
Ararat, Mount 39
Architecture 44, 46-47, 90-91
   cave churches and dwellings **220**,
      222, 224-229
Armenians 32, 92, 112
Arnavutköy 100, 106, 130, 131
Arnoux, J.A. 110
Art nouveau 46, 110, 163, 196
Art and photography 47-48, 78-79,
   121-122
ARTER 48
Ashman, Anastasia M. 51
Asia Minor 36
Asian Istanbul 10, 137-149
Asian Turkey 10, 36
Aspendos 219
Assos 181
At Meydanı 70, 72

Atatürk 10, 25, 28-29, **29**, 32, 34, 47,
   69, 108, 111, 117, 118, 119, 124, 125,
   127-128, 149, 159, 170, 175
   Gallipoli Campaign 183, 185, 188
   mausoleum 155, **170**, 170, 171
Atatürk Cultural Center 48, 117
Atbükü Bay 215
Atik Valide Mosque 21, 146-147
Avanos 226
Aya Nikola Church 92
Aya Yorgi Monastery 163
Ayasofya Pansiyonlari 78
Ayazma 189
Ayla Efimia Ortodoks Kilisesi 141
Ayvansaray 93

B
Babadağ, Mount 210
Bacchus, Saint 73
Bağdat Caddesi 138, 143
Bahariye Caddesi 141
Balaclava 141
Balkan Wars 32
Balyan family 125, 127, 128, 148, 150
Balık ekmek 104, 122
Balık Pazarı 111
Banks 239
Barbaros Park 125
Barbarossa 125
   Tomb of 91, 125
Bartering 81
Basil II, the Bulgar Slayer 30
Basil, Saint 229
Basilica Cistern 73, **76**, 76-77, 132
Batık Şehir 216
Batur, Enis 50
Bayezıt I 25, 31
BEACHES 11, 135
   Black Sea **156**, 156-157
   Bozcaada 181, 189
   Çeşme Peninsula 196-197
   Princes Islands 161
   Turquoise Coast **206**, 207-219
Bebek 100, 106, 130, 131
Belgrade Forest 76, 100, 116, **132**,
   132-133
Belisarius 27, 72
Belly dancing 48, **128**
Beşiktaş 46, 124-128, 131
   İskelesi 125
Beşiktaş Soccer Club **124**, 125
Beylerbeyi Palace 25, 147, **148**, 148-149
Beypazari 175
Bilgi University 114
Bird-watching 169
Black sand cove 214, 215
Black Sea 11, 36, 38, 40, 43, 158, 180
   beaches **156**, 156-157
Blegen, Carl 187
Blogs 16
Blue Mosque 9, **12**, 56, **70**, 70-71,
   72, 79
Bond movies 77, 144
Bookshops 27, 84, 108
Bosphorus 8, 10, **14**, 24, 31, 56, **138**,
   158, 158-159
   boat tours **106**, 106-107, **107**, 129, 154
   Bridge 100, 106, 128, 129, 130
   chain 151
   Fatih Sultan Mehmet Bridge 130
   Maiden's Tower **52-53**, 139, **144**, 144
   Marmaray Tunnel 34, 36, 130, 159
   northern shore 146-147
Bostancı 31
Botter House 110
Boza 43
Bozcaada 180-181, 186, 189-191,
   190, 191
   Castle 190
   Vintage Festival 191
British Consulate 111
Brownworth, Lars 51
Burgazada 160, 161, **164**, 164-165

Burqa 92
Bursa 30, **154**, 154, 166-168
   Emir Han 167
   Great Mosque 167
   Green Mosque and Mausoleum 167
   Hisar 168
   İpek Han 167
   Koza Han 167
   Muradiye Camii Mosque **168**
   Orhan Gazi mausoleum 168
   Osman Gazi mausoleum 168
   Setbaşı Bridge 167
   Yeşil Cami 44
Büyük Mecidiye Mosque 100, 128-129
Büyükada **160**, 160, 162-163
Büyükdere 100, 130, 131, 134-135, **135**
Byzantine Empire 24, 27, 30, 44, 66-67
Byzantine mosaics **26**, 27, 44, 56, 57,
   66, 67-68
Byzantium 22, 23-24, 34, 158
   see also Istanbul

C
Cable cars 95, 96, 118-119, 154, 169, 219
Caferağa Medresesi 64, 68, 90
Cağaloğlu Hamamı 75
Calendar 239
Caliphate 25
Calligraphy 47, **79**, 79, 82, 96, 108, 134
Calvert, Frank 187
Çam Limanı 165
Çanakkale 181, 186, 187-189
   Archaeology Museum 189
   Aynalı Bazaar 188
   Çimenlik Castle 188-189
   Fetvane Sokak 188
   Military Museum 189
   Naval Museum 188
Cap Helles 183, 184
Cappadocia 10, 23, 24, 27, **38**, 39, **220**,
   221-229, **226**
   climate 232
   dovecotes 225, 231
   Rock churches 224-231, **228**
Cappadocian Fathers 229
Caravanserai 44, 90, 172
Caria 22
Carpets 47, 51, 79, **82**, 97
Carthage 22
Cartier Bresson, Henri 105
Caucasian Wars 32
Cave dwellings **220**, 224-231
Cave hotels 223, 226, 229
Çavuşin 224, 230, **230**
Çekirge 168
Çelebi, Evliya 51
Çelebi, Hezarfen Ahmet 108
Çemberlitas Hamamı 75
Çengelköy 138, 150
Ceramics 47, 51, 79, 82, 187-188
   Chinese porcelain 59-60
   tiles 62, 62, 63, 71, 79, 87, 96
Çeşme town 196-197
Çeşme Peninsula 15, 194, 196-197
Çeşme of Sultan Ahmet III 68
Cevahir 100
Cevahir Alışveriş Merkezi 134
Chimaera Flames **215**, 217
Chinatown 111
Chios 196
Christianity 24, 27, 30, 32, **33**, 33-34,
   47, 66-67, 194, 201, 239
   Cappadocia 222, 226-231, **228**
   rock churches 224-229, **228**
Chunuk Bair Cemetery 184
Çiçek Pasajı **110**, 111
Cihangir 100, 117, 120, 122-123
Çiller, Tansu 16
Cinema 50, 262
Çinili Hammam 147
Çinili Mosque 147
Çirağan Palace 125
Çıralı 211, 212, 214-215, 217

Çiya Sofrasi 140
Cleopatra's Pool 205
Climate 36, 228, 232
Clothing etiquette 9, 18, 21, 71
Coastline 11, **20**, 38
   Turquoise Coast **206**, 207-219, 232
Codex Justinianus 24
Coffee 43
Constantine the Great 23-24, 71-72, 158, 201, 228-229
Constantine VI 66
Constantine IX Monomachus 68
Constantine XI Dragases 67
Constantinople 22, 23, 24, 30-31, 44
   sack 30
   sieges 25, 27, 30-31, 93
   see also Istanbul
Çöp şiş 200
Çorba 42
Crafts 51, 129
Crimean War 25, 32, 138, 141-142
Croesus 22
CRUISES 11
   Bosphorus **106**, 106-107, **107**, 154
   Golden Horn 93, 95
   Turquoise Coast 211
Crusades 30, 67, 73
Çukurcuma 100, 120, 122, **123**
Cumhuriyet Caddesi 117
Cuno, Helmut 31
Currency 10
   restrictions 234
Customs 233
Cycling 154, 162, 189
Cyprus 18
Cyrus the Great 22
Çırağan Palace 106
Çıralı 209

D
Dance 48-49, 108
Dandolo, Enrico 67, 68
Dardanelles **178**, 180-181, 188, 190
D'Aronco, Raimondo 110
Demre **216**, 216-217
Denizli 204
Derinkuyu 228, 231
Devrent Valley 231
Didyma 194, 202, **203**, 203
Diocletian, Emperor 23-24
Disabled travelers 240
Divan Yolu 70
Diving 11, **210**, 211
Dolma 42
Dolmabahçe Caddesi 127
Dolmabahçe Palace 25, 29, 32, 46, 47, 100, 106, 124, **126**, 126-129
   Harem 127-128
   Muayede Hall 127
   Selamlık 127
Dolmuş 113
Draperis, Clara Bartola 110
Driving 8, 19, 236
Drugs and narcotics 233-234
Düden Waterfalls 219
Dydyma 32

E
Ebü Eyyüb el-Ensari 93
   tomb 95, 96
Edict of Milan 24
Egirdir, Lake 218
Egyptian Consulate 131
Electricity supply 238
Embassies and consulates 233, 241
Emergency services 241
Eminönü 93
Eminönü Haliç Iskelesi 93
Emirgan 100, 130, 131, 134
Emirgan Korusu **130**, 131, 134
Ephesus 10, 23, 24, 32, 44, 194-195, 198-200
   Library of Celsus **194**, 194, 199
   Temple of Artemis 194, 198, 200-201
   theater **198**, 199-200

Erciyes Dağı 222
Erdoğan, Recep Tayyip 16-17
Erim, Kenan Tefvik 203
Ersoy, Mehmet Akif 50
Esbelli Evi 229
Etiquette 9, 18, 21, 62-63, 71, 238
   bartering 81
Eunuchs 61
European Istanbul (Beyoğlu) 9-10, 15, 27, 46, 98-135
European Passage 111
European Turkey 9-10, 36
EXPERIENCES
   Aqua Fantasy 201
   Atatürk Mausoleum **170**, 171
   Blue Cruise 211
   Caferağa Medresesi courses 64
   Cleopatra's Pool 205
   cooking Turkish food 40
   Ephesus 199
   exploring Bozcaada 189
   Florence Nightingale Museum 142
   Gallipoli's memorials **182**, 183
   Golden Horn boat trip 93
   Grand Bazaar shopping tour 82
   hot-air ballooning **226**, **227**, 227
   Istanbul Eats culinary tours 87
   nargile water pipe **120**, 121, **140**
   Ortaköy's nightlife 129
   Princes Islands activities 162
   riding a dolmuş 113
   sea kayaking around Kekova 218
   shopping malls 134
   Sultanahmet's Baths 75
   tasting naşik ekmek 104, 122
   Termal spas 169
   water sports in Alaçatı 197
   wine-tasting on Bozcaada 191
Eyüp 27, 57, 89, 93-96
   Çeribaşı Mosque 94 Square 94
   Sultan Mosque 93, 94-95, 96
   Zal Mahmud Paşa Mosque 94

F
Fadıllıoğlu, Zeynep 47
Fatih 33, 89, 92, **97**, 97
Fatih Sultan Mehmet Bridge 106, 130
Fatih Mosque 25, 89
Fayton 162, 163
Fener 33, 93
Ferries 8, 19, 31
   Princes Islands 161
Feshane 93, 94
Festivals 262
   Bozcaada Vintage Festival 191
   Contemporary Istanbul 48
   film 50
   religious 239-240
   Tulip Festival 134
   Ürgüp Wine Festival 226
Fethiye 208, 210, 211, **212**, 212
Fethiye Mosque **11**, 21, 89
Fez 29
First Kadın 60
Firuzağa Mosque 123
Fish/fishing 38, 43, **56**, **84**, 103, 104, **146**
   Balık Pazarı 111
Flower Market 85
FOOD AND DRINK 40-43, **84**, 84-85, 129, 195
   alcohol 238
   balık ekmek 104, 122
   Balık Pazarı 111
   Bozcaada 189
   Bursa 167
   Çengelköy cucumbers 150
   Istanbul Eats culinary tours 87
   Kanlica yogurt 147, 150
   Köy kahvaltısı 201
   Kumpir 129
   Ottoman cuisine 40
   pickles **105**, 122
   Selçuk 200
   Wine 43, 191, 195, 226, 238

Fortress of the Infidels 175
Fossati brothers 110
Fountain of the Executioner 58
Fountains 68, 77, 121
Four Seasons Hotel 106
Freely, John 51
French Consulate 117
French Street 122
Frescoes, Cappadocian **228**, 228-231
Funicular railway 102, 104

G
Galata 102-103, 104-105, 108-109
   Whirling Dervish Hall 108, 110
Galata Bridge 100, 102-103
Galata Tower 10, 100, **102**, 102, 105, 106, 108
Galatasaray Hamamı 75
Galatasaray Square 111
Galatasaray University 106
Galip Dede 108, 110
Galip Dede Caddesi 48
Gallipoli Campaign 28, 159, 180, 182-185, **184**, 188, 189
Gallipoli Peninsula 11, 32, **178**, 180-185
   climate 232
Gaziantep 40
Gecekondu 21
Geyikli Yükyeri 189
göbek taşi 75
Göcek 208, 210-211
Gökçeada 181
Gökmen, Jennifer Eaton 51
Gölbaşı Lake 174
Golden Horn 33, 56, 57, **58**, 71, 95, 100, 106
   boat trip 93, 95
   chain 118, 151
   Galata Bridge 102
   northern 112-115
   southern 89, 92-93, 96-97
Göllü Dağ 222
Gördion 22, 174
Göreme 222, 223, 226-229, **228**, **229**, 231
Gözleme 195, 197
Grand Bazaar 70, 79-84, **80**, **82**
Greco-Turkish War 32, 33
Greek-Turkish population exchanges 32, 33, 210
Greeks 22, 32-34, 44, 112, 194, 202-203, 205, 217
Gül, Abdullah **35**
Güler, Ara 48
Gulet 211
Gülhane Park 58, 62, 63
Gümüşsuyu 117
Güneşli Bahçe Sokak 140
Güzelyurt 231
Gyllius, Petrus 77

H
Habbele 189
Haçli Church 225
Haco Pulo Cafe 111
Hacı Baba 117
Hagia Eirene 58
Hagia Sophia 9, 24, **26**, 27, 30, 31, 44, 47, **54**, **56**, **66**, 66-69, 76, 90
   mosaics 66, 67-68
   narthex 67
   sack 67
   upper gallery 67-68, **69**
   weeping column 68
Hammam of Roxelana 68, 92
Hammams 9, 44, **74**, 74-75, 133, 147, 154
Hamsi 38, 40, 43
Harem 59, 60-61
Hasan Dağı 222
Hasan Paşa 93
Hasköy 93, 112-113
   Park 112
Haydarpaşa Cemetery 138, 141-142
Haydarpaşa Station 31, 138, 142-143

Haymana 175
Hellenistic culture 22, 44, 202–203, 205
Helles Memorial 184
Hellespont 180
Heraclius, Emperor 27
Hero and Leandros 144
Herodotus 51, 187, 208
Heybeliada 47, 160, 161–162, 164–165
Hierapolis 44, 194, 204–205
Hikmet, Nazim 50, 123
Hippodrome 24, 30, 70, 71–73, **73,** 79, 88
Historical background 22–35
Hodjapasha Culture Center 49
Holy Trinity Church 111
Holy Trinity Orthodox Church 117
Homer 51, 187, 208
Horse-drawn carriages 154, 162, **163, 232**
Hospitals 241
Hot-air ballooning **226, 227,** 227
Hotels 242–259
Hüseyin Ağa Mosque 111

I
Ibrahim I, the Mad 60–61
İbrahim Paşa 60, 78 I fun
İbrahim Paşa Palace 78–79
Iconoclastic debates 27, 66
Icons 47, 66, 229
Identification papers 241
Ihlara Valley 222, 231
Ildiri 197
İnözü Valley 175
Insurance, travel 233
Internet access 237
Irene, Empress 66, 68, 163
İskander kebab 42, 43, 167
İskele Meydanı 128, 129
Islam 25, 27, 30–31, 32, 47, 67, 74, 239
İstanbul 20–21, 31
  blogs 16
  history 22–35
  population 20–21
  sea walls 89
İstanbul Biennial **46,** 48, 78
İstanbul Eats culinary tours 87
İstanbul Yeni Valide 71
İstiklal Caddesi 9, 46, **98, 100,** 100, 102, 103, 108, 109–111, **110,** 116–117
İzmir 33, 194, 195, 196
İznik 87

J
Janissary guards 59, 61, 90, 120
Jason and the Argonauts 127, 159
Jewish community **112,** 112, 131
John II Comnenus 68
John the Evangelist, Saint 194, 201
Johnston's Jolly 184
Justinian the Great 24, 27, 44, 56, 66, 73, 76, 97, 201

K
Ka'aba, keys to 62
Kabataş 144
Kaçkar Mountains 38
Kadıköy 10, 33, **140,** 140–143
Kale 216–217
Kalkan 211
Kamondo, Abraham 105, 112
Kamondo Staircase 10, 104–105, 112
Kanlica 106, 138, 147, 150, **151**
Kanyon 100
Kanyon Alışveriş Merkezi 134, **135**
Karaköy 100, 102, 103–104
Kariye Mosque 89, 92
Kaş 11, **210,** 211
Kaşık Adası 160, 161, 164
Kasımpaşa 93
Kavacık 130
Kaya **11**
Kayaking 11, **20,** 210, 216, 218, 219
Kayaköy 210

Kaymaklı 228, 231
Kazasker Sokak 141
Kebabs **41,** 42, 43, 200
Kekova **208,** 211, 216, 218
Kemal, Orhan 50, 123
Kemal, Yaşar 50
Kemalism 28–29
Kese 74, 75
Kestane Şekeri 167
Khedive's Palace 131, 149, 150
Kilims 51, 79
Kilitbahir Castle 188
Kilyos 130, 135, 156
Kınalıada 160–161
Kitesurfing **196,** 197
Koç family 114
Köfte 42
Koressos, Mount 201
Korgmann, Manfred 187
Köy kahvaltısı 201
Küçük Mecidiye Mosque 125
Küçüksu Palace 150
Kumbaba Beach 157
Kumpir 129
Kurban Bayram 240
Kurds 16, 21
Kuzguncuk 147
Kılıç Ali Paşa Mosque 90–91, 120–121

L
Lachmacun **42,** 42–43
Landscape 36–39
Languages 18, 34, 210
Laodicea 10, 194, 205
Lavaş **42**
League of Nations 32
Leatherwork 51
Lengerhane 112
Leo III 27, 66, 229
Leo VI 67
Leonardo da Vinci 102
Letöon 209, 211
Liquor laws 238
Lira, Turkish 10
Literature 32, 50, 118
Lone Pine Cemetery 184
Lost property 241
Loti, Pierre 50, 51, 96
Lycia 22, 65, 208, **216,** 217
Lycian Way 208, **212,** 212–215, **215,** 216; 232
Lydia 22

M
Maden Beach 215
Madresseh 44, 90
Mahmud II 32
Mahmud Paşa 94
Maiden's Tower **52–53,** 139, **144,** 144
Mail 237
Malta Köşkü 125, 126
Mantı 42
Marmara, Sea of 43, 56, 158
Marmaray Tunnel 34, 36, 130, 159
Mary, Virgin 194, 201
Marzik Patisserie 110
Massage 75
Mediterranean Sea 36, 43, 180, 208
Mehmet II, the Conqueror 25, 30, 44, 58, 59, 79, 93, 105, 106, 132, 188
  mausoleum 89
Mehmet III 86
  tomb 68
Mehmet VI 25, 63
Mehter band 118
Melendiz River 231
Menemen 42
Meryemana **200,** 201
Metric system 237–238
Mevlevi see Whirling Dervishes
Meze 42
Michelangelo 102
Mihrab 71
Mihrimah Sultan Mosque 145, 147
Mikla 113

Miletus 32, 194, 202–203
Mimar Sinan Çarşısı 145
Minbar 12, 69, 71
Miniatures 84
Miniatürk 112, **115,** 115
Mint 58
Mısır Apartmanı 111
Moda 140, **143,** 143
Modernization 28–29, 34–35, 119
Mohammed's footprint 96
Montagu, Lady Mary Wortley 133
Montreux Convention 159
Monument of the Republic 117
Mosaics **26,** 27, 44, 56, 57, 66, 67–68, 97, 110
Mosque etiquette 9
Muradiye 168
Murat II 69
Murat III, tomb 68
MUSEUMS AND GALLERIES
  Archaeological Museum, Antalya 209
  Archaeology Museum, Çanakkale 189
  Archaeology Museum, Çeşme 197
  Archaeology Museum, Hierapolis 205
  Archaeology Museum, Istanbul 9, 34, 58, 64–65, **65**
  Archaeology Museum, İzmir 196
  Atatürk Museum 119
  Beyoğlu 103
  Borusan 110
  Caricature and Humor Arts Museum 97
  Cer Modern 173
  Chora Museum 30, 92
  Efes Museum, Selçuk 200
  Ethnographic Museum, Antalya 209
  Fethiye 210
  Florence Nightingale Museum 138, 142
  Galatasaray 111
  Göreme Open-Air Museum 226–227, **228,** 231
  Grand Palace Mosaics Museum 97
  Hüsnu Züber Evi 168
  İnönü Evi Museum 162, 165
  Istanbul Modern 10, 44, 100, 106, 120, 121–122
  Kabatepe War Museum 183, 185
  Kristal Istanbul Museum 115
  Maritime Museum 124–125
  Military Museum 118, 189
  Museum of Anatolian Civilizations 155, 170, 172–173, **173**
  Museum of the Ancient Orient 64
  Museum of Divan Literature 108
  Museum of Energy 114
  Museum of the History of Science and Technology in Islam 63
  Museum of Islamic Art 64
  Museum of Painting and Sculpture 124
  Museum of Turkish Calligraphic Art 96
  Museum of Turkish & Islamic Arts 47, 78–79, 96, 97
  Naval Museum 188
  Orhan Kemal Museum 123
  Osmanli Evi Museum 168
  Ottoman Bank Museum 104
  Pera Museum 109
  Pergamum Museum 202
  Rahmi M. Koç Museum 93, 100, 112–113, 172
  Republic Museum 116, 171
  Sadberk Hanım Museum 114
  Sakıp Sabancı Museum 134–135
  Santa Claus Museum 216–217
  Santralistanbul 47, 100, 114
  Suna-Inan Kıraç Kaleiçi Museum 48, 48, 219
  Train Museum 170
  Vakiflar Carpet Museum 96
  Victory Museum 115
  Yıldız Palace Museum 126
  Zelve Open-Air Museum 231

Music 48-49, 108, 110, 118, **219**, 262-263
Mustafa I, tomb 68
Muvakkithane Caddesi 140
Myra **23**, 208, 211, **216**, 216-217

N
Nargile water pipe **120**, 120, 121, **140**
National Parks 39, 166, 168-169, 185, 217, 219, 226
Naval High School 164
The Nek 184
Neolithic cultures 22, 34
Nesin, Aziz 50
Netherlands Consulate 110-111
New Mosque 85-86
Newspapers and magazines 238-239
Nicholas, Saint 216-217
Nightlife 129, 263
Nika Riots 24
Nişantaşı 10, 15, 100, 117, 118, 119
Nomads 39, 79
Norwich, John Julius 51
Nostalgic Tram 110
Nova Roma 22, 23, 24
  see also Istanbul
Nuruosmaniye Mosque 81
Nusretiye Mosque 120, 121

O
Obelisk of Theodosius 72, **73**
Ölüdeniz 210
Olympos 209, 212, 214, **215**, 217, 219
Oracle 205
Orient Express 109
Ortahisar 226
Ortaköy Mosque 100, 124, 128-129
Osman I **25**, 25
Ottoman Empire 9, 25, 30-32, 35, 67, 88-89, 180
  architecture 44, 46
  cuisine 40
Ovacık 212
Özal, Turgut 16

P
Palazzo Corpi 109
Pammakaristos, Church of 10
Pamuk, Orhan 50, 51, 118
Pamukkale 10, 39, 194, **204**, 204-205
Paragliding 210
Patara 210, 211
Paul, Saint 194, 228
Pera Palace Hotel 109
Pergamum 32, 194, 202
Perge 218, 219
Persian Empire 22, 180, 208
Phaselis 209, 217-218
Phrygia 22
Pickpockets 241
Pide 42-43
Pierre Loti 96
Pierre Loti café **94**, 95, 96
Pigeon houses 225, 231
Pilgrimage 25, 62-63, 93, 96, 201, 229
Poetry 50
Polatlı 174
Police 241
Political background 16-19
Polonezköy 156, 157
Pontic Mountains 38
Post offices 237, 239
Priene 32, 194, 202
Princes Islands 11, 27, 31, 33, 142, **152**, 154, **160**, 160-165, **163**, **164**
Printing 32
Proje4L 48
Public holidays 238

Q
Quarantine 234
Quinn's Post 184

R
Rabies 241
Rakı 10, 43, 238
Ramadan 239
Ramadan Bayramı 239-240
Red Valley 222, 231
Religion 9, 239
  festivals 239-240
Restaurants 10, 18, 239, 242-259
Restrooms 240
Ritter, Otto 31
Rock churches 224-231, **228**
Rod of Moses 24
Rogers, Andrew 223
Romans 22-24, **23**, 35, 44, 70, 72, 166, 171, 172, 194-195, 198-200, 202-203, 205, 208, 212, 214, 217
  aqueduct **132**
  baths 74, 199
  theater **198**, 199-200
Rose Valley 222, **224**, 224-225, 230, 231
Rosewater 85
Roxelana 31, 60, 68, 78, 87
  tomb 89
Rumeli Fortress 100, 106, 131, 150, 158, 159
Rumeli Hisarüstü 130
Rumeli Kavağı 130, 131, 135, 151
Rumi 49, 108
Russian Consulate 110
Rüstem Paşa 86-87
Rüstem Paşa Mosque 86-87

S
Safiye 86
Sahaflar Çarşısı
Sahlep 43
Saint Anthony of Padua Church 111
Saint George, Church of **33**, 33
Saint John the Baptist, Church of, Burgazada 161, 164
Saint John the Baptist, Church of, Çavuşin 224
Saint Paul Trail 218
Saint Savior in Chora, Church of 57, 89, 92
Saint Stephen of the Bulgars, Church of 57, 92-93
Saints Sergius and Bacchus, Church of 73
Şakirin Mosque 47
Şalgam suyu 122
Sali Pazarı **136**, 141
Santa Maria Draperis Church 110
Sariyer 100, 107, 130, 131, 135
Savarona 106
Schliemann, Heinrich 180, 187, 188
Scribes of Istanbul 50-51
Sedef Adası 160, 163
Sehzade Mosque 91
Selçuk 195, 200-201
Selim I, the Grim 25, 31, 62
Selim II, mausoleum 68
Selim III 96
Seljuks 44
Sema 108
Semşi Paşa Mosque 144-145
Seraglio Point (Sarayburnu) 56
Sergius, Saint 73
Serpents Column 72
Sevastopol 141-142
Seven Wonders of the Ancient World 194, 201
Shafrak, Elif 50
Shell Green Cemetery 184
Shopping 9, 11, 18, 103, **105**, 260-261
  Ankara 171-172
  antiques 122, **123**, 140-141, 145
  Balık Pazarı 111
  bartering 81
  Bozcaada 190
  Bursa 167
  Çanakkale 188

European Istanbul 100, 103
Flower Market 85
Grand Bazaar 70, 79-84, **80**, **82**, 134
  historical bookshops 27, 84
  Kadıköy 140-141
  Nişantaşı 119   opening times 239
  Ortaköy craftmarket 129
  Sali Pazarı **136**, 141
  shopping malls 134
  Spice Market **83**, 84-85
Shrapnel Valley Cemetery 184
Silahtarağa 112, 114-115
Şile **156**, 157
Silk 167
Silk Route 59, 154, 175, 222, 228
Simena 22, 216
Sinan, Mimar 31, **45**, 46, 58, 68, 70, 86, 88, **90**, 90-91, 94, 125, 132, 145, 146-147
  mausoleum 46
Sinan Pasha Mosque 91
Sinking palace 76
Şirince 195, 201
Şişli 117, 119
Sivriada 160, 161, 164
Skiing 154, 166, 169
Slavery 60, 76, 78
Soccer 10, 15, 100, 106, 111, **124**, 125
Sogukçeşme Sokak 77-78
Soğukluk 75
Spice Market **83**, 84-85
Spoonmaker's Diamond 63
Suada 106, 129
Sufism 49
Süleyman I, the Magnificent 25, **30**, 31, 58, 60, 63, 78, 86-87, 88-89, 90, 94, 132
  tomb 89
Süleymaniye Mosque 10, 31, **45**, 71, 78, 87-89, **91**, 91
Sultanahmet Camii *see* Blue Mosque
Sultanahmet (Old City) 9, **12**, 24, 55-95, **232**
Sultanahmet's Baths 75
Sultanate of Women 32
Sumner-Boyd, Hilary 51
Süreyya Opera House 48, 141
Sütlüce 93
Suvla Bay 183
Sıcaklık 75

T
Mount Tahtalı 217, 219
Taksim Park 117
Taksim Square 100, 109, **116**, 116-119, 133
Tamerlane 25
Tanzimat Period 32
Tarabya 100, 131, 134
Taurus Mountains 38
Tavşan Adası 160, 163
Taxis 8, 237
Tea 43
Teimussa 216
Tekirova 214-215
Telephones 237
Television 239
Terki Dünya Monastery 165
Termal 154, 169
Termessos 219
Tevfikiye 187
Textiles 82, 83
  angora wool 172
  silk 167
Theater 263
Theodora, Empress 27, 73
Theodosian Walls 24
Theodosius the Great 24, 56-57, 72, **73**, 132
Thermal springs 154, 169, 175, 194, 205
Thermopylae, Battle of 180
Time differences 240
Tipping 240
Tophane 100, **120**, 120-122

Tophane Fountain 121
Tophane Kasrı 120
Topkapı Palace 9, 24, 31, 40, 46, 56,
 58, 58–64, **61, 62,** 127, 158
 Apartments of the Queen Mother 61
 Baghdad Kiosk 64
 Chamber of Petitions 62
 Chamber of the Sacred Relics 62–63
 Chief Physician's Chamber 64
 Circumcision Room **62,** 63
 Courtyard of the Eunuchs 61
 First Courtyard 58–59
 Fourth Courtyard 63–64
 Gate of Felicity 61
 Gate of Salutation 59
 Golden Road 61
 Grand Kiosk 64
 Gülhane Park 58, 62, 63
 Harem 59, 60–61, **61**
 Iftar Pavilion 63–64
 Imperial Costume Collection 63
 Imperial Gate 58
 Imperial Hall 61
 Imperial Mint 58
 Imperial Stables 60
 Imperial Treasury 63
 jewelery collection 63
 kitchens 59, 60, 90
 Konyalı restaurant 64
 Library of Ahmet III 62
 Old Treasury 60
 Second Courtyard 59–61
 Third Courtyard 61–63
 Throne Room 61–62
Tourist information 240–241
Trabzon 33
Trains 8, 19, 29, 31, 236
 Haydarpaşa Station 31, 138, 142–143
 Marmaray Tunnel 34, 36, 159
Transport 8, 19, 113, 234–237
Travertine pools **204,** 204
Treaty of Lausanne 32
Treaty of Sèvres 32, 159
Trojan War 180, 186–187

Troy 22, 32, 39, 51, 65, 180–181, **186,**
 186–187, 188
 climate 232
 Megaron building 187
 Temple of Athena 186–187
Tufa 222, 224–231
 Tulip Period 32
Tulum peyniri 195
 Tünel funicular railway 102, 104, 110
 Tünel Geçidi 110
 Tünel Square 104, 108, 110, 117
 Turhan Hatice 86
 Turkish Delight 84, 85, 103
 Turquoise Coast **206,** 207–219, 232
Turşu 122

U
Üçağiz 216
Uçhisar 226
Uludağ, Mount 39, 154, 166, 168–169
Ulupınar 209, 217
UNESCO World Heritage sites 39, 180,
 204, 211, 222, 226
Ürgüp 226
Üsküdar 10, 31, 71, 90, 108, 138,
 144–147, **146**

V
Valide Sultans 32, 60, 86
Vallaury, Alexander 109
Valley of the Fairy Chimneys 226–227
V Beach Cemetery 184
Vegetation 37–38, 133
Veliaht Dairesi 124
Venice 67
Visas 233

W
WALKS
 Burgazada and Heybeliada
 164–165
 Eyüp and Pierre Loti 94–95
 İstiklal Caddesi 110–111
 Lycian Way **212,** 212–215, **215,** 232
 Rose Valley **224,** 224–225

St. Paul Trail 218
Üsküdar 144–145
Walled Obelisk 73
Water, drinking 241
Water sports 195, **196,** 196–197, 210–211
Water supply 76–77, 116, 132–133
Weights and measures 237–238
Whirling Dervishes 48, **49,** 49–50,
 108, 110
Wildlife 39, 132
Wilhelm II, Kaiser 31
Wine 43, 191, 195, 226, 238
World War I 28, 32, 109, 142, 159, 180,
 182–185, 188

X
Xanthos 209, 211
Xerxes I 180

Y
Yachting 210
Yalıs 46, 131, 138
Yanık Kapı 103
Yassıada 160, 161, 164
Yeni Valide Mosque 145, 147
Yenikapı 34, 56–57
Yeniköy 100, 106–107, 130, 131, 134
Yıldız Park 126
Yoros Castle 150–151
Young Turks 28, 32, 111, 149
Yurt 79

Z
Zelve **220,** 230–231
Zeytinyağlılar 42
Zoe, Empress 68, 163

ILLUSTRATIONS CREDITS

National Geographic
TRAVELER
Istanbul &
Western Turkey

Published by the National Geographic Society
John M. Fahey, Jr., *President
and Chief Executive Officer*
Gilbert M. Grosvenor, *Chairman of the Board*
Tim T. Kelly, *President, Global Media Group*
John Q. Griffin, *Executive Vice President;
President, Publishing*
Nina D. Hoffman, *Executive Vice President;
President, Book Publishing Group*

Prepared by the Book Division
Barbara Brownell Grogan, *Vice President
and Editor in Chief*
Marianne R. Koszorus, *Director of Design*
Barbara A. Noe, *Senior Editor*
Carl Mehler, *Director of Maps*
R. Gary Colbert, *Production Director*
Jennifer A. Thornton, *Managing Editor*
Meredith C. Wilcox, *Administrative Director,
Illustrations*

Staff for This Book
Lawrence M. Porges, *Project Editor*
Kay Kobor Hankins, *Art Director*
Olivia Garnett, *Copy Editor*
Michael McNey, David Miller *Map Production*
Leslie Allen, Jackie Attwood-Dupont, Katherine C.
Brazauskas, Linda Makarov, Jane Sunderland,
Contributors

Manufacturing and Quality Management
Christopher A. Liedel, *Chief Financial Officer*
Phillip L. Schlosser, *Senior Vice President*
Chris Brown, *Technical Director*
Nicole Elliott, *Manager*
Rachel Faulise, *Manager*
Robert L. Barr, *Manager*

Windmill Books Ltd.
Lindsey Lowe, *Editorial Director*
Tim Harris, *Managing Editor*
Jeni Child, *Design Manager*
Supriya Sahai, *Senior Designer*
Joan Curtis, *Designer*
Sophie Mortimer, *Picture Manager*
Martin Darlison, *Cartographer*
Clive Carpenter, Joe Fullman, Alastair Gourlay,
Leon Gray, Ben Hollingum, Sally McFall,
Contributors

Founded in 1888, the National Geographic Society is
one of the largest nonprofit scientific and education-
al organizations in the world. It reaches more than
285 million people worldwide each month through
its official journal, *National Geographic,* and its four
other magazines; the National Geographic Channel;
television documentaries; radio programs; films;
books; videos and DVDs; maps; and interactive
media. National Geographic has funded more than
8,000 scientific research projects and supports an
education program combating geographic illiteracy.

For more information, please call 1-800-NGS LINE
(647-5463) or write to the following address:

National Geographic Society
1145 17th Street N.W.
Washington, D.C. 20036-4688 U.S.A.

Visit us online at www.nationalgeographic.com

For information about special discounts for bulk
purchases, please contact National Geographic
Books Special Sales: ngspecsales@ngs.org

For rights or permissions inquiries, please contact
National Geographic Books Subsidiary Rights:
ngbookrights@ngs.org

Printed in China

10/TS/1

**National Geographic Traveler:
Istanbul & Western Turkey
ISBN 978-1-4262-0708-2**

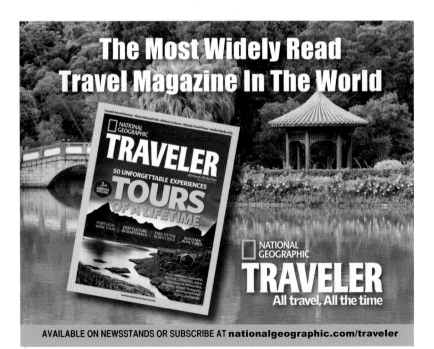